# LEGAL ASPECTS OF FOREIGN INVESTMENT
# IN THE EUROPEAN ECONOMIC COMMUNITY

Legal Aspects of

# Foreign Investment

in the

# European Economic

# Community

*by*

W. H. BALEKJIAN

Dr.rer.pol., Dr.Jur. (Vienna)
Ph.D. (Manchester), University Lecturer,
Institute of European Studies, Vienna

MANCHESTER UNIVERSITY PRESS
U.S.A. OCEANA PUBLICATIONS, INC.

© 1967 Manchester University Press
Published by the University of Manchester at
THE UNIVERSITY PRESS
316–324 Oxford Road, Manchester 13

GBSBN 7190 0297 4

U.S.A.
OCEANA PUBLICATIONS INC.
75, Main Street, Dobbs Ferry, N.Y. 10522
Library of Congress Catalogue Card No. 67-15827

INDIA
N. M. TRIPATHI PRIVATE LTD.
BOOKSELLERS & PUBLISHERS
Princess Street, Bombay–2

Printed by Butler & Tanner Ltd, Frome and London

# FOREWORD

Dr. W. H. Balekjian prepared this work during his two-year stay as Simon Fellow, an office which he filled with academic and social distinction.

The problems of investing in the European Economic Community are at once complex and urgent, and Dr. Balekjian's assessments and solutions have a very real topical interest, whether the U.K. enters the E.E.C. or not. At present similar problems face all would-be investors from outside the E.E.C., and to them this work is seriously commended.

*Faculty of Law*
*University of Manchester*

B. A. WORTLEY

# ACKNOWLEDGEMENTS

The present study is based on a Ph.D. thesis written at the Faculty of Law, University of Manchester. The author feels greatly indebted to Professor B. A. Wortley, O.B.E., LL.D., for his suggestion of the present study, his sustained encouragement and supervision. Special thanks are to be extended also to Dr. K. Martin, Reader in International Economics at the Faculty of Economic and Social Studies, University of Manchester, for his valuable advice, and to Miss Marguerita Oughton for her intensive work in the editorial preparation of the manuscript for the Press. The responsibility for the final text is entirely the author's.

The author would like to acknowledge his debt to the staff of the following libraries: the Central and University Libraries (Manchester), the libraries of the European Communities (Brussels) and of the Court of Justice of the European Communities (Luxembourg), the Peace Palace Library (The Hague), and the Library of the International Bureau for Fiscal Documentation (Amsterdam).

Research for the manuscript was completed at the end of March 1965. Although a few later publications have been taken into consideration, the situations discussed here are as in March 1965.

The whole study was made possible by the generosity of the Trustees of the Simon Research Fellowship of the University of Manchester.

*Manchester, 8 February 1967*                                 W. H. BALEKJIAN

# CONTENTS

CONTENTS                                    ix

PART THREE
*Summary and Speculations on the Future*

# ABBREVIATIONS

| | |
|---|---|
| *A.J.C.L.* | American Journal of Comparative Law |
| *A.J.I.L.* | American Journal of International Law |
| BGB | Bürgerliches Gesetzbuch (German Civil Code) |
| BGBl | Bundesgesetzblatt (Federal Law Gazette) |
| *B.Y.I.L.* | British Yearbook of International Law |
| C.E.E. | Communauté Economique Européenne |
| *C.M.L. Rep.* | Common Market Law Reports |
| *C.M.L. Rev.* | Common Market Law Review |
| E.C.S.C. | European Coal and Steel Community |
| E.E.C. | European Economic Community |
| E.F.T.A. | European Free Trade Area |
| EURATOM | European Atomic Energy Community |
| G.A.T.T. | General Agreement on Tariffs and Trade |
| HGB | Handelsgesetzbuch |
| I.B.F.D. | International Bureau of Fiscal Documentation |
| I.C.J. | International Court of Justice |
| *I.C.L.Q.* | International and Comparative Law Quarterly |
| I.L.R. | International Law Reports |
| I.M.F. | International Monetary Fund |
| *J.D.I.* | Journal du Droit International |
| J.O. | Journal Officiel de la République française. Lois et décrets |
| J.O.(C.E.) | Journal Officiel des Communautés Européennes (French edition) |
| *O.B.R.* | Overseas Business Reports |
| O.E.C.D. | Organization for Economic Co-operation and Development |
| O.E.E.C. | Organization for European Economic Co-operation |
| P.C.I.J. | Permanent Court of International Justice |
| *Rec. A.D.I.* | Recueils, Académie de Droit International de la Haye |
| *Rec. I.C.J.* | Recueils, International Court of Justice |
| *Rev. M.C.* | Revue du Marché Commun |
| RGBl | Reichsgesetzblatt (German Law Gazette) |
| T.I.A.S. | Treaties and International Agreement Series (U.S.A.) |
| U.N.T.S. | United Nations Treaty Series |
| *W.T.I.S.* | World Trade Information Service |

# PERIODICALS

The following periodicals and journals, chiefly economic and financial, are referred to in this study:

British Trade Journal (London)
Cartel (London)
Commerce in Germany (American Chamber of Commerce in Germany, Frankfurt/Main)
Direction (Paris)
The Economist (London)
Entreprise (Paris)
European Community (London)
European Economic Community Bulletin (Luxembourg)
European Taxation (International Bureau of Fiscal Documentation, Amsterdam)
European Taxation, Supplementary Service
The Financial Times (London)
Frankfurter Allgemeine Zeitung (Frankfurt/Main)
The Guardian (Manchester)
Kurier (Vienna)
Le Monde (Paris)
Neue Zürcher Zeitung (Zürich)
Newsweek (New York)
New York Herald Tribune, European edition
Opera Mundi: Europe (Paris)
O.E.C.D. Observer (Paris)
Overseas Business Reports (O.B.R.) (U.S. Dept. of Commerce, Bureau of International Commerce, Washington)
Revue du Marché Commun (Paris)
Time (Chicago)
The Times (London)
The Times Review of Industry (London)
La Vie Française (Paris)
Die Welt (Hamburg)
World Trade Information Service (W.T.I.S.) (U.S. Dept. of Commerce, International Programs Bureau, Washington)

# CASES, DOCUMENTS, TREATIES, CONVENTIONS AND LEGISLATION

## CASES

## TREATIES, CONVENTIONS, AGREEMENTS

# CHAPTER I

## INTRODUCTION

In this survey of the legal aspects of foreign investment in the European Economic Community we are dealing with a region that is, in economic terms, advanced and we are concerned with the legal status and treatment of foreign-owned undertakings under both the municipal laws and the Community law that are operative in that region. A special study is made of the types of legislative rules and administrative controls set up for the supervision of foreign investments and for their co-ordination with the interests of each of the member states and, indirectly, of the Common Market as a whole.

In the Treaty of Rome of 25 March 1957, under which the European Economic Community was established, a process of integration was proposed within which institutions with a supra-national character common to all member states were set up. This will lead, among other things, to changes in the rights of foreign investors and of the nationals of the member states. Attention is given here, therefore, to an assessment of the effects of the process of integration, when it is fully implemented, upon the existing—and at present predominant—municipal laws concerned with foreign investment. The legal impact of the Treaty of Rome on the status of foreign investments is thus discussed in terms of the situation beyond the transitional period. Finally, the nature and extent of investment law in the Community are examined in the context of international legal standards concerned with investment law.

Part One is a survey of the current situation and law of foreign investment in the six member states of the Community. The material presented therein is used for a comparison of similarities and divergences between the respective systems of the six states; at the same time it constitutes the basis for part of the discussions in Part Two, on the harmonization of law within the Community in its relevance to foreign investment. Reasons for the inclusion of some of the material in Part One—for example, the law of restrictive practices and of patents in chapter VIII—are made evident in the text. Here let it suffice to remark that current investment law has to deal more and more with the flow and protection

of technical knowledge, services and personnel, in addition to the
flow of money as investment capital; relations between the principal and subsidiary companies necessitate a discussion of restrictive practices when dealing with foreign investment.

Part Two deals with Community law as it refers to foreign
investment. Part Three reviews points of particular importance
to foreign businessmen and the situation in 1965, and speculates
on the future legal developments in the E.E.C. The section in
Part Three which deals with attitudes of and towards foreign investors is included to illustrate an integral part of the climate in
which the law of foreign investment has to operate.

This book is not intended to serve as an investment manual.
The economic factors that should be considered in such a manual
do not fall within its scope. The statistical data used for reference
here are both incomplete and unreliable, for there are no satisfactory international investment statistics available for detailed
study and methods do not exist for compiling such statistics in a
form common to all the Community states.

## DEFINITIONS

### The European Economic Community and the Treaty of Rome

The Treaty of Rome, of 25 March 1957, established the European
Economic Community. The original text of the Treaty is in the
French, German, Italian and Netherlands languages (see Article
248 of the Treaty). The English text as used in this study is that
published by Her Majesty's Stationery Office.[1]

The European Economic Community (also referred to in these
pages as E.E.C., the Community, or the Common Market) comprises the six member states: Belgium, France, Germany (the
Federal Republic), Italy, Luxembourg, the Netherlands. The
term 'Germany' in the text refers always to the Federal Republic
of Germany. Reference to the member states is made in their
English alphabetical order.

This study covers only the area in Europe of those six states
and legal aspects of foreign investment in their oversea territories
and possessions are not considered.

A member state in which an enterprise originating outside the

[1] Treaty establishing the European Economic Community. Rome,
25 March 1957, H.M.S.O., London, 1962.

Community ('foreign-owned') is established is referred to as the host (member) state.

## Non-member countries

States outside the E.E.C. are referred to as non-member countries. In the Treaty of Rome, as will be seen in the extracts quoted from various of its Articles, they are referred to as 'third countries'. The word 'foreign' (in foreign nationals, foreign-owned enterprise) refers to non-member states, implying anything derived from outside the E.E.C.

## Municipal laws

Municipal laws, legislation or rules are frequently referred to in this work and refer to those laws belonging to a member state individually, made either before the establishment of the Community or later as part of that state's internal legislation. The term here contrasts with *Community law*, which came into being with the E.E.C. and refers to the Community as a whole.

## Investment

This term is used as synonymous with *direct investment*, that is:

i. the establishment of enterprises or subsidiaries, partly or wholly owned, or the acquisition of partial or total ownership in existing undertakings;
ii. capital holdings in new or existing undertakings;
iii. long-term loans intended to establish or maintain lasting relationships.

In the course of the study, reference is made in general to categories i. and ii. Category i. is comprehensive and includes contributions not only in money but also in technical knowledge as referred to in Section 223(a) of the U.S. Act for International Development 1961,[1] namely 'any contribution of capital commodities, services, patents, processes or techniques . . .'

## Foreign investment

This term is used distinctively in this work with a special meaning: investment originating in a country *outside* the E.E.C. and made in one of the member states. It describes, for instance,

---

[1] See E. I. Nwogugu: *The Legal Problems of Foreign Investment in Developing Countries*, Manchester, 1965, p. 71; and G.-Y. Bertin: *L'Investissement des Firmes Etrangères en France 1945–62*, Paris, 1963, p. 10.

investment originating in Switzerland and made in Belgium. It excludes, in the context of this study, investments *between* member states of E.E.C., for example, capital originating in Belgium invested in Italy.

The need to introduce this special usage is brought about by the superimposition of the European Economic Community and all its functions upon social, economic and national matters in each of its member states. Formerly, before the inception of E.E.C., foreign investments, in the ordinary sense of those words, could be made in any of the six states (which became the Community) by any other country in the world, including the future Community members; and legal aspects of such investments were matters concerned solely with the municipal laws of the two countries involved and with international law. Since the E.E.C. was established, external investment in any member state can be considered as one of two kinds:

i. investments by nationals of one member state in another member state. These lie outside the scope of this work;

ii. investments by nationals of a non-member state in a member state.

The latter are the foreign investments which are the subject of our study. Upon the single-tier law relationships that formerly affected such investments, there have been superimposed the effects of Community law, creating a double-tiered legal relationship, which is itself evolving as integration within the E.E.C. proceeds.

In the same way and for similar reasons, foreign nationals within the Community (persons or companies from non-member states) must in the context of this work and of the Community be distinguished from nationals of one member state when present or employed in another member state.[1]

Foreign investments originating in non-member countries *associated* with the E.E.C. or in oversea territories belonging to a member state[2] are not discussed in this work. No analysis is made

[1] See Articles 48–73 of the Treaty of Rome concerning the free movement within the Community of persons, services and capital, especially Articles 52–58. Also, since 1960 direct investment, investment in real property, etc. have been liberalized within the Community: see First Directive of the Council on capital movement, approved 12 May 1960.

[2] The overseas associated countries and territories are as follows (28 February 1965):

Associated countries: Greece, Turkey

of the special status that any foreign nationals may enjoy by virtue
of bilateral agreements between their own non-member countries
and a member state of E.E.C. A separate comparative study would
be necessary to examine all these aspects in detail, though they
are referred to in passing in this study.

## Portfolio investment

This term refers to investment through capital markets.[1] It is of
limited importance in this study.

## Developing regions

The economic context of this term is difficult to define in a uniformly valid way;[2] it refers to countries which have all or many
of the following economic characteristics:

i. an undiversified economy and large dependence on one or a
few major but insufficient sources of national income;

ii. capital or industrial equipment small in amount and in relation to the actual or potential labour force;

iii. widespread unemployment, under-employment and lack of
widespread higher skill in modern production methods;

iv. a low real income per capita.

### THE EUROPEAN ECONOMIC COMMUNITY AS AN
### ECONOMICALLY ADVANCED REGION

The components of an investment climate comprise political,
legal and economic factors, which are interdependent. Economic

---

Associated African states: Burundi, Cameroun, Central African Republic,
Chad, Congo (Brazzaville), Congo (Leopoldville), Dahomey, Gabon,
Ivory Coast, Madagascar, Mali, Mauretania, Niger, Rwanda, Senegal,
Somalia, Togo, Upper Volta

Associated oversea territories: Comore Islands, Djibouti (French Somali-
land), French Austral lands, French Guiana, French Polynesia, Guade-
loupe, Martinique, New Caledonia, Reunion, St. Pierre and Miquelon,
Wallis and Fatuna Islands

Source: *The Europa Yearbook* 1962, vol. 1, p. 79.

[1] For a definition of portfolio investment see G. C. Munn's *Encyclopedia of
Banking and Finance*, 6th ed. by F. L. Garcia, Boston, Mass., 1962, p. 586.

[2] See A. Moyes and T. Hayter: *World III. A Handbook on Developing
Countries*, New York, 1964, p. 1 for definitions formulated by the O.E.C.D.
and U.N.O. See also B. A. Wortley (ed.): *The United Nations. The First Ten
Years*, Manchester, 1957, p. 160 (definition by Mars), and E. I. Nwogugu,
*The Legal Problems of Foreign Investment in Developing Countries*, pp. 1–2.

factors, among others, influence the decisions of foreign investors to invest their capital in one country or region rather than in others. Factors like the need for capital or technical knowledge, the ability to compete with foreign enterprise, etc., are some of the elements that shape the attitudes of the population or authorities of a country or a region to welcome foreign investment; in the absence of such positive factors, the attitude may be to resist such investment. These attitudes, favourable or unfavourable to foreign investment, are reflected not only in opinions but also in legislative and administrative measures. Within the E.E.C. the legal status of foreign investments and acceptance of or interest in them can be better understood *vis-à-vis* the economic situation in each of the member states as well as of the Community as a whole. The data which follow outline briefly this economic situation and show the Community to be one of the economically advanced regions of the world.

With an area of 1,167,500 sq. km. (or less than a hundredth of the world's total surface) and a population in mid-1963 of 178,518 millions (equivalent to more than one-twentieth of the world total), the E.E.C. in 1963 accounted for 28·3 per cent of the total value of world imports and 24·6 per cent of the total value of world exports (excluding U.S.S.R. and Eastern Europe).[1] Among 11 major industrial countries, in the first half of 1964, the export trade of the E.E.C. states showed these increases: Netherlands, 23 per cent compared with the corresponding period of 1963; Belgium-Luxembourg, 21·5 per cent; Italy, 17·5 per cent; Germany, 16 per cent; and France, 12·5 per cent.[2]

The Community is part of one of the three main industrial regions of the world, namely North America, Western Europe and Comecon,[3] and its peoples come within the 30 per cent of world population that claim 75–90 per cent of the total world figures for steel output, energy consumption, transportation facilities and merchant fleet.[4] The population of the E.E.C. is included

---

[1] Source: Statistical Office of the European Communities: *Basic Statistics*, 5th ed., December 1964, Table I and p. 101.

[2] *The Financial Times*, 4 December 1964, p. 1. For more details on developments in 1963, see G.A.T.T.: *International Trade 1963*, Geneva, 1964, pp. 83–6.

[3] Council for Mutual Economic Assistance (U.S.S.R. and East Europe). See *Europa Yearbook 1964*, vol. 1, pp. 110–17.

[4] J. P. Cole: *Geography of World Affairs*, 3rd ed., London, 1964, pp. 92–4. See also the *Oxford Economic Atlas of the World*, Oxford, 1954, Sections 7, 8,

in the 22 per cent 'top income bracket' (roughly representing Europe and North America) of the world population that earns nearly 75 per cent of the world total income.[1]

Since the establishment of the Common Market on 1 January 1958, the gross national product within the E.E.C. has increased by 38 per cent,[2] and according to the estimates of the E.E.C. Commission, its average for 1965 was 5·3 per cent.[3] The investment rate of gross formation of fixed capital represented for 1961–1963 an average, for the E.E.C. as a whole, of 22·6 per cent of the gross national product at current price level, showing an increase of 1·7 per cent compared with figures for 1960.[4] The average per capita gross national product at market prices in 1963 was 1421·5 US dollars (8·8 per cent from agriculture, 46·1 per cent from industry and 45·1 per cent from other activities).[5]

The economically active population of the E.E.C. represents an average of 41·7 per cent compared with the total population. Of the total labour force, some 44·8 per cent are active in industry, and 39·8 per cent furnish services. There is an aggregate shortage of labour within the Community. Unemployment is practically non-existent and large numbers of workers are being recruited

9 and 10 and pp. 108–11. On the energy economy of the Common Market, see G. Blondel: 'La politique énergétique de la Communauté Européenne', *Revue du Marché Commun*, no. 69, May 1964, pp. 225 ff.

[1] Moyes and Hayter, *Handbook on Developing Countries*, pp. 6–7 and pillar-grams 3 and 4 on same pages.

[2] *Le Monde*, 21 January 1965, p. 14.

[3] *Entreprise*, no. 488, 16 January 1965, p. 35; for previsions of the E.E.C. economy see pp. 33 ff. Between 1952 and 1962 the gross national product increased, for the whole of the Community, at an annual average rate of 5·6 per cent. See also Appendix A, Tables 4–7 of the present work.

[4] *Entreprise*, no. 487, 9 January 1965, p. 32. For 1960 see J. F. Dewhurst and others: *The New Europe and its Economic Future* (1964), pp. 23 and 125, based on (same authors) *Europe's Needs and Resources: Trends and Prospects in 18 Countries*, New York, 1961. See also Appendix A, Table 8 of the present study.

[5] *The O.E.C.D. Observer*, no. 13, December 1964, pp. 22–3. See also Appendix A, Table 7. For more details see Tables 9, 10 and 11. For the sake of comparison it may be pointed out that the Netherlands with a population of 11·5 million has a national income 50 per cent (or 1½ times) greater than that of Pakistan with a population of 94 million. See John C. de Wilde: 'International financing of industrial development', *Commercial Banks in Relation to Medium- and Long-term Credit*, Vienna, 1964, pp. 140–59, at p. 143.

outside the Community, in, for instance, Spain, Turkey, Greece, Portugal and Yugoslavia.[1]

Finally, a reflection of the E.E.C. as an economically well-developed area may be seen in its favourable international monetary position. Its external liquidity is as a whole characteristic of an advanced region.[2] It exports capital and is an important contributor to funds for development projects abroad.[3]

OBJECTIVES AND INSTITUTIONS OF THE EUROPEAN
ECONOMIC COMMUNITY IN THEIR RELEVANCE TO
FOREIGN INVESTMENTS

The relevance for our topic of some of the objectives set out in the Treaty of Rome is given by the extent to which Community law affects the application of municipal rules on foreign investment.[4] In this respect, it introduces a common standard of national treatment for Community nationals in the member states[5] and includes, to the extent implied by Community law, also

---

[1] On the labour shortage in Europe, including the Common Market, see *Le Monde*, 16 February 1965, p. 14; *The Financial Times*, and London *Times*, 15 February 1965, pp. 9 and 8 respectively. On migrant labour in Europe, see *Opera Mundi—Europe*, no. 287, 14 January 1965, pp. 9 ff.; tables for France, Germany, Belgium, the Netherlands, pp. 13 ff. In Germany there were 563,400 open jobs in January 1965, *Die Welt*, 6 February 1965, p. 1.

[2] The term 'liquidity' is used as indicating the degree of flexibility to respond and adapt without difficulty to foreign payments demands. See W. M. Brown: *The External Liquidity of an Advanced Country*, Princeton Studies in International Finance, no. 14, Princeton, 1964, p. 2 for definition; for developments related to the six member states of the Common Market, in the period 1953–63, see ibid., pp. 62–3, Tables II-a, p. 65, Tables II-c and II-d; for particulars of the member states, see Tables I-a, c, d, e, and g. See also O.E.C.D.: *Statistics of Balance of Payments*, 1960–1, Paris.

[3] For some information, see Moyes and Hayter, *Handbook on Developing Countries*.

[4] The history and law of the E.E.C. as a whole are not surveyed here. For its history see A. Campbell and D. Thompson: *Common Market Law: Texts and Commentaries*, London, 1962, pp. 1 ff., 13 ff.; on the law of the Common Market, ibid., pp. 9 ff., 12 ff., 20 ff., 28 ff. C. McCormick Crosswell: *International Business Techniques: Legal and Financial Aspects*, New York, 1963, pp. 151 ff. E. Stein and T. L. Nicholson (eds.): *American Enterprise in the European Common Market*, Ann Arbor, 1960, vol. 1, pp. 2 ff. On the aims and institutions of the E.E.C. see D. G. Valentine: *The Court of Justice of the European Communities*, London, 1965, vol. 1, pp. 414 ff., 422 ff.

[5] For example in Article 52 of the Treaty of Rome.

foreign nationals and especially foreign-owned enterprise in the Community standard of treatment.

Thus, in connection with *trading* in the customs union which is an objective of the E.E.C., the Treaty of Rome entitles foreign nationals established in one of the member states to engage, like Community nationals, in trade within the customs union.[1] Community law prescribes, indirectly, that foreign enterprise, once established in one of the six member states in accordance with its municipal rules, will not need special authorization on the part of the other five member states for trading throughout the customs union created by the Common Market. In other words, by virtue of Community law, foreign enterprise established in one of the member states, will be able to participate in the economic life of the other member states, irrespective of their municipal rules on the establishment of foreign nationals in their territory.

Another major objective of the E.E.C., the *right of establishment*,[2] introduces a further limitation on the applicability of the respective municipal rules on establishment in the six member states. For this purpose, Community law draws a distinction between a foreign-owned enterprise not yet established and such an enterprise already established in a member state. The establishment of a foreign-owned enterprise coming from a non-member country will be governed by the law of the host member state; but, once established in a member state, the access of such an enterprise to other member states, for establishment, will be governed by Community law and not by the municipal rules of the other member state where establishment is sought. The relationship between Community law and municipal law, in matters related to establishment of foreign-owned enterprises in the E.E.C., and the extent to which Community law imposes restrictions on municipal rules, may be summarized as follows:

i. If a foreign investor[3] seeks access to a member state in a form which we would propose to call an initial establishment, i.e. coming from a non-member country into the Common Market, the *municipal rules* of the host member state will apply to the entry, disinvestment of capital, and transfer of investment income,

[1] Article 3(a)/9 ff., 30 ff., and Articles 59 and 60.
[2] Articles 3(c), 52, 58, 67.
[3] The term implies in the first place the establishment of foreign investment in the member states of the E.E.C., in the form of a legal personality, e.g. joint-stock company.

c

as well as to the economic sectors, e.g. shipping, insurance, transport, and so forth, to which a foreign investor may have access;[1]

ii. If, however, a foreign investor, i.e. a national of a non-member country, seeks establishment in a member state after having been already established in another member state of the Common Market, the *Community law* will apply.

In this connection, it must be added that the limitations imposed by Community law upon municipal laws on foreign investment apply also to associated overseas territories and countries of the member states of the Community.[2] In other words, foreign-owned enterprise, once established in one of the member states, will be entitled not only to receive Community treatment within the Common Market, but also to claim the same benefits of trade and establishment in associated overseas territories and countries.

The rules of competition in trade between member states in Community law will apply to relationships between foreign-owned enterprises operating in the Common Market and the principal companies situated outside it, to the extent that relationships such as exclusive dealings and other restrictive trading agreements, including licences, may affect trade between member states.[3]

Finally, reference should be made to two other objectives, one aiming at 'the co-ordination of the economic policies of member states and the correction of instability in their balance of payments',[4] and the other at 'the approximation of their respective national laws to the extent required for the Common Market to function in an orderly manner'.[5] Since the current economic policies of the member states and their laws have a significant bearing upon the status of foreign investment in the Common Market, it seems justifiable to assume that their co-ordination and approximation, respectively, will not fail to have some effect on the law of foreign investment too, though it is difficult at present to assess concretely the magnitude of this effect. Economic union

[1] For examples of economic activities inaccessible to foreign investment in the different member states, see chapter III. Divergences between these rules are discussed in the section on harmonization in chapter XII.
[2] Articles 3(k), 131, 132/5, 238.
[3] Articles 85/1 and 86.
[4] Articles 3(g), 72, 103, 104.
[5] Articles 3(h), 100, 102, 220.

within implies unity towards the outside world, including the uniform treatment of investment from non-member countries.[1]

In considering the institutions of the E.E.C. in their relevance to foreign investment, the scope of their competences will be of importance because they are the organs responsible for the implementation and supervision of the economic union set out in the Treaty of Rome.[2]

The *European Parliament*, common to the three Communities, i.e. the E.C.S.C., the E.E.C. and the EURATOM, is a deliberating body with no legislative power (as yet), but it has the essential function under the Treaty to exercise a certain power over the Commission of the E.E.C. It is a forum where aspects of foreign investment and the problems it creates within the E.E.C. may be discussed, as an important reflection of public opinion on foreign capital in the E.E.C.[3]

The *Council* of Ministers[4] and especially the *Commission* of the E.E.C., as the executive organs primarily responsible for the functioning of the Common Market, are of more direct concern for the foreign investor. They are the institutions which give more articulate expression to some of the broadly formulated provisions of the Treaty of Rome, such as Articles 52 and 58 on the right of establishment, and Articles 85 and 86 setting out the Community rules on restrictive trading agreements. In fact, they are developing the law of the Community in the broader sense of the word, namely the concrete application of the vague terms of the Treaty. Moreover, both the Council and the Commission may initiate action and the former is empowered to take decisions

[1] See the general remark by J. Deniau: 'Objectives and the constitutional structure of the E.E.C.' in I.C.L.Q. Suppl. Publ. no. 1, *Legal Problems of the E.E.C. and the E.F.T.A.* A Report of a Conference held in September 1960, London, 1961, p. 5.

[2] Articles 4, 137 ff. (the Assembly), 145 ff. (the Council), 155 ff. (the Commission).

[3] See for example E.E.C. *Bulletin*, no. 12, 1964, pp. 49 ff. For a general survey on the Parliamentary Assembly of the European Communities, M. Forsyth: 'The Parliament of the European Communities', *Planning* (P.E.P.), vol. xxx, no. 478, March 1964. For a discussion of the legal bases, p. 12 f.; on selection and status of members, p. 19 f.; control powers on the executive organs of the E.E.C., p. 47; on participation in legislatory work, pp. 67 ff., 84 ff.; on democracy in the Community, p. 90. See also Campbell and Thompson, *Common Market Law*, pp. 80 ff.

[4] Articles 145–154 of the Treaty. See Campbell and Thompson, *Common Market Law*, pp. 82–8.

concerning the harmonization of municipal laws to the extent necessary for the implementation of the economic union,[1] a process which may bear also upon the current double-tiered foreign investment law in the E.E.C.

As for the *Court of Justice* common to the three European Communities, E.C.S.C., E.E.C. and the EURATOM,[2] this is the institution in charge of ensuring 'the observance of law in the interpretation and application' of the Treaty of Rome.[3] It possesses a correspondingly wide jurisdiction over the member states,[4] the other institutions of the E.E.C.,[5] and over natural or legal persons affected by the application of Community law.[6] Foreign enterprise established in the Common Market and engaged in intermember trade would belong to the category of natural or legal persons concerned. Appeals from decisions of the Commission, e.g. on the Community rules of competition (Articles 85–86), may be lodged with the Court of Justice by foreign-owned enterprises affected by them, on grounds indicated in Article 173/1. The future development and implementation of the right of establishment (Articles 52 and 58) would, in cases of dispute, be just as much dependent on the interpretation given by the Court as on the opinions of the executive institutions of the E.E.C.[7]

Summarizing the relevance of Community law for foreign enterprise in the member states of the Common Market, it may be said that in intermember relations, i.e. on Community level, the Treaty of Rome extends Community treatment, or national treatment in the respective member states, also to foreign-owned enterprise, though it distinguishes between a foreign-owned enter-

---

[1] Article 100.

[2] See Convention relating to Common Institutions.

[3] Article 164. For the composition of the Court, see Article 165; for the office of the advocate-general, Article 166; for the office of the registrar, Article 168. For a detailed study, D. G. Valentine: *Court of Justice of the Eur. Communities.*

[4] Articles 219, 169 and 177.

[5] Article 173.

[6] Articles 173 and 192. For jurisdiction on the status of officials and other personnel of the Communities, see Article 179. For the types of jurisdiction of the court, Valentine, *Court of Justice of the Eur. Communities*, vol. 1, pp. 9 ff.

[7] For more details on this point, see chapter X. On the function and problems of the Court in developing law, see Campbell and Thompson, *Common Market Law*, pp. 92–3, and Valentine, *Court of Justice of the Eur. Communities*, vol. 1.

prise not yet established in any member state and such an enterprise already established in a member state and, therefore, also in
the Common Market. Community law marks a new development,
by affecting conditions of foreign investment on a large regional
basis. Moreover, it provides through the jurisdiction of the Court
of Justice of the European Communities, a permanent judicial
organ competent to deal with interstate investment disputes falling within the ambit of Community law on the right of establishment. The structure of investment law in the E.E.C. is thus a
double-tiered one, in which both municipal and Community rules
exist. While these two sets of rules are in principle delineated,
their parallel application may raise problems of co-ordination as
the economic integration of E.E.C. member states progresses.
What the content of these two sets of foreign investment laws
are and what the future needs for their co-ordination may be, will
be examined in the following pages.

# PART ONE
# FOREIGN INVESTMENT IN THE MEMBER STATES OF THE EUROPEAN ECONOMIC COMMUNITY

# CHAPTER II
# STATISTICAL DATA

The law of foreign investment is primarily economic law which is applied to the interstate flow of investment funds and to the establishment of foreign enterprise in a given country. Its impact is economic in nature and has to be measured with reference to economic data. If it needs change, such change will be prompted by the problems of the economic situation; likewise, its usefulness will be judged in terms of the function it fulfils in economic life. With the economic impact of investment law in mind, it is appropriate to refer to statistical data on foreign investment in the E.E.C.[1] The available data are, however, neither uniform nor complete for the whole of the Common Market.[2] Hence, their correlation for uniform treatment is not possible. Questions on the percentage of foreign investment in the total investment of a member state or of the E.E.C. as a whole cannot be reliably answered, nor can the impact of foreign investment on economic growth in the respective member states be assessed in a reliable manner. These are, however, questions that fall within the competence of statisticians and economists. Such material as is available is included in the conviction that it will prove useful and at the least provide some background for our discussions.

The bulk of foreign investment in the Common Market is from the United States, followed by the United Kingdom, Switzerland, Sweden and other countries.

At the end of 1962, the value of investment from the United States had reached a total of 3,671m US dollars,[3] or about 9·9 per

[1] In accordance with the definition of 'foreign investment' given above, intermember investments are not included in the data presented here. This takes into account the fact that with the implementation of the Treaty of Rome, the legal meaning of the term 'foreign investment' will no longer be applicable to intermember investments (Articles 52, 58; also Article 67/1).

[2] The limitations and incompleteness of available data have been indicated in answers to questions on American investments, addressed to the E.E.C. Commission. See J.O.(C.E.), 1963, Question no. 172, p. 975/63 and J.O.(C.E.), 1964, p. 3725/64; see also J.O.(C.E.), 1965, p. 2154/65.

[3] Data represent cumulated totals of net capital and undistributed earnings. Source: U.S. Department of Commerce, *Statistical Abstract of the United States*, 1964, p. 854.

cent of total American private capital invested abroad (US dollars 37,145m) and about 42·7 per cent of American private capital invested in Western Europe (US dollars 8,607m).[1]

### Total direct U.S. investment in E.E.C. (Cumulated totals)

| Year | million US dollars |
|------|------|
| 1950 | 637 |
| 1959 | 2,208 |
| 1961 | 3,087 |
| 1962 | 3,671 |

Source: U.S. Dept. of Commerce, *Stat. Abstract of the U.S.* (1964), p. 854.

It is difficult to guess what percentage these figures present in the total amount of investment in the member states. A rough guess which should not be too far from reality would be around 2 to 3 per cent.[2]

As for the geographical distribution of American direct investment in the six member states of the E.E.C., the cumulated totals at the end of 1962 were as shown on opposite page .

An important part (about 56 per cent) of the American capital invested in the Common Market has been invested in the manufacturing industries, a fact that lies behind the growing concern about successful competition in the E.E.C. by American firms

[1] Source: O.E.C.D. Economic Surveys: *The United States,* November 1963, Paris, Table 2, p. 10, which also shows for comparison, total U.S. private capital abroad in 1950, 1961 and 1962.

[2] One author, referring to *new* investments by American industry abroad, is of the opinion that such investments would correspond in any country to only 0·5 to 2 per cent of the total investments of that country: E. R. Eggers: in *Commerce in Germany,* no. 131, November 1964, p. 26. According to another opinion, U.S. direct investments do not account for more than 1 per cent of total capital investment in Europe: P. Uri: *Le Monde,* 23 February 1964, p. 14. In the opinion of the E.E.C. this figure was 2 per cent in 1960, 2·3 per cent in 1961: J.O.(C.E.), 1963, p. 977/63; see also Table 4, p. 975/63. Cf. also E. R. Eggers: on the nature and trends of American investments in Europe, *Opera Mundi—Europe,* no. 269, 17 September 1964, pp. 5–12; H. Kremp: on the percentage of American capital in total industrial investment in the E.E.C., *Mitteilungen der Handelskammer Hamburg,* no. 5, May 1963, pp. 270–2; and information reported in *Markt-Informationsdienst,* vol. III, no. 18, January 1963, pp. 1–48, and in *Mondo Economico,* 16 February 1963, no. 7 (Supplement), pp. 1 ff. Also Appendix B, Table 1 of the present work.

| Member state | million US dollars | Percentage of E.E.C. total |
|---|---|---|
| Belgium-Luxembourg | 283 | 7·7 |
| France | 1,006 | 27·4 |
| Germany | 1,472 | 40·1 |
| Italy | 540 | 14·7 |
| The Netherlands | 370 | 10·1 |
| E.E.C. total | 3,671 | 100·0 |

Source: U.S. Dept. of Commerce, *Stat. Abstract of the U.S.* (1964).[1]

with better production and marketing standards. Indeed, the largest American investors in Europe are companies which are responsible for 88 per cent of the industrial research undertaken in the United States.

Of direct investments from the United Kingdom in 1961 £24·8m (11·7 per cent of a total of £211·6m invested abroad) went to the E.E.C.; figures for 1962 were £30·7m or 19·6 per cent of a total of £156·9m invested abroad and overseas.[2] Figures for Swedish subsidiaries in the E.E.C. show that about 30 per cent of a total of 1,084 Swedish subsidiaries established abroad were operating in the E.E.C.[3]

## BELGIUM

Among the E.E.C. member states information on foreign investment is more reliable in Belgium. Where available, data permit an assessment of the impact that foreign investment has had on the economic life of the country. In 1963 the value of new foreign investment projects notified to the Ministry of Economic Affairs represented a total value of Bfrs. 5,444m (about US dollars 108·9m), bringing the total for 1959–63 to Bfrs. 24,793m (about US dollars 495·9m).[4] The number of jobs scheduled for the new

[1] See also The Chase Manhattan Bank, New York: *The European Markets*. January 1964, p. 39; and Appendix B, Tables 1, 5 and 6 of the present work.

[2] Figures do not include investment by oil and insurance companies. Source: Board of Trade Journal, November 1963 (figures for 1962 are incomplete). See Appendix B, Table 3 of the present work; also *Mondo Economico*, 16 February 1963, no. 6 (Supplement), pp. 1 ff.

[3] B. Ekman: 'Swedish Industry goes Abroad', *Featuring Sweden, no. 4,1964*, p. 30. See also Appendix B, Table 5.

[4] Journal of the Belgian Chamber of Commerce in Great Britain, January 1965, p. 32. Also A. van Hissenhoven: in *La Revue de la Banque* (Brussels), 27th year, no. 4, 1963, pp. 426–54, on foreign investments in Belgium; on the

foreign investments in 1963 amounted to 4,265, increasing the total number of new jobs created by new foreign investments in the period 1959–63 to 26,000 (0·7 per cent of a total labour force of 3,525 million in 1963).[1] Of this total, 15,740 jobs or about 60·5 per cent arose from American investments.[2]

## FRANCE

New foreign investment was NF. 741m in 1960 and rose to NF. 1,076·9m in 1961, representing 2 to 3 per cent of gross fixed asset formation of enterprises,[3] and deriving 31 per cent from the United States, 42 per cent from other O.E.C.D. countries, 4 per cent from Canada and other countries (the remaining 23 per cent came from the other E.E.C. member states).[4] It is estimated that 50 per cent of direct foreign investment in the country is of American origin, i.e. American capital that came to France directly or via other countries like Switzerland or Liechtenstein. While the basic sectors of the economy are not dominated or influenced by foreign capital, certain sectors like industries manufacturing ball-bearings, calculating machines, electronics and agricultural machinery are, respectively, 80, 61, 60 and 45 per cent foreign-owned.[5]

---

same topic, see *Notes Rapides sur la Situation Econ. en France et à l'Etranger* (Paris), 15th year, no. 223, 20 September 1964, pp. 4–6, and ibid., no. 192 (Supplement to *Problèmes Economiques*, no. 837), 14 January 1964, pp. 3–7.

[1] O.E.C.D. *Observer*, no. 13, December 1964, pp. 20–1.

[2] For some information on the activities of British firms in Belgium, see *Brit. Trade Journal*, Supplement, 6 December 1963, p. 48.

[3] Source: O.E.C.D. and French authorities. On foreign investments in France, in general, see: *La Vie Française*, 20th year, no. 978, 21 February 1964, p. 7, and no. 980, 6 March 1964, p. 7. Also G.-Y. Bertin: *Direction*, no. 94, April 1963, pp. 401–11.

[4] For more information on American investments in France, see: P. Mordacq: *Problèmes Economiques* (Paris), no. 818, 3 September 1963, pp. 14–18; *La Vie Française*, 19th year, no. 963, 8 November 1963, p. 7; *Neue Zürcher Zeitung*, no. 270, 3 October 1962, Blatt 10, p. 1; *Force Ouvrière—Informations*, no. 123, January 1963, pp. 75–81; *Economie et Politique*, nos. 100–101, November–December 1962, pp. 192–214.

American direct investments (par value) in France at the end of 1961 were given as US dollars 840m (1950: 217m). See Moody's *Municipal and Government Manual—American and Foreign*, 1964, p. 2773.

[5] J. Gervais: *La Vie Française* 20th year, no. 979, 28 February 1964, p. 8, and no. 980, 6 March 1964, p. 7; *Der Volkswirt* (Frankfurt/Main), 18th year,

## GERMANY

Among foreign direct investments in the Federal Republic of Germany, the largest amount is American. Other countries outside the Common Market exporting substantial direct investment capital to Germany are the United Kingdom, Switzerland,[1] and probably Sweden. In 1962 and 1963 American new investments have averaged US dollars 300m per year,[2] and at the end of 1963 their cumulative total was estimated to be US dollars 1,800m,[3] or about 3 to 4 per cent of the estimated total of German industrial investment (US dollars 50,000–60,000m).[4] The estimated yearly average of US dollars 300m for American new investments represented 4 per cent of German yearly investments, considered to be about US dollars 7,500m. One-quarter of American investments is reported to be in Hamburg. Fewer than 30 of a total of 311 (1962) American-owned firms and subsidiaries in Germany were employing 1,000 workers or more; American-owned enterprise employed about 1 per cent of the total German labour force. Of the 35 largest German corporations, three were American-owned, namely Esso (10th largest), Opel (18th largest) and Ford (30th largest), representing together some 40 per cent of American investments in Germany.[5]

---

no. 27, 3 July 1964, pp. 1380–2; G.-Y. Bertin: *Direction*, no. 94, April 1963, pp. 401–11.

According to R. Eggers: *Commerce in Germany*, American companies in France control 90 per cent of the synthetic rubber industry, and 65 per cent of the farm machinery production. For some information on foreign investment in earlier years, cf. *Foreign Investment in France*, publ. Crédit du Nord, Paris, 1963, pp. 4, 5–6. Also P. H. de Vallée: 'Les investissements américains en Europe', *L'Information*, 14 December 1962, on the increase of American investment in France after the establishment of the Common Market.

[1] *Hamburg-Information* (bulletin), no. E/62, 14 January 1965, p. 1.

[2] U.S. Ambassador C. McGhee in a lecture in Frankfurt, on 20 October 1964, reported in *Commerce in Germany*, no. 131, November 1964, p. 9.

[3] Ibid.; see also table on p. 19 above.

[4] On American capital participation in German industry see *La Vie Française*, 19th year, no. 969, 20 December 1963, p. 25; B. Huffschmid, in *Documents*, Revue des Questions Allemandes, 19th year, no. 1, January–February 1964, pp. 62–70.

[5] C. McGhee and also R. E. Eggers in *Commerce in Germany*, no. 131, November 1964. For the 100 largest firms in Germany, see *Frankfurter Allgemeine Zeitung*, 1 December 1962, p. 5. For Europe's 60 largest companies, see E.E.C.: *Europe's 60 largest companies* (in 1961), June 1963.

## ITALY

The most important flow of foreign direct investment in Italy is from Switzerland and Liechtenstein, representing 50 per cent of the total at the end of 1961,[1] followed by capital from the United States (approximately 16 per cent), the United Kingdom (about 7 per cent) (the remaining 12 per cent originated from the Common Market). The net amount of foreign investment (including investment from other E.E.C. countries) in 1962 was US dollars 771·6m (1961: 493·2m) bringing the cumulative total to US dollars 3,438·6m, of which US dollars 431·9m represented US capital (1955: 154m).[2] Part of the investment is effected in the form of machinery, mainly from the United States. Most foreign investment has been directed to the metal, chemical and petroleum industries.

## LUXEMBOURG

Figures on foreign direct investment are not available. A list of industrial firms established since 1959 in the Grand-Duchy of Luxembourg contains names of important foreign firms.[3]

## THE NETHERLANDS

The total value of American direct investment in the Netherlands at the end of 1961 was US dollars 308m (1953: US dollars 124m).[4] In September 1963, of a total of 435 subsidiaries or participating enterprises from non-member countries, 230 firms or approximately 53 per cent were American, 99 firms or approximately 23 per cent were from the United Kingdom, 41 undertakings or

[1] Source: O.E.C.D. On foreign investments in Italy in the period 1956–62, see *France-Italie*, Revue économique de la Chambre de Commerce Italienne de Paris, 78th year, no. 8, November 1963, pp. 24–5; *The Italian Market:* a Contimart Report, no. 7, Zurich, 1962, p. 29. On new trends of foreign investments in Italy, see *Rivista di Politica Economica* (Roma), 53rd year, no. 7, July 1963, pp. 1095–108. On foreign investments in relation to southern Italy, see *Entreprise*, no. 371, Supplement, 20 October 1962, pp. 30–42.

[2] *Moody's Municipal and Government Manual*, p. 2815. The figures given are presumed to include also portfolio investment. For figures in 1959–60, see World Trade Inf. Service (*W.T.I.S.*), 1962, no. 62–51, p. 10.

[3] *Bulletin Economique*, publ. by the Central Service of Statistics and Economic Studies, Luxembourg, vol. IX, no. 2, February 1963, pp. 14–15.

[4] *Moody's Municipal and Government Manual*, p. 2838.

9·4 per cent were Swiss and 34 firms or about 8 per cent from Sweden.[1] Foreign investment has been directed in the first place to the metal manufacturing and chemical industries.

## CONCLUSIONS

While incomplete and lacking uniformity, available data on foreign direct investment in the E.E.C. show that the Common Market has been attracting considerable foreign investment funds at an increasing yearly rate since its establishment in 1958.[2] This development reflects favourably on both the legal and the economic aspects of investment climate in the E.E.C., though it has become, at the same time, a matter of some concern on the part of domestic enterprise in some of the member states, especially France and Germany. The concern expressed is not about foreign investment as such, but about investments from one particular non-member country—the United States. In fact, some of the discussions refer to foreign investment as almost synonymous with American investment. While appreciating the considerable economic and technical contribution that foreign, especially American, capital has made, certain quarters have pointed to some of the disadvantages under which, in the present legal system, domestic enterprise has to compete with the financially and technically better equipped American enterprise. Some of the arguments presented in this respect are examined in chapter XIII. It is sufficient to say here that the situation to which these arguments refer possibly introduces a new dimension in the law of foreign investment between economically advanced countries, and it may

[1] Netherlands Ministry of Economic Affairs, *Economische Voorlichting*, no. 42, 16 October 1963, The Hague; also, by the same ministry: *Guide to the Establishing of Industrial Operations in the Netherlands*, The Hague, 1961, p. 71; *Zeitschrift fur Europäische Wirtschaft/Entwicklungsländer* (Baden-Baden), 1963, no. 1, p. 48. Concerning the activities of British firms in the Netherlands, see *Brit. Trade Journal*, Supplement 6 December 1963, pp. 45–6.

[2] On foreign investments in Europe, in general, before the establishment of the E.E.C., see Ph. Courtney: 'Investment across the Atlantic', in *European American Survey*, publ. by the European Movement, Brussels, July 1957, p. 124; see also for some figures on American investment in the E.E.C. between 1950 and 1956, *The European Common Market*, publ. The First National City Bank of New York, 1958, p. 20. Between 1958 and 1961, American investments in the E.E.C. had increased by 81 per cent: J.O.(C.E.), 1963, pp. 975/63, 976/63 (Table 2), p. 977/63 (Table 3). See also Appendix B, Tables 1 ff. of the present work.

raise fundamental questions about fair competition, in terms of foreign investment, between advanced national economies. This is a problem which exists in general between the respective economies of the member states in the E.E.C., and is duly considered in the Treaty of Rome—the basic principle of co-ordination of national economies within a customs union is behind many of the provisions of the Treaty. The concern of Community enterprise about foreign investment may possibly point to the existence of a similar problem in relation to the massive participation of foreign enterprise in the E.E.C.

The flow of investment capital into the E.E.C. from advanced countries is in line with the long history of capital movements between regions or countries of more or less equal economic development.[1] In the context of the current international situation it represents, however, only one of the two main categories of interstate capital flow: (a) between *advanced* countries, and (b) from *advanced* to *developing* countries (where the need for capital is very marked). Foreign investments in the E.E.C. fall in the first category; moreover the movement of capital into these developed European countries is flowing at an increasing rate.[2]

This trend is to a great extent due to the differential economic and legal factors of investment climate in well-developed and developing regions of the world. In this respect, it is relevant to ask what the impact and interaction of the economic and legal components of investment climate are in their effectiveness to attract foreign capital. With respect to a region like the E.E.C., an outline analysis of this question is undertaken in chapter XIII.

[1] C. K. Hobson: *The Export of Capital*, London, 1914, republ. 1963, chapter VI, p. 121 f. P. Uri, in *Le Monde*, 23 February 1963, p. 14.
[2] *The Britannica Book of the Year for 1963*, p. 266: in 1962-3, the E.E.C. continued to receive more capital from non-member countries than its members invested abroad. On the same trend, O.E.C.D. Economic Surveys: *The United States*, p. 11; X. Zolotas: *Monetary Equilibrium and Economic Development*, Princeton, New Jersey, 1965, p. 132. On the increasing flow of American capital into the E.E.C., see the statement of the Lord Privy Seal in 1961 to the effect that half of the American investments in Europe formerly came to Great Britain, but in 1960 only 41 per cent did so, while over 50 per cent was expected to go to the Common Market: 640 H.C. Debates, Column 1388, 17 May 1961. Western Europe is currently the site of 50 per cent of the total foreign activities of American companies (*The Times*, 16 December 1964, p. 19); one-third of all American foreign investment is estimated to be in Canada. On further American investment in 1964, see *Die Welt*, no. 252, 28 October 1964, p. 13, and *Kurier*, 29 December 1964, p. 6.

# CHAPTER III

# FOREIGN PARTICIPATION IN THE ECONOMY OF MEMBER STATES

In the Common Market, the economic systems of the six member states are marked by a mixture of public and private enterprise. The role of public enterprise varies from one member state to another but in all of them a large section of economic activity is the domain of private initiative.

In sectors where public enterprise is active, such as state monopolies, public utilities or state-owned industries, statutory rules preclude the participation of (domestic and foreign) private capital.[1] In some sectors—for example, the manufacture of explosives—only domestic private capital may be permitted to have access; in others the access of foreign enterprise is governed by certain principles concerned with, say, the extent of domestic participation, reciprocity and national interest. Finally, there is the group of economic activities open to foreigners with no other requirement than an administrative authorization which is equally required from nationals of the host member state.[2] The participation of foreign investment in the economies of the E.E.C. states is discussed here under four heads:

  i. sectors inaccessible to private capital;[3]
 ii. sectors accessible to domestic private capital but not to foreign private capital;
iii. sectors accessible to foreign capital but governed by certain conditions and principles;
 iv. sectors easily accessible to foreign capital.

---

[1] Such preclusion may provide, however, for exemptions so that private capital may participate in the activities of public utilities or public enterprise.

[2] In virtue of Articles 52 and 58 of the Treaty, the distinction between foreigners and nationals of a given member state will not apply to Community nationals: see chapter X below.

[3] In this sector exceptions may exist providing for the access of private capital.

i. *Economic sectors inaccessible to private capital: commercial state monopolies, public utilities, state-owned industries*

Commercial state monopolies[1] in respect of commodities exist in three of the six member states: France, Germany and Italy. In France, they concern tobacco, matches, spirits, explosives, petroleum, potash and newsprint;[2] in Germany, matches and spirits;[3] and in Italy, tobacco, salt, matches, lighters, lighter-flints, cigarette paper, quinine, and all bananas imported from Somalia.[4] Under Article 37 of the Treaty, the monopolies will continue to exist; but in accordance with the objectives of the Common Market, they will be subject to a progressive adjustment so as to eliminate, by the end of the transitional period, all discrimination 'between the nationals of Member States as regards the supply or marketing

[1] For a broad definition of 'monopoly' in the Treaty of Rome, see Article 37/1 par. 2: 'any organization through which a Member State, *de jure* or *de facto*, either directly or indirectly controls, supervises or appreciably influences imports or exports as between Member States'. This definition includes also 'monopolies delegated by the State to other legal entities'. For comments, see H. v. d. Groeben and H. v. Boeckh: *Kommentar zum EWG-Vertrag*, Baden-Baden, 1958, vol. 1, p. 104, n. 6(a); Campbell and Thompson, *Common Market Law*, pp. 224–5 and p. 36. Community law does not prohibit the existence of state monopolies, but governs their adverse and unjustified effect on trade *between* member states: Groeben and Boeckh, *Kommenter*, vol. 1, p. 103, n. 4(c).

[2] For tobacco, see Law of 28 April 1816; matches, Law of 2 August 1872; explosives, Law of 13 August 1797; potash, Law of 19 July 1845. See Groeben and Boeckh, *Kommentar*, vol. 1, p. 102, n. 2; Campbell and Thompson, *Common Market Law*, p. 37; also F. Ridley and J. Blondel: *Public Administration in France*, London, 1964, p. 239.

[3] For matches, see agreement between the German government and the Svenska Tandstickaktiebolaget (Sweden) of 26 August 1926, and Law of 29 January 1930; spirits, Law of 8 April 1922. See Groeben and Boeckh, *Kommentar*, vol. 1, p. 101, n. 2.

[4] For tobacco, see Law of 17 July 1942. Concerning tobacco monopolies in the Common Market and their status in respect to the Treaty of Rome, see M. A. Migot: 'Le Traité de Rome et les monopoles fiscaux des tabacs', in: *Recherches économiques de Louvain*, no. 7, September 1964, pp. 571 ff.

For salt, see Law of 17 July 1942; for matches, Law of 5 April 1925; lighters, lighter-flints, Law of 26 February 1930; cigarette paper, Law 13 January 1936; quinine, Law of 8 March 1936; bananas from Somalia, Law of 2 December 1935. See Groeben and Boeckh, *Kommentar*, vol. 1, pp. 101–2, n. 2; Campbell and Thompson, *Common Market Law*, p. 37. From 1 December 1965, the monopoly on the import of bananas was scheduled to be abolished. The government will require, however, that importers purchase half of the bananas imported from Somalia: see *Die Welt*, no. 284, 5 December 1964, p. 12.

of goods'.[1] In other words, it is submitted that even though a member state may maintain a commercial monopoly, to which its nationals are barred access, those nationals and other Community nationals will in due course have, nevertheless, the possibility of manufacturing competitive products in other member states and of importing them, under conditions prescribed by the Treaty and Common Market organs, into the monopoly-holding member state. Any opinion opposed to the one admitted would be incompatible with the free movement of goods as one of the major objectives of the economic union envisaged by the Treaty. As to the term 'nationals of Member States', it would include also foreign-owned enterprises, as provided for in Articles 58 and 52, established in a member state other than that of the monopoly. Until the end of the transitional period, intermember restrictions on trade concerning state monopoly goods will exist.

In the field of central banking, the respective banks in France, Germany, Italy and the Netherlands are 100 per cent owned by the central government or government-owned corporations.[2] In the sector of public utilities, the railroad systems in Belgium, France, Germany and the Netherlands are state-owned, while in Italy such ownership amounts to 90 per cent. In Luxembourg 51 per cent of the capital of the national railroad company has been subscribed by the state of Luxembourg, and the remaining 49 per cent, in equal shares, by Belgium and France. In all six member states, telephone and telegraph services are state-owned and state-controlled. In radio and television broadcasting, facilities in five of the states (Luxembourg is the exception) are owned either by the central government or by provincial authorities. In power supply services, 93 per cent of electricity production and distribution in France and 94 per cent in Germany are state-owned; in the Netherlands the industry of electric power production is 100 per cent owned either by the state or by local authorities.[3]

State participation in economic activities in the form of public

---

[1] Article 37/1 par. 1; see also Articles 52 and 58. The provision of Article 37/1 par. 1 will equally apply to foreign-owned legal entities constituted in accordance with the law of a member state (Art. 58/1).

[2] Details of the government and management of banking and public utilities are given, for the various states, in the notes at the end of this chapter.

[3] See J. F. Dewhurst and others: *Europe's Needs and Resources: Trends and Prospects in 18 Countries*, p. 437. The percentage figure for electricity in France includes the manufacture and distribution of gas.

enterprise, wholly or partly owned, is more extensive in some member states than in others but it exists in all of them, often side by side with private enterprise, as public utilities, basic industries or manufacturing.

In Belgium the Société Nationale d'Investissement, founded in October 1962, is a joint public and private institution, influenced by the state, to promote the creation or expansion of commercial and industrial undertakings; this body is of significant interest for co-operation between foreign and Belgian investors.[1] In 1960, 50 per cent of ownership in scheduled airlines was by public authorities; in electricity production 7 per cent, in electricity distribution 33 per cent, while, in the same year, 275,494 hectares of forests were administered by the state.[2]

In France, the extent of public enterprise is not easy to determine.[3] The fuel and power industries are almost entirely state-controlled. Coal mines, nationalized since 1945, are operated by a national coal authority (Charbonnages de France).[4] The participation of the state in the field of petroleum is considerable: the state has acquired 35 per cent of the Compagnie Française des Pétroles and exercises control over the subsidiaries of this company, over tankers, refineries and distributing agencies.[5]

In the field of transportation, in addition to a 100 per cent ownership of the national railroad (S.N.C.F.), the airline company, Air France, is 93 per cent owned by the government and the state dominates a great part of the aircraft industry.[6] Since 1933, the state is a majority shareholder of the Compagnie Générale Transatlantique. It also controls 78 per cent of the shipping company Messageries Maritimes and about 40 per cent of total French shipping tonnage.[7]

One-third of the motor car industry is owned by the state: the Renault automobile manufacturing company is wholly state-owned. It is the seventh largest company on the list of world car manufacturers.[8]

[1] Overseas Business Reports (O.B.R.), 1964, no. 64-15, p. 13.
[2] Dewhurst and others, *Europe's Needs and Resources*, p. 437; O.B.R., 1964, no. 64-15, p. 6.
[3] Ridley and Blondel: *Public Administration in France*, pp. 238, 239.
[4] Ibid., p. 235.          [5] Ibid., pp. 238, 233-4.
[6] O.B.R., 1964, no. 64-10, p. 11; Ridley and Blondel, *Public Administration in France*, p. 238; *Le Monde*, 27 February 1965, p. 20.
[7] Ridley and Blondel, *Public Administration in France*, pp. 234 and 236.
[8] *The Guardian*, 27 February 1965, p. 9.

State ownership and control are also prominent in the field of banking[1] and insurance. In 1946, 34 insurance companies were nationalized and a reinsurance institute, the Caisse Centrale de Réassurance, was established to deal with all reinsurers other than the nationalized companies.[2]

Among the state-controlled undertakings are the Union Générale Cinématographique and others that manufacture refrigerators, washing machines, fertilizers and various chemicals.[3] The latest report of the Commission for the Verification of the Accounts of Public Enterprises (Commission de Vérification des Entreprises Publiques) reveals that the state participates in 122 industries with some 1,100 subsidiaries.[4] The state is the largest owner of and customer for French industry: it accounts for 30 per cent of all salaries paid, 15 per cent of the production and 10 per cent of industrial investments.[5] It owns the largest enterprise in the country, the Electricité de France, which ranks eighth in the table of E.E.C.'s 100 largest firms.

In Germany, large industrial and commercial assets are owned by the Federal government. These assets are valued at more than 1,000m US dollars, including holdings in some 3,000 undertakings.[6] It is estimated that the state controls and manages some 48 per cent of the national income.[7] In 1958, publicly owned enterprises delivered 36·7 per cent of the total of iron ore in the country, 25·7 per cent of the coal,[8] 70·1 per cent of the crude aluminium, 45·2 per cent of the zinc and 40·3 per cent of the

---

[1] See Note at end of chapter.

[2] Ridley and Blondel, *Public Administration in France*, p. 236: O.B.R., 1964, no. 64-20, p. 14.

[3] Ridley and Blondel, pp. 237, 238; *Le Monde*, 26 February 1965, p. 20.

[4] *The Guardian*, 27 February 1965, p. 9; *Le Monde* (Paris), 26 February 1965, p. 20; also J.O., 24 February 1965, Annex in the Series 'Documents Administratifs·: The Report of the Commission for the Verification of the Accounts of Public Enterprises.

[5] *Entreprise*, no. 492, 13 February 1965, p. 51.

[6] For a general article on public enterprise in Germany, see S. B. Fay: 'State ownership in Germany', in *Current History*, vol. xviii, March 1950, pp. 129–33; O.B.R., 1963, no. 63-156, p. 8.

[7] *Opera Mundi—Europe*, no. 293, 25 February 1965, p. 2.

[8] The state-controlled VEBA (Vereinigte Elektrizitäts- und Bergwerke AG.) controls three subsidiaries which account for a large production of coal and occupies a prominent position in the field of electric power and chemicals production: O.B.R., 1963, no. 63-156, p. 8; *Die Welt*, no. 253, 20 October 1964, p. 10.

motor cars.[1] Approximately one-third the total of 17 million acres of forest lands in the Federal Republic are in the ownership of the government and over a quarter are owned by regional authorities and co-operative undertakings.[2] The Federal government is also a majority holder of the principal airline company Lufthansa.

The capital of public undertakings in Italy is subscribed by the state and public establishments. Most of these public undertakings are grouped under the Institute for the Reconstruction of Industry (Istituto di Ricostruzione Industriale—I.R.I.) and the National Hydrocarbon Group (Ente Nazionale Idrocarburi—E.N.I.).[3] These two institutions accounted in 1960 for about 6·6 per cent of the gross national product of Italy.[4] The I.R.I. controls or participates in some 130 companies in the fields of nuclear energy, electric utilities, steel production, automotive industry, shipbuilding, shipping lines, radio and television, air transport and banking.[5] The E.N.I. has a complex system of subsidiaries active in mineral and petroleum exploration and extraction, refining and petrochemicals, gas and oil pipelines, gasoline stations and nuclear energy. It is estimated that the power industry is 35 per cent publicly owned.[6] The national airline company, Alitalia, Radio Televisione Italiana in charge of radio and television, and the companies responsible for the telephone service are all government controlled.[7] The state is developing its participation in the tourist trade; the Compagnia Internazionale della Parabola d'Oro, a planning company, has both I.R.I. and I.M.I.

---

[1] The state ownership or control of the Volkswagen car factories ceased in 1961 when shares were sold to private investors: see articles in *Fortune*, August 1962, p. 116. For a similar plan for denationalization of VEBA see *Die Welt*, no. 253, 29 October 1964, pp. 1, 9 and 10.

[2] *O.B.R.*, 1963, no. 63–156, p. 6.

[3] Royal Decree-Law, no. 1398, of 13 November 1931; and Law of 10 February 1953, no. 136. For a study of E.N.I., see Ch. R. Dechert: *Ente Nazionale Idrocarburi—Profile of a State Corporation*, Leiden, 1963; D. Votaw: *The six-legged dog—Mattei and E.N.I.: A Study in Power*, Berkeley–Los Angeles, 1964.

[4] *W.T.I.S.*, 1962, no. 62-51, p. 10.

[5] *Time*, 27 March 1964, p. 66.

[6] *W.T.I.S.*, 1962, no. 62-51, p. 11; also K. Osterkamp: 'Die Organisation der italienischen Energiewirtschaft' in: *Die öffentliche Wirtschaft*, 13th year, no. 1, January–March 1964.

[7] *W.T.I.S.*, 1962, no. 62-51, pp. 12, 13; *Poste e Telecommunicazione* (Rome), no. 1/2, 1964, p. 61.

(Istituto Mobiliare Italiano) among its shareholders.[1] A major part of the planned or projected motorways in Italy are under the control of a subsidiary company of I.R.I.[2] In 1955 government participation in and control of Italian industries were estimated as follows: coal mining, 100 per cent; crude oil, 20 per cent; iron ore, 76 per cent; natural gas, 94 per cent; iron (pig iron), 80 per cent; steel, 50 per cent; general machinery, 13 per cent; electrical equipment, 30 per cent; transport equipment, 40 per cent; automobiles, 10 per cent.[3] The Italian government can exercise an important influence on the trend of economic activities, by investment projects in the public and mixed enterprise sectors.[4]

In the Netherlands, with very few exceptions public utilities are state-owned.[5] The steel industry is a mixed enterprise, in which the majority of the capital is publicly owned. Fifty per cent of the coal production is contributed by the state mines. In the field of agriculture many farms are state-owned.

Taking all these examples into account, the extent of state participation in economic activities is seen to vary from one state to another, but nevertheless that participation commonly concerns sectors of vital or basic importance for the respective national economies. At the same time it constitutes an application of the principle that, in such vital economic sectors, private capital (domestic or foreign) should be excluded, or, if permitted to be active, should be in collaboration with public capital.

ii. *Sectors accessible to domestic but not to foreign private capital*

Although no background material covering all the member states of the E.E.C. is available, a few examples of statutory rules applicable to this category may be given.

[1] *Die Welt*, no. 47, 25 February 1965, p. iii (Supplement). The I.M.I. is another public enterprise (Royal Decree no. 1398, 13 November 1931).

[2] *The Economist*, 17 October 1964, p. 258; *The Times*, 5 October 1964.

[3] Dewhurst and others, *Europe's Needs and Resources*, p. 439; *Le Monde*, 27 October 1964, p. 16.

[4] A further important public enterprise, specializing in development projects in southern Italy, is the Cassa per il Mezzogiorno (Law of 10 August 1950, no. 646): Report of Cassa p.i. Mezzogiorno, *Dodici Anni*, 1950–62, vol. I, Bari, 1962. For a study of the economic problems of Sicily see N. Insam: 'Der Wirtschaftsausbau Siziliens: Probleme, Ziele und Masznahmen eines wirtschaftlich rückständigen Landes', doctoral thesis, University of Vienna, 1961.

[5] P. Sanders: in *Legal Aspects of Foreign Investment*, Friedmann and Pugh, eds., London, 1959, pp. 373–4.

In France, Article 148 of the Decree of 12 January 1939 provides that public transportation services on roads cannot be exploited except by French nationals and companies that are subject to French law, that is, they are French in the sense that their offices are situated in France and persons directing such companies are French nationals.[1] It may be argued that this provision does not necessarily exclude the participation of foreign capital in public transportation services on roads, especially since the same decree provides for exceptions in favour of foreign nationals. However, as the said exception refers to foreigners who were operating such services in France on 21 April 1934, one might conclude that under the decree new applications would be rejected. A similar prohibition concerns fishing and coastal trade along the French coasts: foreigners are excluded. At this point we should remind ourselves that the decree and the exceptions it covers should apply only to nationals of non-member countries, since, under Articles 52 and 58 of the Treaty of Rome, by the end of the 'transitional period' (if not earlier) all Community nationals will be entitled to national treatment in all the member states. The status of Community nationals and foreign-owned enterprise in the E.E.C. are examined in chapter X.

These remarks are equally applicable to the case of Germany, where the manufacture of and trade in weapons of all kinds is an economic field prohibited to the foreign investor. In Italy, airline services run between Italian airports must be entirely Italian, except in particular cases contemplated in international agreements.[2]

iii. *Sectors accessible to foreign capital but governed by certain conditions and principles*

Access by foreign enterprise to specific sectors of economic activities in E.E.C. states depends on several principles. No reference is made here to the administrative formalities that apply to the *establishment* of foreign capital. The principles governing access are:

   a. Approval by the High Authority of the E.C.S.C. or the Council of the EURATOM;

[1] Décret du 12 janvier 1939 relatif à la coordination des transports ferroviaires et routiers: J.O., 18 January 1939. Also E.E.C. Commission: Régime juridique des transports ferroviaires, routiers et fluviaux dans les états membres de la C.E.E., Situation au 1er juillet 1962, p. F-49.

[2] Banco di Roma: *Foreign Private Enterprise in Italy*, Rome, 1959, vol. I, p. 13.

b. Domestic partnership or participation, either in the invested capital or in management, or in both;
c. Reciprocity;
d. Location in the host member state of the main centre of activities or the main office of the undertaking;
e. National interest;
f. Long residence in the host member state.

a. *Approval by the High Authority of the E.C.S.C. or the Council or Commission of the EURATOM.* In its relevance to foreign investment Community law governs the freedom of capital movements and establishment between member states, while the entry of foreign enterprise from non-member countries continues to remain the domain of municipal law. A few provisions in the E.C.S.C. and EURATOM treaties are, however, exceptions to this general rule, in that they subject to Community rules direct investment from non-member countries, in the respective spheres to which the two treaties apply. They do not replace municipal rules in this respect, but provide for a complementary application of Community law.

According to Article 54/5 of the E.C.S.C treaty investments linked with subsidies or indirect assistance fall within the ambit of Community law, necessitating on the part of the High Authority an opinion with binding power. 'If the High Authority finds that the financing of a project or the operation of the installations which it would entail would involve subsidies, assistance, protection or discrimination prohibited by the (E.C.S.C.) Treaty,[1] its unfavourable opinion based on these grounds shall have the force of a decision . . .[2] and shall have the effect of prohibiting the undertaking concerned from resorting to resources other than its own funds to carry out such a project.'[3]

Article 54/5 does not replace municipal law. It does not subject, furthermore, independent investment projects, domestic or foreign, to Community law; it does govern, and prohibit, however, projects of investment supported by subsidies and other

[1] E.C.S.C. Treaty, Article 54 par. 1(c). For the unofficial English translation, see: *Treaty establishing the E.C.S.C., Paris, 18 April 1951*, H.M.S.O., London, 1962.

[2] See Article 14, E.C.S.C. Treaty.

[3] See also Article 11 of the Convention containing the transitional provisions at p. 70 in the unofficial English translation of the E.C.S.C. Treaty and related documents, publ. by H.M.S.O., 1962.

forms of assistance that would be contradictory to the objectives of the E.C.S.C. treaty. Hence, foreign investments falling within this category will also depend on a respective opinion, negative or positive, of the High Authority.

Similar provisions in the EURATOM treaty apply to the participation of foreign enterprise in the field of atomic energy within the E.E.C. Under Article 103 of the EURATOM treaty, 'Member States shall communicate to the [EURATOM] Commission their draft agreements or conventions with a third country, international organization or national of a third country, in so far as such agreements or conventions concern matters covered by the [EURATOM] Treaty.'[1] If the Commission is of the opinion that the draft agreements or conventions submitted are contrary to the objectives and impede the effectiveness of the treaty,[2] the member state concerned 'may not conclude the intended agreement or convention until it has removed the Commission's objections or complied with any ruling which the Court of Justice, adjudicating urgently upon a formal request [requête]', submitted by the given member state, 'shall give concerning the compatibility of the proposed clauses with the provisions of the [EURATOM] Treaty.' Thus, foreign enterprise in the field of atomic energy, as object of agreements or conventions referred to in Article 103 of the EURATOM treaty, will be subject to a final decision or approval resting with the EURATOM Commission.[3]

A similar competence is given to the EURATOM Council by Article 47 par. 4 of the same treaty, with respect to the participation of foreign enterprise in joint ventures: a unanimous consent by the Council of the EURATOM is necessary for the participation by a non-member country or national, or an international organization in the financing or management of joint undertakings.

The provisions of the E.C.S.C. and EURATOM treaties discussed above do not have their parallel in the E.E.C. treaty. The

---

[1] Article 103/1 of the EURATOM Treaty. See unofficial English translation, H.M.S.O., London, 1962.

[2] Article 103/2 of the EURATOM Treaty.

[3] For agreements concluded before the Treaty entered into force, see Articles 104–105. For comments on Articles 103–105 of the EURATOM Treaty, see J. Errera and others: *Euratom: Analyse et Commentaires du Traité* (Bibl. de l'Institut Belge de Science Politique), Brussels, 1958, pp. 184–5. Cf. also Arts. 2(c), 4/1, 41 and Annex II, 112–113, sectors of industry referred to in Art. 41.

latter does not contain clauses which would directly permit the executive organs, namely the Commission or the Council, to supplement existing municipal rules on foreign investment with corresponding Community rules. A possibility is offered, however, by the contents of Articles 92–94 of the Treaty of Rome, under which the E.E.C. Commission may examine among aids granted by member states, any investment incentives which 'in any form whatsoever' distort or threaten to distort 'competition by favouring certain undertakings or the production of certain goods' in so far as they adversely affect trade between member states.[1] It should be borne in mind, however, that the E.C.S.C. and EURATOM treaties with their more specific clauses govern particular and relatively limited spheres of activities, whereas the Treaty of Rome encompasses all the activities in the Common Market; in its context, therefore, it is more difficult to be as specific as are the other two treaties.

b. *Domestic partnership or participation in the invested capital or in management, or in both.* Exceptions to the rules of the various states discussed below arise in connection with other principles, especially those of reciprocity, national interest and long residence. Such exceptions are referred to later in this chapter, under the appropriate heading.

In Belgium, in accordance with special agreements concluded between the state and a number of shipping companies, the latter are to have a majority of Belgian nationals on their board of directors.[2]

In France, mining exploration or exploitation rights can be held only by companies constituted under French law; the president and majority of directors of such companies must be French nationals.[3] No permits have been granted to companies without substantial participation of French capital.[4] Similar requirements apply to foreign publishing companies; the president, directors or

[1] Treaty of Rome, Article 92/1.

[2] J. L. Blondeel: in *Legal Aspects of Foreign Investment*, Friedmann and Pugh, eds., pp. 61–2, n. 50.

[3] Decree of 12 November 1938.

[4] N. Ely: *Summary of Mining and Petroleum Laws of the World*, U.S. Dept. of the Interior, Bureau of Mines, Washington, 1961, p. 75; in which see, for mining laws in the E.E.C.: Belgium, pp. 70 ff., France, pp. 74 ff., Germany, p. 79 f., Italy, 84 ff., Netherlands, pp. 86 ff. For a Dutch bill on concessions in the North Sea, see *Le Monde*, 27 February 1965, p. 24.

shareholders of such companies have to be French nationals.[1] Provisions of Article 148 of the Decree of 12 January 1939 stipulate that public freight carriage by road can be operated or directed only by French nationals or companies governed by French law. Directors of such companies must likewise be French nationals.[2]

In Germany, in the field of inland waterway transportation, corporate bodies must have a participation of more than 50 per cent by German nationals.[3]

Maritime laws in Italy contain a number of special provisions concerning domestic partnership. Thus, two-thirds of the stocks or capital of Italian shipping companies must be owned by Italians.[4] A shipping company is Italian, if, in addition to two-thirds Italian capital, it is established in Italy and its main offices are in the country. The legal effect of these rules is that only ships owned by such companies can be registered as Italian.

Similar provisions apply to admission to the profession of passenger carrier on inland waterways. Again, only Italian ships may be registered, i.e. ships belonging two-thirds to Italian nationals or to Italian companies having their main office in the country, with a capital three-fourths owned by Italian nationals. Furthermore, Italian nationals must constitute a majority in the administrative and directing organs of such companies.[5]

Similarly for aircraft, Article 751 of the Admiralty Code authorizes the registration of aircraft as Italian only if such aircraft are owned by companies formed in Italy with a general manager, general director and two-thirds of its directors of Italian citizenship. In addition, foreign capital may not exceed 33 per cent of the total.

In the field of life insurance, foreign companies in Italy must have an Italian as general representative. For auditing companies, the Law of 23 November 1949, no. 1966, provides in Article 1 that two-thirds of the directors of such a company must be Italian citizens in addition to the Italian general-manager and Italian president.

---

[1] Ordinance of 26 August 1944.
[2] Décret du 12 janvier 1939 relatif à la coordination des transports ferroviaires et routiers: J.O., 18 January 1939.
[3] E.E.C. Commission: *Régime juridique des transports*, p. D-71, also p. D-70.
[4] Article 143/1 of the Admiralty Code, as amended (Codice della Navigazione, Gaz. Ufficiale, 1942, no. 93).
[5] E.E.C., Commission: Régime juridique des transports, p. I-47.

The Netherlands maritime law states that all managers and three-quarters of the board of directors of companies registering their vessels in the Netherlands must be Dutch nationals. A corollary to this rule is that shipping companies managed and directed in the Netherlands by foreigners cannot have their vessels registered in the country.[1]

c. *Reciprocity.* In the field of passenger transportation by road, foreigners in Belgium are entitled to the same treatment as Belgian nationals, provided (i) the administrative offices of the given enterprise are situated in Belgium and (ii) their country of origin extends similar advantages to Belgian nationals on a basis of reciprocity.[2]

In France, as we have seen, Article 148 of the Decree of 12 January 1939, provides that public transportation services on roads cannot be exploited except by French companies and nationals who are subject to French law, and are French in the sense that their offices are situated in the country and that persons directing the companies are French nationals.[3] Exceptions can be made by the Minister of Public Works and Transport, in agreement with the Minister for the Interior and in consultation with the Supreme Council for Transport. Exceptions may apply to foreigners who have been operating public passenger services in France on 1 April 1934 and are nationals of a state that grants similar privileges to French nationals. The principle of reciprocity applies similarly to foreigners operating freight services on roads. A foreigner may obtain an authorization to operate passenger and freight services on inland waterways, if he is a national of a state that extends a similar exception to French nationals.[4] The principle of reciprocity applies also to foreign publishing companies.[5]

---

[1] Both Italian and Dutch laws concerning the registration of ships as respectively Italian or Dutch adhere to the principle of 'genuine link' and not to the principle of flag of convenience in public international law: B. A. Boczek: *Flags of Convenience*, Cambridge, Mass., 1962, for the official attitude of the Italian and Dutch governments, pp. 195 ff. See also F. Florio: *Nazionalità della Nave e Legge della Bandiera*, Milan, 1957, pp. 207–21.

[2] E.E.C. Commission: Régime juridique des transports, p. B-32. For freight transportation by road, ibid., p. B-39.

[3] Ibid., p. F-49.

[4] For these cases see E.E.C. Commission: Régime juridique des transports, pp. F-49/50, F-63, F-83 and F-94.

[5] Ordinance of 26 August 1944.

In Italy, the operation of foreign banks is subject to an authorization by the Treasury, granted on the basis of the treatment which Italian banking companies receive in the applicant's country of origin.[1] The principle of reciprocity is equally applied when considering applications of foreign reinsurance companies interested in activities in Italy.

d. *Location in the host member state of the main centre of activities or the main offices.* This requisite may be assumed to be generally self-evident in rules concerning the establishment of foreign capital in a given country. Nevertheless, a number of legal provisions refer to it explicitly in some of the member states of the E.E.C. In some cases there is a parallel application of the principle of reciprocity as already discussed.

In Belgium, for road transport enterprises (passenger and freight), foreigners must have their main management office in the country; it is not sufficient to have only an agency or branch office in Belgium.[2]

In France, companies operating freight services on roads or passenger and freight services on inland waterways must have their main office in the country.[3]

In Germany, legislation governing passenger services on roads does not distinguish between German and foreign nationals. Authorization for transport services within the Federal territory will be granted, however, to entrepreneurs who have their main office in the Federal Republic. The same provisions apply for freight services on roads.[4]

For shipping companies, aircraft companies and passenger carriers on inland waterways in Italy, reference has already been made to the requirements in the rules regarding foreign participation in such companies that, amongst other principles, their main offices must be situated in Italy. In the field of natural resources, authorization for the exploitation of mines will be granted to Italian citizens or companies with main offices in Italy.[5]

In Luxembourg, for activities as a road carrier, an authorization is required by the Ordinance of 14 August 1934, and the Law

[1] Royal Law-Decree of 14 September 1919, no. 1620.
[2] E.E.C. Commission: Régime juridique des transports, pp. B-32 and B-39.
[3] Ibid., pp. F-83 and F-94; Décret du 12 janvier 1939, J.O., 18 January 1939.
[4] Ibid., pp. D-43, D-45, D-54.
[5] Law of 1 January 1957, no. 6.

of 2 June 1962.[1] A concession will be granted if the place of residence of the concessionnaire is in the Grand-Duchy.

e. *National interest.* We deal here with cases where foreign investors may be admitted as an exception to existing rules preventing foreigners from having access to certain sectors of economic activities.

In France, according to the Decree of 13 February 1961, exceptions on grounds of national interest may be made in the field of public transportation services on roads to foreigners who have rendered valuable services to France in the sector of transportation and who have been active in this field for a period of at least ten years.[2]

Mention has already been made of Article 143 of the Admiralty Code of Italy which governs the status of shipping companies as Italian. Article 144 of the same code provides for an exception in this respect—in the national interest, foreign companies or companies established in Italy by foreigners may be awarded the status of Italian legal entities, in the meaning implied by the Admiralty Code, if their main activities or offices are in Italy or if the founders of such companies are foreigners resident in the country for more than five years. Similarly, an exception to the rules governing the admission to the profession of waterway passenger carrier is possible on grounds of national interest.[3]

f. *Long residence in the host member state.* The condition of long residence in the country is complementary to one or more of the four principles: domestic partnership, reciprocity, location of main office or activities in the country, and national interest.

In France, the Decree of 13 February 1961, concerning road passenger and freight services, makes the exception referred to in the section on National Interest dependent also on residence either in the mainland of France or in the overseas territories for a minimum period of ten years.

[1] Respectively: Arrêté grand-ducal du 14 août 1934, soumettant l'exercice de certaines professions à une autorisation gouvernementale (Mémorial 1934, p. 819); Loi du 2 juin 1962 déterminant les conditions d'accès et d'exercice de certaines professions ainsi que celles de la constitution et de la gestion d'entreprises (Mémorial 1962, p. 488).

[2] Décret du 13 février 1961 relatif aux conditions de nationalité exigées des transporteurs public routiers J.O., 18 February 1961.

[3] E.E.C. Commission: Régime juridique des transports, pp. I-47, I-48.

In Italy the exceptions referred to under National Interest concern foreigners who are residents in the country for more than five years. A similar rule applies to physical persons of foreign nationality active in the field of inland waterway transport—they must be resident in Italy for more than five years.

*Conclusions*

1. Article 54 of the E.C.S.C. Treaty and Articles 47 and 103 of the EURATOM treaty provide exceptions to the general pattern in which municipal and Community rules on foreign investment function in the E.E.C. In the general pattern, municipal law applies to foreign enterprise from non-member countries while intermember investment is governed by Community law. The provisions prescribed in the E.C.S.C. and EURATOM treaties are rules that are to be applied, like Community law, parallel to municipal rules in instances regarding foreign investment and enterprise from non-member countries. As such, they are uniform rules on foreign investment matters common to all member states and a contrast to the individual municipal rules.

2. In the light of the role that public enterprise plays in the economy of member states, it may be said that the distinction between public and private enterprise is of greater importance in the member states of the E.E.C. than a discriminatory distinction between domestic and foreign private enterprise. Indeed, since public enterprise is active in sectors deemed to be of paramount public or national importance, the margin left for a decisive discrimination between domestic and foreign private capital on grounds of public or national interest[1] is a relatively narrow one.

---

[1] For a discussion of the term 'national interest' with regard to the impact of economic activities on economic growth, national income, balance of payments, public revenue and innovational effect, see R. D. Robinson: *International Business Policy*, New York, 1964, pp. 99 ff. The absence of foreign participation in public utilities in Europe is also reflected in the following statistical data. In 1962, the industrial distribution of the book value of American private investment was 13 per cent in manufacturing; 2·9 per cent in trade; 6·4 per cent in petroleum; 1·3 per cent in other industries and 0·1 per cent in public utilities; the total of the above percentages represented 23·7 per cent of American private investment abroad (32·7 per cent in Canada, 22·8 per cent in Latin America and 20·7 per cent in the remaining parts of the world).

Source: U.S. Dept. of Commerce: *Survey of Current Business*, vol. 43, Wash., D.C., August 1963. See also L. B. Krause and K. W. Dam: *Federal Tax Treatment of Foreign Income*, Wash., D.C., 1964, p. 64.

This margin, which includes mainly the manufacturing industries, would still have been wide enough for the purpose of discriminating against foreign enterprises. The fact, however, that such a discrimination is practically non-existent in the E.E.C. may be considered as proof of liberalism towards foreign enterprise in the Common Market.

3. The principles reviewed above show that the member states concerned do not want to exclude the participation of foreign enterprise from some economic activities, for example, shipping in Italy and the Netherlands, though they apply measures to avert foreign domination in these sectors. The principle of domestic partnership fulfils a major function in this respect, though exceptions are possible in the national interest.

Two of the principles reviewed, location of the main centre of activities and long residence in the country, emphasize the necessity of an effective link between the foreign applicant for establishment in the country and the economic life of the host state. Such an effective link is a necessary condition for the authorization to exercise economic activities that are subject to restrictions.

4. The principle of reciprocity is significant in a particular respect. On the level of international law, it is the application of equal treatment of nationals of countries that mutually import and export private capital. In the case of the respective E.E.C. member states, it is one of the principles that they apply with regard to investments by their nationals abroad.

5. Under the impact of Community law in its application to investment between member states of the E.E.C., it is evident that the restrictive clauses in municipal law reviewed in this chapter must be amended with regard to Community nationals, at least by the end of the transitional period.

iv. *Economic sectors easily accessible to foreign capital*

This category concerns the activities of foreign-owned undertakings in economic sectors easily accessible to capital from non-member countries, on a footing of equality with domestic enterprise and hence not subject to any of the rules discussed earlier. Legal aspects of this category illustrate the extent of liberalism which member states of the E.E.C. exercise with respect to foreign-owned enterprise. The extent of liberalism can be assessed in terms of the presence or absence of differential treatment of foreign investment in each of the member states. Such an assess-

E

ment is made in subsequent chapters where the regulations and laws that affect foreign investment are reviewed in turn.

## NOTES

*Government and management of Banking and Public Utilities in E.E.C. states*

BANKING

*Belgium*

Fifty per cent of the shares of the Banque Nationale de Belgique, founded in 1850, is held by the state as registered and non-transferable securities. (See Bank for International Settlements: *Eight European Central Banks: A Descriptive Study*, Basle–London, 1963, p. 12.)

*France*

The Banque de France opened for business on 20 February 1800, was nationalized by the Law of 2 December 1945. In accordance with Article 1 of that Law, all the shares of the bank are in the possession of the state. Together with the Banque de France, three others of the six largest commerical banks of France were nationalized in 1945. These four banks then represented some 55 per cent of the total assets of banking houses in France. (See *Eight European Central Banks*, pp. 124, 125; *Dictionnaire des Sciences Economiques*, Paris, 1956, vol. 1, p. 127; Dewhurst and others, *Europe's Needs and Resources*, p. 440.)

*Germany*

The legal status of the Deutsche Bundesbank is governed by the Law of 26 July 1957. Its capital of DM. 290m is owned by the Federal Republic. (See *Bundesgesetzblatt* (BGBl—Federal Law Gazette), I, 30 July 1957, p. 745; For details on the German central banking system, W. Schmidt and K. Andreas: 'Bank deutscher Länder und die angeschlossenen Landeszentralbanken', *Enzyklopädisches Lexikon für das Geld-, Bank- und Börsenwesen*, vol. I, Frankfurt/Main, 1957; *Eight European Central Banks*, p. 55.)

*Italy*

The Banca d'Italia was created in 1893. In 1936, it ceased to exist as a private joint-stock company and acquired its current legal status of an institution incorporated under public law and for unlimited duration. In accordance with the Law of 1936, Articles 20–21, the private shareholders were refunded in full and the bank's capital of 300m Lire transferred to institutions incorporated under public law, which can transfer their shares only among themselves, with the prior consent of the bank's Board of Directors. The bank's shares are owned by state-owned banks. (See *Eight European Central Banks*, p. 183; Law no. 449 of 10 August 1893; Agreement between the Bank and the Minister for the Treasury, 30 October 1894, approved by Decree no. 533 of 10 December 1894; Articles 3 and 20, par. 1, of the Decree-Law no. 375 of 12 March 1936, converted with various amendments into Law no. 141 of 7 March 1938; Article 20 par. 3 of the Law of 1936, Article 3 of the Statutes

(Decree no. 482 of 19 April 1948), Article 3 par. 3 and Article 4 of the Statutes; Dewhurst and others, *Europe's Needs and Resources*, p. 440. For banking in Italy in general, see E. Bompard: 'The Italian banking system', *Journ. Inst. Bankers*, no. 4, August 1964, pp. 276 ff.)

*Netherlands*

The Nederlandsche Bank was founded in 1814; since 1948 it has been entirely state-owned as a joint-stock company with limited liability. The Statutes of March 1949 have been amended in April 1957. (See *Eight European Central Banks*, p. 232; Staatsblad, I, 1948, p. 166; 1952, p. 35; and 1955, p. 335. Also *Dict. des Sciences Econ.*, vol. I, p. 126.)

## SAVINGS BANKS

In France, postal accounts in 1952 amounted to approximately one-seventh of total demand deposits (Ridley and Blondel, *Public Administration in France*, p. 53).

In Germany savings banks are predominantly public-owned, and with the widespread system of postal savings that enable depositors to make transfers between accounts, the governments, federal and provincial, play an important role both in the savings and commercial banking fields. (See Dewhurst and others, *Europe's Needs and Resources*, p. 440.)

In Italy state-owned agencies play a substantial role in the field of commercial and savings banks. The Istituto per la Ricostruzione Industriale is the chief instrument of state-owned commercial and savings banking operations in the country. Closely akin to a holding company, it acquired in 1936 90 per cent of Banca Commerciale Italiana and of the Banca di Roma, and 78 per cent of the stock of Credito Italiano. By 1945, state-owned institutions were managing 49 per cent of all commercial and savings bank deposits, 30 per cent were managed directly by the state, 13 per cent by private banks and 8 per cent by co-operative agencies. (See *Annual Report* of Banca d'Italia, April 1945, quoted in M. Einaudi, M. Byé and E. Rossi: *Nationalization in France and Italy*, Ithaca, 1955, p. 225.)

## RAILWAYS

*Belgium*

The operation and management of the rail transportation system in Belgium is in the hands of two companies: Société Nationale des Chemins de Fer Belges (S.N.C.B.) and Société Nationale des Chemins de Fers Vicinaux (S.N.C.V.); the latter operates narrow-gauge railroads. The S.N.C.B. was created by the Law of 23 July 1926 (*Moniteur Belge*, 24 July 1926) and given the right of exploitation, for 75 years, of railroads operated until then by state and private concessionaries. The state holds all the shares of the S.N.C.B. whose legal status is that of a commercial corporation *sui generis*.

The S.N.C.V. is older—created by the Law of 28 May 1884. In 1885 it was entrusted with the exploitation of all secondary railroads operated until then by different companies. It is a limited liability company of a particular kind and is in fact a co-operative undertaking. Its shareholders are the Belgian state, the provinces, the city governments and a few individuals. (See E.E.C. Commission: Régime juridique des transports, pp. B-11, B-12, B-14.)

*France*

The company in charge of railways (other than local and limited railroads) is the Société Nationale des Chemins de Fer français (S.N.C.F.). Created by the Decree of 31 August 1937, it took over the then existing independent railway systems. By Article 5 of the Decree, the S.N.C.F. was entitled to exploit the concessions granted earlier to the preceding companies and to construct, whenever needed, new railways. The transferred concessions were prorogated for a period ending on 31 December 1982. At the same time the exploitation rights of the two then existing national railway networks were also transferred by the state to the new S.N.C.F. The dispossessed companies were given as compensation 1,391,024 privileged shares of the S.N.C.F., representing 49 per cent of the company's total shares; their amortization will be concluded on 31 December 1982. The remaining 51 per cent of the company's capital is owned by the state. The S.N.C.F. is a limited liability company. Its status is governed by the provisions of the Commercial Code (of France) and other laws concerning limited liability companies, with due regard however to derogations approved or provided for by the Decree of 31 August 1937. The influence of the state is a predominating one on its organization and administration. (See E.E.C. Commission: Régime juridique des transports, pp. F-25, F-26 ff., F-33.)

*Germany*

According to the legislation governing railroads in the Federal Republic of Germany there are two groups of railroads: (i) those owned and operated by the Federal government; (ii) those managed and controlled by the provincial (Länder) governments. A further distinction is made by the general law of 29 March 1951, governing railways for public and private transportation, as it does not apply to tramways or transportation similar to tramways, mountain railways or other special rail systems.

The German Federal Railways (Deutsche Bundesbahn) are to a large extent an autonomous corporation. The non-federal railroads are subject to concessions granted by the Länder and to control by the provincial transport authorities. The principal participants in such concessions are mostly public corporate bodies. Indeed, so far, concessions by the Länder have been granted only to provincial and local corporate bodies, but there are no specific legal rules opposed to the participation of foreign or domestic private investors. (See E.E.C. Commission: Régime juridique des transports, pp. D-17, D-21, D-22.)

*Italy*

The railroad network has been largely taken over by the state from private companies since 1905. At present it is exploited by an autonomous administration, the State Railways (Ferrovia dello Stato). Lines not included in the network of the F.S. are subject to state concessions. (See E.E.C. Commission: Régime juridique des transports, pp. I-15, I-16.)

*Luxembourg*

Among the six states in the E.E.C., Luxembourg is the only one where financial participation in the State railways from other states exists: 49 per cent of the capital having been subscribed, in equal shares, from Belgium and France. Up to 1944 the railways network was exploited by independent companies. Since then it is operated by the Société Nationale des Chemins de Fer Luxembourgeois (C.F.L.). (See E.E.C. Commission: Régime juridique des transports, pp. L- 9.)

## Netherlands

The Railway Re-organization Law of 26 May 1937 (Staatsblad 520, 27 May 1937) effected the dissolution of the two then existing private railway companies and the transfer of their assets and liabilities to the new limited liability company, Nederlandsche Spoorwegen (N.S.). All shares were acquired by the state, with the exception of two representing a value of 1,000 florins each, attributed to the two dissolved private companies. (See E.E.C. Commission: Régime juridique des transports, pp. N-14, N-15.)

### TELEPHONES AND TELEGRAPHS

## Belgium

After an initial period of private concessionnaires, the system became a complete governmental monopoly in 1896, controlled and operated by the Régie des Télégraphes et des Téléphones. (O.B.R., 1964, no. 64-15, p. 9.)

## France

In 1889 the government took over the entire private system. The service is operated by the Postal, Telephone and Telegraph (P.T.T.) administration. International radio-telegraph and submarine cable services are operated by both French and foreign entities. (O.B.R., 1964, no. 64-10, p. 11.)

## Germany

There has been a governmental monopoly since services started. The Deutsche Bundespost has a monopoly and an extensive system of motorbus services, postal accounts and postal savings banks.

### RADIO AND TELEVISION

In Belgium the radio monopoly is held by a public corporation, the Institut National Belge de Radiodiffusion (I.N.R.). Television services are also publicly owned with financial support from public funds. French radio and television broadcasting services are state monopolies, operated by the Radiodiffusion-Télévisions Française (R.T.F.). In Germany seven regional (Land) networks operate under public law. Radio Televisione Italiana is government controlled. A privately owned broadcasting company operates in Luxembourg; there is also a commercial broadcasting system in the region of the Saar. Under Dutch law, the radio and television system, with programmes sponsored by various social and cultural organizations, comes under central co-ordinating bodies with the status of foundations (Stichting) (See Internationales Handbuch für Rundfunk und Fernsehen, Hamburg, 1964, pp. F6 ff., F23 ff., C1 ff., F95 ff. and F99 ff.)

# CHAPTER IV

# EXCHANGE CONTROL REGULATIONS

The movement of investment capital from non-member countries into the E.E.C. is governed by the municipal rules of each of the member states. There is no uniform law on exchange control for the whole of the Community though there are strong similarities amongst the municipal systems, which are reviewed here in terms of: entry of capital; transfer of investment income; disinvestment; and the administrative formalities ancillary to the application of exchange control regulations.

## BELGIUM

The basic legislation on the regulation of capital movements is the Decree-Law of 6 October 1944, as amended, which also affects foreign investments in the country.

*Entry of capital.* Foreign capital may enter the country through the official or the *free* exchange markets at the investor's choice. In the official exchange market, transactions may be carried out only through authorized banks; exchange rates may vary within official limits, whereas on the free market rates may fluctuate freely; (they have varied, in practice, by one per cent). Transactions through the official market enjoy a number of legal advantages affecting the re-transfer of foreign capital.

The administrative body in charge of the official exchange market is the *Institut Belge–Luxembourgeois de Change* (I.B.L.C.), managed by a group of nine members. It issues guarantees for the repatriation of foreign investment in an amount equivalent to the original capital imported into Belgium.

*Transfer of profits.* There are no restrictions on the transfer abroad of profits accruing to foreigners from investment in Belgium. Transfer may be effected at the investor's choice through the official or free exchange markets. Under the heading of profits fall also payments of royalties by residents or companies in Belgium to foreigners abroad. An authorization by the I.B.L.C. for a contract in this respect is tantamount to a guarantee that foreign exchange needed for royalty payments will be provided by the authorized banks.

*Disinvestment and repatriation of capital.* Repatriation of disinvested capital can be provided for at the time of the initial establishment in the country, when the capital is imported, provided such establishment is effected through the official exchange market. In such a case, the I.B.L.C. will issue a guarantee to the effect that repatriation of the originally imported and invested capital will be allowed.

*Indirect investment.* There are no restrictions on the purchase of securities quoted on the Belgian stock-exchange markets.[1]

## FRANCE

*Entry of capital.* The main provisions governing capital movements between France and non-member countries are found in Regulation 669 of the Exchange Office.[2] The control of exchange operations is shared between the Ministry of Finance and the Banque de France. The provisions of Regulation 669 distinguish between two categories of foreign investors and investments. Both categories are subject to authorization by the respective administrative authority. The main difference between the two categories concerns the extent to which a planned investment will participate in the economic life of the country. Thus, non-resident investors can carry out the following transactions through an authorized bank but without special authorization from the Exchange Office of the Ministry of Finance:

i. Purchase or sale, for cash, of real estate located in the country;
ii. Loans to residents, up to an amount of NF. 2m for a period not exceeding five years;
iii. Purchase or sale of French securities listed on the French stock-exchange markets.

Investors falling within the second category need a special authorization from the Ministry of Finance for the following transactions:

i. Participation in or creation of a business undertaking in the country;

[1] Code of Liberalization of Current Invisible Operations. O.E.C.D., Paris, December 1964. See also the O.E.C.D. *Observer*, no. 13, December 1964, p. 10.      [2] J.O., 21 January 1959, pp. 1130 ff.

ii. Investment financed by contributions in assets other than cash, such as capital equipment, technical services and licensing or patent agreements, including trademarks;

iii. The purchase of unlisted securities or of foreign securities in the French stock-exchange markets.

Applications falling under the second category have to be filed with the Ministry of Finance, Direction des Finances Extérieures. They must include detailed information concerning the planned investment, with a description of the contribution that the said investment will make to the economy of the country. If the envisaged investment is worth NF. 500,000 or more, the application cannot be approved by the Direction des Finances Extérieures, but has to be referred to the *Comité d'Investissements*, a committee of six members who are representatives of the Ministries of Finance, Industry and Commerce, and Economic Affairs; of the Governor of the Bank of France and of the Commissariat du Plan. An approval of the submitted application is equivalent to a guarantee that proceeds from disinvestment will be transferred for repatriation at the exchange rate prevailing at the time of repatriation.

While no special authorization is required for establishing an agency or a branch office in France, income accruing from such offices need authorization for transfer abroad. Such authorization has to be secured while the planned agency or branch office is being established.

As the French government has been concerned for some years about the extent to which certain sectors of the country's industry are being penetrated by foreign capital, especially American, stricter criteria in granting investment authorizations are to be applied. From January 1965 the French government is making a clear distinction between investments that are conducive to new economic activities on the one hand, and such investments that lead to a take-over of part or of the whole of existing undertakings on the other.[1]

*Transfer of profits.* A special authorization is required for transfer of profits accruing from each investment, granted in accordance with prescribed formalities for application.[2] The term 'profits' includes royalties and other income accruing from technical services.

[1] *Financial Times*, 13 January 1965, p. 13; *Le Monde*, 14 January 1965, p. 14.
[2] Regulation 669, J.O., 21 January 1959.

*Disinvestment and repatriation of capital.* Rules prescribed by Regulation 669 provide for the liquidation and disinvestment of imported capital and re-transfer abroad. The necessary procedure is laid down in the Regulation.

*Indirect investment.* The purchase of French securities listed on the stock-exchange markets is liberalized, while transactions with unlisted French securities or foreign securities are subject to authorization granted by the Ministry of Finance.

## GERMANY

*Entry of capital.* The entry of foreign investment capital into the Federal Republic, including West Berlin, is governed by the fifth revised version of the Memorandum on Foreign Investment of May 1959, and in the Foreign Trade Law of May 1961.[1] There are no restrictions on long-term direct investment, one formal requirement being the notification to the German Federal Bank of any transactions and the amount of money they involve.[2]

On the basis of the Memorandum on Foreign Investment non-resident investors are permitted (i) to establish or acquire enterprises in the country; (ii) to acquire participation in already existing undertakings or in planned activities; (iii) to contribute in the form of cash or material assets or rights; (iv) to acquire real estate and rights thereto. If the planned investment is not in one of these four categories, a special authorization has to be issued by the regional (Land) bank, acting as a representative of the German Federal Bank.

In Germany, a distinction is made between rules affecting the entry of foreign capital and those permitting the establishment of an undertaking with the imported capital. Rules pertaining to the latter are part of the law of trade licences, which are applicable equally to nationals and foreigners.[3] Foreigners investing in the

[1] Respectively: Bundesanzeiger no. 86, 8 May 1959; and Auszenwirt-schaftsgesetz, BGBl, I, 5 May 1961, p. 29. See also Decree for the Implementation of the same Law: Verordnung zur Durchführung des Auszenwirt-schaftsgesetzes (Auszenwirtschaftsverordnung), BGBl, I, 31 August 1961, p. 69.

[2] Sections 23 and 26 of the Foreign Trade Law (Auszenwirtschaftsgesetz).

[3] Many handicraft trades require a master's roll obtained after a period of training and a number of examinations. See the Handicraft Law, BGBl, I, 17 September 1953, p. 1411; also the Retail Trade Law, BGBl, I, 5 August 1957, p. 1121.

country and establishing an undertaking are required to obtain a permit from the Federal Ministry of Economic Affairs.[1]

*Transfer of profits and repatriation of capital.* Neither is subject to restrictions.

*Indirect investment.* Under the Memorandum the acquisition of German securities is permitted, though there are regulations regarding taxation of income from securities (see page 119).

## ITALY

*Entry of capital.* Of the six member states of the E.E.C., Italy has the most elaborate legislation for foreign investments. The special Law no. 43 of 7 February 1956 regulates, among other matters, the conditions under which capital from abroad may be imported and later repatriated, including the transfer of profits and royalties.[2]

This Law permits foreigners to invest in the form of cash, material assets such as imported equipment, or licensing. Formalities concerning the establishment of an enterprise are to be distinguished in terms of 'productive' and 'non-productive' undertakings as indicated in Articles 1 and 2 of Law no. 43. The Presidential Decree of 6 July 1956, no. 758, defines productive enterprises as economic activities which aim at the production of goods or services 'such as reclamation or improvement of land; installation of factories, power generators and power transmission lines, digging of wells and tunnels; the exploitation of transportation systems, construction of buildings (including hotels) and roads'.[3] The enumeration in the above quotation is not exhaustive and the State Treasury is the authority competent for individual decisions.[4] Plans of the contemplated productive undertaking

[1] Section 12, Law on Trades (Gewerbeordnung), RGBl, 1900, p. 871, as amended; Section 292 of the Corporation Law (Aktiengesetz), RGBl, I, 30 January 1937, p. 107, as amended; Section 105 of the Law concerning the Supervision of Private Insurance Companies and Building and Loan Associations, RGBl, I, 6 June 1931, p. 315, as amended.

[2] Gazzetta Ufficiale, no. 43, 21 February 1956. For an English text, see Credito Italiano: *Useful Information for Investing Capital in Italy*, Rome, 1961, Appendix I, pp. 101 ff.

[3] Gazzetta Ufficiale, no. 189, 30 July 1956. For English text, Cred. Ital.: *Useful Information*, Appendix no. 2, pp. 108 ff.

[4] Cred. Ital., *Useful Information*, p. 72.

are to be submitted to the Ministry of the Treasury, with details for the evaluation of its merits. Within a statutory time-limit of 90 days, the Treasury is held to make a statement of approval or refusal for the given individual project.[1] For the category of non-productive business activities, including portfolio investments, no specific administrative formalities prevail other than those mentioned below in conjunction with exchange control regulations.

On the level of exchange control rules, the distinction between productive and non-productive undertakings implies different standards of treatment as far as the transfer of profits and the repatriation of the originally invested capital are concerned.

*Transfer of profits.* No limits are prescribed for profits accruing from productive undertakings, whereas income derived from non-productive investment may not be transferred at a yearly rate higher than 8 per cent of the originally invested capital.[2]

*Repatriation of capital.* In the case of productive enterprises, dis-invested capital is not subject to transfer restrictions. There is, however, one exception in this respect: recovered capital derived from investments in material assets, such as machinery and other type of equipment, can be repatriated only after a period of two years counted from the date of investment. In accordance with the Circular of 17 August 1956, no. 137, issued by the Ministry of Finance, Section of Superintendence of Customs and Indirect Taxes, a compulsory customs declaration is required for material assets when these are brought into the country for investment. Such a declaration will facilitate in due course the repatriation of proceeds from the liquidation of the equipment brought into the country.[3]

The transfer of capital disinvested from non-productive enterprises is not possible until two years from the date of investment and in an amount not exceeding the foreign capital originally imported. Funds exceeding these limits may be used in conformity with the other currency control regulations, i.e. not applying to the favourable treatment of foreign investments, in force at the

---

[1] Article 3 of the Presidential Decree of 6 July 1956.

[2] Article 1 of Law no. 43 of 1956.

[3] Article 8 of the Presidential Decree of 6 July 1956; Article 5 par. 3 of Law no. 43 of 1956. On disinvestment of capital generally see Cred. Ital., *Useful Information*, pp. 75-7; Banco di Roma: *Foreign Private Enterprise in Italy*, vol. 1, p. 23.

time when such re-transfer of funds is made. In other words, sums derived from non-productive investment will not be transferable abroad at the official rate of exchange; they may be transferred abroad in foreign currency at rates prevailing in the foreign exchange market, or deposited in Italy as 'capital account'.[1] 'Capital accounts' are held in Italian Lire with Italian banks, by persons or corporate entities residing abroad.[2] No authorization is required to open them and no limits are set to the amounts involved.

As for the administrative control of foreign capital entering or leaving the country, banks, notaries, exchange agents and public officials are required to notify the complete particulars of transactions involving foreign investment in Italy to the Italian Exchange Office within 30 days from their conclusion.[3] The transfer abroad of capital and income thereof is effected through the Bank of Italy or its authorized agents.

*Indirect investment.* All shares in Italy are registered in accordance with legal provisions. Only in Sicily, Sardinia and Trentino–Alto Adige district can bearer shares be issued in certain cases. The sale or purchase of securities is permitted to foreigners or to Italian nationals residing abroad. Companies and enterprises operating in Italy are required to inform the Italian Exchange Office of sales of shares and debentures to such purchasers within 30 days from the conclusion of the transactions. The transfer of shares registered in the name of non-residents can be made without restrictions and without distinction, to other persons residing abroad or in Italy, though in the latter case (to persons residing in the country) the transaction and transfer must take place through a bank.[4]

## LUXEMBOURG

Many similarities exist between the exchange control regulations in Belgium and Luxembourg, as a result of the Economic Union

[1] Their origin goes back to the *conti loro* created by the Law of November 1935.
[2] Circulars issued by the Italian Exchange Office; 16 April 1955, and No. A-52, 22 January 1958; see also Banco di Roma, *Foreign Private Enterprise in Italy*, vol. 1, p. 17.
[3] Article 7 of Law no. 43 of 1956; Banco di Roma, vol. 1, p. 15.
[4] Banco di Roma, vol. 1, p. 15; Cred. Ital., *Useful Information*, p. 42.

(B.L.E.U.). The Institut Belge-Luxembourgeois de Change (I.B.L.C.) is an institution common to both countries.

*Entry of capital.* An authorization is required by the I.B.L.C. for direct investment in existing companies or in undertakings yet to be established. This requirement is distinct from the authorization of the Ministry of Economic Affairs needed for a new business or industry in the country. The latter authorization will be based on considerations taking into account the economic needs of the country.[1] As in Belgium, there are official and free exchange markets.

*Transfer of profits.* Similar to provisions in Belgium, profits from investment can be transferred either through the official or the free exchange markets. For transfers through the official exchange market, a guarantee from the I.B.L.C. can be obtained upon application at the time of the original investment, to the effect that the necessary authorization for foreign exchange to cover the transfer of dividends will be granted. Without such prior authorization or guarantee, the transfer of dividends to foreigners is subject to a special permit, which is granted, however, without difficulty. No upper limit is prescribed for the transfer of investment income.

As in Belgium, an authorization allowing a Luxembourg resident to accept the payment of royalties or other fees to a non-resident constitutes a permit for the exchange necessary to cover such payments.

*Repatriation of capital.* Regulations are similar to those prevailing in Belgium. Disinvested capital may be transferred abroad with the least formalities through the free exchange market. Transfers through the official market are subject to the two types of approvals referred to above: (*a*) approval under general regulations, or (*b*) in virtue of a guarantee issued by the I.B.L.C. upon application at the time of the initial investment.

*Indirect investment.* Conditions governing this type of investment are the same as those prevailing in Belgium.

---

[1] Grand-Ducal Decree of 14 August 1934. See *Luxembourg and the Common Market: Establishment of New Industrial Enterprises*, publ. by the Banque Internationale à Luxembourg, Luxembourg, 1959, p. 5.

## THE NETHERLANDS

*Entry of capital.* Regulations are governed by the Foreign Exchange Decree of 1945, as amended, which makes every international financial transaction subject to a licence issued by the Exchange Control Division of the Bank of Netherlands. Applications therefore are to be submitted to the Directorate-General for Industrialization and Power Supply, Ministry of Economic Affairs (The Hague), accompanied by full details as to the merits and scope of the contemplated investment. The Directorate-General may act in an advisory capacity on technical matters related to the planned enterprise, and also handle all formalities required by other governmental authorities. If the Directorate-General approves the submitted project, the Bank of Netherlands will issue the required exchange licence. This will entitle the holder to the right of transferring profits abroad and repatriating disinvested capital, under the regulations administered by the Bank of Netherlands.[1]

In addition to this administrative formality, the Dutch government may require, in virtue of the Act on Licensing Industrial Activities,[2] a further licence which affects, however, both foreign and domestic enterprises. In order to promote an equilibrium between the supply and demand sectors of the economy, the government may restrict the establishment of new (foreign or domestic) enterprises in certain industrial branches.[3]

*Transfer of profits.* The transfer of profits and dividends is not subject to a special licence other than the one applicable to the entry of capital. Similarly, royalties, fees and income from licensing agreements are not subject to restrictions, if agreements related to them have been approved by the Bank of Netherlands at the time they were concluded.

*Repatriation of capital.* No further authorization is required for the repatriation of disinvested capital if the required licence has been obtained from the Exchange Control Division of the Bank of Netherlands at the time of the initial investment.[4]

[1] Min. of Econ. Affairs: *Guide to the Establishing of Industrial Operations in the Netherlands*, p. 4.

[2] Bedrijfsvergunningswet of 7 July 1954 (Staatsblad no. 339, 1954).

[3] Licensing requirements are to be established in the event of existing or potential over-capacity in production.

[4] Foreign Exchange Notice 6/54, quoted in *Guide to the Establishing of Industrial Operations in the Netherlands*, p. 34.

*Indirect investment.* The purchase of securities is not subjected to restrictions.

## CONCLUSIONS

1. All member states of the Common Market treat the entry of investment capital, transfer of investment income and the repatriation of disinvested foreign capital in an integrated manner; at the time when capital for investment is imported, assurance may be obtained or implied that no restrictions will apply to the transfer of investment income and to the repatriation of subsequently disinvested capital. In Belgium and Luxembourg, investors may choose, for their transactions, between the official and free exchange markets; the former offers obvious advantages in the form of a guarantee issued by the I.B.L.C. In Italy foreign investors cannot avail themselves of the official exchange market if they intend to invest in non-productive industries and transfer profits or disinvested capital in a manner not provided by law.

2. While the purpose of exchange regulations is the exercise of some administrative control over foreign investment, the scope of such measures varies from one member state to another. In Belgium, Germany and Luxembourg, the criteria of control seem to be more general while in France, Italy, and also in the Netherlands, they are more specific in distinguishing between the more welcome and the less desirable foreign investments. In the Netherlands, investment in certain sectors may be restricted in the interest of an equilibrium between demand and supply; in France the magnitude or economic importance of the proposed investment is taken into account, while in Italy a distinction is made between productive and non-productive investments. The former enjoy certain advantages. In this respect, foreign exchange regulations in Italy, as applied to foreign enterprise, are in effect incentives—they attract and encourage certain categories of investment in preference to others.

3. Indirect investment is liberalized in all of the member states. It involves a minimum of formalities.

### Exchange control regulations and the International Monetary Fund

The factors behind the liberal exchange control regulations currently applied to foreign investment in the member states of the E.E.C. are not only motivated by a desire to liberate international capital movements as much as possible, but they are also greatly favoured by the fact that the economic position of the member states and of the E.E.C as a whole enables the maintenance of such a liberal policy. This policy corresponds to the objectives of the International Monetary Fund, concerning the establishment and maintenance of convertible currencies, and the widest extension of multilateral payments.

All six member states of the E.E.C. have accepted the obligations of Article VIII, Sections 2, 3, 4 of the Fund Agreement, under which they have undertaken not to impose, without the approval of the Fund, 'restrictions on the making of payments or transfers in respect of current international transactions', unless such restrictions have been authorized under Article XIV/2 or Article VIII/3 of the Fund Agreement.[1]

*Future co-ordination of exchange control regulations*

As for the continued application of the current rules beyond the transitional period of the Common Market, that is probably after 1968–9, it may be suggested that their effectiveness will diminish and one or other of the functions they presently fulfil will become illusory as far as the individual economic life of member states is concerned. At present, foreign exchange rules are applied in conjunction with other administrative rules affecting the establishment of undertakings, for the purpose of controlling, in the first place, the establishment of foreign-owned enterprise in the country, secondly the extent of alienation of the country's industrial and commercial assets, thirdly the participation of foreign enterprise in the economic life of a member state, and fourthly the role that investment capital and investment income movements may play in the balance of payments. After the end of the transitional period the application of the existing rules unmodified would be ineffectual, for in any one case a foreign-owned enterprise would have the opportunity to establish itself in another (more liberal) state member of the Common Market

[1] The six member states accepted the obligations of Article VIII, Sections 2, 3 and 4, on 15 February 1961: Int. Monetary Fund, 14th Annual Report on Exchange Restrictions, 1963, Washington, D.C., pp. 35, 118, 131, 199 and 261. For the text of Article VIII, see Cmd. 6885, I.M.F., Articles of Agreement. For a discussion of Articles VIII and XIV of the Fund Agreement, see J. Gold: *The Int. Mon. Fund and Private Business Transactions: Some Legal Effects of the Articles of Agreement*, publ. I.M.F., Wash., D.C., 1965, especially pp. 16 ff.

and to operate in the Common Market from there. It would have access to all the national markets of the E.E.C. More than that, while cumbersome in practice but legally nevertheless feasible, it would be possible for a foreign-owned enterprise under the Community law of intermember establishment and free movement of capital, to find its way into a member state where its initial establishment would have been difficult or even impossible. Thus, the continued maintenance of current foreign exchange rules, as they apply to foreign enterprise from non-member countries, and of establishment formalities ancillary to them, will not be justified in order to fulfil the main functions of excluding or controlling the penetration of foreign-owned enterprise into the economic life of a given member state.

The Treaty of Rome does not contain specific clauses on foreign investment, but it provides for 'the progressive co-ordination of the exchange policies of Member States in respect of the movement of capital between those States and third countries'.[1] The purpose of such progressive co-ordination is 'the highest degree of liberalization'. Under the Treaty, member states have the obligation to keep the Commission of the E.E.C. 'informed of any movements of capital to and from third countries which they know about'.[2] These clauses indicate that exchange control policies and their co-ordination fall within the ambit of Community affairs. Moreover, competence of some sort seems to have been given to the Commission by the vague terms of Article 72, since it may be assumed that it is not for purely formal and self-contained reasons that it places such an obligation on member states with regard to movements of capital. The elements of a vaguely implied competence are contained in the second sentence of the same Article 72: 'The commission may address to Member States any comments which it deems appropriate on this subject.'

On the basis of Articles 70 and 72 of the Treaty of Rome, it may be said that the authors of the Treaty envisaged the need for the highest possible degree of liberalization, based however on the *co-ordinated* exchange policies of member states.[3] Otherwise, the efficiency of rules in one member state would become illusory

[1] Article 70/1, Treaty of Rome. See Campbell and Thompson, *Common Market Law*, p. 51. Groeben and Boeckh, *Kommentar*, vol. 1, p. 220, n. 1 ff.
[2] Article 72, Treaty of Rome. See Groeben and Boeckh, *Kommentar*, vol. 1, p. 223. See also Article 213.
[3] Groeben and Boeckh, *Kommentar*, vol. 1, p. 220.

under the effect of corresponding but diverging rules in one or more of the other member states. Each member state controls, in the form of its foreign exchange rules and establishment formalities governing foreign investment, the key for the access of foreign enterprise from non-member countries not only to its own territory, but also to the whole of the Common Market.[1]

Initiative on the part of the Community organs—the Commission and the Council—for progress towards the co-ordination of the rules concerned will depend on a broad interpretation of the term 'exchange policies' in Article 70/1 as inclusive also of 'rules' pertaining to the entry of foreign investment capital, transfers of investment income and repatriation of disinvested capital.

The above comments relate to the relevance of Treaty provisions to foreign investment and to their controlling power at the level of exchange policies. Disregarding for a moment the complex situation in which foreign investments in and from the E.E.C. are involved, the co-ordination of exchange policies could be said to consist in the application of uniform rules affecting the promotion or restriction of foreign enterprise in all of the six member states. A further possibility would consist in restricting the initial establishment of foreign enterprise in some of the member states but promoting it in others where there would be good economic reasons for doing so. The ultimate exclusion of foreign enterprise from the markets of a given member state, and of its establishment there through intermember transfer of its seat under the Community law of establishment, will be impossible, however, once foreign enterprise has entered into one of the member states.

While unilateral action against foreign investment on the part of individual member states would be possible, the acceptability of such action will be questionable in the light of two facts: (*a*) the E.E.C. exports capital and a member state could not take unilateral action oblivious of the effects that such action might have on E.E.C. investment abroad; (*b*) member states have individual treaties with non-member countries on establishment of enterprises. Since the inception of the Common Market on 1 January 1958, because of the liberal attitude in the E.E.C. towards foreign enterprise, no conflicts have arisen between such individual treaties and the provisions of the Treaty of Rome.

---

[1] R. Savatier, in: *Rev. critique de droit international privé*, 1959, no. 2, p. 249; L. Cartou, in: *Rev. de Science Financière* (1963), vol. 55, no. 3, p. 342.

Once, however, action by member states under the obligations of the Treaty becomes necessary, a legally difficult situation may be created, because 'in so far as such agreements are not compatible with [the Rome] Treaty, the Member . . . States concerned shall take all appropriate steps to eliminate any proven incompatibilities).[1] The elimination of such incompatibilities might involve the consent of the non-member countries which are parties to the individual agreements with member states on establishment and commerce. Finally, unilateral action on the part of the E.E.C. members will not be easy or indeed necessary, because the situation (as in March 1965) is not characterized by a concern about foreign enterprise in general, but about investment originating from one non-member country (the United States). Despite this concern, the application of regulations to all foreign investment is excluded as undesirable. It does not offer any solution by means of the application of measures against investment originating from a particular country, like the United States, with which some of the member states of the Common Market already have bilateral agreements on establishment.

In the light of such a complex situation, some quarters in the Community have appealed to the authorities of the United States to devise ways and means for curbing the pressure of American investment capital in the E.E.C. A solution will have to be sought not only on the level of co-ordination within the Common Market, but also on the level of co-ordination with the United States.[2]

If bilateral efforts fail, and 'if the present influx of capital into the Community were to continue, there would be a danger of fresh balance of payments surpluses and this would lead to new inflationary pressure', and if other measures such as capital exports, envisaged to offset the said surpluses do not lead to satisfactory results, 'fundamental importance should be attached to restricting excessive imports of capital from countries outside the Community'.[3] The Seventh Report of the E.E.C. Monetary Committee quoted here indicates clearly what the impact of foreign investment in the individual member states can be on monetary stability in the E.E.C. as a whole. In the absence of co-ordinated

[1] Article 234/2, Treaty of Rome.
[2] See the statements of Professor W. Hallstein, President of the E.E.C. Commission, in: *Entreprise*, no. 496, 13 March 1965, p. 31.
[3] Seventh Report of the E.E.C. Monetary Committee (1 March 1965), quoted in *Opera Mundi—Europe*, no. 295, 11 March 1965, p. 11.

measures to restrict 'excessive imports of capital from third countries', member states could individually resort to the application of Article 70/2 and 'take appropriate measures [on intermember level] to overcome . . . difficulties' caused by differences between municipal exchange and establishment rules affecting foreign investment in the member states,[1] subject to the control of the Commission, as set out in Article 70/2.

[1] For comments, see Groeben and Boeckh, *Kommentar*, vol. 1.

# CHAPTER V

# COMPANY LAW AND THE
# MAIN FORMS OF BUSINESS

Companies constitute the main legal form under which foreign investment operates in a host country. Very frequently, such companies are subsidiaries established in accordance with the law of the host state; and if the latter has a uniform company law, the question of choice between different legal systems does not arise. If, on the other hand, in an area like the E.E.C. six different systems of municipal law exist, foreign enterprise may be guided in its decision to invest in one or the other of the member states, all other legal and economic factors being assumed equal, by considerations concerning legal requirements of minimum capital, possibility of sole ownership, protection of minority interests and power of the top managerial personnel. These and similar questions may affect the efficiency and competitiveness of the planned undertaking. The relevance of company law for the foreign investor in the E.E.C. goes, however, further than a few considerations bearing on efficiency and competition. It involves, in fact, the question to what extent the dynamics of the current process of integration will necessitate the harmonization or unification of the existing municipal company laws. The right of establishment, that is, the right to set up agencies, branches or subsidiaries in the member states of the E.E.C., and, just as paramount, a workable system of competition, both major objectives of the Treaty of Rome, necessitate an examination of that question in its relevance to the foreign investor.

The text of the Treaty implies directly in Articles 58 and 220 the incidence which the establishment of the Common Market is expected to have on company law. Departing from the existence of six different national laws on companies, the Treaty prescribes the recognition, in all member states, of companies constituted in accordance with the law of a member state. Thus it lays down the principle of Community treatment which, in its concrete application, is an extension of national treatment to all Community companies operating in a given member state. This indeed is one

61

of the basic foundations on which the right of establishment and the mobility of enterprise in the Common Market will rest.

The right of establishment of companies in relation to foreign-owned enterprise will be examined in chapter X and the possible trends of future development are discussed in the section on the harmonization of laws (chapter XII). In the present chapter the two main legal forms of enterprise in the member states are reviewed, a review intended as an illustration of some of the problems arising from the existence of different law systems in the envisaged economic union of the E.E.C. The two types of companies to be examined are the *limited liability company* and the *joint-stock company*, which correspond approximately to the *private* and *public* (joint-stock) companies of British law.[1] These are the commonest and most important types of companies for our purposes. As the (private) limited liability company does not exist in the Netherlands, only one type of company will be examined in the section on Dutch company law.

## BELGIUM

Belgian commercial law recognizes six forms of business organization.[2] Of the six types two will be examined here as being of direct interest to foreign investors contemplating the establishment of large or medium-sized enterprises: (*a*) the *société de personnes à responsabilité limitée* (partnership with limited liability, which corresponds to an English private limited liability company) and (*b*) the *société anonyme* (S.A.) (corporation).

---

[1] The translations used in the state sections which follow do not in any way imply an exact correspondence of the types of company under the laws of each state to those known by those terms in Anglo-American law.

[2] Code de Commerce, Section VI. The six types are:

   i. société anonyme (corporation) (Articles 26 ff.);
  ii. société de personnes à responsabilité limitée (limited liability company) (Articles 116–140);
 iii. société en commandite par actions (limited partnership with shares) (Articles 105–115);
  iv. société en commandite simple (limited partnership) (Articles 18–25);
   v. société en nom collectif (partnership) (Articles 15–17);
  vi. société coopérative (co-operative) (Articles 141–164).

## (a) *Société de personnes à responsabilité limitée*[1]

*Creation.* Only physical persons can form a *Société de Personnes à Responsabilité limitée* (S.A.R.L.) (Art. 119/1). There must be at least two and not more than 50 partners (Art. 119/3); a notarial instrument is required certifying that the basic conditions for the establishment of the company have been fulfilled. A S.A.R.L. may be formed for a maximum period of 30 years which may be renewed upon application (Art. 130).

The minimum capital requirement is Bfrs. 50,000 of which one-fifth must be paid in cash at the time of formation (Art. 120). Partners' shares (*parts sociales*) have a minimum value of Bfrs. 1,000 each (Art. 124/1). Their transfer is possible between members of the company and between members of their families. Shares are excluded from listing or public offering (Art. 131). For transfer to persons other than partners or members of their families, the consent of at least 50 per cent of the partners owning at least 75 per cent of the company's capital is required (Art. 126).

Publicity requirements prescribe that certain parts of the articles of association be published in the annexes of the *Moniteur Belge* (*Official Gazette*). After business has started, the balance sheet and the statement of profit and loss must be filed annually with the Commercial court, without parallel publication in the *Moniteur Belge*.

*Operation.* No board of directors is prescribed. One or more managers, not necessarily the partners, may be in charge of the company (Art. 129/1). Their appointment and powers may be determined by the articles of association (Art. 129/2). A manager designated by the articles as *gérant-statutaire* without limitation of time is presumed to have been appointed for the duration of a company's existence. In such a case, dismissal may be only for cause, entailing the complications of lawsuits for alleged unjustified termination of employment (Art. 62).

If the number of partners of a S.A.R.L. exceeds five, the appointment of one or more controllers (*commissaires*) becomes mandatory. These may be members or other persons (Art. 134/3).

The scope of activities precludes the engagement of a S.A.R.L. in insurance or banking (Art. 118).

A S.A.R.L. may be dissolved in accordance with provisions in

[1] References in parentheses within the text are to Articles in the Code de Commerce, Section VI, Articles 116–140.

the articles of association, by decisions of its partners and by bankruptcy (Art. 140).

## (b) Société anonyme[1]

*Creation.* The articles of association must be drawn up before a notary by at least seven founders who can be natural or legal persons (nationals or foreigners) (Art. 29). For creation by public subscription, the following requirements are prescribed: publication of a draft charter in the *Moniteur Belge*; subscription by future shareholders, and, following public subscription, a general meeting of all future shareholders (Art. 32 and 33). At this stage, a majority vote can prevent the formation of the proposed company and all subscribers are thereby released from their commitments.

Founders are liable for all debts incurred in connection with the company contemplated until such time as at least seven shareholders have been subscribed (Art. 35). This liability includes also the effective payment of one-fifth of the shares subscribed. Payments may be made in cash or in material assets (Art. 29bis and 34).

The establishment of a company becomes definite with the obligatory publication in full of the minutes of subscribers' general meeting in the *Moniteur Belge*. The published minutes must include a list of subscribers and a statement of the payments made for stock (Art. 30). Within two months after its establishment, a company must be registered at the *Registre de Commerce* with the payment of a registration fee equivalent to 0·1 per cent of the par value of the corporate capital.[2]

The nationality of the company will be determined by the location of its head office; hence, companies with their main

---

[1] References in parenthesis within the text are to Articles in the Code de Commerce, Section VI, Articles 26–104.

For the texts of laws see Arrêté Royal, 30 November 1935 (*Moniteur Belge*, 12 December 1935) as amended by the laws of 7 June 1949 (*Mon. Belge*, 18 June 1949), 9 February 1953 (*Mon. Belge*, 16–17 February 1953), 10 November 1953 (*Mon. Belge*, 28 November 1953), 1 December 1953 (*Mon. Belge*, 16 December 1953), 6 January 1958 (*Mon. Belge*, 16 January 1958), 30 June 1961 (*Mon. Belge*, 6 July 1961), 14 March 1962 (*Mon. Belge*, 17 March 1962), and 31 July 1962 (*Mon. Belge*, 8 August 1962). For the uniform text currently in force see Ch. Wauters-de Néeff: *Code des Lois sur les Sociétés par Actions en vigueur dans les Pays du Marché Commun*, Brussels, 1964, pp. 10 ff.

[2] Article 122 of the Code on Registration Fees (Code des Droits d'Enregistrement).

establishment in Belgium will be treated as Belgian companies (Art. 197).

The statutory limit for a company's existence is thirty years; it is renewable (Art. 102/3). The corporate purpose, clearly stated in the articles of association, cannot be subsequently changed to the extent of modifying the essential character of the company (Art. 30 and 70bis/3). For any amendments within the statutory limits indicated, a special shareholders' meeting is required to deal with the corporate purpose (*l'objet social*) (Art. 70bis). At such a special meeting, 50 per cent of the capital shares and 50 per cent of beneficiary shares, if any exist, must be represented. If the required quorum cannot be achieved, a second meeting with 25 per cent of each class of the respective shareholders may be held (Art. 70bis/4). Valid amendments require four-fifths of the votes present (Art. 70bis/5). The right of beneficiary shares to vote on charter amendments regarding the corporate purpose cannot be annulled by stipulations in the articles of association, but such shares have no voting rights on other matters (Art. 74/2). Charter amendments may be made subject to a substantial majority by including stipulations to this effect in the articles of association. [1]

There is no minimum statutory capital required. The agreed capital must be subscribed in full at the time of the company's creation, and one-fifth of the subscribed shares must be paid at the time of incorporation (Art. 35). In case of a subsequent increase in capital, founders and directors of a company are jointly liable for unsubscribed parts.

Shares may be at par or no-par value, registered or bearer, with equal voting rights which cannot be restricted (Art. 41). Title to ownership of registered shares depends on the inscription of the owner's name in the register of the company; the share certificate is not sufficient (Art. 43). Additional restrictions on the transferability of shares may be prescribed by a decision of stockholders, for example, making transfers dependent on a majority consent of shareholders or directors. [2]

As to stock types, these can be capital shares (*actions de capital*) issued for contributions in cash (*actions de numéraires*) or in kind (*actions d'apport*) (Art. 29). The articles of association must describe in detail and contain an assessment of contributions in kind, and list the persons to whom capital shares have been

---

[1] L. Frédéricq: *Traité de Droit Commercial Belge*, Ghent, 1950, vol. 5, no. 505.
[2] J. van Ryn: *Principes de Droit Commercial*, Brussels, vol. 1, 1954, no. 545.

issued (Art. 30). Shares received for contributions in kind cannot be transferred until the tenth day following the publication, in the annexes of the *Moniteur Belge*, of the second annual balance sheet after the date of issue of such shares (Art. 47/1). Prior to this time-limit, transfer may be effected only by assignment certified by a notary or competent court official, and by notice to the company concerned within 30 days following the transfer. If capital shares for contributions in kind are bearer shares, they must remain deposited with the company until the end of the time-limit indicated above (Art. 47/2).

A further type of stock is the *part bénéficiaire* (beneficiary shares) issued to promoters, founders or persons who have rendered valuable services to the company (Art. 41/1). If the articles of association so provide, beneficiary shares may participate in the distribution of profits, and may have additional voting rights. Similarly, they may be entitled to a share in the assets of the company, in case of dissolution, after the reimbursement of capital shares. The total number of beneficiary shares may not exceed, however, half of the total number of votes allocated to holders of capital shares, nor can they be counted for more than two-thirds of the votes cast by holders of capital shares. As for their rights to transfer shares, holders of beneficiary stock are subject to the same limitations as those applicable to holders of capital shares for contributions in kind (Art. 41/1).

Other types of stock are the founders' shares (*parts de fondateurs*) as opposed to common stock (*actions ordinaires*). The former may be entitled to a higher rate of return on the capital contributed and to other advantages concerning surpluses (Art. 41/1). The *action de jouissance* is a type of stock for which the initial investment capital has been reimbursed but dividends continue to be paid. It is not entitled to rights regarding the company's capital except after reimbursement of all other types of stock.[1]

*Operation.* A minimum of three directors is statutorily required. They are elected for one or more periods of six years (re-election is possible). Foreign directors need the professional permit card (which is not difficult to obtain) required for business activities in the country (Art. 55). The power of directors may be extended or restricted by stockholders' decision (Art. 65).

As the executive persons in charge of managing the affairs of a

[1] J. van Ryn, *Principes*, vol. 1, no. 822.

company, directors incur certain liabilities and as such they must give certain guarantees in the form of a number of company shares deposited with the company. These shares may belong to the directors or to third persons (Arts. 57, 58 and 62); their number may be increased by a resolution of the shareholders' general meeting (Art. 58/3). Directors may be removed by the general meeting, even if their designation is recorded in the articles of association (Art. 55/3).[1]

In case of improper performance of their duties, directors may be sued by the company but not by individual shareholders. Individual shareholders may sue at civil law for tortious conduct of one or more directors or other higher management personnel, or on the part of the company (Art. 62/2).[2]

Directors of companies need not be shareholders of the one they serve (Art 58/2). A predominant view is of the opinion that even corporations can be directors.[3] Delegation of power by the board of directors is possible and may include part or all of the current management affairs. One or more of the board's members (*administrateur-délégué*) or other persons (*directeur-gérant*) may be charged with the powers delegated (Art. 63).

The management of a company and its records is supervised by one or more controllers (*commissaires*), who are auditors appointed by the general meeting of shareholders, for a maximum period of six years (Art. 64/1 and 2). They can be relieved of their functions, similarly, by the general meeting (Art. 64/3). If a given company has offered or is offering securities to the public, at least one of the *commissaires* must be an independent public accountant (Art. 64bis/1, par. 1 and /2 par. 1).[4]

The auditors (*commissaires*) have the right of unlimited control of all matters related to the affairs of a company (Arts. 64/1 and 65/1). They may inspect the books, correspondence, minutes and records of the company. The directors are responsible for

---

[1] A provision in the articles of association or contractual agreement to the contrary would be void. See van Ryn, *Principes*, vol. 1, no. 586.

[2] See also Article 1382 of the Belgian Civil Code; van Ryn, *Principes*, vol. 1, no. 609. For judicial examples, see *Répertoire Pratique du Droit Belge*, vol. 12, no. 898, 1951; L. Frédéricq: 'De veranwoorderlijkheid van de beheerders in de naamloze Vennootschap', in *Rechtskundig Weekblad*, 24 November 1957.

[3] Van Ryn, *Principes*, vol. 1, no. 37.

[4] Public accountants in Belgium, as in many European countries, have a semi-public function. For Belgium, see Law of 22 July 1953.

presenting to them a semi-annual statement on the company's assets and liabilities (Art. 65/2). On their part, the auditors report annually to the stockholders' general meeting (Art. 65/3). In case of need, expert assistance may be claimed by the auditors for checking the books and accounts of the company (Art. 65/6). The assisting experts must be approved by the company and, in case of conflict, a decision may be taken by the competent commercial court (Art. 65/7). Like the board of directors, auditors must deposit a guarantee in the form of shares of the company's stock. No minimum is required and the amount of security offered does not restrict the auditors' liability (Arts. 57/2, 58/2 and 3, 59 and 69).

In addition to the annual meeting of stockholders, specific meetings can be convened, called by the board of directors, by the auditors or by stockholders representing at least one-fifth of the shares issued (Art. 73/2).

While the procedure to be followed during the general meeting can be governed by by-laws, three rules are mandatory by law: every shareholder must have the right to vote (Art. 74); no one person or corporate body owning shares of the company may vote more than one-fifth of the shares issued, or more than two-fifths of the shares actually voting at the given meeting (Art. 76); and shareholders of shares not yet fully paid cannot vote if they have been called upon to make further payments but have not yet paid. Until the required payments are effected, their voting rights are suspended (Arts. 74, last par., 73/3 and 77, last par.).

Shareholders' meetings may be held outside Belgium if the articles of association so provide.[1] The annual balance sheet and profit-and-loss statement approved by the stockholders' general meeting must be published in the *Moniteur Belge*, within ten days following their deposit with the appropriate Commercial Court (Arts. 80 and 81); such deposit must take place within 15 days after approval by the stockholders (Arts. 10, 11 and 80/2).

The distribution of profits can be made subject to provisions in the articles of association or to decisions of the annual stockholders' meeting. Statutory requirements prescribe that annually 5 per cent of net profits must be set aside for capital reserves until such time as the reserve fund has reached 10 per cent of the corporate capital (Art. 77/4).

The question of liquidation of a company must be discussed by

[1] Van Ryn, *Principes*, vol. 1, no. 696.

a special shareholders' meeting when the corporate capital drops
to 50 per cent of the nominal value. Stockholders representing 25
per cent of the shares participating in the meeting may decide to
proceed with the liquidation (Art. 103). A clause in the articles of
association may provide for liquidation at a specified higher capital
loss expressed in a percentage. If a company has had less than seven
shareholders for more than six months, request for liquidation
may be made by an interested party (Art. 104).

*Conclusions*

Belgian company law offers a wide margin for special provisions
that can be included in the articles of association, to suit the
particular intentions of shareholders. Thus, while little statutory
protection is offered to minority shareholders, their interests can
be considered when the articles of association are drawn up. Safe-
guards may be included against abuse of majority rights (Art. 70);
clauses may insure that all reports on the company's activities will
be duly communicated to stockholders.[1] The right of appointment of one or more directors may be reserved for minority
stockholders.

### FRANCE

Personal associations or partnerships (*sociétés de personnes*) recognized by French commercial law will not be treated here, and of
the three types of capital companies (*sociétés de capitaux*) two will
be considered which offer the most suitable form for business
activities by foreign investors in France: (*a*) the *société à responsabilité limitée* and (*b*) the *société anonyme*.[2] Similarities between

---

[1] J. L. Blondeel, in: *Legal Aspects of Foreign Investment*, Friedmann and
Pugh, eds., pp. 66–7.

[2] The three personal partnerships without limited liability are:

i. associations en participation (joint ventures);

ii. société en nom collectif (general partnership) (Code de Commerce,
Articles 20–22);

iii. société en commandite simple (limited partnership) (Code de Commerce,
Articles 23–28).

The three capital companies are:

i. société en commandite par actions (limited partnership with shares)
(Law of 24 July 1867, Articles 1 ff.);

ii. société à responsabilité limitée (limited liability company) (Law of
7 March 1925);

iii. société anonyme (corporation) (Law of 24 July 1867).

Belgian and French company law exist; both Belgian and Luxembourg commercial law have been extensively influenced by French law.

## (a) Société à responsabilité limitée (S.A.R.L.)[1]

Creation. At least two partners (natural or legal persons; nationals or foreigners) are required for the establishment of a private limited company (S.A.R.L.) which comes into existence when the association agreement is signed.[2] In the absence of a provision in the agreement, determining the length of time during which the company is to exist, the company will have been established for an indefinite duration. In this case, each associate is entitled to dissolve the company at will.[3]

The minimum capital prescribed by law is NF. 10,000.[4] Each partner must make a contribution which may be either in cash or in kind in return for shares (i.e. business interest) in the company. The required capital must be fully paid when the company is created.[5]

With the signature of the association agreement, the company is created and its shareholders are bound by their agreement, but the company cannot yet begin activities as far as third parties are concerned until public notice is given in the prescribed form.[6] Four formalities are to be fulfilled within 30 days after the signature of the association agreement: (1) deposition of the company contract with the Commercial Court, (2) publication of an extract of the association contract in a local newspaper carrying legal items; (3) similar publication in the Bulletin des Annonces Légales Obligatoires; and (4) listing in the Commercial Register.[7]

---

[1] Law of 7 March 1925 as amended by the Decree-Law no. 15 of 30 October 1935, Decree of 9 August 1953 and the Law of 1 August 1957. For a detailed study of limited companies in French law, see E. M. Church: Business Associations under French Law, London, 1960, chapter 6, pp. 189 ff. Reference to this work is made, in subsequent footnotes, under the author's name.

[2] Article 5 of the Law of 7 March 1925; Church, p. 142 f.

[3] See Church, p. 142 with reference to Article 1869 of the French Civil Code, concerning the right of an associate in a S.A.R.L. to dissolve the company.

[4] Article 6, Law of 7 March 1925, as amended by the Decree of 9 August 1953; Church, p. 143.

[5] Article 7, Law of 7 March 1925, Church, pp. 144, 145.

[6] Church, pp. 146 f., 547 ff.

[7] Articles 13, 14, 16 and 20 of Law of 7 March 1925; Church, p. 147.

*Operation.* The association contract may specify that one or more managers, who may be associates or third (natural or legal) persons, appointed by shareholders, will be in charge of the company's affairs, Similarly, the contract may indicate the scope of their competence, within which commitments with third parties will be binding. The appointment of managers may be for a limited, or for an indefinite period. For a private limited company (S.A.R.L.) with more than 20 partners, a supervisory council (*conseil de surveillance*) is mandatory.[1]

Business shares or interests cannot be transferred to third parties without the consent of partners representing at least three-fourths of the capital.[2] Transfers are necessarily made by contract.

While the same principles in general apply to the liquidation of both partnerships and private limited companies, in the case of the latter, death, interdiction, bankruptcy or insolvency of one of the partners do not lead to the dissolution of the S.A.R.L.[3]

## (b) *Société anonyme (S.A.)*[4]

*Creation.* The articles of association may be drawn up by a notary or by the founders themselves numbering at least seven.[5] The proposed capital, for which there is no statutory minimum, must be subscribed in full; 25 per cent of the par value of each share, with a minimum value of NF. 100 each, must be paid at the beginning; payment thereof must be completed within five years of the company's effective existence. A notarial declaration must be issued to the effect that the prescribed payments for 25 per cent of the shares subscribed have been made. Contributions may be made in cash or in kind.[6] If contributions are only in cash, a general constitutive meeting will be convened for adopting the statements of subscription, and appointing the company's directors and supervisory auditors. The company comes into existence with the acceptance, on the part of the directors and auditors, of the appointments proposed by the constitutive meeting.[7]

---

[1] Articles 24 and 30; Church, pp. 157, 142, 159 ff.

[2] Article 22, Law of 7 March 1925; Church, p. 149.

[3] Article 36; Church, p. 175.

[4] For the texts of the main laws on joint-stock companies, see Ch. Wauters-de Néeff: *Code des Lois sur les Sociétés par Actions en vigueur dans les Pays du Marché Commun*, pp. 101 ff.

[5] Article 1, Law of 24 July 1867; Church, pp. 182, 189 ff., 219.

[6] Articles 1, 4 and 24, Law of 24 July 1867; Article 1, Law of 4 March, 1943.

[7] Articles 24 and 25, Law of 24 July 1867.

If contributions are made also in kind, it is mandatory to appoint special auditors who will be in charge of the assessment concerning the contributions in kind, or special advantages offered to part of the future shareholders. The special auditors report on their assessment to a second general constitutive meeting.[1] If the said report is approved, the meeting proceeds with the appointment of directors and controlling auditors. With the acceptance of the proposed appointments, the existence of the company begins.[2] Lastly, the requirements of public notice and registration must be fulfilled. Within two months after a company has begun to operate an entry must be made in the list of the Commercial Register.[3]

The nationality of a company created in France will be French beyond doubt if both its legal domicile (*siège social*) and real head office are situated in France.[4] A company is created for an indefinite period, unless otherwise stipulated in the articles of association.[5]

Dual classification of stock types includes cash shares (*actions de numéraire*) and contribution shares (*actions d'apport*); capital stock (*actions de capital*) and reimbursed stock (*actions de jouissance*); preferred stock (*actions privilégiées or actions de priorité*) and common stock (*actions ordinaires*); and bearer shares (*actions au porteur*) and registered shares (*actions nominatives*). Mixed shares (*actions mixtes*) with a combination of bearer and registered share characteristics may be also issued. There is no par stock in French law.[6]

The ownership of registered shares is based on registration of the owner's name with the company.[7] All holders of common or preferred stocks are entitled to vote at the stockholders' general meeting. A 'double vote' may be granted by the articles of association or by a subsequent special stockholders' meeting to fully paid nominal stock or to shares that have been in the ownership of the same holder for two years.[8] Voting by proxy is possible.

*Operation.* The management of a company is entrusted to a board of directors (*conseil d'administration*) consisting of at least

---

[1] Article 4, Law of 24 July 1867.          [2] Article 25, ibid.
[3] Church, pp. 547 ff.; Article 47, Commercial Code.
[4] Church, pp. 540 f.
[5] Article 1865, Civil Code; Church, p. 517.
[6] Articles 3 and 4, Law of 24 July 1867; Church, pp. 261 ff.
[7] Cass. 31 July 1887, S. 88.1.307, quoted in Church, p. 415.
[8] Article 1, Law of 13 November 1933; Church, pp. 425 f., 428 ff.

three and not more than twelve members appointed for a specified period not exceeding six years, by the shareholders' general meeting.[1] The chairman (*président*) of the board of directors is the person in charge of the top management and of carrying out decisions taken by the board of directors.[2] As a guarantee, all directors must deposit a minimum number of shares with the company; they may deposit only their own shares, and hence have to be themselves stockholders of the company.[3]

The president's powers may be extended by delegation on the part of the board of directors. He may be summarily dismissed by the shareholders' meeting, or by the board. His replacement can take place by the board of directors and not by shareholders. Not more than two French companies may have the same president, nor can companies be president of other companies.[4] Upon the recommendation of the president, the board of directors may appoint a vice-president (*directeur général adjoint*) who may not necessarily be a member of the board.[5] The vice-president acts as a general manager under the orders of the president.

On the level of liability, directors are individually responsible for decisions or actions of the board in which they participate. In addition to legitimate excuses such as incapacity to participate in the board's activities at a given time, individual directors may escape liability for a particular action of the board, by proving that they voted against the action. In case of outvoting, directors may submit their resignation and request the convocation of a stockholders' meeting.[6]

Supervisory auditors (*commissaires de surveillance*), elected by the shareholders, are in charge of control of the company; they verify the company's accounts and have the right of access to any information they may need for the proper exercise of their function.[7]

For companies with more than 50 employees, a board representing the latter, known as the *comité d'entreprise*, is prescribed for

[1] Article 1, Law of 16 November 1940; Church, p. 183 f., 365 ff.

[2] Article 2, Law of 16 November 1940, as amended by the Law of 4 March 1943; Church, pp. 183, 380 ff.

[3] Articles 22 and 26, Law of 24 July 1867; Church, pp. 365 ff. and the cases cited on p. 366.

[4] Article 12, Law of 4 March 1943; Church, p. 381 and the cases cited there.

[5] Article 2, Law of 16 November 1940, as amended by the Law of 4 March 1943; Church, p. 382.

[6] Church, pp. 390-1, and the court decisions quoted on p. 391.

[7] Article 32, Law of 24 July 1867; Church, pp. 184, 399 ff.

G

representing the workers and employees of the company. It is elected by the personnel and has the function of submitting opinions to the board of directors. It has no voting rights in the board's meetings.[1]

Foreigners acting as presidents or directors of French companies need the *carte de commerçant* required as a permit for commercial activities.

Shareholders' general meetings may be convened only at the company's domicile, hence only in France. Voting by proxy is possible.[2] The quorum required for the first meeting is 25 per cent of the capital stock. This may be increased by provisions in the by-laws; similarly, a specific quorum may be fixed for the second meeting; in the absence of specific provisions, a second meeting is valid no matter what proportion of the capital is represented.[3] At extraordinary stockholders' meetings, valid decisions depend on a quorum representing 50 per cent of the capital stock, for the first meeting; one-third for the second, and one-fourth for a third meeting.[4] In all cases a majority of two-thirds of those voting is required.[5]

Profits may be distributed only if they are real and not fictitious, i.e. without impairment of the capital stock. A minimum of 5 per cent of yearly profits have to be allocated to a reserve fund until the reserve fund equals one-tenth of the capital stock.[6] By provisions in the articles of association, it is possible to pay a fixed interest on shares independently from profits.

Companies may be judicially dissolved if within a period of a year the number of shareholders drops below the statutorily required number of seven, all of whom must be genuine and not men of straw.[7] A judicial dissolution may also take place upon a corresponding decision or a resolution of a shareholders' extraordinary meeting, following the loss of at least 75 per cent of the capital.[8] The articles of association may prescribe a smaller proportion.

[1] Ordinance of 22 February 1946, Laws of 16 May 1946 and of 7 July 1947.
[2] Church, p. 417.
[3] Article 29, Law of 24 July 1867; Church, pp. 440-1.
[4] Article 31, Law of 24 July 1867, as amended by the Law of 25 February 1953; Church, p. 469.
[5] Law of 1 May 1930; Church, pp. 470 f.
[6] Article 36, Law of 24 July 1867; Church, pp. 451, 452.
[7] Article 38, Law of 24 July 1867.
[8] Article 37, ibid.; Church, p. 519.

*Conclusions*

In both France and Belgium, a minimum of seven shareholders is required for the formation of a company, and the reduction of this number may lead to the dissolution of a company; there are no requirements for a minimum capital; there is a great similarity in the types of stock that a company may issue; while there are minor differences, the same basic principles apply to the management of companies in both countries. In terms of protection for minority shareholders, both systems provide for a margin of special provisions that may be included in the articles of association, for example, on a specified number of representatives on the board of directors.

A company established as a subsidiary in France or in Belgium cannot be owned by a single principal. In France, a one-man company is a contradiction in terms—a company is based on a contract *between* physical or legal persons (see Article 18, Commercial Code; Article 1832, Civil Code). None of the seven shareholders required as a minimum may be men of straw.[1]

## GERMANY

For the purposes of this study, among the different forms of business organization recognized by German law, the two major forms of capital association, (a) *Gesellschaft mit beschränkter Haftung* (GesmbH. or GmBH.) (limited liability company) and (b) *Aktiengesellschaft* (AG.) (joint-stock company or corporation) will be surveyed.[2]

[1] Church, p. 219 and the case quoted there.
[2] The types of partnership or association recognized by German commercial law are:

  i. Gesellschaft bürgerlichen Rechts (association of civil law) (Bürgerliches Gesetzbuch (BGB) (German Civil Code), Section 705); both natural and legal persons can be partners; no business can be conducted, however, under a common name;
  ii. Offene Handelsgesellschaft (general partnership) (Handelsgesetzbuch (HGB) (German Commercial Code), Sect. 105–160); for the definition of partnership in German law see Sect. 124, 184, 185, HGB and Sect. 705, BGB.
  iii. Kommanditgesellschaft (limited partnership) (HGB, Sect. 161–177);
  iv. Stille Gesellschaft (silent partnership) (HGB, Sect. 335);
  v. Kommanditgesellschaft auf Aktien (limited partnership with shares) (Aktiengesetz (Corporation law), Sect. 219–232);

(a) *Gesellschaft mit beschränkter Haftung (GmbH. or GesmbH.)*[1]

*Creation.* Two or more natural or legal persons, foreigners or nationals are prescribed for the valid formation of a GmbH. The contract and by-laws of association must be drawn up before a notary or a court official (Sect. 2/1). A minimum capital of DM. 20,000 is required; each associate must contribute at least a sum equal to DM. 500 (Sect. 5/1). Of the required capital, which must be entirely subscribed, one-fourth must be initially paid up; each associate must contribute at least DM. 250 to the capital amount paid up at the beginning (Sect. 7/2).

The business interest (*Geschäftsanteil*) of each partner depends on the initial contribution (*Stammeinlage*) made in the form of cash or material assets (Sect. 14). For their later transfer, the consent of partners is required if the contract of association contains a stipulation to this effect; otherwise their transfer may be by assignment or inheritance (Sect. 15). Sole ownership of a GmbH. by subsequent concentration of all business shares in the hands of a single or natural or moral person is possible.

The contract of association may prescribe that supplementary contributions are to be effected at some later date, in proportion to the initial contributions made by the partners (Sect. 26–28). If a partner fails to make the prescribed contribution, the difference must be balanced by additional amounts paid by the remaining partners in proportion to their respective business shares (Sects. 24, also 21 and 25).

The existence of a company is established, in relation to third parties, by its entry in the Commercial Register of the region where the company is domiciled (Sects. 7, 8 and 10).

*Operation.* One or more managers (*Geschäftsführer*), not necessarily partners of the company (Sects. 6 and 35), are appointed by a corresponding inclusion in the contract of association, or subsequently by the partners and in case of necessity by a court.[2]

---

vi. Gesellschaft mit beschränkter Haftung (GesmbH. or GmbH.) (limited liability company) (Gesetz betreffend GmbH.) (law concerning limited liability companies);

vii. Aktiengesellschaft (AG. or A.G.) (joint-stock company, corporation) (Aktiengesetz).

[1] References in parenthesis within the text are to sections of Gesetz betreffend GmbH., 20 April 1892, RGBl, 1892, pp. 447 ff., as amended by Law of 10 August 1937, RGBl, I, 1937, p. 897.

[2] See BGB, Section 29.

Managers may be removed at any time (Sect. 120). They are jointly liable for damages caused by a lack of proper diligence on their part (Sect. 43/1–2, also Sects. 82 and 83). The contract of association may specify the scope of power delegated to a manager, to the board of managers or to different members of a board (Sects. 6/2–3, 37).

The contract of association may provide for a board of directors. Their election and powers are the same as in the case of joint-stock companies (Sect. 52).

The general meeting of partners may be convened whenever necessary for the affairs of the company, upon request of its managers or directors (Sect. 49). It may be held in or outside Germany. Partners representing one-fifth of the business shares may convene a general meeting (Sect. 50/1).

Each partner has a vote proportional to his business share (Sect. 47/1–2). Voting by proxy is feasible, and a proxy may vote for more than one partner (Sect. 47/3). The right to act as proxies may be reserved by the contract of association to the company's partners. If resolutions are adopted in writing (i.e. by correspondence), it may not be necessary to adopt them at a general meeting. For voting at general meetings, the function of which is mainly a supervisory one, the contract of association may provide for a qualified majority; in the absence of a corresponding clause, resolutions at the general meeting will be passed by simple majority of votes cast (Sect. 47/1).

In German law, the increase or decrease in capital is equivalent to an amendment in the contract of association, for which rules on procedure and publication are to be observed (Sects. 55–58). A pre-emptive right for old partners may be stipulated by the contract of association. A reduction in capital is more difficult than an increase in capital and may be effected after all creditors have been satisfied or given adequate security (Sect. 58/1). Obviously, capital reduction cannot extend below the statutory minimum of DM. 20,000 prescribed as corporate capital (Sect. 58/2).

Requirements of public notice prescribe that a list of the partners (names, addresses, occupations, amount of business shares) must be filed annually with the Commercial Register (Sect. 40); likewise, amendments in the contract of association, increase or reduction of corporate capital must be communicated to the Commercial Register (Sect. 39). Requirements about business information to be made available to the public are less stringent for private limited companies than they are for joint-stock companies. In recent years thirteen of the 100 largest German companies, in terms of turnover figures, were private limited entities.[1] As a result, certain quarters in Germany have been advocating that the compulsory publicity presently applicable to joint-stock companies be extended also to private limited companies. It is argued that the law does not prescribe a limit to the scope of activities of limited companies,[2] and that such companies, while as active as joint-stock companies, are not subject to the same strict provisions of company law.[3]

For amendments of the contract of association, a majority vote of 75 per cent in favour of the proposed amendments is statutorily prescribed (Sect. 53/1–2). A larger majority may be stipulated by the contract of association (Sect. 52). Any amendment affecting the imposition of new obligations on partners must be adopted in unanimity (Sect. 53/3).

For the dissolution of a GmbH., court action is necessary. A request in this respect may be filed by partners representing at

[1] On the size and criteria used in the measurement of big enterprise in Germany, in terms of turnover figures, labour force involved, see *Die Welt*, no. 256, 2 November 1964, p. 10, on the basis of a study published by Werbeagentur Pritchard, Wood GmbH. (Hamburg). Of the 100 largest enterprises in Germany, in terms of turnover figures, 79 were joint-stock (AG.), 13 GmbH. and 3 Kommanditgesellschaften auf Aktien (limited companies with shares).

[2] The scope of activities of a GmbH. includes all activities of a commercial nature (Sect. 13, par. 3).

[3] See *Frankfurter Allgemeine Zeitung*, 27 February 1964, p. 18, and *Neue Zürcher Zeitung*, 13 October 1964, leaf 3 verso. The 45th Conference of German Lawyers dealt with the given question extensively. In the Federal Parliament a draft law was submitted by the Socialist Party (SPD). The draft provides for compulsory publicity for limited liability companies with more than 2,000 employees with yearly turnover figures of DM. 50 million or more, or with yearly balance figures of DM. 100 million or more. It is believed that interested economic quarters wish to have, in this way, access to information concerning the economic position of foreign-owned subsidiaries playing an important role in the country's economic life. Leading German lawyers are of the opinion that stricter regulations for publicity by limited liability companies will in the course of time become unavoidable. The Conference of German Lawyers dealt also with a directive proposal of the E.E.C. Commission favouring publicity for limited liability companies in the E.E.C. with a yearly balance of at least DM. 4,000,000. The Commission proposes that legislative action in this respect should be taken on the municipal level.

least one-tenth of the corporate capital (Sects. 61/2, 60, 61/1, 62, and 65–74).

## (b) *Aktiengesellschaft (AG.)*[1]

*Creation.* Five natural or legal persons foreigners or nationals are required to draw up as founders (*Gründer*) the articles of association (*Satzung*) of the company planned (Sect. 2). The articles must be drawn up before a court official or public notary (Sect. 16/1). With the inscription of the articles of association in the Commercial Register, the existence of the Aktiengesellschaft (AG.) begins (Sect. 34/1).

The basic capital required is DM. 100,000 which may be contributed in cash or in material assets (Sect. 7). All contributions, in cash or in assets, must be expressed, however, in German marks (Sects. 2, 6/2 and 7).

The principal place of business, which establishes the nationality of a company, is the location where the company's management is situated (Sect. 5).

Stock shares must have a minimum value of DM. 100 (Sect. 8/1) and may not be issued below par (Sect. 9, also 34/4). They may be registered (*Namensaktien*) or bearer (*Inhaberaktien*) (Sect. 10) and all have the same voting rights (Sect. 12), though preference shares may be excluded from voting rights (Sects 11 and 12/1). If shares are issued before the capital has been fully paid, their registration becomes mandatory (Sect 10/2). Title to the ownership of registered shares is based on their registration in the company's books (Sect. 62/3).

*Operation.* A supervisory council (*Aufsichtsrat*) must be appointed by the founders. This council has direct supervisory functions over the board of managers. Its members cannot be less than three, and depending on the amount of capital, not more than 9, 12 or 15 members, all of whom must be natural persons (Sect. 86). Statutory rules, such as in the Law of Enterprise Constitution

[1] References in parenthesis within the text are to sections of the Aktiengesetz (law concerning joint-stock companies and partnerships limited by shares) of 30 January 1937, RGBl, I, 1937, p. 187 (AktG.) with a last amendment on 11 October 1952, BGBl, I, 1952, p. 681. A further amendment is being elaborated; see *Die Welt*, no. 49, 27 February 1965, p. 9. The amended law came into force on 1 January 1966. The tendency is towards stricter control of concentration.

(*Betriebsverfassungsgesetz*) of 1952, prescribe the representation of employees in the supervisory council. This will consist of an equal number of representatives appointed by shareholders and by employees.[1]

The competence of the supervisory council includes the appointment of members of the board of managers (*Vorstand*) consisting of natural persons only. This board is in charge of the management and representation of the company (Sect. 70 ff.).

The shareholders' general meeting, which must be held in Germany, can be convened by one or more shareholders representing at least 5 per cent of the corporate stock or even less if a clause to this effect is contained in the articles of association (Sect. 106/2). The management is under obligation to comply with the desire of the given shareholder(s), otherwise application may be made to the competent court (Sect. 106/4). The judge concerned can authorize the convention of the requested general meeting. Expenses in this case may have to be borne by the requesting shareholders, if a decision to this effect is taken by the general meeting (Sect. 106/5). Voting rights at a general meeting may be exercised by proxy (Sect. 114/3). If deliberations of a general meeting concern amendments of the articles of association, a resolution with a majority vote of at least three-fourths of the share capital represented at the meeting is required; a larger majority may be stipulated by the articles of association (Sects. 145 and 146/1).

Special provisions are to be observed when adopting amendments affecting the basic capital. Three types of capital increases are recognized in law: (*a*) general increase (Sect. 149 ff.), (*b*) contingent increase, dependent on a right to exchange shares or acquire additional shares (Sect. 159 ff.), and (*c*) authorized capital increase issued by the management of the company (Sect. 169 ff.). The last two forms of capital increase are subject to a resolution of the general meeting with a majority of at least three-fourths of the capital represented (Sects. 160 and 169/2). The first form of capital increase (general increase) may be decided by a simple majority, provided a corresponding clause is included in the articles of association (Sect. 149/1). For a capital reduction, a majority of at

[1] For a study on employee representation in corporate management, see M. P. Fogarty: *British Journal of Industrial Relations*, vol. II, no. 1, March 1964, pp. 79 ff., and by the same author: *Companies beyond Jenkins*, P.E.P. publication, vol. XXXI, no. 486, February 1965, pp. 66 ff.

least three-fourths of the capital represented is required (Sect. 175/1).

A statutory reserve of one-tenth of the corporate capital or any higher percentage thereof fixed by the articles of association is prescribed (Sect. 130/1). No less than 5 per cent of the annual net profits are to be paid for the accumulation of the reserve fund. If shares are issued above par, the premium must be allocated to the reserve fund.

For the annual report which is required to be submitted by the board of managers and the supervisory council to the shareholders, and for the profit-and-loss statement, minimum contents are prescribed (Sects. 125 ff., 128). The required information must contain reference to any existing cartel arrangements and to membership of the company in any associations (Sect. 128). Omissions are permissible if they are in the interests of the company or of a linked undertaking, or are dictated by considerations of public interest (Sect. 128/3).

At the general meeting, any shareholder may request additional information related to the given point of the agenda. Additional information sought in this way may be withheld only on grounds of company interest, or interest of a linked enterprise, or on grounds of public interest (Sects. 112 and 125).

A general meeting may appoint, by simple majority, a special auditor for a study of the circumstances under which the company was created or is being managed (Sects. 118 and 136/1). Shareholders representing at least 10 per cent of the company's capital may apply to the Commercial Court requesting the appointment of a special auditor; the court may accept the request if it finds that there are good reasons for it (Sect. 136/2 and 3).

Any resolution of the general meeting may be challenged by a shareholder if he applies to the Commercial Court (Sects. 197–199). In case of grave violation of statutory provisions, the Court may declare the given resolution(s) null and void (Sects. 199 and 195). Shareholders who abuse their voting rights to obtain advantages for themselves or for third parties against the interest of the company or of its shareholders may, similarly, be challenged (Sect. 197/2). A shareholder who challenges resolutions must, however, have attended the general meeting in question and his objection to the resolution(s) concerned must be registered in the minutes of the meeting (Sect. 198/1). In case of absence from the meeting he can have the right to challenge on grounds that he was not duly invited or that the meeting itself was not properly called or the object of the given resolution was not appropriately announced or explained. Members of the management board and of the supervisory council are also entitled to challenge a given resolution if they would by not doing so be made subject to criminal or civil liability.

Legal action may be taken against the management: a minority of 10 per cent of the shareholders may submit claims on behalf of the company for damages caused by members of the management board or supervisory council (Sect. 122/1). Upon application, and in case of need, the Commercial Court may appoint a legal representative for minority shareholders.

## Conclusions

The choice between the creation of a GmbH. (private limited company) or an AG. (joint-stock company) may be based mainly on considerations of relative simplicity in the case of a private company; the scope of activities of such a company is as wide as that of a joint-stock company. An existing difference in the publicity requirements of the two kinds of companies will very probably disappear as more and more pressure by public opinion favours a statutory alignment of requirements.

Whereas in Belgian and French law, a minimum of seven shareholders must be maintained for joint-stock companies, in Germany the AG. and also the private company may survive with a single shareholder or associate, respectively. This fact may enable a parent company wholly to own a subsidiary. Obviously, the joint-stock company presents advantages over a private company as far as the desire to attract capital is concerned. Similarly, rules affecting the minority shareholders of an AG. are, in comparison, more elaborate than rules for minority associates in the case of a private company, though in the latter case protection may be provided by the inclusion of specific clauses in the contract of association. In a comparison of minority protection in German law, on the one hand, and Belgian and French law, on the other, protection in the former is embodied in the first place in statutory rules, whereas in Belgium and France such protection is vaguely expressed in the law but may be elaborated in the form of special clauses in the articles of association.

## ITALY

Provisions governing the different types of business enterprise recognized by Italian law are contained in Book V of the Civil Code (*Codice Civile*). A first distinction is made between sole ownerships (*imprese individuale*) and partnerships or companies (*società*). Both groups concern enterprises engaging in commercial activities.[1] As for the types of partnerships or companies, the law recognizes five forms of capital association.[2] In this section two of them, (*a*) *società per responsibilità limitata* (limited liability company) and (*b*) *società per azioni* (SpA) (joint-stock company, corporation), will be examined as the most suitable for commercial activities by foreign capital in Italy.

### (a) *Società per responsabilità limitata*[3]

*Creation.* A minimum capital of 50,000 Lire and the participation of at least two partners are required for the creation of a limited company (Arts. 2474/1 and 2329/1). The basic share of each partner must be at least 1,000 Lire; if it is higher than this sum, it must be in multiples thereof, 2,000, 3,000 and so on. The contract of association, drawn up before a notary, must be entered into the Commercial Register (Arts. 2475, 2328, last par., 2330/1 and 2188). The legal existence of the company begins with its listing in the Register (Art. 2331/1). Until then, the founders of the company remain personally liable for obligations incurred in respect of the company planned (Arts. 2475, last par., 2331/2 and 1292).

The transfer of business shares can be restricted by provisions in the contract of association (Art. 2479). If these shares are

[1] See Codice Civile, Article 2195.

[2] The five forms are:

i. società in nome collettivo (general partnership) (Codice Civile, Article 2291);

ii. società in accomandita semplice (limited partnership) (Codice Civile, Article 2312);

iii. società in accomandita per azioni (limited partnership with shares) (Codice Civile, Article 2462);

iv. società per responsibilità limitata (limited liability company) (Codice Civile, Article 2472);

v. società per azioni (joint-stock company, corporation) (Codice Civile, Article 2325).

[3] For the definition of a limited company, see Codice Civile, Articles 2472 and 2473. References in parentheses within the text are to articles of the Italian Civil Code.

subsequently concentrated in the hands of a single person, the existence of the company is thereby not affected (Art. 2497).

*Operation.* Only partners, one or more, can be in charge of a company's management (Art. 2487). At the general meeting, each partner has at least one vote corresponding to the basic share of 1,000 Lire prescribed for each partner; additional votes must correspond to the multiples of basic shares (Arts. 2484–2485). Resolutions at an ordinary general meeting can be adopted by simple majority; at an extraordinary meeting, a majority representing three-fourths of the capital is prescribed (Art. 2486).

If the corporate capital exceeds one million Lire or if the contract of association so prescribes, the participation of a *collegia sindacale* (auditors) in the management becomes mandatory (Arts. 2488/1 and 2397 ff.). In any case, partners representing at least one-third of the corporate capital are entitled to subject, at their own expense, the accounts of the company to an annual inspection (Art. 2489).

Provisions governing the increase or reduction of capital in joint-stock companies apply equally to limited companies.[1] For a decision affecting the liquidation of the company, a majority vote representing three-fourths of the corporate capital is required (Arts. 2497, also 2486 and 2448–2457). In cases of insolvency, debts and liabilities incurred during the period in which the company was owned by a single person are to be borne by the unlimited liability of that person (Arts. 2497 and 2362).

(b) *Società per azioni (SpA)*

*Creation.* At least two founders are prescribed (Art. 2247). For a corporate capital exceeding 500m Lire and for activities in the fields of banking, insurance, mining, operation of power plants, or sea, air and land transportation services, a special authorization from the Ministry of the Treasury is required.

Subscription to the corporate capital, which must not be less than one million Lire, can be private or public (Arts. 2333 and 2327). Three-tenths of the subscribed capital must be deposited with the Bank of Italy prior to the company's registration (Art. 2329). Contributions may be made in cash or in material assets, and

---

[1] For amendments of the contract of association, see Articles 2494, 2436–2437: for capital increase, Articles 2495, 2438–2441, 2474; for a reduction in capital, Articles 2496, 2445–2447, 2474.

additional contributions may be stipulated in the articles of association. These must be drawn up before a public notary (Art. 2328). Founders and subscribers can be natural or legal persons, nationals or foreigners and can participate in the creation of the planned company directly or by proxy. For the founders' meeting, a quorum of 50 per cent is required (Art. 2335). Each subscriber, regardless of the amount subscribed, is entitled to vote. Terms set forth in the draft articles of association may not be amended without the unanimous consent of all subscribers.

Upon formation, the new company may start its activities (Art. 2331). Its legal existence will be established, however, by its registration in the Register of Business Enterprises (*Registro delle Impree*) and a corresponding notice in the official bulletin (Arts. 2330 and 2331). Until then, founders remain liable for all obligations incurred and all expenses caused by the planning of the company. For the prescribed entry into the Register of Business Enterprises, all the capital must have been subscribed, and three-tenths of the subscribed capital paid into the Bank of Italy, and, if necessary, any required authorization obtained (Art. 2329). After the registration of the company, the Bank of Italy will reimburse the three-tenths of the corporate capital paid in at the stage of the creation. No shares may be issued or sold prior to the registration (Art. 2331).

The duration of the company may be fixed in the articles of association (Art. 2328). The nationality of the company will be determined by the law of its domicile, i.e. the location of its main office.

As to corporate stock, shares may be issued only at par value, must all be equal in value and have the same rights within a given class (Arts. 2346 and 2348). Preferred shares with limited voting rights may not represent more than 50 per cent of the company's capital. After the creation of a company, all shares may be concentrated in the hands of a single shareholder without affecting the existence of the company. A shareholder owning all the shares of a company is liable without limitation, however, for obligations incurred during the period in which he held all the stocks (Arts. 2362 and 2497). Shares assigned to former holders of redeemed stock (*azioni di godimento*) may participate in dividends and be excluded from voting (Art. 2353).

Bearer shares are recognized by law only in Sicily, Sardinia and the province of Trentino–Alto Adige (Art. 2355). Thus, registered shares are the rule in Italy. When partly paid shares are transferred, the transferor remains liable for the amount still due jointly with the transferee, if the latter fails to pay (Art. 2356). The articles of association may include special provisions affecting the transfer of shares (Art. 2355). No new shares may be issued, that is, corporate capital may not be increased, before already issued shares are fully paid.

A company may not buy its own shares if funds from net profits are not used for the purpose, with prior authorization from the stockholders' general meeting. The given shares must be fully paid. Voting rights attached to them remain suspended so long as they remain in the ownership of the company (Art. 2357). Neither reciprocal subscription nor ownership or stock between two or more companies is authorized, not even through an intermediary (Art. 2360); nor is it permissible to own shares in the capital of a company controlled by the other company (Art. 2359). Ownership of shares of other companies is, moreover, not possible, if such ownership is incompatible with the corporate purpose or modifies it. For contributions other than in cash, the control of an expert appointed by the court is mandatory (Art. 2343).

*Operation.* The management may be entrusted to a single director or to a board of directors (Art. 2380). These may be persons other than shareholders. The appointment of a sole director or the chairman of the directors' board may be effected by stockholders. Management power may be delegated to managing directors who must be members of the board (Art. 2381). All directors are appointed for a period not exceeding three years (Art. 2383/2).

Within 30 days following their appointment, directors are required to deposit a guarantee equal to not less than one-fiftieth of the corporate capital. The deposited guarantee may consist of registered stock of the company or of registered securities issued or guaranteed by the State (Art. 2387/1). Failure to comply with the guarantee requirement within the prescribed 30 days following appointment debars the directors concerned from office (Art. 2387/2). Directors and managers may be sued by the general meeting of stockholders.[1]

Under Italian company law, a supervisory power is exercised

---

[1] For the remuneration of directors, see Article 2389. For liability, Articles 2393–2395; for managers, Article 2396.

by the board of auditors (*collegio sindacale, sindaci*) (Art. 2397).
Members of this board not only audit the corporate accounts, but
also have supervisory functions to see that the company functions
in accordance with the law and provisions of the articles of
association (Art. 2403). Their appointment may be included in the
articles of association and later effected by the shareholders' meetings (Art. 2400). They may not necessarily be shareholders (Art.
2397/1). For companies with a capital exceeding 50m Lire, the
appointment of auditors is mandatory (Art. 2397/2). The board
of auditors may consist of three or five members: within a board
consisting of three auditors, one must be selected from the list of
Certified Public Auditors (*Ruolo dei Revisori dei Conti*); in a board
with five members, two must be certified public auditors (Art.
2397/1 and /2).

Companies with capital totalling less than 50m Lire must have
at least one auditor and an alternate auditor, both from the professional list with a period of appointment of three years (Arts.
2397/3 and 2400/1). While directors may be dismissed at any time,
the dismissal of auditors is permissible only for cause and is
subject to an approval of the court (Arts. 2383/2, 2400 and 2402).
As to their liability, they may be sued, like directors, by the
general meeting, both for civil and criminal sanctions (Arts. 2407,
2393 and 2394). They are responsible for supervising the orderly
management of the company and they are empowered to convene
the shareholders' meeting if the directors fail to do so (Arts. 2403
and 2406).

The shareholders' general meeting may be convened at places
other than the principal office, within or outside Italy.[1] For a valid
quorum, half of the capital stock must be represented (Arts.
2368–2369). Voting by proxy is possible. Directors or employees
of a company may not act as proxies (Art. 2372).

For amendments in the articles of association, a quorum
representing more than 50 per cent of the corporate capital is
required (Art. 2368). If a first meeting fails to attain this quorum,
a second meeting may proceed with a representation equal to one-
third of the corporate capital (Art. 2369). These requirements may
be made stricter by the insertion of corresponding clauses in the
articles of association.

The corporate purpose or the form of the company may be

[1] R. Nobili: in *Legal Aspects of Foreign Investment*, Friedmann and Pugh,
eds., p. 312.

changed by votes representing 50 per cent of the capital stock, even at a second meeting. The same majority vote is required to dissolve a company, or to issue preferred shares.

Dissenting stockholders, who oppose resolutions which they think modify the corporate purpose or form, or effect the transfer of the company's office abroad, can withdraw. Notice of withdrawal must be given within three days following the end of the given general meeting. This rule applies for stockholders who attend the meeting (Art. 2437). Absent shareholders must notify the company of their withdrawal within fifteen days from the entry of the resolution concerned in the Register of Business Enterprises. Withdrawing shareholders are entitled to reimbursement for their shares at the average market value of their stock over the previous six months (Art. 2437/1). In case the reimbursed stock is not quoted, reimbursement must be proportional to the company's assets as shown by the balance sheet for the last business year. The right of withdrawing shareholders to reimbursement cannot be restricted by provisions in the articles of association or by special agreements (Art. 2437/3).

Individual shareholders have the right to report to the board of auditors any matters deemed to be important for the company (Art. 2408). They may present objections to procedural irregularity of general meetings (Arts. 2377 and 2369). They may sue directors for damage to them as individual shareholders; such damage must have resulted from fraud or negligence. Damage inflicted to shareholders as a whole is tantamount to damage inflicted to the company; in this case, the liability of directors concerns their duty towards the company (Art. 2393). Directors who dissent are liberated from their liability in relation to the resolution or decision that caused the damage (Art. 2392).

Minority stockholders can demand a general meeting if they represent one-fifth of the corporate capital (Art. 2367/1). During a general meeting, stockholders representing one-third of the capital may demand the postponement of the meeting for three days if they feel that they are in need of additional information on a given matter. A given point on the agenda cannot be the object of such a postponement for more than once (Art. 2374). While a company may renounce its right of action for liability against directors, stockholders representing one-fifth of the capital can prevent a resolution to this effect (Art. 2393/4). Stockholders representing one-twentieth of the corporate capital may submit a complaint to the board of auditors. The board must, in such a case, investigate and report with conclusion and proposals to a general meeting. A general meeting may be called immediately if the board of auditors considers it urgent (Art. 2408/2). Stockholders representing one-tenth of the corporate capital may request a court investigation with regard to justified suspicion of a breach in duty on the part of the company's directors or auditors. The court may take precautionary action, may convene a stockholders' meeting and in serious cases even discharge the directors and auditors and appoint a manager (Art. 2409).

Concerning liquidation, if losses amount to more than one-third of the corporate capital, directors must convene a general meeting to discuss the situation (Art. 2448).

*Conclusions*

Among the company laws of four countries so far outlined, Belgian and French laws prescribe a minimum of seven shareholders the reduction of which may affect the existence of the company. In Germany and Italy, five and two founders are respectively required for the creation of a joint-stock company; later, however, the given company may pass into the sole ownership of a shareholder. In Italy, in such a case, the sole stockholder will be exposed to an unlimited liability for obligations incurred by the company.

For the protection of minority shareholders, French and Belgian laws leave a wide margin for provisions to be included to this effect in the articles of association, whereas German and Italian company laws are more specific in statutory rules. In Italy, a dissenting shareholder may withdraw without suffering material losses, since the stock he owned must be reimbursed.

In terms of minimum corporate capital, the amount required is not prescribed in Belgium or France, while in Germany it is approximately £9,092 (DM. 100,000) and in Italy £5,581 (Lire 1,000,000).

### LUXEMBOURG

Six different forms of business associations and companies are recognized in Luxembourg.[1] As in the case of Belgium, France,

[1] Recueil de Lois concernant les Sociétés Commerciales, Holdings, Association sans but lucratif, et établissements d'utilité publique, 2nd ed., Luxembourg, 1960, in German and French. Article 2, Law of 10 August

H

Germany and Italy, two of the more common types of business
organization in Luxembourg will be outlined: (*a*) the *société à
responsabilité limitée* (private limited company) and (*b*) the *société
anonyme* (joint-stock company).

(a) *Société à responsabilité limitée (S.A.R.L.)*[1]

*Creation, operation.* The law of S.A.R.L. in Luxembourg has
many aspects in common with the corresponding Belgian or
French law. In the following lines, mention will be made of
the most important characteristics of the law in Luxembourg;
reference may be made to the Belgian or French law for further
details.

The scope of activities of a S.A.R.L. in Luxembourg does not
include banking or insurance (Art. 180). For drawing up a
notarial instrument creating a S.A.R.L., there must be at least
two partners (physical persons), nationals or foreigners; their
maximum number is limited to 40 (Art. 181). The minimum
capital prescribed is Lfrs. 100,000; shares must represent minimum values of Lfrs. 500 and be multiples thereof (Art. 182). At
the time of creation, the total capital must be subscribed (Art.
183). Public subscription is precluded (Art. 188).

One or more managers may be appointed by the articles of
association or, later, by partners. Their power may be likewise
specified (Art. 191). Unless it is specifically so stipulated in the
articles of association, the existence of a S.A.R.L. does not end
with its bankruptcy, or the death of one of its partners (Art. 202).

(b) *Société anonyme (Aktiengesellschaft)*

*Creation.* For the valid creation of a joint-stock company, at least
seven founders are required, for drawing up the articles of associa-

---

1915, concerning commercial companies, as amended by the Laws of
13 April 1922, 15 January 1927, 6 June 1930, 18 September 1933, 2 April
1948. For uniform text see Wauters-de Néeff, *Code des Lois.*
The six forms are:
i. société en nom collectif (general partnership);
ii. société en commandite simple (limited partnership);
iii. société à responsabilité limitée (private limited company);
iv. société en commandite par actions (stock partnership);
v. société cooperative (co-operative association);
vi. société anonyme (joint-stock company).

[1] References in parentheses within the text are to Articles in the Law of
10 August 1915, as amended.

tion before a notary (Arts. 26 and 4/2). Founders may be natural or legal persons, nationals or foreigners. No minimum capital is prescribed, but the agreed capital must be wholly subscribed and one-fifth of it paid up initially (Arts. 26 and 28). Since amounts paid in this form may not be less than Lfrs. 50 for each subscription share, representing one-fifth thereof, and at least seven shareholders are required, it may be said that statutorily Lfrs. 1,750 (£12 10s. 0d.) will be required as a minimum capital.

Contributions may be in cash or in material assets. For the latter, the articles of association must contain information as to their nature, conditions of contributions and the names of their subscribers (Art. 27). All documents related to the creation of a company must be published in their entirety in the annexes of the *Mémorial* (Official Gazette) within fifteen days following their execution (Arts. 8 and 9/1 and /2). Subscription to the corporate capital may be *private* or *public* (Arts. 29 and 33). Prior to the legal existence of a company, founders are liable for all obligations arising from the creation of the company, for instance, for unsubscribed parts of corporate capital (Art. 32). The duration of a company is for 30 years; this term can be prolonged, under conditions which may be included in the articles of association, by the general meeting of shareholders (Arts. 99/1 and 67). If the main establishment of the created company is in Luxembourg, the company will be, as to its nationality, a Luxembourg legal entity (Art. 159).

Shares of the capital stock may be at par or no-par value (Art. 37/1). Privileges attached to beneficiary shares can be stipulated in the articles of association (Art. 37/2). Stock may consist of bearer or registered shares (Arts. 37 and 41). The title of ownership depends on a corresponding entry in the register of the company (Art. 40). Bearer shares may be transferred by simple tradition, but only after the valid constitution of the company and payment of one-fifth of the corporate capital (Arts. 42–43). Unless otherwise provided by the articles of association, owners of bearer shares can apply for their conversion into registered shares or vice versa (Art. 43). Shares issued for contributions in material assets may not be negotiated before the tenth day after the publication of the second annual balance statement following their creation. Prior to this time-limit, they may be transferred by a notarial act accompanied by due notification to the company within a month following the transaction (Art. 44).

*Operation.* At least three managers are required; they are appointed
by the general meeting of shareholders or nominated in the articles
of association (Arts. 51, 52 and 53/1). Their term of office is for
six years but they may be re-elected (Art. 52). They may be summarily discharged by the stockholders' general meeting at any
time (Art. 51). Managers may be shareholders or other persons
(Art. 50). Their powers can be restricted or extended by the
articles of association (Art. 53/1). As a guarantee, registered
shares must be deposited by the managers of the company (Art.
54). The extent of this guarantee can be fixed in the articles of
association (Art. 55/1). The registered shares may belong to third
persons (since managers may be persons other than shareholders)
(Arts. 50, 54 and 55/2). The required guarantee must be effected
within one month following the appointment of managers
(Art. 56).

Managers are responsible under company law to the company
for the orderly administration of corporate affairs, and are liable
under civil law also to third parties, unless they can prove that
they did not participate in the given tortious decisions or actions
(Art. 59).

Management powers can be delegated to administrative directors and other agents who may be shareholders or third persons,
as stipulated in the articles of association (Art. 60/1).

The supervision of the company must be entrusted to one or
more *commissaires* appointed by the stockholders' general meeting.
They may be shareholders or other persons, and they serve for a
period of six years. Re-election is possible. Their mandate may be
withdrawn by the shareholders' general meeting (Art. 61). *Commissaires* have unlimited power to supervise and control all
activities of the company (Art. 62/1).[1] The management must
submit to them a six-monthly report on the situation of the company (Art. 62/2). They may avail themselves of any expert assistance they may need; the commissioning of the given experts
must, however, be confirmed by the company, and if this is not
possible, by the competent Commercial Court (Art. 62/4 and /5).

The articles of association may provide for the constitution of
a General Council (*conseil général, Generalrat*) consisting of the
managers and *commissaires* (Art. 65).

In the general meeting, every shareholder has a voting right

[1] For the guarantee to be given by the *commissaires*, see Articles 66 and
54-56.

(Art. 67/2 and /3). For deliberations concerning the purpose and form of the company, a quorum representing 50 per cent of the corporate capital is required (Art. 67/4). The same rule applies for discussions affecting the increase or reduction of corporate capital (Art. 69). If the required quorum cannot be attained, a second meeting with a quorum representing one-third of the subscribed capital may be convened (Art. 67). In both cases, however, for valid resolutions a majority vote of three-fourths of shareholders present at the meeting is necessary. No single shareholder can cast votes representing more than one-fifth of the issued shares, or two-fifths of the shares represented at the general meeting (Art. 71).[1]

If the corporate capital decreases below 50 per cent, the situation must be discussed by the general meeting; if the capital is reduced by 75 per cent, one-fourth of the shareholders represented at the general meeting can effect the dissolution of the company. Any interested party may request at the Commercial Court the dissolution of a company, if six months have elapsed since the reduction of its shareholders to a number less than seven.

## Conclusions

The similarities between Belgian, French and Luxembourg company law are obvious. The law in Luxembourg too is characterized by a margin of clauses that may be inserted in the articles of association to suit the particular needs of minority shareholders or to limit the powers exercised by managers. Unlike German or Italian joint companies, Luxembourg companies cannot have less than seven shareholders without affecting the existence of the company.

## THE NETHERLANDS

Dutch company law recognizes only one of the two business forms that have been discussed in this chapter: the private limited company does not exist in the Netherlands.[2] Hence, the present

---

[1] See Articles 72 ff. for annual balance sheet and profit-and-loss statement; Articles 76 f. for publicity requirements.

[2] Business forms recognized under Dutch law are:

  i. private firm (individual ownership);
 ii. general partnership;
iii. silent or sleeping partnership;

section will deal only with the joint-stock company (*naamloze vennootschap*).

## Naamloze Vennootschap

*Creation.* A minimum of two founders, who may be natural or legal persons (nationals or foreigners) is required (Sect. 36/1).[1] The articles of association, drawn up before a notary and in Dutch (Sects. 36b and 36/2) must be approved by the Ministry of Justice (Sect. 36c/1), prior to registration in the Register of Trade Names (Sect. 36f) and publication in the Official Gazette (*Nederlandse Staatscourant*). The ministerial approval is also dependent on founders' subscription to at least one-fifth of the agreed capital (Sect. 36c/2). The main office must be in the Netherlands and indicated in the articles of association (Sect. 36e).

There is no prescribed capital minimum (Sect. 38c/1). Shares can be in different forms (Sect. 39d), bearer or registered stock, but must be issued at par value. Shares may be issued for contributions in assets other than cash, including goodwill; information on contributions in material assets or in form other than cash must be included in the articles of association and in the report annexed to the balance sheet and profit-and-loss statement for the given financial year (Sects. 40a–40c). There is, on the other hand, no statutory guarantee required that the value of material assets corresponds to the shares issued in return.

While there is no minimum capital required by the law, for listing shares on the stock-exchange market a minimum capital of Fl. 500,000 (approximately £50,000) will be required.

*Operation.* The current management of a company will be the responsibility of the *bestuurders* (*directeuren*—managers) under the supervision of the *commissarissen* (directors) (Sect. 50).[2] The appointment of directors is optional.

---

iv. co-operative association;

v. joint-stock company.

A Royal Commission unanimously recommended in January 1965 several important changes in company law: *The Financial Times*, 25 February 1965, p. 5.

[1] References in parenthesis within the text are to sections of the Dutch Commercial Code (Wetboek van Koophandel) as amended by the Law of 2 July 1928 (Sections 36–56 apply).

[2] The changes recommended in January 1965 by the Royal Commission for company law included the introduction of the compulsory election of

Managers and directors may be initially appointed by the articles of association and subsequently, by the shareholders' general meeting (Sects. 48 and 50c). They may be dismissed by the meeting at any time (Sects. 48b and 50d). A procedural characteristic of Dutch company law is the fact that the articles of association may include a clause for a list of at least two candidates for vacant managerial or directorial posts (Sect. 48a). Out of the list submitted, the general meeting appoints the required manager(s) or director(s). The requirement of a candidates' list can be ruled out by a resolution passed by a majority of two-thirds of the votes cast representing more than 50 per cent of the corporate capital (Sect. 48a/2).

While a company is being created and its legal existence is not yet established in respect to third parties, the managers of the new company are held to be jointly and individually responsible in relation to third parties (Sect. 36g). The same liability applies if shares have been paid up by less than 10 per cent.

General meetings of shareholders must be held in the country at the place provided for in the articles of association. In the absence of such a clause, the general meeting must be convened within the municipality where the main office of the company is situated (Sect. 44).

Proxies for attendance at general meetings may not be issued to directors or other employees of the company (Sect. 44a). Each shareholder has at least one vote; the number of votes to be cast by a single shareholder can be restricted by the articles of association (Sect. 44b). Commitment by contract to cast one's vote in accordance with the decision of a third person is possible.[1]

Amendments to the articles of association require a qualified majority of two-thirds in a meeting representing at least 50 per cent of the corporate capital. The possibility of amendments may be excluded by a clause in the articles of association, but they would still be possible by a unanimous vote at a meeting representing the whole of the subscribed capital (Sect. 45). Amendments are subject to the approval of the Ministry of Justice. Such approval may be refused on grounds of public order or violation of the existing articles of association. In case an increase in capital

---

workers' representatives to the managerial boards of companies: *The Financial Times*, 25 February 1965, p. 5.

[1] Decision of the Dutch Supreme Court (Hoge Raad), 30 June 1944.

is envisaged, approval may depend on the subscription of at least one-fifth of the new capital (Sect. 45d/2). The binding effect of amendments is also dependent on prescribed publication in the *Nederlandse Staatscourant*, following the approval by the Ministry of Justice (Sects. 45d/3 and 45e/1). The same rules apply to resolutions affecting the existence, i.e. dissolution, of a company (Sect. 55b).

A minority of one-tenth is sufficient to request a general meeting and convene it (Sect. 43c). In court, the nullity of a resolution may be claimed by one-fifth of the shareholders or even less than one-fifth if a corresponding clause is present in the articles of association (Sect. 53). Such an assertion must be based on the claim that the given resolution is contrary to the law or to the articles of association. For protecting minority shareholders, it is possible to stipulate in the articles of association that a number of company's directors shall represent minority stockholders (Sect. 50c/2). The same articles of association may prescribe a unanimous vote in a meeting representing the whole of the subscribed capital, for amendments in the articles (Sect. 45). As for the management of a company, one-fifth of the shareholders can call for an inquiry (Sect. 53/1). An even smaller minority than the one indicated by section 53 of the Commercial Code may be prescribed by the articles of association. The competent district court may appoint, upon application by the required minority, one or more persons other than the current managers or directors of the company, in order to control the affairs of the company, to the extent indicated by the submitted request (Sects. 53b and 53c).

A company may be liquidated after the expiration of the period specified in the articles of association, or by a resolution of the shareholders' general meeting, or in case of insolvency, after bankruptcy has been declared (Sect. 55).

*Conclusions*

Dutch company law, like Italian law, requires at least two natural or legal persons as founders of a joint-stock company, as against seven in Belgium, France and Luxembourg, and five in Germany. With no prescribed minimum capital, except for listing of shares or bonds on the stock-exchange market, it is similar to company law in Belgium, France and Luxembourg. For contributions in material assets, approval of their valuation by shareholders and publication of the approved valuation are the only guarantees afforded for the correspondence of the undertaken valuation with the real value of the contributed assets.

In managerial structure, a joint-stock company in the Netherlands does not belong to the system applied in Germany where corporate administration is entrusted to two bodies, a board of directors (*Vorstand*) and a supervisory council (*Aufsichtsrat*), the latter having a controlling function in the first place; nor is Dutch law comparable with the system applied in Belgium, Italy or Luxembourg, where one or more auditors are in charge of supervising the corporate affairs—in Dutch law, the management of a company is in the hands of *bestuurders* (managers); the appointment of a second body with supervisory functions is optional.

Statutory rules for the protection of minority shareholders may be supplemented by clauses in the articles of association; the former prescribe, however, some minimum standards in favour of the minority. Thus, one-tenth of the shareholders can request and convene a general meeting; one-fifth may initiate judicial action aiming at nullifying a resolution or call for an inquiry.

As for sole ownership, this is not excluded by Dutch law, once a company has been created by at least two founders.

## GENERAL CONCLUSIONS

From the foregoing survey of company law dealing with the two main forms of business organization that foreign investors have most frequently used in the Common Market, the following conclusions may be summarized:

1. The law governing private limited or joint-stock companies in the member states of the E.E.C. does not impose any restrictions on the participation of foreign nationals in the capital or management of an undertaking. Naturally, this applies to economic sectors easily accessible to foreign investment, which include most of the manufacturing industries, among them important ones like the chemical, electronics or automobile industries, where foreign participation has been important and valuable. Though by law, undertakings could be 100 per cent owned and managed by foreigners, practical considerations will indicate the desirability of domestic participation. It is thus significant that the

liberalism of legal provisions is not subject to restrictions through discrimination but to the limits imposed by practical necessities related to the interests of the investors.

Decisions to establish a foreign-owned enterprise in one of the member states cannot be primarily influenced by the forms of business organization. The fact that a well-organized law on business organization is available should be, nevertheless, considered as a substantial contribution to the favourable investment climate of the E.E.C. A wide choice is available for foreign enterprise to operate through branch offices, partnerships, limited or joint-stock companies.[1] As for the choice between a limited or joint-stock company, it is difficult to evaluate and recommend a decision on the basis of legal considerations. The decision will depend on the scope and objectives of the planned investment.[2] Market conditions and personal preferences might influence the choice, but no particular form is required of or imposed upon foreigners by the state authorities. Existing rules are equally applicable to nationals.

2. If sole ownership of a subsidiary is envisaged, this is impossible in three of the six member states, Belgium, France and Luxembourg, where the basic principles of company law are the same: sole ownership there is not possible because a company is considered to have a contractual basis and this can only exist between at least two persons. In other words, the legal personality of a company rests upon its creation and ownership by a contract between at least two persons.

A further restriction applies in Belgium, where it is not possible to participate in a limited liability company (S.A.R.L.) set up as subsidiary—all founders and owners of such a Belgian company must be physical persons.

In Germany, the scope of activities envisaged should not be of particular importance in choosing between forming a GmbH. (limited) and an AG. (joint-stock) company. As shown by statistics, the former are as active and as developed as joint-stock

---

[1] For a comparison of advantages and disadvantages arising from doing business abroad through branch offices or subsidiaries, see C. McCormick Crosswell, *International Business Techniques*, pp. 60 ff.; Campbell and Thompson, *Common Market Law*, pp. 137 ff.; W. G. Friedmann and R. C. Pugh, eds., *Legal Aspects of Foreign Investment*, pp. 754 ff.

[2] For the different advantages offered in general by business activities through limited companies and joint-stock companies, see Friedmann and Pugh, pp. 757 f.

companies and figure as 13 of the leading 100 firms in Germany.
They seem to enjoy, in some respects, even more advantages than
joint-stock companies, as requirements for the publication of their
corporate accounts are less stringent.

3. Under company law in the E.E.C., the amount of capital
mentioned in the articles of association is an integral part thereof
and cannot be modified without amending those articles. Under
Anglo-American law, a company may come into existence before
all of its capital has been subscribed and the capital actually
issued may not correspond to the total shareholding specified in
the articles of association, which nominal capital may be higher.[1]
In all of the E.E.C countries, the minimum capital as prescribed by
law or as stipulated in the articles of association must be totally
subscribed and the prescribed shares thereof actually paid up before formalities can be concluded for establishing the existence of
a company.

Thus, in Belgium, Luxembourg, and the Netherlands, one-
fifth of the agreed capital must be paid up when creating a
company, but the totality of the capital must be subscribed. In
France and Germany, the corresponding proportion is one-fourth
of the subscribed capital, while in Italy the proportion is three-
tenths.

In all six countries, contributions to capital may be made in
material assets instead of cash. In France the importation of such
assets will be authorized if they are not available in the country. In
Italy technical knowledge as contribution to corporate capital
has to be in the form of specific patents. As to protection against
exaggerated assessments of material assets as contribution to
corporate capital, there is no statutory guarantee required in the
Netherlands; in the remaining five member countries, varying
forms of guarantees are required to provide for a correspondence
between the value of material assets and the shares issued in
return. Assets other than in cash have to be evaluated under
official supervision or subsequent control. In France and Germany
the evaluation of material assets must be done by special auditors,
while in Italy, in addition, statutory rules prescribe subsequent
adjustment, whenever necessary, after the company starts its
operations. In Belgium and Luxembourg shares issued in return
for contributions in material assets may not be transferred until the

[1] R. R. Pennington: *The Principles of Company Law*, London, 1959, pp. 102,
119 ff. Tophams' *Company Law*, 12th ed., London, 1960, p. 146.

tenth day following the second annual balance statement after the shares have been issued.

4. Owing to liberal exchange control, dividends can be easily transferred abroad. In Belgium and Luxembourg, the transfer may be effected through the free exchange market. This applies to dividends in Italy from non-productive enterprises, which may not transfer yearly more than 8 per cent of their capital abroad in the form of dividends.[1]

5. In Germany, the corporate management is clearly lodged in two bodies, the supervisory council (*Aufsichtsrat*) and the board of managers (*Vorstand*). The first has an overall supervisory function while the second body is responsible for the operational administration. In Belgium, France, Italy, Luxembourg and the Netherlands, the supervisory function of an *Aufsichtsrat* of a German company (AG.) is either within the competence of a board of auditors, who fulfil their function on behalf of the shareholders, or optionally within the competence of a board of *commissarissen* as in the Netherlands. The board of auditors enjoy wide supervisory powers over all aspects of corporate operations. Thus, their function is clearly different from that of auditors of German or Anglo-American companies.[2]

It is noteworthy that the principle of *ultra vires* known to Anglo-American law does not operate in the E.E.C. systems of company law.[3] Thus, administrative officials acting on behalf of a company in the Common Market are not limited by the objectives in the articles of association, in so far as, in relation to third parties, their acts are binding. Under French law, if there is a specific limitation on the powers of corporate directors, an act in violation of such limitation may become binding for the corporation by ratification on the part of shareholders. In Germany, the powers of managers to whom the administration of the corporation is entrusted cannot be restricted in relation to third parties. The company will be bound by the acts of its manager even if the transaction in question is in violation of the company's rules.

6. The nationality of directors and managers of foreign-owned enterprises is not legally subject to restrictions. For practical

---

[1] A number of banks are authorized by the government to carry 'on the spot' exchange transactions in foreign currencies.

[2] Compare Pennington, *The Principles of Company Law*, London, 1959, p. 471; Tophams' *Company Law*, 12th ed., London, 1960, pp. 267 f., 274.

[3] Compare Pennington, ibid., pp. 66 f., 69 f., Tophams, pp. 219, and 29.

reasons however, it may be as well to appoint a local director acquainted with the administrative system and conditions in a given country. The statutory rules regarding both foreign and national directors or managers require that guarantees in the form of company shares be deposited. In all six member states, it is necessary to secure the consent and authorization of local authorities when appointing foreigners as directors or managers of a company.[1]

7. If foreign persons or companies participate in an undertaking in the E.E.C., the question of protecting minority shareholders may become relevant.

In all six countries, provisions for the protection of minority stockholders may be included or made more stringent in the articles of association. Thus, in Belgium, France, Luxembourg and the Netherlands, great importance is attached to the drafting of corresponding clauses, while in Germany and Italy already elaborate statutory rules may be made stricter. The measures adopted could effect the permanent representation of the minority group by one or more directors, or the requirement of unanimity or of qualified majority required for decisions of directors, in addition to high quorum requirements for meetings of the board of directors. In case of difficulties when dealing with the interests of shareholders in general or with interests of a minority group, appeal to judicial authorities—for example, in Italy and the Netherlands—is possible, under statutory rules binding on the court. In Italy, the law provides for the withdrawal of dissenting shareholders from a company. They need not incur losses if they observe the relevant statutory requirements.

8. Reforms of company law proposed in France, Germany and the Netherlands (up to 31 March 1965) concern minor aspects of the existing systems.[2] For example, in Germany, they deal with the competence of the stockholders' general meeting in deciding on the employment of the net profits of a company. In the Netherlands they affect the participation of personnel in the managerial bodies of a company. The reforms in question do not concern the interests of the foreign investors directly. An aspect of company law that does interest them, however, is that of the possible

[1] The employment of aliens is discussed in chapter VII.
[2] *The Financial Times*, 23 March 1965, p. 5, and 25 February 1965, p. 5; *Neue Zürcher Zeitung*, no. 79, 21 March 1965, Blatt 11. For a reform project concerning French company law, *Le Monde*, 14–15 March 1965, p. 11.

evolution, the co-ordination or unification of the current municipal systems, into a law uniform for the whole of the Common Market. This aspect is considered in greater detail under the heading of 'harmonization' in chapter XII.

In the existing situation of separate municipal company laws, a foreign investor cannot set up in the E.E.C. one legal entity that would be equally valid and able to operate without limitation in all six member states. If he finds it necessary to invest simultaneously in more than one member state, a separate incorporation or the creation of separate companies will be necessary in each state concerned. When availing himself of the right of establishment under Community law, he would have to adapt his subsidiary, set up in one of the member states, to the requirements of company law in the other member state(s).

These administrative and technical difficulties of company law in the E.E.C. are, however, only part of a larger and more complex situation that concerns domestic more than foreign-owned enterprises. It involves the economic and technical necessity of concentrating and increasing the size of firms in accordance with an expanding and integrating market. The need for legal provisions that would promote adaptation in this respect has been pointed out.[1] Opinions expressed have referred to the large size of American companies that are investing and operating in the Common Market. It is argued that company law in the E.E.C. must be reformed as one factor among many others in order to promote the development of Community firms comparable in size and technological equipment with American firms. In the present situation, co-operation between firms of different member states falls within the ambit of the Community rules of competition. Mergers in the form of a single company equally valid in two or more member states are not possible, for municipal company laws do not allow them. Any merger has to be effected, under the current system, in the form of new but separate companies in the respective member states. In this way, the present system of municipal laws does affect the competitiveness of domestic undertakings by hampering their co-operation or development on a Community-wide level, in accordance with a developing mass market. The financially and technologically better equipped American firms are not affected by it, since they can bring into the Common Market the results of extensive research and financial

[1] See for example *Die Welt*, no. 64, 17 March 1965, p. 11.

concentration achieved under conditions not governed by the separate municipal laws of E.E.C. countries. In other words, a few of the competitive aspects of foreign and domestic undertakings in the E.E.C. are related to the limits that the present system of municipal company law imposes. This topic is reconsidered in chapter XII.

# CHAPTER VI

# TAXATION

In examining the municipal laws on taxation in relation to companies, our purpose is to ascertain the extent to which tax rates are applied differently to foreign enterprises as opposed to domestic companies. We are concerned with foreign shareholders of companies operating in the Common Market, and with parent companies which are situated outside the E.E.C. but own or participate in subsidiaries active in the Community.[1]

## BELGIUM

The new income tax system, effective since 1963,[2] distinguishes four categories of taxes:

i. a personal income tax (*impôt des personnes physiques*);

ii. a tax on public bodies and non-profit enterprise (*impôt des personnes morales*);

iii. a tax on companies and other profit-making legal entities (*impôt des sociétés*);

iv. a tax on income derived by non-residents (persons or legal entities) from sources in Belgium (*impôt des non-résidents*).

All four categories are reviewed below, the first two summarily, and the last two in greater detail.

---

[1] The standardized treatment of the fiscal rules selected for the purpose of this review should in no way mislead the reader as to the great complexity which is inherent in taxation in general and in the relevant tax systems of the six member states in particular. Bilateral double taxation agreements are mentioned but not discussed.

[2] On Belgian income taxation see V. Pauwels and others: *Traité des Impôts sur les Revenus* (loose-leaf), Brussels, 1963. It contains the legislative texts, with commentaries, together with the royal decrees supplementing the new tax code of 1962. See also Income Tax Code, *Mon. Belge*, 10 April 1964. Unless otherwise specified, all references to Articles here are to the new income tax law of 1963.

## PERSONAL INCOME TAX
### (IMPÔT SUR LES PERSONNES PHYSIQUES)

This tax is payable on total income by individuals resident in Belgium, at progressive rates up to 55 per cent.[1] Individuals temporarily resident in the country, e.g. foreign directors, managers and employees, are given special allowances, which are, as explained below, in addition to deductible business and professional expenses.

*Taxation of temporary residents.* Persons or personnel temporarily assigned for work in Belgium, for a period not exceeding five years, in one or more branches or subsidiaries of a foreign parent company, are entitled to the status of temporary resident. Their temporary work in Belgium must be related to the establishment and initial operation or later expansion of offices or plants, or deal with the supervision or co-ordination for a given period, of enterprises belonging to a foreign company.[2] An important criterion for qualification for the status of foreign temporary resident is the effective possession of a tax domicile abroad.

The taxable income of foreign temporary residents is the amount earned or collected in return for work in Belgium. Tax concessions granted to such residents are not in the nature of differential rates as compared with those applicable to permanent residents, but in the form of higher deductions allowed for professional expenses. Thus, while actual expenses or allowances at the rate of 20, 15 or 10 per cent of the total income may be deducted both by temporary and permanent residents, foreign taxpayers are entitled to an additional allowance of 20 per cent for expenses on that part of their income in Belgium not exceeding 1,000,000 Belgian francs. This applies also to foreign company directors who qualify as temporary residents. They may deduct the special allowance of 20 per cent of their income in Belgium in addition to the standard rate of 5 per cent for expenses applicable to all directors in Belgium.

The additional allowance of 20 per cent deductible from the taxable income will not be granted to foreign directors, managers

[1] Articles 3–5 (Persons subject to the tax); Articles 6 ff. (taxable base); Articles 77 ff. (computation of individual income tax).
[2] International Bureau of Fiscal Documentation; *European Taxation*, Amsterdam, vol. 3, 1963, pp. 110, 122–3.

I

or employees who take up work of a permanent character in Belgium performed mainly in that country. In this case the foreign personnel will be liable to the tax rate of 50 per cent on their total annual income earned in Belgium. A technical point of legal nature worth mentioning is the fact that foreign directors of companies appointed for a period of six years, that is, for the maximum period of appointment recognized by Belgian company law, cannot be temporary residents, the maximum period for such personnel being five years.

The deduction of professional expenses, applicable to resident taxpayers, may be made on the basis of; (i) standard rates varying inversely with income, at rates between 10 and 20 per cent, (ii) a statement submitted to and approved by the fiscal authorities. Special allowance rates apply for individuals over sixty-five, for social security contributions and for certain insurance premiums (within fixed limits).

## TAX ON PUBLIC BODIES AND NON-PROFIT ENTERPRISES
### (IMPÔT DES PERSONNES MORALES)

Levied on public bodies such as the state, provinces, municipalities and other local legal entities and non-profit making enterprises, this is due solely on income derived from movable capital and real property.[1]

## TAXATION OF COMPANIES AND OTHER PROFIT-MAKING
### LEGAL ENTITIES
### (IMPÔT DES SOCIÉTÉS)

This tax applies to companies and other profit-making legal entities; i. registered in Belgium, or ii. with their administrative centre (*siège social*) or main place of activities in Belgium.[2]

The law makes a distinction between *sociétés par actions* (joint-

---

[1] Articles 136–138.

[2] The *siège social* is at the place designated by the articles of association and not one of fact (Article 24/1); see also Articles 94–95. On taxation of joint-stock companies, see J. Kirkpatrick: *Le Régime fiscal des Sociétés belges par Actions*, Brussels, 1963.

One of the following would be sufficient to make a company subject to Belgian tax law: principal establishment (*établissement principal*), control and management (*siège de direction et d'administration*) in Belgium.

stock companies) and *sociétés de personnes* (partnerships). The first category, *sociétés par actions*, includes limited companies (*société anonyme*) and partnerships with shares (*société en commandites par actions*); the category of partnerships includes the *société de personnes à responsabilité limitée* (limited liability company), *société en commandite simple* (limited partnership) and *société coopérative* (co-operative society). A characteristic feature of Belgian tax law for companies is that partnerships may be taxed, as provided for by the law in the same way as companies similar to those included in the first category mentioned above.

Company tax is payable on income from all sources in Belgium or abroad, remitted or unremitted.[1] An exception to this rule is made for dividends by a company to a parent company. Such 'inter-company' dividends are deductible up to 85 per cent of their gross amount and up to 95 per cent of their net amount, i.e. the amount actually received after the deduction of all related expenses, including foreign income or withholding taxes.[2]

The deduction of 85 or 95 per cent allowed from taxable dividends paid by a company to a parent company depends on the type of the recipient company. If this is an *industrial* enterprise engaged in the manufacture or processing of goods, or in the extraction of raw materials (minerals) and, furthermore, holds portfolio investments not exceeding in value the limit fixed by law, the deduction rate of 95 per cent for dividends received, will apply; if the recipient company is a *financial* one, i.e. an industrial enterprise holding portfolio investments beyond the maximum value prescribed by law, or is a trading firm, agricultural enterprise, company of services or a holding company, the deduction of received dividends may not exceed 85 per cent of the taxable amount of dividends.[3]

For income in the form of patent royalties, the recipient company may apply for a standard allowance of 15 per cent of the gross amount for expenses related to the income. This provision is similar to that relating to the deduction of 85 per cent of the

[1] Articles 96 ff.

[2] This exception applies, however, only for that part of income which is taxed at the rate of 30 per cent. For the rate of corporate tax, see the next section. 'Withholding taxes' are those which are deducted at source, prior to payment of dividend.

[3] Articles 98–99. Also *The Taxation of Patent Royalties, Dividends, Interest in Europe*, publ. by the Int. Bureau of Fiscal Documentation, Amsterdam, 1963: Belgium, pp. 2.01 ff.

total amount received as dividends by a company. The rule for patent royalties does not, however, apply if the main purpose of a given company is the exploitation of patents.

*Rate of company tax.* Different rates apply for distributed and undistributed profits. The basic rate for the taxation of distributed profits is 30 per cent. For undistributed profits a reduced rate of 25 per cent applies for amounts up to 1,000,000 Bfrs.; on the next 250,000 Bfrs. the tax rate is 50 per cent; total profits beyond 1,250,000 Bfrs. and up to 5,000,000 Bfrs. are taxed at the rate of 30 per cent. Profits in excess of the 5,000,000 Bfrs. limit are subject to a 34 per cent rate.[1] The higher rates will be reduced to 30 per cent for profits subsequently distributed *prior* to liquidation or in redemption of stock, i.e. no tax will be refunded for profits distributed at the time of liquidation or for the purpose of redeeming stock belonging to the company.

Oil prospecting companies are exempt from tax on undistributed profits, provided such undistributed profits do not exceed 50 per cent of the company income and are re-invested in Belgium within a period of five years.

### TAX ON INCOME EARNED FROM SOURCES IN BELGIUM BY NON-RESIDENTS IN THE COUNTRY (IMPÔT DES NON-RESIDENTS)

Individuals non-resident in Belgium are taxed on income earned in Belgium at rates equal to those of standard income tax. Non-resident companies are subject to a tax rate of 35 per cent on income from business activities, immovable property and capital (including royalties, dividends, and interest).[2]

A withholding tax is levied on patent royalties, dividends and interest paid by a Belgian company to a non-resident company. The rates of this withholding tax (*précompte mobilier*) are 15 per cent for patent royalties and interest, and 18·2 per cent for dividends. Other provisions may apply in virtue of double taxation treaties.[3] Beginning in 1965, patent royalties, dividends and

---

[1] Articles 126–134.

[2] For taxable items, see Articles 140 ff. For a definition of non-resident company see Article 139; see also *Eur. Tax.*, vol. 4, 1964, pp. 190, 193, 194; for a concrete case, p. 67.

[3] I.B.F.D., *Taxation of Patent Royalties*, Belgium, pp. 2.09 ff.

interest are subject to an additional withholding tax of 15 per cent (unless otherwise specified by a taxation treaty) levied on the gross income less prepayments (*précomptes*) and expenses incurred in connection with the income.[1]

Five per cent of annual profits may be appropriated for tax-free reserves.

For *depreciation allowances*, the value of assets, fixed or movable, tangible or intangible, may be, under certain conditions, depreciated by the declining-balance method. Otherwise, the straight-line method will prevail.[2]

A municipal surcharge of 5 per cent is levied on the company income tax.

## TAXES BASED ON CAPITAL[3]

These are registration taxes levied on the creation of a company or increase in company capital. The law distinguishes between registration tax rates for Belgian companies (companies incorporated in Belgium) and foreign companies with a branch or establishment in Belgium. Incorporation is the sole test for liability to this tax. Under Belgian law, the registered and real seat must be in Belgium.

At the time of creation of a Belgian company, the gross value of the assets contributed for the company's capital is taxed at the rate of 1·6 per cent. The same rate applies to any increase in

[1] Ibid. The elaborate system of collecting taxes through prepayments plays an important part in the new income tax system. For details of the system see Articles 153 ff. of the new Law of November 1962 and *Eur. Tax.*, vol. 4, 1964, pp. 175–85.

[2] Royal Decree of 8 October 1963 (*Mon. Belge*, 19 October 1963, no. 210). For the depreciation rules of the new income tax Law of November 1962, see Articles 96 ff. Also *Eur. Tax.*, vol. 3, 1963, pp. 182–3.

The straight-line method provides for the division of the depreciable cost of the given asset minus estimated scrap value, if any, into equal parts corresponding to the estimated number of years of useful life of the asset. The declining-balance method is based on the use of a percentage rate which is applied to the declining value of the given asset each year. This percentage rate (e.g. 40 per cent) is usually higher than the deduction rate used for the straight-line method. For more details, see F. L. Garcia, ed.: *Munn's Encyclopedia of Banking and Finance*, 6th edn., pp. 193–4; E. L. Kohler: *A Dictionary for Accountants*, 3rd edn., New Jersey, 1963, pp. 169–82; T. H. Lewis, ed.: *The Business Encyclopedia and Legal Adviser*, 6th edn., 1956, vol. 2, pp. 365–73.

[3] See Federation of British Industries (F.B.I.): *Taxation in Western Europe*, London, October 1964, p. 51 f.

capital. When a foreign company with an establishment in Belgium is created or the capital of an already existing foreign company with an establishment in Belgium is increased, 0·1 per cent of the capital of the newly founded company or of any increase in capital of such a company must be paid by way of registration taxes. There is a statutory maximum fee of 1,000,000 Bfrs. and a minimum fee of 18,000 Bfrs. In any case, the real property situated in Belgium of a foreign company will be subject to a registration fee of 1·6 per cent. Moreover, the minimum fee of 18,000 Bfrs. will not be required for the increase in capital of a company whose creation has been duly recorded in Belgium. The registration tax is due when the documents of incorporation of the foreign company are published in Belgium.[1]

The registration tax rate for a limited liability company (*société de personnes à responsabilité limitée*) is uniformly 0·35 per cent on statutory capital or subsequent increase in capital.

Company stocks, shares and bonds are subject to stamp taxes, and when issued a tax of 0·7 per cent is levied on the statutory capital, the increase in capital or on the total value of the loan. The stamp tax rate is reduced to 0·35 per cent, however, if the loan contracted is for a period not exceeding five years.

### DOUBLE TAXATION RELIEF

The tax system of Belgium provides for both *unilateral* and *bilateral* double taxation relief. Unilateral double taxation relief applies in the absence of double taxation treaties, for income derived from abroad. The form of tax relief is exemption through tax credit or reduction of tax rates, depending on the type of income. Thus, income earned through business transactions abroad will be subject to a tax rate reduced by 75 per cent; income in the form of patent royalties and interest received from abroad will be subject to company income tax for their *net* amount only, that is, less all expenses, *including all* foreign turnover taxes deducted at source and income taxes.[2]

At the bilateral level, Belgium has signed double taxation

[1] For a suggestion aiming at a reduced registration tax liability, see J. L. Blondeel, in *Legal Aspects of Foreign Investment*, Friedmann and Pugh, eds., p. 59.
[2] I.B.F.D., *Taxation of Patent Royalties*, Belgium, p. 2.03.

treaties with the following countries:[1] Finland, France, Italy, Luxembourg, the Netherlands, United Kingdom, United States of America, Sweden.

## CONCLUSIONS

The tax system of Belgium outlined above does not contain discriminating provisions applicable to foreigners. On the level of individual income tax, it takes into account the position of temporary residents by allowing for higher expense allowances to compensate for additional costs caused by the temporary transfer to Belgium. On the level of company income tax, the standard rate of income tax of 35 per cent levied on the earnings of non-resident companies is only marginally different from the rates of 25–35 per cent applicable to resident companies. This marginal difference is based on technical considerations of fiscal legislation and does not have a penal character. As to foreign shareholders, non-resident in Belgium, they are subject to the standard provisions of individual income tax valid for residents.

## FRANCE

### PERSONAL INCOME TAX
(IMPÔT SUR LE REVENU DES PERSONNES PHYSIQUES)

Residents are taxed on their total income in France; non-residents are subject to taxation on their income derived from sources in France, such as the following categories: income from real property; industrial or commercial profits; remuneration of directors of private companies, partnerships or joint-stock companies; income from agriculture; salaries, wages, pensions, etc.; profit such as interest and dividends. While the tax levied is on total income from all categories, losses under one category may be set off against a positive balance in another category; and if losses exceed total income, the negative balance may be carried forward and set off against profits of the next five years.[2]

---

[1] As in January 1965. See *Eur. Tax.*, vol. 5, 1965, pp. 21–2. On tax treaties in relation to the new income code of November 1962, see *Eur. Tax.* vol. 4, 1964, p. 196.

[2] For details of legislative texts, see *Code Général des Impôts*, Ministry of Finance and Economic Affairs, Paris, 1963. For a summary survey of French taxation, see F.B.I., *Taxation in W. Europe*, pp. 85 ff.

For income from commercial activities such as partnerships or limited liability companies, no distinction is made, for taxation purposes, between distributed or non-distributed profits. The total income is subject to tax which is paid by the recipients.

Rates of the tax range from 5 to 66·5 per cent, the lowest rate being applicable to income up to 2,400 NF. per annum and the highest for income over 64,000 NF. per annum. In addition to the personal income tax, a surcharge is levied at the rate of 6 per cent. Deductible allowances are applicable for social security, superannuation schemes and other types of contributions.

Foreigners are subject to the same rates of income tax that apply to residents, if

(*a*) their permanent residence is in France;
or (*b*) the centre of their income interests is situated in France;
or (*c*) they have taken up temporary residence in the country for more than five years.

Exemption from tax on income from foreign sources is granted if such income is already taxed in its country of origin.

If foreigners have not resided in France for more than five years, they are taxed only on the portion of their total income which is derived in France, or are required to pay in taxes a lump sum amounting to five times the rental value of their residence in the country. The choice of one of these two possibilities will be made by the fiscal authorities in favour of the higher amount.[1]

There are no special deductible allowances granted to temporary residents attached to foreign companies. Moreover, no distinction is made between royalties, dividends and interest paid to non-resident individuals or to companies.

### TAXATION OF COMPANIES
### (IMPÔT SUR LES SOCIÉTÉS)

In addition to companies recognized as such by law, that is, the *société anonyme* and the *société de personnes à responsabilité limitée*, partnerships limited by shares (*société en commandite par actions*) and other types of partnerships may be liable to company tax if partners prefer to be taxed as companies.[2]

[1] F.B.I., *Taxation in W. Europe*, p. 99.
[2] *European Taxation*, Supplementary Service Section A, France. Changes in corporate taxation were imminent in March 1965; the Council of Ministers

The tax rate for all company income is 50 per cent. Tax is withheld at source at the rate of 24 per cent on dividends or income considered similar to dividends, and 12 per cent on payments derived from debentures interest.[1] On the recipient's side, for the purpose of personal income tax, the gross amount received as dividends or interest, less 6 per cent of the dividend amount or 3 per cent of the interest, is included in the total income of an individual; three-fourths of the tax withheld, i.e. 18 per cent of the dividend or 9 per cent of the interest, is credited against the total amount of personal income tax. The remaining 6 per cent of dividends or 3 per cent of interest received is a deductible allowance.

If dividends or interest are paid to a company not closely related to the paying company, that is with no parent–subsidiary link, the gross amount received as dividends or interest will be part of the total income of the receiving company and will be taxed accordingly, but the total amount of withholding tax, 24 per cent on dividends and 12 per cent on interest, will be credited against the company's payable income tax. The law provides for reduced rates applicable to companies with portfolio holdings. Thus, the following rates will apply if a company holds registered securities of another company for more than two years:

| Amount of holdings | Percentage of dividend income exempt from company tax |
|---|---|
| 20–35 per cent | 80 |
| 36–50 per cent | 90 |
| over 50 per cent | 95 |

---

approved a bill on March 24 that year which would become effective in 1966. Under these changes the tax on corporate profits will remain at the level of 50 per cent, but dividends distributed to resident shareholders will no longer be taxed at source. Moreover shareholders will get a credit representing part of the tax paid by the company. This tax may be deducted from the shareholder's personal income tax. Dividends paid to non-residents will still be subjected to a withholding tax at a rate of 25 per cent. Various other adjustments are also to be made to taxes on capital gains. Corporate mergers are to be encouraged by more favourable terms of taxation than those previously applied to assets owned by the absorbed undertakings. See *The Times*, 25 March 1965, p. 12.

[1] See F.B.I., *Taxation in W. Europe*, pp. 88–90 for this and subsequent details of company tax.

While dividends received from a subsidiary company are exempt, at varying rates, from company income tax (as indicated above), the withholding tax of 24 per cent is to be retained by the paying subsidiary and cannot be credited against the company tax to be paid. Dividends so received will be, however, exempt from the tax of 24 per cent, provided they are distributed in the same year by the parent company to its shareholders. Shareholders, on their part, when assessed for personal income tax on dividends received, will get credit and deduction as though the 24 per cent withholding tax retained by the subsidiary had been directly charged to them.

With regard to the withholding tax on dividends and royalties paid to non-resident individuals or companies, if the royalty paid to non-residents is related to property used in France, the withholding tax rate will apply for 70 per cent of the amount of royalty. Otherwise, 80 per cent of the royalty paid will be taxed at the rate of 24 per cent.

Interest paid on debentures to non-resident individuals or companies is subject to a withholding tax of 12 per cent. Other types of income accruing to non-residents from sources in France are subject to a minimum tax rate of 24 per cent. This figure includes the 5 per cent surcharge.

Companies carrying on commercial activities in France are liable to tax on their profits and, in addition, to the withholding tax for part of their distributed dividends. This part (*quotité*) of dividends distributed by the non-resident company will be based on the assessment of that portion of dividends which is deemed to have been derived from sources in France. For the computation of such a *quotité* two methods may be used. One of the methods of assessment will take into consideration the proportion of the given non-resident company's shares which circulate in France (*quotité titres*). The second will consider the proportion which certain factors, such as turnover figures, assets, or payroll of the French branch or subsidiary of the non-resident company, bear to the corresponding total figures of the company (*quotité activité*). Finally, both methods of assessment may be replaced by specific provisions included in a double taxation agreement, such as the one signed between the United Kingdom and France.

For taxation purposes, the method of depreciation of assets used is the straight-line method for movable assets acquired or made before 31 December 1959. Otherwise, the declining-balance method will be the only one prescribed for movable assets acquired after 31 December 1964.[1] Losses may not be carried back but may be taken forward to be set off against profits in the following five years.

On profits earned abroad through a branch or subsidiary, only a withholding tax of 24 per cent is payable on the total amount of dividends regardless of their source in France or abroad. As to tax on income from immovable property situated abroad, companies are not liable to tax. No distinction is made, for taxation purposes, between dividends received from subsidiaries in France or abroad.

### TAXES BASED ON CAPITAL

The subscription of capital is subject to a tax rate of 1·6 per cent on capital subscription of new assets and 12 per cent on the capitalization of reserves.[2] An additional tax of 0·6 per cent must be added if payment for the new stock is effected in the form of real estate. A tax of 4·2 per cent is levied on the sale of shares by means of a formal instrument. The sale of bonds and debentures is not subject to this tax.

When a merger takes place, that part of the capital of the absorbing company which is represented by the issued capital of the absorbed company is taxed at the rate of 0·8 per cent while the remainder is subjected to a tax of 1·2 per cent.

Reductions in registration tax may be granted for carrying out reorganization of business or for moving out to certain development areas. The purchase of land and buildings is subject to a conveyancing tax of 16·6 per cent of the cost of the property. A reduced rate of 4·2 per cent applies, however, when land or buildings are purchased for the purpose of modernizing or decentralizing industry within the framework of specially approved projects.

A tax of 16 per cent is levied on the price of goodwill.

### DOUBLE TAXATION RELIEF

Double taxation agreements have been signed with the following countries:[3] Austria, Belgium, Canada, Denmark, Finland,

[1] F.B.I., *Taxation in W. Europe*, pp. 92–4; also *Eur. Tax.*, vol. 3, 1963, pp. 184–5.      [2] F.B.I., *Taxation in W. Europe*, pp. 100–1.
[3] As in January 1965. See *Eur. Tax.*, vol. 5, 1965, pp. 21–2.

Germany, Greece, Italy, Japan, Luxembourg, The Netherlands, Norway, Spain, Sweden, Switzerland, United Kingdom, United States of America.

Only treaty relief is available; in the absence of a treaty arrangement foreign taxes will be deductible in assessing taxable income.

## CONCLUSIONS

Taxation rates of corporate income do not show differential treatment between domestic and foreign companies. In some cases double taxation agreements effect a taxation rate for non-residents (e.g. in the U.S.A.) with income in France lower than that for residents in France. The heavy fiscal burden is to be alleviated by changes in corporate taxation, in favour of companies.

## GERMANY[1]

### INCOME TAX (EINKOMMENSSTEUER)

This tax is levied on the total income of residents and on the income of non-residents from German sources. The rate varies from 20 per cent[2] on income up to DM. 8,000 (for married persons, DM. 16,000) to 53 per cent on income above DM. 110,040 (for married persons, DM. 220,080). In addition to deductible allowances for children, old-age and expenses incidental to the earned income, special personal expenses (*Sonderausgaben*) may be deducted, for example for payment of interest on personal loans, life-insurance premiums, sickness, donations or contributions for charitable, religious or scientific purposes.[3]

Unless their tax position is otherwise regulated by a double taxation treaty or unless their earned income consists of wages or salaries, *non-residents* will be subject to a minimum tax rate of

---

[1] For reference see W. Blümlich and L. Falk: *Einkommensteuergesetz*, 9th edn., Berlin, 1964, vols. I and II. For the system of taxation, R. Fechner: *Grundrisz des Steuerrechts*, 3rd edn., Berlin, 1960. For a commentary on income and corporate taxes, C. Hermann and others: *Kommentar zur Einkommensteuer und Körperschaftssteuer*, 10th edn., Köln, 1964, 6 vols.

[2] The Revenue Bill of 1964 provided for a reduction of this rate to 19 per cent. For more details see *Eur. Tax.*, vol. 4, 1964, p. 59, and vol. 3, 1963, p. 79.

[3] For further details see *Eur. Tax.* Suppl. Serv. Section B, Germany. Also F.B.I., *Taxation in W. Europe*, pp. 110–11.

25 per cent on their taxable income. Moreover, deductible allowances are granted to a limited extent, with the exception of professional expenses (*Werbekosten*) the claim of which must be supported by proof.

For income earned through work extending over more than a fiscal year, a reduction of 50 per cent of the minimum and maximum rates (10 per cent and 26·5 per cent, respectively) may be applied. On income from partnerships, partners with full liability are taxed at the rates of income tax; limited partners are subject to the rates of company tax.

Income accruing to non-residents is subject to withholding tax on a more extensive range, e.g. a withholding tax (*Aufsichtsratssteuer*) of 30 per cent is levied on the remuneration of directors, 25 per cent on dividends, interest (*Kapitalertragssteuer*) and royalties, unless special provisions of a double taxation treaty apply. For example, dividends paid to a resident of the United Kingdom are taxed at the withheld rate of 15 per cent.

### COMPANY TAX (KÖRPERSCHAFTSSTEUER)

The rates of capital-yield tax (*Körperschaftssteuer*) are 51 per cent on undistributed profits, 15 per cent on distributed profits and a withholding tax of 25 per cent on dividends.[1] A number of special provisions apply for companies with assets of DM. 5,000,000 or less. Thus, if shares representing at least 76 per cent of the nominal capital of such companies are held by individuals and not listed on the securities market, the special tax rate of 26·5 per cent may be applied for distributed profits, while graduated rates between 39 and 49 per cent will be applied on undistributed profits ranging from DM. 10,000 (rate: 39 per cent) to over DM. 50,000 (rate: 49 per cent).[2]

Non-resident companies, whose seat or management is situated abroad, are taxed on income from certain specified sources at the uniform rate of 49 per cent.[3] This rate may be modified by

[1] On fiscal aspects of GmbH. see G. Meissner: in *Commerce in Germany*, no. 135, March 1965, pp. 20-1. See also *Eur. Tax.* Suppl. Serv. Section A, Germany.
[2] F.B.I., *Taxation in W. Europe*, p. 108.
[3] I.B.F.D., *Taxation of Patent Royalties*, vol. 1, p. 6.10. Also F.B.I., *Taxation in W. Europe*, pp. 108-9; and R. J. Niehus in: *The Accountant*, 6 October 1962, pp. 412-15 on tax considerations when setting up a business in Germany.

taxation treaty, for example through the provisions of Articles 12 and 14 of the Austro-German treaty and Article VII of the taxation treaty with the United Kingdom.[1]

Patent royalties accruing to non-resident companies will be subject to a special withholding income tax of 25 per cent if the tax is paid by the recipient and 33·33 per cent if the tax is borne by the paying company. If the foreign company has a permanent establishment in the country, the normal rate of 49 per cent on the amount of patent royalties will be applied.[2]

As for dividends already taxed once as part of the total profits of a company, a second levy will be imposed on them as part of the total income of an individual shareholder or of the total profits of a recipient company. An exception to this rule is provided by the stipulation that companies holding 25 per cent or more of the share capital of another company will be exempt from such taxation, provided, however, dividends received are distributed. Otherwise, a supplementary tax (*Nachsteuer*) of 36 per cent will be due by the receiving company. Naturally, dividends received and distributed by a parent company will be subject to income tax in the hands of the individual shareholders.[3]

For depreciation, the straight-line method is the rule; the reducing or declining-balance method at a rate not exceeding 20 per cent may be applied for movable assets. Furthermore, for specified assets, an accelerated depreciation rate is allowed, with initial allowances between 30 and 50 per cent applicable in the first year. Losses may not be carried back; for a period of five years they may be carried forward unless they could have been written off earlier.[4]

## TAXES BASED ON CAPITAL[5]

### Net wealth tax (*Vermögenssteuer*)

This is levied on all capital assets, movable, immovable, tangible, intangible, both in and outside the country, owned by resident

---

[1] Austro-German Double Taxation Treaty of 4 October 1954; Double Taxation Treaty with the United Kingdom, 18 August 1954. See I.B.F.D., *Taxation of Patent Royalties*, pp. 6.04, 6.08–6.09.

[2] Ibid., p. 6.10.        [3] F.B.I., *Taxation in W. Europe*, p. 109.

[4] F.B.I., *Taxation in W. Europe*, p. 115. See also B. Gubbels: *Die steuerliche Abschreibung im In- und Ausland*, Heft 76, Inst. Finanzen und Steuern, Bonn, 1964 (a comparative study on depreciation allowances in W. European countries). Also *Eur. Tax.*, vol. 3, 1963, pp. 80, 186.

[5] F.B.I., *Taxation in W. Europe*, pp. 119–21.

individuals or companies. Non-residents are liable to this tax in relation to certain specified assets with a value higher than DM. 2,000 held in the country, for example, a permanent establishment in Germany, or patents. Certain allowances are deductible for individuals. As for companies, the minimum basis for levying the net wealth tax on companies is DM. 50,000 for *Aktiengesellschaften* and DM. 20,000 for limited liability companies (GmbH.). The tax is a deductible item for the income tax but not for company tax. Its rate is 1 per cent; and the proceeds flow to the Provincial Governments (*Länder*).

*Capital transactions tax (Kapitalverkehrssteuer).*
This tax consists of three parts:

i. *Tax on the acquisition of company rights (Gesellschaftssteuer).* This levy on the formation or increase in capital of a company, including contributions made by a foreign company to the assets of its branch or subsidiary, is also levied on loans in replacement or substitution of capital share, on the initial acquisition of shares in a German company, hence also on contributions made by a shareholder, and in certain cases on the sale by a company of its own shares. The rate is 2·5 per cent on the value of the transaction; in cases of company reorganization, a reduced rate of 1·0 per cent is applied.

ii. *Securities tax (Wertpapiersteuer).*[1] The first holder of German or foreign registered or bearer bonds is subject to this tax. It is also payable when rights (e.g. shares) in foreign companies are sold for the first time in Germany, or when rights or mortgage or lien on securities are acquired. The basis of assessment, in respect of securities, is the nominal value; in respect of rights in foreign companies, on the purchase price. The rate is 2·5 per cent.

iii. *Stock-exchange turnover tax (Börsenumsatzsteuer).* This tax is levied on transfers of securities in German stock-exchange markets or when at least one party in the transfer is a person domiciled or ordinarily resident in Germany or has a permanent representative in the country. The rates vary from 0·1 to 0·25 per cent in accordance with the type of securities and are based on the transfer price.

[1] On 27 January 1965 the Bundestag adopted a law subjecting foreigners' income from securities to a tax rate of 25 per cent; see *Wiener Zeitung*, no. 22, 28 January 1965, p. 6, and *Neue Zürcher Zeitung*, no. 211, 15 October 1964, Blatt II.

Half of the rate is due whenever only one party is a resident in Germany.

## OTHER TAXES

*Equalization of burdens-property contribution (Lastenausgleichsvermögens- abgabe):* This is payable on all property owned on 21 June 1948. The rate is 50 per cent; the resulting liability must be paid off, however, over a period of 30 years beginning 1 April 1949.

*Bill of exchange tax (Wechselsteuer).* At the rate of 0·15 per cent, this tax is payable on the face value of bills drawn in Germany. The tax is payable by the drawer and by the first German holder of bills drawn abroad.

*Insurance tax (Versicherungssteuer).* Insurance premiums are subject to this tax at the rate of 5 per cent, when the insured property is located in Germany or the insured person is a resident of the country.

*Land purchase tax (Grunderwerbssteuer).* This tax is also levied on real property belonging to a company or enterprise the assets and real property of which are concentrated in the hands of the purchaser. The rate of 7 per cent is levied on the purchase price or equivalent value in case assets are transferred.

## DOUBLE TAXATION RELIEF

Unilateral relief is possible. Credit is given for taxes that are paid abroad and that correspond to German income or company tax. The credit granted is up to the level of German tax. As an alternative, taxes paid abroad may be deducted as expenses.[1]

On the level of interstate double taxation agreements, the Federal Republic of Germany has signed treaties with the following countries:[2] Austria, Canada, Ceylon, Denmark, Egypt (U.A.R.), Finland, France, Greece, India, Ireland, Israel, Italy, Luxembourg, The Netherlands, Norway, Pakistan, Sweden, Switzerland, United Kingdom, United States of America.

---

[1] See *Eur. Tax.*, vol. 5, 1965, pp. 21–2; and I.B.F.D., *Taxation of Patent Royalties*, vol. 1, pp. 6.13 ff. On unilateral taxation relief see *Eur. Tax.*, vol. 3, 1963, pp. 95–6.

[2] As in January 1965.

## CONCLUSIONS

No discriminatory provisions affecting the taxation of income
earned by foreign individuals or companies are found in German
fiscal legislation. On the contrary, a few provisions in the existing
legislation amount to an effective discrimination in favour of non-
resident individuals and companies. This situation has led to the
operation of originally resident or German capital through companies established abroad, for the purpose of avoiding the higher
rates of taxation applicable to residents. Thus, whereas dividends
to a foreign, i.e. non-resident, company are subject to a withholding tax of 25 per cent, German shareholders receiving the same
amount of dividends may find themselves taxed at substantially
higher rates,[1] the amounts of which being dependent on total income. It is true that dividends paid to non-residents will very
probably be taxed again abroad, but inequities arise as differential
rates of taxation are lower in some of the countries concerned than
in Germany. This does not apply, of course, to German shareholders who have a substantial interest (25 per cent or more) in a
company *situated* abroad.

The inequities result from the application of provisions to companies with substantial holdings (*wesentliche Beteiligung*) in another
company. If a holding company is German, dividends received
from a subsidiary will be exempt from additional taxes other than
the withholding tax of 15 per cent, provided, however, that the
received dividends are distributed to shareholders; otherwise an
additional tax (*Nachsteuer*) of 36 per cent will be levied, bringing
the dividend tax rate to 51 per cent borne by the holding company. If the holding company is non-resident, no such additional
tax of 36 per cent on dividends will be levied. The foreign holding
company will pay the standard withholding tax of 25 per cent.[2]

---

[1] *Eur. Tax.*, vol. 4, 1964, p. 215; ibid., Supp. Serv. Section D, no. 12,
December 1964, on the views of state authorities in Germany; *Die Welt*,
no. 11, 14 January 1965, p. 15; according to *Die Welt*, no. 42, 19 February
1965, measures envisaged would not become effective before April or May
1965.

[2] *Eur. Tax.*, vol. 4, 1964, pp. 216–18. It is to be noted that the qualification
as a non-resident company is not wholly dependent on formal criteria of law.
The control and management of a company claiming to be non-resident must
in fact be exercised outside Germany. Such a company may be subjected to
German tax law if it is found to constitute a link in the economic activities
of a German undertaking (sect. 5/2 and 6 of the Fiscal Adaptation Law

Pursuant to the provisions of many double taxation treaties, income from licence fees and royalties will not be taxed in Germany as the country where such income originates. Income from interest on bonds accruing to non-residents is subject to a tax rate of 25 per cent.

## ITALY

### INDIVIDUAL INCOME TAX[1]

The rates of individual income tax depend on the type or category of income and the total income of individuals. There are four categories of individual income with four corresponding types of taxes:

i. General income tax (*imposta di ricchezza mobile*);
ii. Tax on land (*imposta sui terreni*);
iii. Tax on buildings (*imposta sui fabbricati*);
iv. Tax on income from agricultural activities (*imposta sul reddito agrario*).

i. *General income tax* (*Imposta di ricchezza mobile*)[2]

This is subdivided as follows:

*Category A* (*Ricchezza mobile, cat. A*). This category comprises income from the use of capital, including interest on loans, bonds, etc. but excluding dividends and royalties (which are classified under Category B as income from commercial activities).

Taxes of Category A are usually withheld at source at the rate of 26 per cent. Additional quotas for local authorities bring the rate to an effective level of 31 per cent.

*Category B* (*Ricchezza mobile, cat. B*). This category concerns profits from commercial and industrial activities. The tax is based on the combined use of labour and capital. Aggregate rates, including regional or local surcharges, vary from 18 per cent (for income

---

(*Steueranpassungsgesetz*)). In fact the fiscal advantages enjoyed by a non-resident may be nil or limited to a substantial extent; see *Die Welt*, no. 11, 14 Jan. 1965, p. 11.

[1] For a general survey of Italian taxation see E. Morselli: *Le Imposte in Italia*, 7th edn. Padova, 1962; also V. Uckmar in: *La Fiscalité du Marché Commun*, no. 9 July 1964, pp. 203 ff.

[2] F.B.I., *Taxation in W. Europe*, pp. 159–161.

above 240,000 Lire and less than 960,000 Lire, for individuals and partnerships) to 36 per cent for amounts over 100m Lire. Joint-stock companies, limited liability companies and partnerships limited by shares are taxed at the following rates:

28 per cent (including local surcharges and taxes) for income up to 4m Lire, 36 per cent for amounts over 100m Lire.

Two more categories (C.1 and C.2) concern income from self-employment and income from salaries, wages, etc. Aggregate rates for tax on income from self-employment (Cat. C.1) range from 10·6 to 14·7 per cent (including local surcharges and taxes) with an initial amount exempt from tax (for example, in Rome, 240,000 Lire). Director's personal income from remuneration comes under this Category C.1. It is levied partly as a withholding tax.

Category C.2 (tax on salaries, wages, etc.) is a withholding tax and its basic rates of 4 and 8 per cent are supplemented by local surcharges and taxes.

## ii. *Tax on land (Imposta sui terreni)*[1]

This is a tax levied on income accruing from ownership of land in Italy. It is based on the annual cadastral revenue as valued in 1939 and multiplied by revaluation coefficients. Subject to this tax are lands suitable for agriculture, as distinct from land used for urban housing projects, for free public services or commercial activities. Its basic rate is 10 per cent. Certain categories of land are exempt from this tax and relief may be granted under circumstances defined by the law.

## iii. *Tax on buildings (Imposta sui fabbricati)*[2]

Since 1 January 1962, this tax is also based on the cadastral income (see *tax on land*, above). Industrial or commercial buildings are exempt from this tax since they fall under *Category B* of the general income tax as part of the business investment. The basic rate of 5 per cent is raised to 34 per cent by various surcharges.

## iv. *Tax on income from agricultural activities (Imposta sul reddito agrario)*

This tax is based on individual valuation, with a rate of 10 per cent based on the cadastral valuation of 1939 multiplied by a

---

[1] F.B.I., *Taxation in W. Europe*, pp. 159 ff.          [2] Ibid., p. 158.

regionally varying coefficient (for example in Rome: 138 per cent).[1]

## Complementary tax[2]

This tax is due from individuals whose annual income exceeds 960,000 Lire. There are certain allowances and the rates vary between 3·17 per cent (for 1m Lire) and 65 per cent (for 500m Lire and over). Surcharges raise the nominal rates—the top rate is effectively 78 per cent.

### COMPANY TAX[3]

This is payable by joint-stock companies, limited liability companies and partnerships limited by shares, and it is additional to those enumerated above and applicable to companies.

One of its rates, 0·75 per cent, is applied to the issued capital and reserves; the other rate, 15 per cent, is applied to all types of company income which together exceed 6 per cent of the total amount of capital and reserves. Local surcharges bring the two rates to an effective level of, respectively, 0·825 and 16·5 per cent. Dividends taxed once already as part of the company profits are not taxed a second time in the hands of the shareholders, but may be taxed under the category of the complementary tax referred to above. Dividends paid by a company to another company are not subject to tax on general income but may be taxed under the provisions of company tax.

Banking and holding companies possessing at least 60 per cent of their total assets in the form of financial holdings in other companies enjoy a reduction of 25 per cent applicable to both elements of the company tax. The corresponding rate of reduction is 40 per cent if the shareholder is the Italian government. In any year that ends with a loss the company tax element of 0·75 per cent (above), applied to the net assets of a company may be reduced by ten times the ratio of loss to net worth, with a maximum reduction limit of 90 per cent.

[1] F.B.I. *Taxation in W. Europe*, p. 158.
[2] Ibid., p. 161.
[3] *Eur. Tax.*, Suppl. Serv. Section A, Italy (as in January 1965); cf. *A Guide for Foreign Investors in Italy*, publ. Banca Nazionale del Lavoro, Rome, 1962, pp. 69 ff., and F.B.I., *Taxation in W. Europe*, pp. 161–2.

*Dividend withholding tax (tax deductions from dividends)*

Since 24 February 1964, shareholders may pay either a 30 per cent withholding tax as a final levy or a 5 per cent withholding tax. In the first case, the dividends received need not be included in taxable income for the purpose of company or complementary tax. In the second case, when a withholding tax of 5 per cent is preferred, the dividends received have to be included in income taxable for company or complementary tax; credit is granted, however, for the 5 per cent already paid and any excess of tax paid will be refunded[1]

*The taxation of non-resident individuals and companies*[2]

Unless double taxation treaties provide otherwise, certain non-residents will be subject to a 30 per cent rate. It is possible to apply the withholding tax of 5 per cent on dividends. Income accruing to non-residents from interest will be taxed at source at the aggregate rate of 31 per cent, the corresponding rate for royalties and licence fees will be 24·75 per cent when paid to a company and 17·16 per cent when paid to an individual. These rates include surcharges. The effective rates are, however, lower —16·5 and 11·44 per cent respectively—since the nominal rates are applied to two-thirds of the sums paid. For instance, for taxable income from royalties totalling £1,000, the rates of 24·75 and 17·16 per cent would be, respectively, applicable to two-thirds of this sum, £666, thus resulting in lower effective rates. There is a turnover tax of 3·3 per cent to be paid on royalties and licence fees. These rates constitute a final levy, unless the non-resident individual or company has a permanent establishment in Italy. In this case, the tax withheld will be credited against final liability.

For the depreciation of assets, the straight-line method is used, with varying rates for different items, for example 3 per cent for buildings, 30 per cent for special machinery. Losses may be carried forward for the following five years and set against profits for the purpose of tax on movable wealth but not for the purpose of company tax.

[1] See *Eur. Tax.*, vol. 4, 1964, p. 146.
[2] F.B.I., *Taxation in W. Europe*, pp. 162–7; *Eur. Tax.*, vol. 3, 1963, p. 187.

## TAXES BASED ON CAPITAL

### Registration tax (*Imposta di registro*)

Paid when a company is formed, this is based at the rate of 1·1 per cent on the subscribed capital, at the rate of 3·15 per cent on the value of contributed industrial assets or buildings, immovable property, in which case the rate is applied to the sale value of the property (usually about 11 per cent). Similar rates apply when a capital increase is effected. These rates are aggregate ones; they include various local surcharges and supplements.[1]

### Tax on bonds and debentures (*Imposta sulle obbligazioni*)

This tax is payable by companies on the value of bonds and debentures issued. The rates are 0·5 per cent on the value of bonds issued by companies, and 0·125 per cent for bonds and debentures issued by banking and holding companies.[2]

In case loans are contracted against mortgages, a mortgage tax of 2·5 per cent is due on the value or amount of the registered mortgage.

Various rates are applied when taxes are levied on insurance, e.g. usually 3·3 per cent on the value or premium for maritime insurance, 4·7 per cent for non-maritime transport, 3·3 per cent on the annual premium for accident or life insurance. Levies are also made in the form of stamp duties and advertising tax.

## DOUBLE TAXATION RELIEF

The Italian tax authorities do not grant any unilateral relief other than the deduction of foreign taxes paid as expenses. On the bilateral level Italy has agreements with the following countries:[3] Austria, Belgium, France, Germany, The Netherlands, Spain, Sweden, United Kingdom, United States of America.

## CONCLUSIONS

A comparison of rates applicable to the income of resident and non-resident individuals and companies shows that while marginal differences exist, the differential rates do not amount to

[1] F.B.I., *Taxation in W. Europe*, p. 168.
[2] Ibid., p. 169.
[3] As in January 1965. See *Eur. Tax.*, vol. 5, 1965, pp. 21–2.

a discriminatory taxation of income accruing to non-residents. Non-residents enjoy, in addition, advantages provided in the respective double taxation treaties.

## LUXEMBOURG[1]

### GENERAL INCOME TAX (EINKOMMENSSTEUER)

This has progressive rates ranging from 0·22 per cent to 54 per cent applied to net income after the deduction of professional expenses and allowances. If directors, managers or shareholders of companies have no habitual residence in the country, the tax is levied on the income that originates in Luxembourg or is earned in the country. The normal taxation of non-residents is in accordance with the progressive rates applicable to married persons without children (with a minimum liability of 12 per cent on taxable income or income received as licence fees and patent rights).

### TAX ON BONUSES

A tax is levied on bonuses and other profit-sharing payments made to directors and executives of companies at the rate of 20 per cent if the recipient pays the tax himself as resident in the country; the rate is 25 per cent if the recipient is a resident in Luxembourg and the company pays the tax; a rate of 28 per cent is applied if the recipient pays the tax but is non-resident; the rate of 38·88 per cent becomes applicable when the recipient is a non-resident and the company bears the burden of the tax.

### TAXATION OF COMPANIES

*Tax on company profits (Körperschaftssteuer)*

The law distinguishes between Luxembourg companies and foreign companies. The former are taxable in full while the latter may be taxed, under circumstances, on profits earned in Luxembourg only.

No distinction is made between distributed and retained profits. The rates vary from 20 per cent on profits under Lfrs. 400,000 to 40 per cent on profits over Lfrs. 1,000,000. Deductions for depreciation are allowed within specified limits. Losses may be carried

[1] See J. Sinner: *Code de la Législation Fiscale Luxembourgeoise*, vols. 1–4, Luxembourg, 1964. Also F.B.I., *Taxation in W. Europe*, pp. 174–6.

over for the next two years. For depreciation, the method used is the straight-line one as a general rule; the reducing or declining-balance method may be used if it can be justified.[1]

A withholding tax of 15 per cent is levied on dividends distributed to shareholders and 5 per cent withheld as tax on bonds and interest.

Dividends and interest paid by holding companies and dividends received by a Luxembourg company holding more than 25 per cent of the shares of the paying company are exempt from tax on company profits.

*Holding companies*[2]

These enjoy a special status in the Luxembourg tax system. Firstly, they are not limited to holding shares of other companies, but may also own bonds, debentures and other securities. Furthermore, they may own patents, trademarks and industrial technical knowledge of a non-patentable nature.

They are subject to taxes as follows:

(*a*) They pay an annual fee (*droit d'abonnement*) of 0·16 per cent of the average market value of securities issued by the individual companies. The minimum fee is, however, Lfrs. 1,500.

(*b*) They pay a tax (*droit d'apport*) on the subscribed capital at the time of their formation, capital increase or renewal of their respective statutory duration periods, at a rate of 0·32 per cent. The minimum amount payable is Lfrs. 3,000.

(*c*) They pay a stamp duty (*droit de timbre*) when they issue shares or other securities, at a rate of 0·1 per cent on the nominal value of shares or other securities. The minimum payable is Lfrs. 1,000.

Within the category of holding companies, the so-called holding *milliardaires* constitute a group by themselves. They are companies with assets worth at least Lfrs. 1,000m. They are not subject to the payment of an annual fee (*droit d'abonnement*) and pay but reduced rates for the tax on subscribed capital (*droit d'apport*) and for stamp duties (*droit de timbre*). They pay a maximum tax rate of 3 per cent on interest paid on bonds and on dividends distributed to shareholders. Salaries and other remunerations paid

---

[1] *Eur. Tax.* Suppl. Serv. Section A, Luxembourg, Corporate Tax rates. For depreciation and loss allowances, see also *Eur. Tax.*, vol. 3, 1963, p. 188.
[2] *Eur. Tax.*, vol. 3, 1963, p. 148.

to the managers and directors who are non-resident in the country for more than six months a year are exempt from income and director's tax.

## TAXES BASED ON CAPITAL[1]

*Net wealth tax (Vermögenssteuer)*

This tax is paid by resident individuals and legal entities on total net wealth, movable or immovable, tangible or intangible, in the country or abroad. The law provides for a scheme of allowances for individuals. The minimum taxable net wealth of a company (joint-stock company) is Lfrs. 500,000; for limited liability companies (S.A.R.L.) the corresponding amount is Lfrs. 200,000. A holding by one company in another resident company of 25 per cent or more is not included in the amount taxable as net wealth of the holding company.

Non-resident individuals or companies are subject to this tax only for certain specified assets in the country. There are, however, no personal allowances deductible as in the case of resident individuals; nor is there a minimum amount for liability by non-resident companies. The rate is 0·5 per cent on the value of the assets as determined in accordance with the rates laid down in the valuation Act of 1934.

The capital transaction taxes for companies other than the holding companies mentioned above, are as follows:

*Tax on subscribed capital (Droit d'apport).* Payable at the time of creation of the company or increase in capital, the rate is 0·3 per cent.

*Tax on the value of securities issued (Droit d'abonnement).* This levy is due annually on the value of securities issued, at a rate of 0·36 per cent (0·18 per cent for small companies).

*Stamp duty (Droit de timbre).* This is payable when securities are issued, bills of exchange drawn and promissory notes and other negotiable instruments are issued, at a rate of 0·1 per cent.

Further types based on capital are the *registration duty (droit de transcription)* payable when a mortgage is entered in the registry

[1] F.B.I., *Taxation in W. Europe*, pp. 180–2. Also *Eur. Tax.*, vol. 3, 1963, p. 188.

of real property at a rate of 1 per cent; the *conveyancing tax* (*droit d'enregistrement*) on the sale value of real or personal property, at a rate of 6 per cent; *immovable property tax* with a rate of 0·5 per cent on property in excess of a value of Lfrs. 500,000.

## DOUBLE TAXATION RELIEF[1]

As unilateral relief, there is the possibility of deducting taxes paid abroad as expenses incurred in earning the given income.

Luxembourg has double taxation agreements with the following countries: Austria, Belgium, France, Germany (Federal Republic), United States.

## CONCLUSIONS

While fiscal law in Luxembourg distinguishes between local and foreign companies, the distinction is not to the disadvantage of foreign companies since income of the latter is taxable to the extent that it is earned in Luxembourg. Special rates applicable to the category of the so-called holding *milliardaire* companies make investment in such companies attractive to foreign investors.

## THE NETHERLANDS[2]

### INCOME TAX

This tax has progressive rates between 0·5 per cent (for married persons with three children) and 58·9 per cent and is levied on total income. Income accruing from partnerships is taxed without any distinction between distributed and non-distributed profits.

Directors' remuneration are subject to a special withholding tax with progressive rates. For remuneration received from any one

---

[1] As in January 1965. See *Eur. Tax.*, vol. 5, 1965, pp. 21–2. See J. Sinner: *Etudes Fiscales*, Luxembourg, 1963, for a survey of tax conventions concluded by the Luxembourg government.

[2] For a survey of Dutch fiscal laws, see W. E. C. de Groot and others: *Nederlandse Belastingwetten*, 6th edn. Alphen aan deu Rijn, 1965. For a discussion of proposed fiscal reforms, D. Booy: *Belastingrecht in wording, de ontwikkeling van de belastingsontwerpen en de vergelijking met het bestaande recht*, Arnhem, 1964 (loose-leaf). For a summary of Dutch taxation system, F.B.I., *Taxation in W. Europe*, The Netherlands, pp. 185–6.

company, the withholding tax rate is 30 per cent for amounts
between Fl. 1,001 and 5,000, and 50 per cent for amounts over
Fl. 5,000. For the individual income tax liability of directors, only
the net amount of the fees received need be included in the
taxable income.

## COMPANY TAX[1]

On company profits the rate levied is 42 per cent for amounts up
to Fl. 40,000. For profits between Fl. 40,000 and 50,000, the first
Fl. 40,000 are taxed at the rate of 42 per cent and the excess at the
rate of 57 per cent. For profits exceeding Fl. 50,000, a uniform
rate of 45 per cent on total profits is applied.

Dividends paid by a company are taxed twice: once as part of
the company profits, and a second time as part of a shareholder's
personal income.[2]

Dividends received by companies and partnerships limited by
shares from shareholdings of at least 25 per cent are exempt from
tax on dividends. This provision applies equally to holdings in
foreign companies. Moreover, a holding of less than 25 per cent
may qualify for exemption by special consent of the Ministry of
Finance. Portfolio holding companies are exempt from dividend
tax independently from the size of their holdings in the paying
company. To qualify for this exemption, it is necessary, however,
to distribute at least 60 per cent of dividends received by a holding
company in any one year to shareholders, or to have its shares
listed on the Amsterdam or Rotterdam stock-exchange markets.

For depreciation, both the straight-line and the declining-
balance methods may be used. Rates vary from one asset to
another; the conventional depreciation rate for machinery is 10 per
cent, for buildings 1·5 to 3 per cent. Depreciation can begin from
the date a contract is passed for the purchase of the given asset.
A Ministerial Decree of 31 January 1964 has suspended all
acceleration allowances.[3]

Losses may be carried back or forward. They may be carried
back and set off against profits of the preceding year, or carried

[1] *Eur. Tax.* Suppl. Serv. Section A, Corporate Tax Rates (as in January
1965).
[2] *Eur. Tax.*, vol. 4, 1964, p. 149.
[3] *Eur. Tax.* Suppl. Serv. Section A, The Netherlands; *Eur. Tax.*, vol. 3,
1963, pp. 145, 201.

forward against profits of the following six years. Moreover, losses arising in the first six years of a business may be carried forward indefinitely. From any one year, the order for setting off losses is: (*a*) losses of the first six years; (*b*) losses of the preceding six years; (*c*) losses of the last year.[1]

## TAXES BASED ON CAPITAL[2]

A *net wealth tax* is due by individuals on the market value of their net property, i.e. assets minus debts. The rate is 0·5 per cent and there are tax-free allowances. Non-residents are subject to this tax on only certain specified assets located in the country and enjoy the same allowances as residents. In order to be deductible, debts must have, however, an organic link with the taxable items.

A *land tax* is levied on land without buildings at the rate of 6 per cent. The rate of tax on land with buildings is 4·86 per cent multiplied by a coefficient of 130 per cent and increased by possible local surcharges.

A *registration duty* is to be paid on capital subscribed at the time of formation of companies and limited partnerships. For capital subscribed but not yet paid up, 0·25 per cent is due, and when the payment of such capital is effected, the rate of 2·5 per cent is to be completed by the payment of a further 2·25 per cent.

*Stamp duties* at varying rates are due on domestic bonds and debentures, at the rate of 0·75 per cent on the nominal value of such securities. The importation of foreign shares, bonds and debentures is subject to a stamp duty of 2 per cent on their nominal value.

## DOUBLE TAXATION RELIEF[3]

Unless specific treaty provisions apply, amounts paid in foreign taxes for income from foreign sources may be deducted up to a level equal to that part of Dutch tax which is similarly proportional to the total amount of tax due in the Netherlands as the

[1] F.B.I., *Taxation in W. Europe*, p. 190; *Eur. Tax.*, vol. 3, 1963, p. 202.
[2] F.B.I., *Taxation in W. Europe*, pp. 191–3; *Eur. Tax.*, vol. 4, 1964, p. 236.
[3] As in January 1965. See *Eur. Tax.*, vol. 5, 1965, pp. 21–2 and also I.B.F.D., *Taxation of Patent Royalties*, pp. 12.03 f.

amount of foreign income is proportional to the total income taxable in the country. In case of dissimilarity between the given tax paid abroad and taxes payable in the Netherlands, the foreign tax may be deducted from the income subject to Dutch tax.

Double taxation treaties have been signed by the following countries: Belgium, Canada, Denmark, Finland, France, Germany (Fed. Republic), Italy, Norway, Sweden, Switzerland, United Kingdom, United States.

## CONCLUSIONS

Dutch corporate taxation is characterized by non-discrimination of resident and non-resident companies. This general rule is supplemented by a number of double taxation treaties that duly regulate the flow of income between the Netherlands and the respective signatory states.

## GENERAL CONCLUSIONS ON THE TAXATION OF FOREIGN INVESTMENT IN THE E.E.C.

A study of fiscal regulations in their relation to income derived from foreign investment in the member states of the Common Market shows that they do not discriminate between foreign-owned and domestic enterprise. A distinction is made between resident and non-resident physical or legal persons; but each of these two categories could include enterprises owned by foreigners or nationals of the member states. Hence, the term 'foreign-owned' is not a legal term for the purpose of taxation in the Common Market—the principle of control does not apply, thus excluding the basis of differential treatment.

Fiscal treatment uniformly applicable to foreign and domestic enterprise in the Common Market may be considered as a valuable incentive to attract foreign investment, particularly in conjunction with other factors that constitute the favourable investment climate of the E.E.C. The differential rates that exist are intended to align the fiscal burden of foreign enterprise with that of domestic undertakings without being penal to the former.

It is wellnigh impossible to assess, without a detailed approach, the reasons why and the extent to which foreign enterprise prefers one member state more than the others in respect to fiscal considerations. According to one source, Germany has the heaviest overall fiscal charges in the E.E.C. while France ranks as fourth among the six member states.[1] According to another source, among the three member states, Belgium, France and the Netherlands, corporate taxation in France is the least conducive to the accumulation of reserves and effects the highest reduction in the amount of net dividends.[2] If fiscal factors were strong foreign investment incentives or deterrents, they should have been sufficient to direct the bulk of foreign capital to the four remaining member states, Belgium, Italy, Luxembourg and The Netherlands. In fact, however, the considerable amount of foreign investment in France and Germany has led to concern in these two countries far greater in extent than any complaints, if any, in those four countries. More subsidiaries of American companies have been established in France than in any other member state of the Common Market, in spite of high fiscal rates.[3] This proves that taxation, by itself and particularly in combination with other factors, is not a determining element in directing foreign enterprise to a given country.[4] Naturally, these apply within certain limits and situations where even the penal character of differential rates can be balanced by other factors acting as advantages. A highly interesting question in this connection, but one that is beyond the scope of the present study, is whether advantages implied in or incidental to double taxation treaties more than offset the disadvantages of higher fiscal charges in a country like France. An answer to this question would necessitate an exhaustive comparative study of double taxation agreements and of taxation in the

[1] *Le Monde*, 17 October 1964, p. 22.

[2] *Entreprise*, no. 482, 5 December 1964, pp. 39 ff., especially pp. 45, 47; ibid., no. 492, 13 February 1965, the opinions of M. Drancourt, pp. 43 ff., especially p. 51. L. B. Krause and K. W. Dam: *Federal Tax Treatment of Foreign Income*, p. 51, Table 2. For an economic analysis of taxation of foreign investment, see P. B. Richman: *Taxation of Foreign Investment Income*, Baltimore, 1963.

[3] C. McCormick Crosswell: *International Business Techniques*, p. 162; on differential rates in their effect on competition, pp. 51 ff. For comparative tables of tax rates as applied to commercial companies in the E.E.C., see P. Cheynet: *Tableaux comparatifs des Impôts et Taxes, applicables aux Sociétés commerciales dans les Pays du Marché Commun*, Paris, 1963. For a general survey of the tax systems of the E.E.C. countries, L. Trotabas: *Finances Publiques*, Paris, 1964, pp. 380 ff.

[4] Krause and Dam, *Federal Tax Treatment*, p. 92. McCormick Crosswell, *Int. Business Techniques*, p. 162.

two countries concerned.[1] Independently of the results of such a study, it can be said that unilateral non-discriminatory provisions affecting the income of foreign enterprise in the E.E.C. are supplemented by numerous bilateral agreements on double taxation. These agreements offer particular advantages to investors coming from non-member countries.

Clearly none of the six member states of the E.E.C. considers taxation as a suitable instrument for encouraging and particularly discouraging foreign investment. In other terms, measures applied for the restriction and control of foreign enterprise are not to be found, in the E.E.C., on the level of fiscal rules. Such measures of restriction and control are incorporated in legislative and administrative rules affecting certain sectors of activities inaccessible or conditionally accessible to foreigners, and in rules that deal with the exchange control and authorization of foreign enterprise at the stage of initial entry and establishment in the country. Beyond this stage, and once admitted into the country, a foreigner can operate on a footing of equality with nationals of the host member state. Foreign-owned companies constituted in accordance with the law of a member state will also enjoy, under the Treaty of Rome (Arts. 52 and 58), Community treatment when extending their activities on an intermember level. Thus, in general and also in the sphere of taxation, the member states of the E.E.C. have excluded the (elusive) principle of ownership or control when dealing with foreign enterprise.

[1] For a discussion of tax treaties and their effect on business operations, see McCormick Crosswell, *Int. Business Techniques.*

# CHAPTER VII

# INVESTMENT INCENTIVES AND EMPLOYMENT OF ALIENS

## INVESTMENT INCENTIVES

We have earlier referred to the interdependent political, legal and economic factors that contribute towards a country's favourable investment climate, and discussed briefly the economic situation in the E.E.C. Turning to the legal factors, we can see that legislative measures and official or public attitudes that both allow and stimulate foreign enterprise will be incentives to foreign investment in a country. In assessing the extent of investment incentives as embodied in the laws of each of the E.E.C. states, we shall be examining such measures as state assistance in the form of loans or grants for the promotion of industrial activities and the training of labour, and the absence of discrimination between foreign and domestic enterprise in the application of these measures.

### BELGIUM

The *general* law of 17 July 1959, as amended by that of 14 February 1961, aims at the encouragement of economic expansion.[1] It does so by promoting the creation, expansion, conversion and modernization of industrial undertakings. Administered by the Ministry of Economic Affairs, it applies to industrial operations, whether by domestic or foreign enterprise, that are in the general interest of the country and are directly related to the country's economic life by being carried out in Belgium.[2] It provides for state assistance in the form of subsidized low-interest loans, generally for a period of three years.

Loans with low interest rates may be granted in the form of general, special or additional aid. In the category of *general* aid, interest rates of loans may be reduced by 2 per cent for invest-

[1] *Mon. Belge*, 29 August 1959 and 15 February 1961. For a summary of special laws concerning the promotion of industrial investments, see *Digest of Special Laws designed to promote industrial investments in Belgium*, publ. by the Ministry of Economic Affairs and Energy, Brussels.

[2] *Digest of Special Laws*, p. 3.

ments contributing to an overall expansion of the country's economy.[1] A *special* aid may effect a further 2 per cent reduction in interest rates on loans if recipients comply with the aims of the government for a given industrial sector. Global interest rate reductions (these two forms of aid added together) may not, however, exceed a maximum or total reduction of 4 per cent.[2] Finally, in periods of economic depression as declared by Royal Decree, *general* or *special* aid may be supplemented by an *additional* aid up to a point where the interest paid by the recipient may not be below 3 per cent for *general* aid and 1 per cent for *general and special* aids combined.

If natural or legal persons applying for loans are unable to satisfy the guarantee requirements of credited institutions approved by law, the state may undertake the required guarantee for part or whole of the loan together with the interest and costs incidental to it.

Undertakings investing in building in accordance with conditions that apply to special or additional aid may be exempted for five years from tax on real estate income.[3] Such an exemption will apply automatically if the investment is undertaken with state aid, and in particular cases that have been approved by the Ministry of Economic Affairs. In exceptional cases, the government may even undertake the construction of buildings or acquire premises and let or sell them for the envisaged industrial project.

For intangible investments, for example, research in and promotion of new techniques, interest-free loans representing up to 50 per cent of the research costs may be granted. They are repayable as soon as the investment becomes sufficiently profitable.[4]

A second (*regional*) law (18 July 1959 as amended 14 February 1961),[5] relates the provisions of the general law to the promotion of economic expansion in specified regions where the need for economic development is felt.[6] Like the general law, it applies equally to foreign enterprise planning operations in development regions. The list of development regions currently determined by law will be in force until 15 December 1965.[7]

---

[1] Ibid., p. 4.    [2] Ibid., p. 5.    [3] Ibid., p. 6.    [4] Ibid., p. 7.
[5] *Mon. Belge*, 29 August 1959 and 15 February 1961.
[6] Capital grants are possible but in very exceptional cases: *Digest of Special Laws*, p. 12.
[7] *Digest of Special Laws*, p. 10, in which see also Annex III, pp. 27 ff. for a list of the development regions. For some regional developments in

L

138 LEGAL ASPECTS OF INVESTMENT IN THE E.E.C.

A third legislative incentive to industrial investment is assistance given by the state for the adaptation of labour to changing conditions. Such changing conditions may involve the creation of new industries, or the extension or conversion of existing ones.[1] The relevant legislation provisions govern the conditions under which the National Employment Office (*Office National de l'Emploi*) may participate in expenses related to the selection, training, re-adaptation and travel of qualified or semi-qualified personnel. The Ministry of Labour has, however, wide discretionary powers in determining the conditions under which assistance may be extended and the amount of assistance fixed.[2]

In addition to the above legislative measures affecting state assistance both for industrial investments and adaptation of labour to changing conditions, provisions on depreciation of assets, contained in the fiscal law of 20 November 1962, may also be considered as investment incentives. Under Article 13 of that law, a Royal Decree may authorize the application of the declining-balance method instead of the straight-line method.[3] Furthermore, under Article 29 of the same fiscal law, tax exemptions may apply favourably to mergers. For the category of investment incentives, mention should lastly be made of special rules that govern the favourable tax treatment of foreign nationals temporarily resident in the country; these rules are examined here under the heading on employment of aliens.

Legislative measures governing state assistance in industrial investments contribute to the favourable investment climate in Belgium by their non-discriminatory application to domestic as well as to foreign-owned enterprise. This functional approach to domestic or foreign initiative useful to the economic life of the country is marked, in addition, by a considerable degree of flexibility and takes into account the particular needs of development regions. The relevant legislation lays down general rules, the concrete application of which is left to a wide margin of discretionary power exercised by administrative authorities such as, in the first place, the Ministry of Economic Affairs. This is in accordance

---

Belgium, see *Journ. Belg. Chamber of Commerce* (in Great Britain), October 1964, pp. 7 ff., and *The Times Review of Industry*, June 1962, p. 64.

[1] *Mon. Belge*, 28 March 1961, for Royal Decree of 24 March 1961; Royal Decree of 20 March 1961 (*Mon. Belge*, 23 March 1961).

[2] *Digest of Special Laws*, pp. 22–3.

[3] Ibid., p. 16.

with the need for easily adaptable legislative and administrative action to influence the general trend of economic activities.

These flexible and adaptable legislative rules are applied in a field that is comprehensive, and which involves all the major needs of current industrial and economic life of a country like Belgium—state support for private initiative where such initiative is short of investment funds for expanding or adapting existing enterprises, or for establishing new ones; and, not least, funds for mobilizing research and for the training or re-adaptation of skilled personnel to changing conditions of industrial life.

### FRANCE

As in Belgium, French regulations on state aid to industrial and regional investments affect the establishment of new undertakings, and the development, adaptation or conversion of existing ones. The regulations must also take into account the decentralization of industries concentrated in the region of Paris.[1] Aid is offered in the form of grants, low-interest loans and tax reductions or exemptions. Grants for establishing new plants, or for renovating, partially or basically, existing ones may amount to 20 per cent of investment expenses. Loans with low interest rates may be granted for improving productivity, for decentralization plans and for labour housing projects. Local authorities may grant preferential rates for power supply (gas, electricity).

Loans for research may be contracted for a period extending up to 12 years. They may be converted into grants under specified conditions.

On the level of tax incentives, special deductions from taxable profits may be granted by the authorities.[2] All provisions governing industrial investment incentives do not distinguish between

---

[1] The new guide and code on industrial decentralization published in January 1965 by the Ministry of Industry. For a short report on assistance to be given by the French government to industries established outside Paris, see *The Times*, 3 June 1964, *The Financial Times*, 1 May 1964, and *The Guardian*, 23 March 1964. For a survey of regional economies and state planning, *La Documentation Française: Notes et Etudes Documentaires*, Paris, September 1964, no. 3118. Also *Le Monde* 29–30 November 1964, pp. 9, 12. *Industrial Decentralization in France* (pamphlet), publ. by the French Embassy in London, 1963. For further regional studies, see contemporary issues of *Entreprise*, e.g. no. 488, 1 January 1965, and 30 January 1965.

[2] F.B.I., *Taxation in W. Europe*, pp. 85, 89.

foreign-owned and locally-owned enterprises. There are, on the other hand, no special rules for the favourable treatment of alien nationals working, for instance, as technicians in a newly established foreign-owned enterprise.

## GERMANY

The pattern of industrial and regional investment incentives in Germany is similar to the systems in Belgium and France: no discrimination is made between foreign and domestic enterprises; incentives consist of grants, loans and tax reductions or exemptions. The responsible authority is the Federal Ministry for Economic Affairs in Bonn. In addition, regional authorities may grant various facilities such as aid for the construction of plants or for leasing sites for plant construction.

Loans for the establishment of new enterprises may be made available for a maximum period of 15 years at a rate of 3·5 per cent. In addition, loans at a 2 per cent interest rate may be contracted for vocational training. Preference may be given to industries in regions specified as areas in need of assistance, such as those near the demarcation line between West and East Germany. Tax incentives in the form of reductions in income or company tax, higher depreciation allowances, turnover tax, will be granted to undertakings operating in West Berlin or to income derived from sources in West Berlin.[1]

## ITALY

The Italian system of investment incentives also shows no discrimination between enterprise owned by the country's nationals and that owned by foreigners, and its assistance is in the form of grants, loans and tax reductions. The main geographical area where investment incentives are applied is the region south of Rome, and including Sicily and Sardinia. In this region, the situation has been marked for decades by a lack of adequate economic development and consequent high rates of unemployment. The main organization in charge of influencing economic development in southern Italy is the *Cassa per il Mezzogiorno*.[2]

[1] F.B.I., *Taxation in W. Europe*, p. 112.
[2] *Neue Zürcher Zeitung*, Fernausgabe, no. 76, 18 March 1965, Blatt 10, the article by C. Mötteli on economic development in southern Italy. Also *The European Markets*, The Chase Manhattan Bank, New York, January 1964.

Grants for financing industrial enterprises may represent 20–25 per cent of initial costs required for buildings, roads and supply lines, and 10 per cent of expenses for production equipment. Medium-term loans may be approved for a period not exceeding 15 years and may cover up to 70 per cent of the total investment amount at an interest rate of 3–4 per cent.

Tax exemptions may be granted to new industrial undertakings for a period extending up to ten years; higher rates of depreciation allowances may be applied. Additional incentives are provided for undertakings that are set up in specified urban regions, for instance, in or near towns with 10,000 inhabitants.

Investment incentives in Italy concern not only special grants, loans or tax exemptions, but also certain exchange control advantages granted to foreign investors that establish productive undertakings in the country, as specified by Law no. 43 of 1956, under which special rules are applied to investment profits from productive undertakings.[1] The transfer of such profits and the repatriation of imported capital are entitled to favourable treatment.

### LUXEMBOURG

The forms of aid in Luxembourg are basically the same as those already examined in this chapter and the principle of non-discrimination for foreign-owned enterprise is applied.[2]

The Law of 2 June 1962 provides for aid in the form of low-interest loans, state guarantees, investment subsidies, tax reductions and acquisition by the State of real estate needed for industrial purposes.[3] Undertakings contributing to the improvement of productivity standards and to national economy in general will be entitled to the benefits of the said law.[4] Regulations for low-interest loans are similar to those in Belgium, as are those for state guarantees for the repayment of loans and interest incidental to them.[5] Subsidies granted by the state may not exceed 15 per cent

[1] See page 50 ff above.

[2] Law of 2 June 1962 (Mémorial A, no. 31, 19 June 1962, pp. 492–7). Grand-Ducal Regulation of 31 July 1962 (Mémorial A, no. 50, 9 September 1962, pp. 921–7). For a survey of regional problems, *Bulletin Economique*, publ. by the Ministry of Economic Affairs, vol. viii, no. 3, March 1962, pp. 18 ff. For a summary of incentives, *Brit. Trade Journal*, Suppl., 12 December 1963, pp. 14–15, and 48.

[3] Articles 2, 6 and 8, Law of 2 June 1962.

[4] Article 1, Law of 2 June 1962.          [5] Articles 3 and 4.

of investments for buildings, and 10 per cent of investments for production equipment (machinery).[1]

## THE NETHERLANDS

A few problem areas exist in the Netherlands, in relation to which the Ministry of Economic Affairs may apply regional investment incentives. The pattern is basically the same as in the other member states of the E.E.C.: aid may be extended in the form of grants, loans and tax reductions. A characteristic for grants is the fact that they are scaled according to useful floor space. Loans may be obtained at favourable interest rates for repayment in ten years. As for tax reductions, these may be in the form of accelerated depreciation, or investment allowances deductible from taxable income, or carrying losses forward for six years; losses in the first six years being carried forward indefinitely.[2] All of the incentive measures apply equally to foreign-owned enterprise.

## CONCLUSIONS

Governmental measures designed as investment incentives do not discriminate between foreign-owned and domestic undertakings in all six member states. The principle of control or ownership is not applicable, and foreign and home investors are equally entitled to the benefits of grants, low-cost loans, tax exemptions and other forms of investment incentives. The use of grants is much less frequent than other forms of incentives; in some of the member states the application of incentives is related to the application of governmental plans for economic development. In this respect, one of the implications is that, if member states extend incentives equally to foreign investors, they consider the latter as welcome participants in official plans for economic development. The principle of national treatment thus makes a further contribution to the favourable investment climate of the E.E.C. by its application to investment incentives.[3]

While municipal laws on investment and investment incentives

[1] Article 5.

[2] Chase Manhatten Bank: *The European Markets.*

[3] For a summary survey of governmental measures applied as investment incentives and for solving regional problems in a number of Western European countries, see the O.E.C.D. *Observer*, no. 13, December 1964, pp. 14 ff.

fall within the competence of the member states, the executive organs of the E.E.C. may interfere in so far as subsidies and other aids granted by member states distort competition on an inter-member, Community level. The Commission of the E.E.C. is authorized under Articles 92 ff. of the Treaty of Rome to take action concerning governmental aids which are deemed to be incompatible with the objectives of the Common Market.[1]

## EMPLOYMENT OF ALIENS

Not infrequently, industries or businesses established as a result of foreign investment give rise to the introduction into the host country of new techniques, which in turn require foreign technical experts to be brought in. Moreover, the foreign-owned enterprise may best be operated, in its initial stages, by directors or managers who have experience in similar operations elsewhere and may have to take up residence, at least on a temporary basis, in the host country. Thus foreign investment may involve the participation not only of foreign capital but also of foreign personnel; and the conditions under which such personnel, managerial or technical, may enter and reside in the host country can be, to some extent, additional incentives or deterrents to foreign investment.

In the E.E.C. the personnel brought in from non-member countries and primarily needed in the operations of foreign-owned enterprise are in a category of non-salaried or non-wage-earning activities, and it is to this category that subsequent comments apply.

In none of the Common Market countries are there basic rules prohibiting the recruitment of foreign personnel in connection with foreign investment. The application of statutory rules is left to the discretionary power of the administrative bodies in charge of the authorization of the employment of aliens.[2]

In Belgium, non-wage-earning activities accessible to foreigner

[1] For Community views on this point, see E.E.C. *Bulletin,* no. 12, 1964, pp. 10 ff. and 52.

[2] 'Aliens' and 'foreign' used in this text refer, of course, to persons from non-member countries; Community nationals will be subject, under the Treaty of Rome (Articles 48 ff.: labour, and 52 ff.: the right of establishment), to *national* treatment in all the member states. See G. le Tallec, in: *Rev. M.C.,* no. 72, September 1964, pp. 371 ff.

are regulated by the Law of 19 February 1965.[1] which prescribes that aliens must obtain a *carte professionnelle* from the Ministry of Economic Affairs (which is also in charge of questions related to foreign investment). As we have seen foreign directors and managers temporarily resident in Belgium enjoy special tax reductions related to expenses incurred as a result of their activities in the country.

In France, a *carte de commerçant* is required for aliens active in the country as managers or directors of companies, in addition to the residence permit connected with the entry and establishment of aliens in the country. (The latter requirement applies to all six member states.) In Germany, an approval concerning the appointment of aliens as directors or managers of a company will be issued in connection with the permission that a foreign company needs from the Federal Ministry of Economic Affairs for establishment in the given Land or Province.[2] Similar rules apply in Italy.[3] In Luxembourg, for managerial positions in foreign-owned enterprise a professional card will not be required; visa and residence permit formalities must be fulfilled.[4] The same applies for managerial activities in the Netherlands.[5]

In conclusion, it may be said that formalities and provisions governing the employment of alien personnel in managerial positions in the member countries of the E.E.C. are not prohibitive; they are moreover reduced to a minimum, even if in

---

[1] *Mon. Belge*, 26 February 1965.

[2] Sect. 12 of the Order on Trades and Professions (*Gewerbeordnung*) of 21 July 1869, as amended by the (4th) Law of 5 February 1960, and Sect. 292 of the Law on Joint-Stock Companies (*Aktiengesetz*). For the residence of aliens, see Police Order of 22 August 1938, RGBl, p. 1053, replaced by a new law adopted by the Bundestag on 12 February 1965 (*Le Monde*, 14–15 February 1965, p. 3).

Germany employs large numbers of foreign labour at the wage-earning level. The total was over one million or less than 5 per cent of the total labour force in 1964 (1954: 72,900 or 0·4 per cent). For a few details on labour in the E.E.C., see *Entreprise*, no. 483, 12 December 1964, pp. 53 ff.

[3] Orders of 18 June 1931 and 6 May 1940.

[4] On entry and visa, Law of 30 December 1893, as amended by the Law of 18 July 1913, and Order of 25 April 1945; the Law of 28 October 1920, the Orders of 30 November 1919, 21 February 1920 and 11 November 1936.

[5] For aliens' entry and residence in the Netherlands, Law of 13 August 1849 (Vremdelingenwet), Staatsblad no. 39, as amended on 21 December 1951 (Staatsblad no. 594); Laws of 17 June, 1918 and 10 January, 1920, as amended on 21 December 1951 (Staatsblad no. 594).

some of the member countries administrative formalities take longer to perform than in others; and they take into due consideration the technical need for alien personnel who can supervise the operations of foreign-owned enterprises at least in their initial years.

A matter related to municipal rules on alien employment is the status of foreign personnel under Community rules of establishment. Foreign managers or directors would not be, as individuals, entitled to the same free movement as nationals of states within the Community. In Article 54/3(f) of the Treaty of Rome, 'the progressive abolition of restrictions on freedom of establishment in every branch of activity under consideration' shall be effected by measures initiated by the Council and the Commission, 'both as regards the conditions for setting up agencies, branches or subsidiaries in the territory of a Member State and as regards the conditions governing the entry of personnel belonging to the main establishment into managerial or supervisory posts in such agencies, branches, and subsidiaries'. This text can be said to reflect an awareness of the technical necessity to transfer managerial or supervisory personnel to agencies, branches and subsidiaries. Now, under Articles 52 and 58 of the Treaty, foreign-owned enterprises 'formed in accordance with the law of a Member State and having their registered office, central administration or principal place of business within the Community shall . . . be treated in the same way as individual nationals of Member States'. If Article 54/3(f) is to apply to Community enterprises and their managerial or supervisory personnel, it is difficult to see how it could not also apply to foreign-owned enterprises which fulfil the requirements of Article 58/1, and to their (alien) managerial or supervisory personnel. Article 54 does not imply any differentiation between Community and non-member nationals but seems to have been inspired by the technical necessities that dictate the transfer of managerial or supervisory personnel. In fact, on the level of establishment within the Community, the Treaty does not apply the test of nationality or control once the requirements of Article 58 are satisfied. It should be added, on the other hand, that reference in Article 54/3(g) to 'the main establishment' refers to the content of Article 58/1 and cannot imply *any* main establishment *within or outside* the E.E.C. The right of establishment incorporated in Community law is a body of rules specifically governing *intermember* relationships and does not concern natural or legal persons situated *outside* the Community. Finally, the concrete implementation of Article 54/3(f) will be subject to the competence of the Council and the Commission 'as regards the conditions' under which managerial and supervisory personnel, including aliens, may be transferred from one member state to another.

Thus, in conclusion, the municipal liberalism affecting the employment of alien managerial or supervisory personnel will be supplemented by a corresponding liberalism on Community level, in the interest of investment activities that need the participation of qualified personnel, without regard to their origin or nationality.

# CHAPTER VIII

# MUNICIPAL LAW

## RESTRICTIVE PRACTICES

The law on restrictive practices in the Common Market is double-tiered. Within each of the member states, the respective municipal rules apply, but intermember trade is governed by the Community rules on competition. The Community law on restrictive practices is surveyed in chapter XII. In the present chapter the corresponding municipal laws are outlined in terms of their nature, scope and similarities.

## BELGIUM

In Belgium the law on restrictive practices is of recent origin and dates from 1960 when the Law on Protection against Abuse of Economic Power was passed.[1] It is functional in its approach as it aims at the prevention of abuse based on economic strength in a manner contrary to public interest. It does not prohibit, therefore, the establishment and existence of monopolies or cartels, since these do not constitute an abuse of economic power by themselves in the meaning of the law; their effects, and the public interest involved thereby, are the bases upon which the application of the law is founded. In application of the same principle of effect, abusive effects of a dominant position also fall under the provisions of the law.

The procedure provided for the implementation of the law is an administrative one: the qualification of given practices as 'abuse' is entrusted to a Reporting Commission led by a Reporting

---

[1] Law of 27 May 1960 (*Mon. Belge*, 22 June 1960, p. 4674). See also *Wirtschaft und Wettbewerb* (Düsseldorf), 1960, p. 704. For an English translation, O.E.C.D.: *Guide to Legislation on Restrictive Business Practices—Europe and North America*, Paris, 1964, vol. I, Belgium. For the history of the Law of 27 May 1960, see Ch. del Marmol: *La Protection contre les Abus de Puissance Economique en droit belge*, Liège, 1960. For a history of the Law and its enforcement since 1960, L. P. Suetens: 'Belgian Antitrust Law in action', *C.M.L. Rev.*, vol. 2, no. 3, December 1964, pp. 325–39.

Commissioner. He is appointed by the King from among members of the Public Prosecutors; other members are recruited from the judiciary or from the executive organs.[1] A Council for Economic Disputes, created in 1935[2] and attached to the Ministry of Economic Affairs, can intervene, when it is deemed to be necessary by the Council, in the findings of the Reporting Commission.[3] The final decision about a given case rests with the Minister for Economic Affairs.[4]

In case the Minister for Economic Affairs decides that action is warranted against an abuse of economic power, he makes binding recommendations to the persons or undertakings concerned. The recommendations made by the Minister become definitively binding when they are accepted by the persons concerned and duly published in the *Moniteur Belge*. If the persons or undertakings concerned cannot agree with the Minister's recommendations, the latter can take unilateral confirmatory action which becomes duly binding. If the ministerial recommendations are accepted by those concerned but there is subsequent failure to comply with them, a Royal Decree can be promulgated for the termination of the given abusive practices. Non-compliance with the requirements of a Royal Decree leads to imprisonment from eight days to one year, and/or a fine ranging from Bfrs. 10,000 to 1,000,000. Further abuses may lead to imprisonment terms between eight days and two years, and/or to fines equivalent to Bfrs. 10,000 to 2,000,000.[5]

A point of interest for foreign investors is the provision of Article 20/2 of the Law of 1960, according to which a principal will be liable for the payment of any fine incurred by any of its subsidiaries.

In summary, Belgian law on restrictive practices governs not the existence as such of monopolies, cartels and dominant positions but their effects to the extent that they amount to an abuse of economic power. The term 'abuse' is comprehensive and could

[1] Articles 3, 4–6, Law of 27 May 1960.

[2] Royal Decree no. 62, 13 January 1935. See Suetens, *C.M.L. Rev.* for details, pp. 327 f.

[3] Articles 7–9, 13, Law of 27 May 1960.

[4] Articles 13–14, Law of 27 May 1960. A negative opinion by the Council is binding for the Minister (Art. 13/3). For controversial aspects of implementing the law through judicial or administrative authorities, see Suetens, *C.M.L. Rev.*, pp. 337 f.

[5] Articles 18–20, Law of 27 May 1960.

include the negative effects of any dominant position. The broad
content of the term is necessitated by the non-existence of case
law in Belgium on restrictive practices, and by a need to adjust the
application of the law to economic necessities as required by
public interest, without subjecting it to the rigidity of a too
formal approach. The application and supervision of the law is in
charge of an administrative body. Its effects upon foreign-owned
enterprise consist not only in its application to any enterprise
active in Belgium, but also to the principal of such a subsidiary—
fines imposed on subsidiaries incur the liability for payment of
the principal companies irrespective of their location in or outside Belgium.


## FRANCE

The French law on restrictive practices is not a specialized law to
the extent found, for instance, in Germany. It is part of a larger
body of regulations that govern prices and commercial activities.
and as such constitute further rules on commercial offences.[1] Like
other offences, breaches of the law on restrictive practices are
punishable by heavy fines and imprisonment imposed by Commercial Courts. Action by the judiciary may, however, be averted
by agreement between the parties concerned, under the supervision of the Economic Enquiry Branch which acts as an administrative body.

The legislative instruments currently in force for restrictive
practices are the Decree of 9 August 1953, as amended by the
Decrees of 24 June 1958 and 17 August 1959; and the Finance
Act of 2 July 1963 (Arts. 3–4). They govern commercial practices
that discriminate, such as refusal to sell or making sale dependent
on the purchase of unwarranted goods or on a minimum quan-
tity, and fixing minimum resale prices, and the abuse of dominant
position.[2]

---

[1] See Ordinance No. 45-1483 (Arts. 37, 59bis ff.) and no. 45-1484 of
30 June 1945, as supplemented and amended by Decrees no. 53-704, of
9 August 1953, no. 58-545 of 24 June 1958 and no. 59-1004, of 17 August
1959, and by the Law no. 63-628 of 2 July 1963. Also Article 419 of the
Penal Code.

[2] Decree no. 54-97 embodying a Ministerial Order in application of the
provisions of Decree no. 53–704 of 9 August 1953, concerning the maintenance or restriction of free industrial and commercial competition. Also
Circular of 31 March 1960, on the prohibition of restrictive practices;

Selling practices are supervised by the Economic Enquiry Branch which acts as an administrative body. It enjoys complete freedom of action.[1] If it fails to induce the discontinuation of given practices, parties concerned may appeal to the court by a complaint lodged with the Public Prosecutor. As for cases involving abuses of dominant position, the approach taken is a functional one. It is irrelevant whether one or more undertakings are involved in them, if the effect of the practices in question is tantamount to (i) restraint on competition and (ii) an adverse effect on prices or on the normal activities of a given market. In both cases, the agreements or practices conducive to the said effects are prohibited and hence null and void under civil law. The same functional approach of the law provides for exceptions that are in accordance with legal provisions or result in their effect to a promotion of economic progress without prejudice to the public. The assessment of each situation considered for an exception is subject to the evaluation of the Technical Commission on Combines and Dominant Positions.[2] This Commission has a consultative function and submits advisory opinions to the Ministry of Economic Affairs. Its 14 members are recruited from the judiciary or from civil servants who have served in the economic departments of the government, representatives of trade and industry and economic experts. The Technical Commission on Combines and Dominant Positions takes action either through a request on the part of the Ministry of Economic Affairs or upon its own initiative. Its chairman appoints one or more Rapporteurs with extensive powers of investigation. A procedural requisite is that both sides of a complaint are to be heard.[3]

As in Belgium, a decision to pursue or drop a given case is taken by the Minister for Economic Affairs, based on the opinion submitted by the Technical Commission on Combines and

Law no. 63-628 of 2 July 1963, on the prohibition of loss leader selling and of misleading advertisement.

[1] Opinion of the Cour de Cassation, 19 November 1959, in: *Juris-Classeur periodique* (Paris), 1960, no. 11, p. 448; *Recueil Sirey*, Paris, 1960, p. 283.

[2] For opinions delivered by the Technical Commission on Combines, see J.O., edition for administrative documents, 1960, no. 11 (January 14), pp. 211-24. For comments on the same, see O.E.C.D., *Guide to Legislation on Restrictive Business Practices*, vol. III, France, pp. 3.1.0.–1 ff.

[3] Articles 1, 4, 7 and 10 Decree of no. 54-97 of 27 January 1954, as amended,

Dominant Positions. The decision of the Minister will be either to invite the parties concerned to discontinue the given practices; or to refer the case to a court. In practice, the first alternative is the one most frequently adopted.[1]

In summary, French rules on restrictive practices have a wide margin of application for the functional approach, through which practices or dominant position will fall under the law if they have any adverse effect on the market. The implementation of the existing rules is entrusted in the first place to administrative bodies attached to the Ministry of Economic Affairs, with the ultimate power of decision resting with the Minister. If an agreement or discontinuation of the practices concerned cannot be achieved, the matter may be referred to a court.

### GERMANY

The law on restrictive practices in Germany is based on the Law against Restraints of Competition of 27 July 1957; it was introduced to the Parliament in 1952 and underwent many amendments.[2] Its scope of application covers all types of formal or informal agreements which influence competition adversely (Sect. 1/1). It provides for a closer supervision on the part of authorities with a system of notification (Sect. 2/3). It distinguishes between permissible agreements and others which are conducive to abuse (Sect. 2/1). Permissible agreements must be characterized by a

---

[1] Ibid., Articles 17 ff. For a statement expressing the policy of the government on matters related to restrictive practices, see Circular of 31 March 1960, which is not, however, legally binding (on the courts or private persons). See Judgments of the Conseil d'Etat of 5 May 1961, 14 June 1961 (*Juris-Classeur périodique*, 1961–11–11, 135bis; *Gazette du Palais*, 1 September 1961, p. 411). For comments on the legislation, see O.E.C.D., *Guide to Legislation on Restrictive Business Practices*, vol. III, France, pp. 2.1 ff. For an application of the Finance Act of 2 July 1963, to a case on combines see J. O. (Docs. adm.), no. 12, 15 June 1964.

[2] Gesetz gegen Wettbewerbsbeschränkungen (GWB), 27 July 1957, BGBl, I, p. 1081. References in parenthesis within the text are to sections of this law. For an English translation, O.E.C.D.: *Guide to Legislation on Restrictive Business Practices*, vol. II, Germany. For commentaries, E. Langen: *Kommentar zum Kartellgesetz*, 3rd edn., Neuwied, 1958; H. Müller and G. Gries: *Kommentar zum GWB*, Frankfurt/Main, 1958; H. Müller-Henneberg and others: *GWB, Kommentar*, Köln, 1958; H. Rasch: *Wettbewerbsbeschränkungen gegen Kartell- und Monopolrecht. Kommentar*, Berlin, 1958; H. Kaufmann and others: *Kommentar zum GWB*, Köln, 1958.

uniform application of terms of trade and can become valid in the absence of objections raised by the Cartel Authority within a period of three months after notification. Thus, rebate cartels of a non-discriminatory nature are permissible (Sect. 3/1). Moreover, emergency cartels in times of crisis, authorized by the Federal Ministry of Economic Affairs, and rationalization or specialization cartels conducive to better standards of efficiency will be permissible (Sect. 5/2–3).[1] An important criterion for the positive evaluation of the latter is the benefit derived from them both for those undertakings which are directly concerned and for others competing in the given market (Sect. 5/3). Export cartels which do not interfere with competition on the domestic market will be allowed, but they have to be notified to the Federal Cartel Office. In case of interference with the domestic market, an authorization will be required (Sect. 6/1–3). As for import cartels, these will be permissible if they prove to be necessary for facing restrictive competition on the foreign suppliers' side. Again, however, such import cartels should not interfere significantly with competition on the domestic markets (Sect. 7). The above-mentioned cartel forms concern *horizontal* agreements (Sects. 1–14).

*Vertical* agreements, i.e. between participants on different levels, can be valid if they are in agreement with types specifically enumerated in Section 16 of the Law of 27 July 1957 and with provisions of civil law (Sects. 15–21).[2] Nevertheless, the Cartel Office is empowered to invalidate them whenever it deems it necessary to do so, as in the case of abuse (Sects. 17, 18, 26). Licensing agreements are valid as long as they concern the protection of the interest involved (Sects. 20–21).

As for market domination and concentration, the functional approach applies to them, whereby they are not *per se* prohibited if they are not coupled with an abuse (Sect. 22/3–4). This applies to monopolies or oligopolies (Sect. 22/1–2). All types of concentration are to be reported to the Cartel Office if 20 per cent or more of a given market is affected by the concentration or acquisition in question (Sect. 23). An acquisition of a share representing 25 per cent of the voting stock of an enterprise is equivalent to such a concentration (Sect. 23/5). A Bill for introducing amend-

---

[1] Emergency cartels are subject to an authorization by the Federal Ministry of Economic Affairs: *Wirtschafts- und Wettbe-werbsrecht*, 1959, Düsseldorf, p. 385.

[2] See also Sect. 826 of German Civil Code (BGB).

ments is in this respect being currently discussed by the Bunde-stag.[1]

Coercion or boycott and discrimination are prohibited *ab initio* (Sects. 25–26). Discrimination which does not go beyond the interests of parties concerned will not be interpreted as prohibited if it is not unfair (Sect. 26/2).

The administration of the law is entrusted in the first place to federal authorities, and is divided between the Federal Ministry of Economic Affairs, the Federal Cartel Office (in Berlin), and the Cartel authorities of the federal provinces (Sects. 8, 44, 48–50).[2]

Parties affected by restrictive practices do not have a direct right of action (Sect. 22), but can lodge a complaint with the Cartel Office to initiate action. A direct right to action may arise under Section 826 of the German Civil Code (BGB). Once the illegality of the given restrictive practices is established, the injured or affected parties may take direct action for sanctions or to obtain relief. The law provides also for the imposition of administrative fines (Sect. 38).

Since the German law on restrictive practices applies the criterion of effect on the domestic market, any agreement apt to have an adverse effect on the market, irrespective of its place of conclusion, will constitute a breach of the law (Sect. 98/2).

Among the municipal laws on restrictive practices reviewed under the present section so far, evidently Germany has the most specialized system. It has the functional approach in common with the systems in Belgium and France, but it provides for a closer supervision on the part of (cartel) authorities. The law defines the types of agreements that are permissible; but the ultimate decision

[1] The proposed amendment Bill provides for alternative criteria as a test of concentration. Accordingly, a minimum share of 20 per cent of the given market, *or* more than 10,000 persons employed, *or* turnover figures of at least DM. 500m yearly *or* a yearly balance sum of at least 1,000m DM. are the criteria envisaged. *Die Welt*, no. 60, 12 March 1965, p. 13.

[2] See also Verordnung über das Verfahren bei der Eintragung von Wettbewerbsregeln und über die Anlegung und Führung des Registers für Wettbewerbsregeln, 10 January 1958 (BGBl, I, p. 57) (Ordinance concerning the procedure of registration of competition rules and the establishment and keeping of the Registry for competition practices); and Verordnung über die Anlegung und Führung des Kartellsregisters, 15 January 1958 (BGBl, I, p. 59) (Ordinance concerning the establishment and keeping of the Cartel Registry).

M

rests with the authorities which have to be kept informed about both permissible and other types of agreements.

The system of implementation is largely administrative, and resembles basically those in Belgium and France, where ultimate appeal to a court is also possible.

## ITALY

Italy has neither a special law applicable to restrictive practices nor special machinery to deal with them.[1] The beginnings of legislation go back to 1932 when the Law no. 834 of 16 June 1932 was promulgated; it has been subsequently declared ineffective.[2] This Law concerned the formation and operation of trade associations within a given business sector. It was followed in 1937 by the Law no. 961 of 22 April, 1937 dealing with the voluntary trade associations for production and sale.

Provisions which are currently effective beyond doubt are Articles 2595–2620 of the Codice Civile, dealing with the regulation of competition and trade associations. They are based on the principle that free competition must be subordinated to public interest. Article 2595 reflects a functional approach by referring to the principle of abuse. Article 2596 regulates the conclusion of agreements which must be in written form, for a maximum duration of five years, and dealing with a specific area or branch of economic activity. Article 2597 applies the principle of non-discrimination, whereby persons or undertakings in control of a permissible monopoly are obliged to transact business without discrimination and supply the goods or services which they offer. A contrary attitude would amount to an abuse as defined in Article 2595 of the Codice Civile.

Article 2603 prescribes that an agreement for the establishment of a trade association must be made in writing, in order to be legally binding, and must specify its object. Its duration cannot exceed a maximum period of 10 years, but it is renewable (Art. 2604).

Articles 2359–2360 of the Codice Civile set limits to the formation of trusts. Thus, companies may not invest all or part of their capital in the shares of another company which controls them or

---

[1] For a summary of the historical background, see O.E.C.D., *Guide to Legislation on Restrictive Business Practices*, vol. IV, Italy, pp. 0.3 ff.

[2] Presidential Decree no. 1036, of 9 November 1958.

in the shares of other companies which they control. Such control will be deemed to be existent when a company holds shares of another to the extent of having a majority of votes in the stockholders' meeting or has a dominant influence over the other company. Hence, companies cannot mutually subscribe to each other's shares, even through third parties.

In Italy, therefore, as in France, the existing rules are part of the general law of commercial practices. They are incorporated in the Codice Civile, which, in Articles 1567–1568, contains also provisions on exclusive dealings.[1]

## LUXEMBOURG

There is no municipal law on restrictive practices.

## THE NETHERLANDS

The beginnings of legislation in the Netherlands on restrictive practices go back to 1935 when some supervision of industrial groupings favourable or unfavourable to national economy was envisaged. The Law on Economic Competition now in force dates from 1956, though it came into force in 1958. It regulates competition through agreements and governs the limits of influence exercised on the basis of a dominant position.[2] Its approach is basically a functional one, since it does not condemn monopolistic tendencies *ab initio* but gives the government the right to intervene whenever warranted by public interest. On the other hand, the government can approve a cartel by qualifying it as binding upon all undertakings in the given sector of activities (Sect. 7).

The control machinery set up for the implementation of the law is one consisting of administrative authorities and the judiciary; the function of the courts is a supervisory one in respect to the legality of administrative acts. Courts control the policy of the administrative authorities but they do not participate in the creation or development of a cartel policy (Sect. 33 ff.).[3]

[1] R. Morera in: *Le Droit Européen*, no. 53, 1963, pp. 297 ff.
[2] Wet economische mededinging (Law on economic competition) (Staatsblad, 1958, p. 413), Sect. 1/1. Subsequent references within the text under this heading are to Sections of this law.
[3] Also Wet regelende het berope tegen beschikkingen krachtens de Wet economische mededinging (Staatsblad, 1958, p. 412).

Cartel agreements are subject to registration, from which exemptions are possible (Sect. 4). The Ministry of Economic Affairs, the administrative authority in charge of the government's cartel policy, may qualify given agreements as ineffective if these are deemed to be contrary to public interest (Sect. 5).[1]

As for the abuse of a dominant position, the nature of its prohibition is similar to the one in force in the other member states of the Common Market (Sect. 24).

The basic principles of the law on restrictive practices in the Netherlands are the same as in the other E.E.C. states where rules in this respect exist (Luxembourg is the exception). The language used is broad and adaptable to economic necessities as required by public interest. The main responsibility for supervision rests with an administrative body, beside which the courts have a controlling function to guarantee the legality of administrative acts.

## CONCLUSIONS

In five of the six member countries (i.e. with the exception of Luxembourg) legislative instruments for regulating economic and trade competition exist in different forms. In France and Italy, the law is part of the larger body of rules governing commercial and industrial life. In Belgium, and the Netherlands, special legislation exists as in Germany where the relevant law is the most elaborate of all.

These five member states apply the functional approach, in the light of which the effect of practices is the decisive factor in invalidating a given agreement or practice. With a limited background and experience of case law, concepts incorporated in the rules, such as abuse, dominant position, are interpreted as having a broad content. This system offers the advantage of flexibility and adaptation to changing market conditions and to public interest and avoids the rigidity of a too legalistic approach.

The emphasis for the implementation of the law is on administrative bodies, thus reserving the judiciary as a last resort after earlier efforts or measures of agreement or discontinuation fail. The use of an administrative machinery is thus apt to be more economical in terms of time and money than one dependent on the judiciary.

[1] See Sects. 28 and 29 for the Economic Competition Committee. Its members are appointed and removed by the Crown.

The relevance of the respective rules to foreign-owned enterprise or subsidiaries rests on the principle of functional approach, in accordance with which the end effect of a certain practice or agreement on a given municipal market and not the place where such action could have been planned or effected, will be the decisive element for governmental intervention or action. This is very clearly expressed in the German system, for instance in respect to export and import cartels. A further point of relevance for the foreign investor is the fact that, if he has extensive activities within the Common Market, he will have to observe within it *six* different sets of rules on restrictive practices, five on a municipal and one on a Community level. Within each of the member states, the respective municipal system will be effective, while for trade between member states, the Community rules on competition (Articles 85 ff. of the Treaty of Rome) will be applicable.

It may be suggested that with the progressive alignment of economic and trading standards throughout the Community, an ultimate alignment of municipal rules on competition will also be gradually effected, though this may not be urgent. If some of the member states, for one reason or other, decide to elaborate the presently existing municipal rules, for example on export or import cartels, they may create rules that present a similarity to the intermember rules of Community law. Such a correspondence already exists between the export and import cartel rules of German law and the intermember rules of the E.E.C.; in case of divergence between the two sets, Community law will prevail.

## Industrial Property: Patents

In the period following the Second World War, the international flow of private investment capital has been accompanied by an important parallel flow of technological skill, as shown by the example of many American and other foreign firms investing in the Common Market. The investing companies are equipped not only with monetary capital, but also with valuable assets in the form of new industrial processes that have been developed through systematic research. The need for new processes has influenced the magnitude of international capital movements and the size of activities in the host countries.

The impact of the international exchange of technological skill has been beneficial for both investors and host countries. The use of patents and licensing agreements constitute an important part of the investment picture in a region like the E.E.C. According to one report, in 1964, France spent 450m US dollars more for the use of foreign patents than she received for the use of French patents abroad; the corresponding figures for Germany and Italy were respectively 600m and 176m US dollars.[1] These figures have been interpreted as indicative of a 'technological gap'; and competition between more efficient foreign enterprise and domestic enterprise exposed to the pressure of foreign technological skill has been an object of concern in some of the member states of the Common Market, e.g. in France and Germany. The situation reflects, it has been claimed, the (undesirable) technical dependence of the Common Market on foreign technological skill.[2] Whatever the extent of this dependence may be, the current situation clearly illustrates how both monetary and technological assets play an important role in international investment.

In the sphere of legal matters, the international exchange of industrial property is dependent on rules that govern the protection of such property and the transfer of income therefrom. The question of transfer in respect of royalties is related to regulations governing exchange control and the availability of foreign currency. Exchange control regulations in the E.E.C. countries, in their relevance to foreign investment and the transfer of investment income accruing from royalties have been examined above in chapter IV. It is now necessary to outline the laws of patents of the Common Market countries in order to indicate the way they contribute to the favourable investment climate of the E.E.C.

All six member states of the E.E.C. are partners to the Paris Convention on Patents of 20 March 1883:[3] Belgium, France, Italy and the Netherlands since 7 July 1884; Germany since 1 May 1903 and Luxembourg since 30 June 1922.[4] Article 2 of the Convention stipulates that a country party to it shall extend the

---

[1] *Newsweek*, 8 March 1965, p. 48. For some details concerning Germany, see *Commerce in Germany*, no. 128, August 1964, p. 5.

[2] *Le Monde*, 7–8 February 1965, p. 9. See chapter XI below, on competition between foreign and domestic enterprise in the E.E.C.

[3] As revised in Brussels (14 December 1900), Washington (2 June 1911), The Hague (6 November 1925), London (2 June 1934), Lisbon (31 October 1958). The current text of the Paris Convention is effective since 4 January 1962.

[4] W. W. White and B. G. Ravenscroft: *Patents throughout the World*, New York, 1963 (loose-leaf).

same protection of industrial property both to its nationals and to nationals of other signatory countries.

In summary of a review of the laws of patents:

i. Patents of invention are granted for a period of 20 years after application in Belgium, France and Luxembourg; for a period of 18 years after application in Germany and the Netherlands; for a period of 15 years after application in Italy.

ii. The patentee may be an individual or a company, and application may be lodged through an assignee in all of the six member states, but an *assignment* will be required in Germany and Luxembourg. If an assignee applies under the International Convention, an assignment will be required in five of the member states, i.e. with the exception of the Netherlands.

iii. Examination as to *novelty* is prescribed in two of the member states, viz., Germany and the Netherlands.

iv. There are no *opposition* provisions in four of the member states, viz., Belgium, France, Italy, and Luxembourg, the exceptions being Germany and the Netherlands, where the opposition periods are respectively three and four months.

v. The *application* of a granted patent must be effected within three years in five of the six member states. The exception is Belgium, where working within one year is required; three years, however, under the Paris Convention. The use of a patent when granted should not be discontinued for more than 12 consecutive months in Belgium, and for three consecutive years in France and Italy. In four of the six member states, the patentee may be compelled to grant a licence, viz., France, Germany, Luxembourg and the Netherlands.

While a foreign applicant finds a properly functioning law of patents and trademarks[1] in each of the six member states, within the context of the progressive integration of the E.E.C. the existence of six different sets of rules on the protection of industrial property raises a number of problems for a foreign investor entering the E.E.C. for the exploitation of technological skill which is his property. The administrative chore of applying for patents in each of the six countries will be inevitable; but this would not be his major difficulty. The major problems will be

---

[1] For the law of trademarks in the E.E.C. countries, see W. W. White and B. G. Ravenscroft: *Trade Marks throughout the World*, New York, 1963 (looseleaf).

related to the divergence between the substantive rules as they are applied to patenting in each of the member states.[1] The difficulties inherent in the current situation have been recognized and work is progressing on Community level for the introduction of a Community patent law which will be in force together with the co-existing national patent laws. While the advantages of a Community patent law are beyond doubt as far as Community nationals are concerned, the benefits that would thereby accrue to foreign investors are still open to debate. It is not yet settled whether non-member countries will be allowed to join the planned Patent Convention; in case of an affirmative reply, another major question concerns the co-ordination of the planned Patent Convention with the national patent laws of the respective non-member countries.

The economic aspects of foreign patents in the E.E.C. do not present particular problems. The deficit due to royalties remitted abroad can be easily borne by the favourable position of balance of payments of the E.E.C. countries. This fact contrasts with the situation in developing regions of the world. The question of competition between foreign and domestic technological skill is, however, one that equally exists in the E.E.C. If the inflow of foreign capital is indicative of the availability of investment funds abroad and of opportunities for their use in the E.E.C., so is the greater inflow of technological knowledge in the form of patents and licensing agreements an indication that there is a 'patent or technological gap' in a region like the E.E.C., compared with the United States. The existence of such a gap is at the root of concern expressed in respect of American enterprise. It reflects the competitive pressure which is being generated by the activities of foreign undertakings in many cases better equipped, technologically, than their homologous domestic undertakings. It involves the question of whether the legal organization in the E.E.C. is adequate to regulate the resulting competition: Does it adequately

---

[1] For particular aspects of problems related to patents and trademarks under the current system in the E.E.C., S. Delvalle Goldsmith: 'Difficulties facing American business in patent applications in Europe', in: *Doing Business in the Common Market*, Chicago, 1963 (addresses presented at the Eur. Common Market Conference at the Nat. Law Center, The Georgetown Washington University, Washington D.C., 9–10 April 1963), pp. 107 ff. R. D. Lippman: 'American business interests and a uniform Common Market Trademark Law', in: *A.J.C.L.*, Spring 1963, pp. 255 ff.

provide for the adaptation and development of domestic undertakings concerned to meet the given challenge? This question is
under discussion in the E.E.C.[1] It constitutes in fact another legal
aspect related to foreign investments, as it may necessitate the
revision of existing legal rules affecting technological research and
the creation of firms of a Community size. It concerns the legal
control of competition between foreign and domestic firms. These
points are elaborated in the section on the harmonization of laws
in the E.E.C. in their relevance to foreign investment in chapter
XII.

## GENERAL CONCLUSIONS ON THE STATUS OF FOREIGN INVESTMENTS UNDER THE MUNICIPAL LAW OF COMMON MARKET COUNTRIES

Having up to this point surveyed the status and treatment of
foreign investment in each of the six member states of the E.E.C.,
we can now see the similarities in the rules and administrative
formalities of the various states. All member states have sectors of
economic activities which they hold to be of public and national
importance; chief amongst these is the sector of public utilities
which are not accessible for domestic and foreign private capital
or for foreign capital alone. In some other sectors, the participation of foreign capital is subject to certain conditions which also
govern the degree of penetration of the given sectors by foreign
capital. Outside these sectors there is, however, a large margin of
economic activities in which foreign investment may participate.
This is best illustrated by the total amount of foreign, especially
American, capital operating in the E.E.C. and its leading position
in certain industrial fields, such as electronics and chemicals in
France, which certain Community industrialists believe should be
dominated, in the interest of the E.E.C. countries, by domestic
enterprises. It also indicates how attractive the Common Market
is for financially and technologically well-equipped foreign investors and how favourable the legal conditions in E.E.C. countries are towards the operations of foreign-owned firms in the
Community.

The legal and administrative treatment of foreign enterprise in
the member states of the E.E.C. is characterized by a barrier

[1] *Newsweek*, 8 March 1965, p. 48; *Le Monde*, 7–8 February 1965, p. 9.

beyond which, once admitted, foreign investors become entitled to national treatment. The barrier in question is the one of initial establishment and exchange control regulations. Beyond this stage, foreign capital becomes entitled to national treatment.

The municipal company laws do not discriminate against foreign investors. Ownership and management of undertakings can be arranged at investors' choice in most cases. Technical requirements of personnel peculiar to foreign undertakings can be satisfied as there are practically no restrictions concerning the appointment of foreigners to managerial posts. The fiscal systems do not have punitive aspects in their application to foreign-owned undertakings. Numerous bilateral double taxation agreements with non-member countries offer advantages to foreign investors. Investment incentives apply equally to foreign-owned firms; the sole criterion applied in this connection is the one of the functional utility of a given enterprise for the economy of the member state concerned. The law of industrial property contributes its share to the legal components of the favourable investment climate in the E.E.C. Not least, the favourable foreign exchange position of the member countries enables the transfer of investment profits or of disinvested capital.

In all six member states, a guarantee is nearly always obtainable for the re-transfer abroad of assets brought into the country. This implies the legal obligation to allow and provide for the repatriation of invested capital independently of non-legal factors that may later affect the foreign exchange situation. In two member states, Belgium and Luxembourg, an investor can choose between official and free exchange markets, conditions of guarantee applying obviously on the official exchange market to investments approved by the authorities.

The legal aspects we have reviewed together constitute that element of certainty and predictability which is the particular contribution that law can make to economic life and international investment. The investment climate of the E.E.C. is characterized as a whole by properly functioning and dependable legal rules which are not exposed to the disturbing effects of political factors, and together with the economic aspects of the E.E.C. make the Common Market highly attractive to foreign investment. This is supplemented by advantages that Community law offers to foreign investors. In addition to the opportunities offered by the municipal laws and economies of the member states and by the

expanding economy of the E.E.C. as a whole, the law of the
E.E.C. itself adds new dimensions to the favourable status of
foreign-owned undertakings in the Common Market. The extent
to which provisions of the Treaty of Rome apply to foreign investors is the topic of Part II of this study.

## CHAPTER IX

# THE PROTECTION OF FOREIGN INVESTMENT AND JUDICIAL CONTROL OF INVESTMENT DISPUTES

The legal system that ensures the protection of foreign investment and investors' rights in the E.E.C is characterized, as we might expect, by a plurality of rules and institutions. First, under municipal law, separate constitutional provisions and judicial systems prevail in each of the six member states. Secondly, certain rights and interests are protected by Community law, under which disputes are subject to the jurisdiction of the Court of Justice of the European Communities. Thirdly, the protection of foreign investment falls also within the ambit of the European Convention for the Protection of Human Rights and Fundamental Freedoms. The mutual delimitation and supplementation of the rules of the several institutions involved in this subject are worthy of consideration.

In the context of this chapter the terms 'expropriation' and 'nationalization' refer to action taken by virtue of sovereign power as a result of which a foreign investor is dispossessed of his property in the host country.[1] 'Nationalization differs in its scope and extent rather than in its juridical nature from other types of expropriation.' Nationalization 'usually signifies expropriation in pursuance of some national or political programme

---

[1] B. A. Wortley: *Expropriation in Public International Law*, Cambridge, 1959, p. 36. For further definitions, I. Foighel: *Nationalization—a Study in the Protection of Alien Property in International Law*, Copenhagen, 1957, pp. 13 ff.; I. Seidl-Hohenveldern: *Internationales Konfiskations- und Enteignungsrecht*, publ. Max-Planck Institut für Ausländisches und Internationales Privatrecht, Beiträge no. 23, Tübingen, 1952, pp. 5, 173 ff.; K. Katzarov: *Théorie de la Nationalisation* (Travaux et Recherches de l'Institut de Droit Comparé de l'Université de Paris, no. 17). Neuchâtel, 1960, p. 226; M. Domke, in *A.J.I.L.*, vol. 55, 1961, p. 587; F. Münch: 'Les effets d'une nationalisation à l'étranger', *Rec. ADI* 1959 (III), pp. 418, 419 f. For definitions similar to that used by Wortley, see Sir Gerald Fitzmaurice and F. Castberg, in *Ann. de L'Inst. de Dr. Int.*, vol. 44, ii, 1952, pp. 255 and 265 respectively; contra, see G. Scelle, ibid., p. 26 f.

PROTECTION OF FOREIGN INVESTMENT 165

intended to create out of existing enterprises, or to strengthen, a
nationally controlled industry'.[1]

## THE PROTECTION OF FOREIGN INVESTMENT UNDER MUNICIPAL LAW

The Treaty of Rome established a double-tiered system of
municipal and Community law in the E.E.C. without affecting
matters related to expropriation. Member states have not re-
linquished under the Treaty any of their sovereign rights in
respect of nationalization. Article 222 of the Treaty clearly de-
limits the competence of Community law in this respect by stating
that the Treaty 'shall in no way prejudice existing systems and
incidents of ownership (*propriété*)'.[2] Community law has recognized the principle accepted in international law that states may
expropriate or nationalize private property within their respective
territories.[3] This recognition has been effected without any reference to the limitations or conditions that international law imposes
in respect of nationalization concerning the public interest, due
process of law and compensation for expropriated foreign property. Indeed it is difficult to see how such a reference could have
been included in a legal instrument like the Treaty of Rome which
governs trade and economic activities and not ownership of
property under municipal law. For the purpose of Community
law, nationalization *per se* is a matter which falls completely outside the business of the Treaty. This implies, however, a major
reservation: expropriation remains outside the operation of
Community law and the jurisdiction of the Community Court of
Justice only if it is genuine, that is, is in accordance with inter-

---

[1] B. A. Wortley, *Expropriation in Pub. Int. Law*, p. 36. On the subject of
nationalization in general, Wortley, op. cit., especially pp. 115 ff.; *Ann. de
l'Inst. de Dr. Int.*, vol. 44, ii, 1952, p. 251; records of the conference on international aspects of nationalization (Int. Bar Assoc., 1954); Nwogugu, *Legal
Problems of Foreign Investment*, p. 21; Katzarov, *Théorie de la Nationalisation*.

[2] For comments see Campbell and Thompson, *Common Market Law*, p. 297;
T. L. Nicholson, in: *American Enterprise in the Eur. Common Market*, Stein
and Nicholson, eds., vol. 2, p. 177; J. Thiesing: in Groeben and Boeckh,
*Kommentar*, vol. 1, p. 264, also vol. 2.

[3] On ownership, sovereignty and expropriation, see Wortley, *Expropriation in Pub. Int. Law*, pp. 12 ff.; Nwogugu, *Legal Problems of Foreign Investment*,
pp. 21 ff.; Foighel, *Nationalization*, pp. 72–3; G. White: *Nationalization of
Foreign Property*, London, 1961, pp. 32 ff.; Katzarov, *Théorie de la Nationalisation*, pp. 387 f.

national law and not a disguised attempt to diminish the effective-ness of the Treaty of Rome. For instance, if the nationalization act of a member state affects the property and ability to do business under the Community right of establishment of non-nationals only, such nationalization will come within Community law.

In a concrete case related to a nationalization act in Italy, the Court of Justice of the European Communities tacitly applied Article 222 of the Treaty of Rome. The Court did not discuss the merits of nationalization as such, but dealt with its different aspects in so far as they possibly affected the functioning of the Common Market. Under (Italian) Law no. 1643 of 6 December 1962, and subsequent decrees, the Italian Republic had national-ized the production and distribution of electric energy and trans-ferred the property of the undertakings concerned to E.N.E.L. (Ente Nazionale per l'Energia Elettrica), a new organization created for the purpose. In its decision on the case (*Costa v. Ente Nazionale per l'Energia Elettrica*, no. 6-64, 15 July 1964), the Court of Justice did not refer to the validity of nationalization as such, but to the effects of the nationalization act in so far as they concerned the operation of the Common Market. If provisions ancillary to nationalization produce a distorting effect on trade between member states, then their incompatibility with Commun-ity law can be examined by the Court.[1] In so far as the transfer of property from private to public ownership is concerned, no com-petence is given to the Court. The question of invalidity of the expropriation cannot arise under Community law. Substantive rules affecting the protection of private property, domestic or foreign, are part of municipal law in the E.E.C. and of other international legal rules that are not related to Community law.

## CONSTITUTIONAL PROVISIONS

The protection of private property is anchored in all six member states in constitutional provisions. These provisions enunciate

[1] The Court of Justice examined the nationalization law in respect of arguments submitted by the plaintiff (Costa) and with reference to the con-tents of Treaty Article 102 (distortion of competition in the Common Market), Article 93 (state aid), Article 53 (the right of establishment), and Article 37 (state monopolies). In the Court's opinion, the nationalization act of the Italian government did not have any aspects incompatible with the provisions of the above articles. See *Costa v. E.N.E.L.* in Common Market Law Reports, vol. III, Part 12, December 1964.

that (i) expropriation shall be effected in the public interest; (ii) it shall be subject to due process of law; and (iii) it shall be dependent on just and previously determined compensation.

Article 11 of the Belgian constitution of 7 February 1831 (as amended) reads: 'No one may be deprived of his property except for a public purpose and according to the forms established by law, and in consideration of a just compensation previously determined.'[1] The French constitution of 4 October 1958[2] has integrated the Declaration of the Rights of Man and of the Citizen of 26 August 1789, Article 17 of which states: 'The right to property being inviolable and sacred, no one shall be deprived of it, except in cases of evident public necessity, legally ascertained, and on condition of a previous just indemnity.'[3] The integration of this text is based on the Preamble of the constitution of 28 September 1946, which has remained unchanged in the constitution of 1958. In its first paragraph it sets out: 'Le peuple français proclame solennellement son attachement aux Droits de l'Homme et aux Principes de la souveraineté nationale tels qu'ils ont été définis par la Déclaration de 1789, confirmée et completée par la préambule de la Constitution de 1946.'[4] The Preamble emphasizes the sovereign right of expropriation in the public interest: 'All property and all enterprises that now have or subsequently shall have the character of a national public service or a monopoly in fact must become the property of the community'; the same Preamble refers to international law and affirms that 'the French Republic, faithful to its traditions, abides by the rules of international law'.[5] No similar reference can be found in the Belgian constitution.

The Basic Law of Germany of 23 May 1949 guarantees the sanctity of property and the right of inheritance thereto, but

---

[1] A. J. Peaslee: *Constitutions of Nations*, 2nd edn., The Hague, 1956, vol. 1, p. 154; cf. also Articles 12 and 128.

[2] J.O., 5 October 1958.

[3] Peaslee, *Constitutions*, vol. 2, p. 21.

[4] J. Chatelain: *La Nouvelle Constitution et le Régime Politique de la France*, 2nd rev. edn., Paris, 1959, p. 360.

[5] Peaslee, *Constitutions*, vol. 2, pp. 6 and 7; also United Nations, General Assembly (VIII), Fourth Committee, 370th meeting (17 November 1953) for the statement of the French representative: 'Le droit public français repose sur le principe constitutionnel de la supériorité du droit international sur les lois internes.' Reported also in A.-Ch. Kiss: *Répertoire de la Pratique Française en Matière de Droit International Public*, vol. 1, Paris, 1962.

proclaims that property shall simultaneously serve the general welfare and as such it may involve limitations (Art. 14/1 and 2).[1] Expropriation in the public interest and by legislation is admissible, but the law concerned 'shall regulate the nature and extent of compensation' (Art. 14/3). German constitutional law is more specific than Belgian and French constitutional law about the nature and extent of compensation. Both aspects 'shall be determined after just consideration of the interests of the general public and the participants'. While the determination of compensation is left to legislative and administrative authorities, the control of compensation disputes is subject to the competence of ordinary courts to whom appeal may be made (Arts. 14/3 and 15). It is noteworthy that a concurrent legislative power is vested in both the federal and provincial (Länder) authorities concerning matters of expropriation specified by the Basic Law (Arts. 74 and 14). These can easily concern foreign property. Finally, similarly to the French constitution, Article 25 of the German Basic Law of 1949 proclaims that 'the general rules of international law shall form part of the federal law', and adds that general rules of international law 'shall take precedence over the laws and create rights and duties directly for the inhabitants of the federal territory'.

The constitution of Italy of 1 January 1948 distinguishes between public and private property.[2] 'Economic assets belong to the State, to institutions, or to private persons.' The law specifies the limits within which private property may be acquired and enjoyed, 'in order to assure its social function . . .' As under Belgian, French and German constitutional provisions, expropriation for reasons of public interest is subject to the due process of law providing for compensation. In Article 43 the Italian constitution refers to 'certain enterprises or categories of enterprises which relate to essential public services or to sources of energy or to monopolistic conditions and which are of pre-eminent general interest in character'. It is noteworthy that the French and Italian constitutions apply the principle of public interest in specific provisions dealing with the property and undertakings that have the character of a national public service or a monopoly. Under French and Italian law they are *per se* of pre-eminent general interest.

---

[1] Peaslee, *Constitutions*, vol. 2, p. 32.
[2] Law of 1 January 1948, Article 42. See Peaslee, *Constitutions*, vol. 2, p. 487.

The constitution of the Grand Duchy of Luxembourg of 17 October 1868 provides under Article 16 that expropriation may be effected for the public use in the manner established by law and upon just and prior indemnity.[1] The corresponding clauses of the Dutch constitution of 24 August 1815, as amended,[2] are similar to those in the other member states: expropriation can take place (i) for reasons of public utility, (ii) under previous declaration by law and (iii) against previously received or assured compensation. 'The requirement that the compensation shall be paid or assured beforehand shall not apply if war, danger of war, riot, fire or flood require that possession be taken immediately.'[3]

As far as the protection of property under the constitutional provisions of the Common Market countries is concerned, it can be concluded that there is general agreement among them. All of them make expropriation dependent upon justification for a public purpose,[4] upon prior legislative authorization and upon compensation.[5] The French and Italian constitutions specify that undertakings and utilities which fulfil essential public functions, or which occupy a monopolistic position, may be transferred into public ownership.

The presence of adequate constitutional provisions for the protection of private property in the member states of the E.E.C. eliminates the necessity of involved discussions about the principle of 'equal treatment' between domestic and foreign nationals.[6] Equality of treatment does indeed exist but in respect of compensation to be paid to foreigners as well as to domestic nationals. In addition, in terms of general principles of international law, with respect to the E.E.C. countries the inference is justified that since the constitutional provisions reviewed above concern foreign property as well, the international legal principle of expropriation in the public interest, by due process of law against compensation, is well established in the E.E.C. This principle has

[1] Ibid., p. 645.
[2] Ibid., pp. 754 ff.
[3] Constitution of 24 August 1815, Articles 158, 159 and 160.
[4] For a discussion on the meaning of public utility in France, see Wortley, *Expropriation in Pub. Int. Law*, pp. 25 f.
[5] On compensation in case of expropriation, cf. Wortley, *Expropriation*, pp. 23 f., 115 ff., 117; Nwogugu, *Legal Problems of Foreign Investment*, pp. 23, 56 f.; A. A. Fatouros: *Government Guarantees to Foreign Investors*, New York, 1962, pp. 164 ff., 168 f., 302 ff., 325 ff., 331 ff.
[6] In this connection see Wortley, *Expropriation*, pp. 120 ff.

N

been concretely applied in cases of nationalization after 1945 in member states like France and Italy, and in cases involving the recognition of nationalization acts before the municipal courts of member states and in the relations of member states with non-member countries. A few examples are quoted below. Public enterprise in a member state like France goes back to the eighteenth century (e.g. gunpowder factories, gobelin workshops).[1] A major development in nationalized industries took place in the decade preceding the Second World War, particularly in France, Germany and Italy. In the post-war period, important nationalizations were effected in France (car factories, mineral fuels). The latest nationalization in the E.E.C. (of electric power generation and supply industry) took place in December 1962 in Italy.[2]

With the exception of a few expropriations of a penal nature and therefore without compensation, nationalizations in the post-war period in France have all been accompanied by compensation which was higher for foreigners than for French nationals. The confiscatory expropriations without compensations were effected on grounds of collaboration with the enemy during the occupation of France.[3] The remaining nationalizations with compensation affected the Gnome motor factories,[4] banking,[5] electricity

[1] For a general article on the topic of nationalized industries in western Europe, see C. Jones, in: *European Community*, no. 5, May 1965, pp. 6 f.

[2] On nationalization in France see M. Waline: *Traité Elémentaire de Droit Administratif français*, 5th edn., Paris, 1950, Laws on nationalization, pp. 294 ff.; B. Chenot: *Les Entreprises nationalisées*, Paris, 1956; Wortley, *Expropriation*, pp. 25 f., 29, 118 ff.; M. Einaudi and others: *Nationalization in France and Italy*, Ithaca, 1955. In Germany public ownership is ramified with various majority and minority shareholdings by the federal, regional and local governments; see Jones, in: *European Community*, no. 5, May 1965, p. 7. On expropriation in Germany, see P. Leverkuehn: *Die Nationalisierung und das Privateigentum*, Beiträge zum öffentlichen Recht, Berlin–Tübingen, 1950, pp. 773–90. For nationalization in Italy, Einaudi, op. cit.; *Neue Zürcher Zeitung*, 21 August 1958, on Italian public participation in economic activities. In Belgium, Luxembourg and the Netherlands, public enterprise is limited to the category of public utilities, in contrast to large public participation in the manufacturing industries in France, Germany and Italy; see Jones, op. cit., and R. Bailey, in: *The Spectator*, 6 April 1962, pp. 434 f.

[3] For the nationalization of the Renault car factories, see J.O., 17 January 1945, p. 222. For other firms affected by confiscatory expropriation, see Einaudi, *Nationalization in France and Italy*, pp. 34 and 76.

[4] Ordinance of 29 May 1945, J.O., 30 May 1945, p. 3082, Article 2.

[5] Law of 2 December 1945, J.O., 3 December 1945, p. 8001, Articles 2 and 8.

and gas works,[1] 35 insurance companies,[2] and mineral fuels.[3] Compensation was in the first place in the form of redeemable interest bonds in return for expropriated shareholdings. The compensation value of shares in coal companies was based on an average price multiplied by certain coefficients.[4] Under compensation agreements, France undertook to indemnify foreign shareholdings.[5] In Italy, as a result of the nationalization that affected the electric power industry in December 1962, the Government undertook to pay the equivalent of 2,400m US dollars over a period of ten years.[6] In the Netherlands the central bank was nationalized in accordance with the Law of 14 June 1947. The expropriated shareholders received compensation in the form of government stock that had an interest rate of 2 per cent up to an amount representing double the nominal value of each share.

While constitutional provisions in France and Italy prescribe compensation in case of nationalization, the application of *adequate*, *prompt* and *effective* compensation in the examples mentioned above has been a debatable one. This fact has been pointed out by a number of authors[7] and as it involves extensive reference to different economic and legal arguments it will not be examined here in detail. It is sufficient to state that the types of compensation in question may be considered as complying with the minimum of international law, as regards France, Italy and the Netherlands, in the post-war period.

---

[1] Law of 8 April 1946, J.O., 8–9 April 1946, p. 2951, Articles 9, 10, 11 ff.

[2] Law of 25 April 1946, J.O., 29–30 April 1946, p. 3566. For list of companies, Article 1; for compensation clauses, Articles 7, 9 ff.

[3] Law of 17 May 1946, J.O., 18 May 1946, p. 4272, Articles 11 ff.

[4] Wortley, *Expropriation*, pp. 118–19; Fatouros, *Government Guarantees*, pp. 320–1; White, *Nationalization of Foreign Property*, pp. 204–5.

[5] Following the nationalization of gas and electricity undertakings in 1946, France concluded compensation agreements with Belgium (18 February 1949) (U.N.T.S., vol. 31, p. 173), Canada (26 January 1951) (J.O., 6 May 1951), Switzerland (21 November 1949) (*Annuaire Suisse de Droit International*, vol. 7, p. 136), the United Kingdom (11 April 1951) (U.N.T.S., vol. 106, p. 3).

[6] *Moody's Municipal and Governmental Manual* 1965, p. 2925.

[7] Wortley, *Expropriation*, p. 119; Fatouros, *Government Guarantees*, p. 321; Katzarov, *Théorie de la Nationalisation*, p. 417. On the topic of compensation, see also M. Domke; in *A.J.I.L.*, vol. 55, 1961, pp. 603 ff.; White, *Nationalization of Foreign Property*, pp. 15–17, 183 ff., 235 ff.

THE POLICY OF MUNICIPAL COURTS AND GOVERNMENTS

In addition to the concrete cases of post-war nationalization in France, Italy and the Netherlands in which compensation was paid, municipal courts in the E.E.C. have dealt with the question of validity of expropriation without compensation.

In Belgium, the Commercial Court at Brussels held in *Lowit v. Banque de la Société Générale de Belgique* (1939) that an expropriation effected in Germany without indemnity conflicted with Article 11 of the Belgian constitution and as such could have no effect in Belgium.[1] French courts have refused to recognize the validity of expropriation or nationalization without compensation. In the case of *Compagnie Nord de Moscou v. Phenix Espagnol*, the Court of Appeal of Paris argued in 1928 that expropriation without compensation (in the Soviet Union) was opposed to the respect of private property embodied in French law.[2] In 1956, the Tribunal de Commerce de la Seine noted favourably, in *Ilitch v. Banque Franco-Serbe*, that by Article 8 of the nationalization law, the Yugoslav government undertook to compensate the owners of nationalized enterprises.[3] In 1958, the Court of Appeal of Paris denied any extra-territorial effect to expropriation without compensation in Czechoslovakia. In the opinion of the Court, such an expropriation was incompatible with French public policy.[4]

In Germany, the policy followed by courts is not uniform. The extra-territorial effects of confiscatory measures in East Germany are generally accepted by German courts.[5] There are, on the other hand, a few cases in which the incompatibility of confiscatory expropriation with international law or German public policy is maintained by courts.[6] A line followed by the High Court of Bremen seems to admit first the existence of a general principle of expropriation subject to compensation in international law; there is, however, nothing in the opinion of the court to establish the existence of an international rule which requires German

---

[1] B. A. Wortley: 'The general principles of private international law', in *Rec. ADI*, 1958 (II), p. 217. See also *La Belgique Judiciaire*, 1 July 1939, col. 505.

[2] A.D., 1927–8, p. 66.

[3] I.L.R., vol. 23, 1956, pp. 19–20.

[4] J.D.I., vol. 86, 1959, p. 1099; also Münch: 'Effets d'une nationalisation à l'étranger', *Rec. ADI*, 1959 (III), pp. 416–17.

[5] Münch, ibid., p. 417.

[6] *Süddeutsche Juristenzeitung*, 1950, p. 277, and 1951, p. 445.

courts to treat expropriation effected contrary to international law as *ipso facto* null and void.[1]

The Italian judiciary has denied any legal effects in Italy to expropriation without compensation in other countries.[2] Dutch courts have also referred to the right to compensation involved in measures of nationalization. In *Hahn Röhren-Walzwerk v. Stokvis* (1952), the Court of Appeal of Arnhem upheld that an act of nationalization without compensation by the Czech government was contrary to Dutch *ordre public*; the manner in which the expropriation concerned was effected was at variance with Article 158 of the Netherlands constitution, the Court argued.[3] Similar views were expressed by other Dutch courts on confiscatory measures in East Germany[4] and on sequestration measures in Indonesia.[5] In the case concerned, the Court of Appeal of Amsterdam qualified the Indonesian measures of sequestration as discriminatory and opposed it on these grounds.

In a number of international agreements, the given member states of the E.E.C. have confirmed the principle that expropriation must be accompanied by compensation. The Belgian government arranged for the compensation of Belgian nationals who held shares in Czech nationalized undertakings.[6] A similar agreement was concluded between France and Czechoslovakia.[7] The Convention of Establishment between France and the United States (25 November 1959), refers in Article IV/3 to expropriation and sets out that this shall be based on public interest and be

[1] Judgment of 21 August 1959; See also *J.D.I.*, vol. 90, 1963, p. 1129.

[2] Court of Cassation, 5 October 1959: Foro Italiano, 1959, I, p. 1463, with an enumeration of previous cases.        [3] I.L.R., vol. 19, 1952, p. 17.

[4] Court of Appeal of Amsterdam (28 March 1957) and Court of Appeal, 8 November 1957; see *J.D.I.*, vol. 91, 1964, p. 619.

[5] Court of Appeal of Amsterdam (4 June 1959), ibid., p. 622.

[6] Belgian-Czechoslovak agreement of 19 March 1947 (U.N.T.S., vol. 23, p. 35).

[7] See also the French Decree no. 64-1233 of 11 December 1964, concerning the compensation of French nationals who were shareholders in French companies (J.O., 15 December 1964); and the reply of the French government to a parliamentary question in the National Assembly (19 February 1957) on compensation (global) to be paid to French nationals by the Bulgarian government: Kiss, *Répertoire de la Pratique Française*, vol. 1, p. 230, no. 443. For French insistence on compensation of her nationals expropriated by the Soviet Union (Parl. Debates, Chamber of Deputies, 1 June 1922), ibid., vol. 4, pp. 392–3, no. 664; also the Serbian and Brazilian Loans Case, P.C.I.J. series A, no. 20/I.

accompanied by just and adequate compensation effected in an effectively realizable form ('without needless delay').[1] The treaty of friendship, commerce and navigation between Germany and the United States (29 October 1954) prescribes just compensation in cases of expropriation (Article V/4).[2] The application of the principle of fair and equitable compensation is provided in the German-Indian investment guaranty agreement (1965) and in other agreements similar to it.[3] While this agreement concerns German investments in India in the first place, it is, nevertheless, an example of German policy in matters of expropriation. Finally, the Dutch note of 18 December 1959, regarding nationalization of Dutch-owned enterprises in Indonesia, reflects the Dutch government's objections to expropriation not accompanied by prompt, adequate and effective compensation. The Dutch note refers to the discriminatory nature of the nationalization in question and argues that nationalization should be based on the general interest.[4]

In summary conclusion the following can be said on the protection of foreign property in the member states of the E.E.C.:

1. The law for the protection of foreign property is the law for protecting private property in general. No distinction is made between foreign and domestic private property.

2. The protection of foreign investment is not based on a special investment code; it is part of the fundamental rights anchored in constitutional provisions. These provisions are, therefore, part of the basic norms of the legal hierarchy in the

---

[1] Text in *J.D.I.*, vol. 88, 1961, p. 285. For a reference to compensation as incorporated in fundamental principles of international law, see parliamentary question and answer on 24 March 1953, reported in Kiss, *Répertoire*, vol. 4, p. 393, no. 665.

[2] For text see BGBl, II, 1956, p. 488.

[3] Text in *International Legal Materials—Current Documents*, vol. IV, no. 3, May 1965, pp. 492–3. For a similar treaty with Pakistan (29 November 1959), BGBl, II, 1961, p. 794, also Nwogugu, *Legal Problems of Foreign Investment*, Appendix A, pp. 285 ff. Germany has concluded similar agreements with Iran (28 February 1961), Greece (27 March 1961), Togo (29 April 1961), Morocco (31 August 1961), Thailand (22 November 1961), Liberia (11 December 1961): see Keesing's Contemp. Arch., 1961, 8985D, 9006E, 9100C, 9328A, 9504A and 9544B.

[4] Text in: *A.J.I.L.*, vol. 54, 1960, p. 485. On compensation for Dutch property nationalized in Poland, see *Het Parool* (Amsterdam), 11 September 1963, p. 1.

member states and are correspondingly difficult to amend by legislative action.[1]

3. There is agreement between the respective constitutional provisions ensuring the protection of private property. In all six member states, constitutional rules provide that expropriation shall be admissible in the public interest, by due process of law and dependent upon legally determined compensation. The constitutions of France and Germany refer to the validity of principles of international law; German law proclaims the priority of international over municipal law. On the basis of the similarities in question and of the fact that they concern foreign property, it can be said that as far as the E.E.C. is concerned, the principle of expropriation for public interest, by due process of law and with compensation, has an international legal character beyond discussion.

4. The constitutions of two member states, France and Italy, establish the public interest of undertakings that fulfil an eminently public function or occupy a dominant position in the country's economy. It may be suggested that foreign enterprise fulfilling these conditions would be *ipso facto* exposed to nationalization in France and Italy to a greater extent than foreign enterprise in a similar position in the remaining member states. The prospects of nationalization in general may, however, be considered as insignificant in the E.E.C., as undertakings of an eminently public character have already been nationalized in the post-war period and it is consequently unlikely that a foreign investor would develop activities that would be of corresponding importance. There is, on the other hand, no legal barrier to stop a member state like France from qualifying new industrial sectors, such as

[1] For provisions governing the amendment of constitutions in the E.E.C. member states see:

Belgium, Article 181 of the constitution, Peaslee, *Constitutions*, vol. 1, p. 168;

France, Article 89 of the constitution of 1958, Chatelain, *La nouvelle Constitution*, pp. 383 f.;

Germany, Article 83 of the Basic Law of 1949, Peaslee, Constitutions, vol. 2, p. 71;

Italy, Article 138 of the constitution, Peaslee, op. cit., vol. 2, pp. 502–3;

Luxembourg, Articles 113–115 of the constitution, Peaslee, op. cit., vol. 2, p. 655;

The Netherlands, Articles 202–206 of the constitution, Peaslee, op. cit., vol. 2, p. 782.

that of electronics or computers, as being of national, and therefore of public interest,[1] and to decree their nationalization. The
sovereign right to expropriate belongs to the individual states.
They may expropriate under the conditions provided by their
municipal law, subject of course to any diplomatic claims.

5. The principle that compensation must be effected in cases of
expropriation is not only anchored in the municipal law of member states; it has been, in addition, frequently applied by municipal
courts and in relations with other states.

### THE PROTECTION OF FOREIGN INVESTMENT UNDER THE EUROPEAN CONVENTION OF HUMAN RIGHTS AND FUNDAMENTAL FREEDOMS

The Protocol to the European Convention for the Protection of
Human Rights and Fundamental Freedoms (Rome, 4 November
1950),[2] signed on 20 March 1952, sets out in Article 1/1: 'Every
natural or legal person is entitled to the peaceful enjoyment of his
possessions. No one shall be deprived of his possessions except in
the public interest and subject to the conditions provided for by
the law and by the general principles of international law.' In
paragraph 2, Article 1 continues: 'The preceding provisions shall
not, however, in any way impair the right of a State to enforce
such laws as it deems necessary to control the use of property in
accordance with the general interest or to secure the payment of
taxes or other contributions of penalties.'[3]

Article 1 of the Protocol establishes three general conditions
for the lawfulness of expropriation: (i) it is admissible in the public
interest, (ii) it must be effected in accordance with the conditions
provided for by the law and (iii) it must be in accordance with the
general principles of international law. Whether an expropriation
is or is not in the public interest may be a question of opinion,
but it falls legally within the discretionary power of a sovereign

[1] What constitutes national or public interest has been only vaguely defined
in international law. It is subject to the sovereign power of states. See in this
connection Wortley, *Expropriation*, p. 25; R. G. Robinson: *International
Business Policy*, New York, 1964, p. 88.

[2] For the text of the Convention, see *A.J.I.L.*, vol. 45, 1951, Suppl., p. 24,
and A. H. Robertson: *Human Rights in Europe*, Manchester, 1963, Appendix 1,
pp. 179 ff.; for the text of the Protocol, Roberton, on pp. 196 ff.

[3] The phrase 'or other contributions of penalties' leaves the impression that
the authors of the text looked upon taxes as 'contributions of penalties'.

state. If a state nationalizes a whole sector of industry, without discrimination between its own nationals and foreigners, and thereby claims to effect it in the public interest, the opinion of that state will have to be accepted in the absence of a competence by an international judicial organ to interpret a given situation. As the Convention has provided for a judicial machinery, the interpretation of the terms 'in the public interest' could fall within its jurisdiction. It is, however, difficult to establish whether the European Court of Human Rights would have authority to decide that an act of expropriation is or is not in the public interest. If the authority of the Court were absolute in this respect, its negative decision would mean that states which are parties to the Convention, and have accepted the compulsory jurisdiction of the Court, would be bound to annul an act of expropriation if such an act, in the opinion of the Court, was not justified on the grounds of public interest. This implies an important restrictive power on the part of the Court in respect to the sovereign right of states to expropriate. This does not seem to be the intention of the contracting parties. The Convention is not an agreement that governs the right of the states concerned to expropriate or not to expropriate, but is an instrument that establishes standards of behaviour which the contracting parties are bound to respect when an expropriation takes place. The Convention governs the consequences of an expropriation in respect to private property and not the right of states to expropriate.

The Convention and Protocol are about the protection of human rights and freedoms, including the right to and respect for private property. The terms 'except in the public interest' included in Article 1 of the Protocol are, therefore, of no primary importance or a *sine qua non* in case of an expropriation.[1] An argument to the opposite would have to be supported by the contention that the European Court of Human Rights had competence to annul a municipal act of expropriation on the grounds that it was not effected 'in the public interest'. There is no evidence in support of this argument in the text of the Convention or of the Protocol concerned. The validity of expropriation acts in cases arising under the Convention will therefore depend on the essential question whether compensation is provided. On the other hand, the presence of the phrase in question in Article 1 puts the

---

[1] See the same remark by M. Domke: in *A.J.I.L.*, vol. 55, 1961, also Castberg: in *Ann. de l'Inst. de Dr. Int.*, vol. 44, ii, 1952, p. 264.

contracting parties under obligation to defend an act of expropriation by arguments of public interest and, above all, not to expropriate for the sake of transferring discriminatively property from foreign private to domestic private ownership. In other words, the phrase 'in the public interest' as used in international law implies a sovereign right to transfer foreign private property into domestic *public* ownership and not a *sine qua non* obligation to prove that such transfer is in the social or economic interest of the public in the state concerned.

The phrase 'subject to the conditions provided for by the law' found in Article 1 is not an element on which the binding obligation that expropriation must be accompanied by compensation could be based. It imposes, it is true, on the contracting parties the duty to regulate by legislation the conditions of an expropriation. Its general content could allow states, however, to apply 'equality of treatment' between its own nationals and those of foreign states and to prescribe 'by the law' that no compensation shall be paid.[1] The inclusion of 'subject to the conditions provided for by the law' indicates that expropriation must be accompanied by legislative action but not necessarily by compensation.

The decisive part of Article 1 of the Protocol in respect of compensation is the phrase 'subject to the conditions provided for . . . by the general principles of international law'. There is, in the first place, recognition on the part of the signatory states that general principles of international law exist in respect of private property. In the absence of a clear statement as to what these general principles of international law are in respect of property, it may still be argued that reference to them in Article 1 of the Protocol does not necessarily imply an obligation under international law to pay compensation in case of expropriation. As a result, the application of 'equality of treatment' as a general principle of international law could again be upheld. Such an inference does not make much sense, however, with the main objective and nature of the European Convention and its Protocol. It is a Convention for *the Protection of Human Rights and Freedoms*. It would be contradictory, both to the main objective of the Convention and to the objective of Article 1 of the Protocol itself, to maintain that the contracting parties did not undertake to protect private property. A denial of the duty to pay compensation for expropriated

---

[1] On 'equality of treatment', see Wortley, *Expropriation*, pp. 120 ff.; Nwogugu, *Legal Problems of Foreign Investment*, pp. 122 f.

private property under Article 1 of the Protocol would be tantamount to a denial of protecting private property; in such a case,
Article 1 would be superfluous and a foreign body in the system of
Human Rights and Fundamental Freedoms established by the
Convention. This Convention is not about the right or fundamental freedom of states to deny the payment of compensation
in case of an expropriation; it is about the defence of rights and
freedoms of 'every natural or legal person' who, the contracting
parties recognize, 'is entitled to the peaceful enjoyment of his
possessions'. It would be a remarkable feat of logic and imagina-
tion to claim that expropriation without compensation is tantamount to 'the peaceful enjoyment' of private possessions. Reference in Article 1 of the Protocol to 'the general principles of
international law' is, therefore, reference to the duty to pay compensation for expropriated property.

As for the argument that Article 1 of the Protocol concerns the
payment of compensation for expropriated *foreign* property, it
must be pointed out, in support of it, that the Convention and
Protocol are not municipal but international legal instruments.
Sovereign states do not need to conclude international agreements for undertaking duties towards their own nationals. If an
obligation is incurred under an international convention, it is to
be assumed that the obligation in question was intended for legal
effects extending across municipal boundaries. The duty to compensate for expropriated private property includes therefore, in
Article 1 of the Protocol, the international obligation of the signatory states in respect of foreign property. This is corroborated
by the provisions of Article 48/1(b) of the Convention, under
which a high contracting party 'whose national is alleged to be a
victim' may bring a case before the European Court of Human
Rights.

The conclusion is that, as far as the protection of foreign property is concerned, the internationally binding nature of Article 1
of the Protocol hinges on the inclusion of 'general principles of
international law'. It is intended as a guarantee to pay compensa-
for the expropriation of foreign property.[1]

For ensuring the observance of the rights and freedoms guaranteed by the Convention and Protocol, two organs, a Commission

[1] Robertson, *Human Rights in Europe*, p. 32; and the decision of the Commission on application 511/59: Yearbook of the Convention, vol. 3, 1960,
p. 424.

and a Court, have been created under Article 19 of the Convention. Under Article 25, petitions may be addressed by 'any person, non-governmental organization or group of individuals claiming to be the victim of a violation by one of the High Contracting Parties' of rights guaranteed by the Convention, under condition, however, that a signatory state 'against which the complaint has been lodged has declared that it recognizes the competence of the Commission to receive such petition'.[1] The Commission may only deal with the petition, however, 'after all domestic remedies have been exhausted, according to the generally recognized rules of international law.'[2]

The first function of the Commission is to attempt a friendly settlement between the parties.[3] If a friendly settlement fails, the Commission is empowered to draw up a report and submit it to the Committee of Ministers of the Council of Europe,[4] or to refer

[1] Article 25/1 of the Convention on Human Rights. For a history of the Convention, see Robertson, *Human Rights in Europe*, pp. 1 ff.; of the Commission, pp. 43 ff.; of the Court, pp. 85 ff.

[2] Article 26 of the Convention. On the exhaustion of local remedies see Wortley, *Expropriation*, pp. 140 ff., and also in *Tulane Law Review*, vol. 35, 1961, pp. 749–50; Nwogugu, *Legal Problems of Foreign Investment*, pp. 105ff. It is difficult to assess the solely procedural or solely substantive character of the local remedies rule. In the case of Article 26 of the Convention of Human Rights, this rule will tend to have a procedural character in the first place as any act by a signatory state contrary to the Convention and the Rights guaranteed under it will constitute a breach of international law. If the same act would be at the same time contrary to the municipal law of a signatory state, the substantive character of the remedies rule will exist side by side with its procedural character. Difficulties will be relatively easy to overcome, in the case of the European Convention on Human Rights, as under Article 45 of the Convention, the signatory states have accepted the interpretive competence of the European Court. It will be the task of the Court to determine in each individual case the manner in which the phrase 'after all domestic remedies have been exhausted . . .' shall apply. A possibility for the co-ordination of municipal remedies and the provisions of the Convention is provided under Article 57: 'On receipt of a request from the Secretary-General of the Council of Europe any High Contracting Party shall furnish an explanation of the manner in which its internal law ensures the effective implementation of any of the provisions of this Convention.'

[3] Article 30, also 28–29, of the Convention. Wortley, in *Tulane Law Review*, vol. 35, 1961, pp. 749–50.

[4] Article 31/2 of the Convention. For the Committee of Ministers of the Council of Europe, see Articles 10, 13 ff. of the statute of the Council of Europe. Text in: A. H. Robertson, *The Council of Europe*, 2nd edn., London, 1961, appendix 1, pp. 257 ff., also pp. 24 ff.

the question to the European Court of Human Rights within three months from the date of the transmission of the report to the Committee of Ministers.[1] If the question is not referred to the Court but submitted as a report to the Committee of Ministers, the Committee of Ministers will decide by a majority of two-thirds whether there has been a violation of the Convention.[2] If in the opinion of the Committee of Ministers a violation of the Convention has been committed by a signatory state, the Committee will require the signatory state concerned to take the required measures. In this respect, the signatory states undertake to regard as binding any decision which the Committee of Ministers may take.[3]

If, on the other hand, the question is referred by the Commission to the Court, the Court will have jurisdiction to settle the given question.[4] It is to be noted that cases may be brought before the Court by (i) the Commission and (ii) states whose national is alleged to be a victim, or states which referred the case to the Commission, or states against which the complaint has been lodged.[5] In addition, only states that have accepted the Court's jurisdiction are liable before it.[6]

At the end of 31 December 1964, five member states of the E.E.C. (i.e. with the exception of France) had ratified the Convention and Protocol for the Protection of Human Rights and Freedoms.[7] Four member states of the Common Market (the exceptions being France and Italy) had accepted the right of individual petition to the Commission and the compulsory jurisdiction of the Court.[8] As a result, the jurisdiction of the European Court of Human Rights is not applicable to foreign investments in France and Italy.

The following observations may be submitted as conclusions on the protection of foreign property under the European Convention of Human Rights and Fundamental Freedoms:

1. Compared with the United Nations' Universal Declaration

---

[1] Articles 32 and 48 of the Convention.
[2] Article 32/1 of the Convention.
[3] Article 32/2 and 3 of the Convention.   [4] Article 49 of the Convention.
[5] Articles 44 and 48 of the Convention.   [6] Article 46 of the Convention.
[7] Council of Europe *News*, Strasbourg, January 1965, p. 8. Also *The Rights of the European Citizen*, Council of Europe publication, Strasbourg 1961, p. 85; Robertson, *Human Rights in Europe*, pp. 199 f. See also Article 66/1 of the Convention and Article 6 of the Protocol.
[8] Articles 25/1 and 46 of the Convention.

of Human Rights (1948), which is not legally binding, the European Convention for the Protection of Human Rights and the Protocol to it are applicable law. Article 17/2 of the Universal Declaration of Human Rights states in broad terms that 'No one shall be arbitrarily deprived of his property.' Article 1 of the Protocol of 20 March 1952 to the European Conventions of Human Rights sets out in clearer terms that expropriation shall be effected in the public interest, subject to the conditions provided for by the law and by the general principles of international law.[1] Under it, the right to compensation is proclaimed as a basic right without discrimination between nationals and foreigners in a signatory state where expropriation takes place.

2. The judicial control of disputes arising under the application of the Convention and the Protocol concerned is entrusted to an institutional system of international law. A Court and a Commission are responsible for the observance of the guaranteed rights and freedoms. In this respect, the judicial system of the signatory states is co-ordinated with the respective provisions of the Convention; this corresponds to a general rule of international law which requires that in the judicial hierarchy of a state, a judgment for a given case must be rendered in a final form, that is, by the supreme court or highest court of appeal, before it can be settled under international law.[2]

3. The right of petition of natural and legal persons is recognized under the Convention. A valuable contribution has thus been made to the position of individuals in international law. Under the Convention, the right of individual appeal is not only possible, but it is also subject to the competence of an international institution and not to the discretionary power of the states concerned.[3] This right is subject to a system in which a state

[1] Wortley, *Expropriation*, p. 150.
[2] 'La règle selon laquelle il faut épuiser les recours internes avant de présenter une requête internationale est fondée sur le principe que l'Etat défendeur doit pouvoir d'abord redresser le grief allégué par ses propres moyens dans le cadre de son ordre juridique interne': Judge Lauterpacht, in the Affair Interhandel, *Rec. I.C.J.*, 1959, p. 27. See also Wortley: in *Tulane Law Review*, vol. 35, 1961, pp. 745 and 749; L. Oppenheim: *International Law*, H. Lauterpacht, ed., 8th edn., 1962, vol. 1, pp. 361 f.
[3] Wortley, *Expropriation*, p. 150; Nwogugu, *Legal Problems of Foreign Investment*, pp. 238 f. G. L. Weil: in *A.J.I.L.*, vol. 57, 1963, p. 821; E.-H. Böckstiegel. Die allgemeinen Grundsätze des Volkerrechts über Eigentumsentziehung. Eine Untersuchung zu Artikel 1 des Zusatzprotokolls zur

cannot at one and the same time be judge and party to a dispute,[1] as the signatory states have recognized the capacity of individuals to take international procedural action.[2]

Individuals have a *locus standi* before the Commission and not before the Court of Human Rights. That this provision has, however, more a procedural than substantive character was indicated in the case *Lawless v. Ireland* (1961).[3] The Commission represented the individual applicant before the Court. In the opinion of the Court, the Commission's role should not be reduced to that of a postbox destined to reproduce and submit the individual applicants' views. On the other hand, since the judicial character of proceedings before the Court necessitates an impartial hearing of both sides, individual applicants' relevant arguments may be used by the Commission or by the given contracting state representing the case of an individual.[4] The effective representation of individuals before the European Court of Human Rights is thus possible.

4. Beyond the stage of appealing to the Commission, the representation of private rights guaranteed under the Convention before the European Court is indirect, i.e. a case may be brought before the Court by the Commission or by a contracting state the national of which the given natural or legal person is, or which has referred the case to the Commission, or by a contracting state against which the complaint has been lodged. These contracting states must have accepted the compulsory jurisdiction of the Court.[5] This procedural approach marks a departure from traditional attitudes about the nationality of claims.[6] Since the

---

Europäischen Menschenrechtskonvention, vol. 27 in the series *Neue Kölner Rechtswissenschaftliche Abhandlungen*, Berlin, 1963; Lord McNair in Preface to *The Rights of the European Citizen*, publ. Council of Europe, Strasbourg, 1961, pp. 19–20; M. St. Korowicz: in *A.J.I.L.*, vol. 50, 1956, p. 561; I. Seidl-Hohenveldern; in *Mélanges Séfériadès*, Athens, 1961, pp. 255 ff.

[1] Lord McNair, Preface, *Rights of Eur. Citizen*, pp. 19–20.
[2] Korowicz, in *A.J.I.L.*, vol. 50, 1956, p. 561.
[3] Publications of the European Court of Human Rights, Series A, Judgments and Decisions, *Lawless v. Ireland* (July 1961).
[4] See the very valuable discussion of the Lawless case by Robertson, *Human Rights in Europe*, pp. 112 ff., especially pp. 120 ff., 126 ff.; also Nwogugu, *Legal Problems of Foreign Investment*, pp. 238 f.
[5] Robertson, *Human Rights in Europe*, pp. 97 ff.
[6] On the nationality of claims, see Wortley, *Expropriation*, pp. 143 ff.; Nwogugu, *Legal Problems of Foreign Investment*, pp. 101 ff.; also W. G. Friedmann: *The Changing Structure of International Law*, London, 1964, pp. 242 ff.

Commission or a contracting state may refer a case to the Court independently of the nationality of the natural or legal persons concerned, the traditional approach that individual interests must be represented in international forums by a state, the nationals of which the individuals concerned are, does not hold here. As to the provision that a case may be referred to the Court by a contracting state whose national is alleged to be a victim, this may remind of the traditional doctrine of diplomatic protection. There is a difference, however, between the two systems. The system of representation under the Convention is not subject to preliminary and often tedious interstate negotiations and a subsequent contractual agreement in which the negotiation parties are at one and the same time judge and party to a given dispute. The right of a contracting state to refer a case to the Court cannot be contested on grounds of the nationality of plaintiffs. It is a right founded on the Convention of Human Rights. Even if the natural or legal persons concerned were not nationals of the contracting state which is referring the case to the Court, the jurisdiction of the European Court would still apply (Articles 24 and 48(c)).

5. Obviously the Convention and the Protocol of 20 March 1952 cannot apply against states which have not accepted the right of appeal to the Commission and the compulsory jurisdiction of the Court. In the E.E.C., foreign investment cannot be protected, under the Convention and the Protocol, in France and Italy. Furthermore, the Convention and Protocol may apply to the interests of individuals who are nationals of non-signatory states only under certain conditions. For instance, the interests of investors from Austria or Denmark can be protected by these states before the European Court, because both countries are signatory parties to the Convention and have accepted the compulsory jurisdiction of the European Court. The interests of investors from the United States can be brought before the European Court only if the Commission or a contracting state decide to do so, as the United States is not a signatory state and does not have access to the European Court (Article 48 of the Convention).

THE PROTECTION OF FOREIGN INVESTORS' RIGHTS
UNDER COMMUNITY LAW

The Treaty of Rome implies or specifies the conditions under which foreign nationals and foreign investment may be entitled to Community treatment. The main provisions in this respect are on the freedom to carry on business across municipal boundaries by setting up agencies, branch offices or subsidiaries in the different member states.[1] These provisions and others on freedom to supply services, on restrictive practices across municipal boundaries and on aids granted by member states fall, as Community law, under the jurisdiction of the Court of Justice of the European Communities.[2] This Court is responsible for the observance of Community law, and as Community law includes certain rights for foreign investors, the protection of these rights also falls under the jurisdiction of the Court.

As matters related to property and expropriation do not fall within the ambit of Community law,[3] the competence of the Court of Justice of the European Communities can concern only matters related to rights of foreign investors under Community law. These rights of foreign investors do not constitute the object of any special jurisdiction but fall under the jurisdiction that the Court has in relation to any natural or legal person under Community law.

The right of foreign investors to appeal to the Community Court of Justice can be examined with respect to the acts of Community organs and of the administrative and judicial authorities of member states. Like any natural or legal person, foreign investors or foreign-owned enterprises may appeal against a decision of the Community executive organs addressed to them, 'or against a decision which, although in the form of a regulation or decision directed to another person, is of direct and individual interest to (them)'.[4] They may also lodge a complaint with the Court 'on the ground that one of the institutions of the Community has failed to send (them) a formal document, such document not being a recommendation or an opinion'.[5] Appeals of undertakings, for

[1] Articles 52 ff. of the Treaty of Rome.
[2] Ibid., Articles 164 ff.    [3] Ibid., Article 222.
[4] Article 173/2 of the Treaty of Rome. The Treaty does not define the term 'enterprise'; in this respect see Valentine, *Court of Justice of the Eur. Comm.*, vol. I, p. 290; G. Bebr: *Judicial Control of the European Communities*, London, 1962, pp. 58 and 66. On actions that can be brought before the Court of Justice by enterprises, associations of enterprises, other legal persons and individuals, see Valentine, op. cit., vol. I, pp. 290 ff., 299 f., also 287 ff. and 10 f.; Bebr, op. cit., pp. 58 ff.
[5] Article 175/3 of the Treaty of Rome. See Valentine, loc. cit., and Bebr, op. cit., pp. 128 f. Also Friedmann, *Changing Structure of Int. Law.*, pp. 224 f.

instance, from decisions of Community organs with respect to restrictive trading agreements under Article 85 will be possible under the provisions of Articles 173/2 and 175/3 of the E.E.C. Treaty.

As the Court of Justice has sole jurisdiction to determine upon Community matters when these figure in cases before certain municipal courts, the Court will be competent to judge the validity of and to interpret the acts of Community institutions in any action before municipal courts where these matters are at issue.[1] In this manner, a uniform application and interpretation of Community law will be effected in the municipal courts of member states and if the rights and interests of foreign investors are thereby involved, the function of the Court of Justice will be similar to that of a central court of interpretation.

With respect to the competence of the Court of Justice over *administrative* (and *not judicial*) acts of member states in which Community law is involved, the Treaty of Rome is not very explicit. The jurisdiction of the Court for municipal administrative acts involving the application of Community law is indirectly envisaged under Articles 169–170 of the Treaty. While ordinary judicial organs of member states may request from the Court of Justice a ruling on a case related to Community law (Article 177/2), and the highest municipal courts are 'bound to refer' a similar matter to the Court of Justice (Article 177/3), there is no corresponding provision for administrative organs of member states to refer a question on Community law to the executive organs or to the Court of Justice of the E.E.C. Failure to fulfil an obligation by a member state under Community law may, however, be referred to the Court, under Articles 169 and 170, by the Commission or a member state respectively.

The application of Community law will depend not least on the administrative acts of member states. For instance, many questions ancillary to the freedom of carrying on business through agencies, branches or subsidiaries across municipal boundaries in the E.E.C., under Articles 52 and 58 of the Treaty, will depend on the application of Community law by administrative organs of member states. What action can, for instance, a foreign-owned or Community-owned German company take under Community law if it meets discrimination on the part of the administrative authorities of another member state where the company intends to set up

[1] Article 177/1 of the Treaty of Rome. See Valentine, op. cit., vol. 1, p. 15.

a subsidiary? The matter obviously involves Community law and it falls within the competence of the Community Court of Justice. Community law does not provide, however, for the right of action before this Court by a natural or legal person against a member state. For bringing such a case before the Community Court of Justice, a number of possibilities can, however, be envisaged:

i. If overriding importance is attached to Article 155 of the Treaty, under which the Commission shall 'ensure that the provisions of [the] Treaty and the measures taken by the institutions by virtue of [the] Treaty are carried out', the plaintiff company may bring the discriminating administrative act of a member state to the attention of the Commission. If the Commission considers that under Article 169/1 the member state concerned has failed to fulfil an obligation under the Treaty, it can ex officio issue 'a reasoned opinion on the matter after giving the State concerned the opportunity to submit its comments'. 'If the State concerned does not comply with the terms of such opinion within the period laid down by the Commission, the latter may refer the matter to the Court of Justice.'[1]

ii. The case of the company discriminated against may be taken up by any member state which considers that the other member state concerned has failed to fulfil an obligation under Article 58 of the Treaty, and may refer the matter to the Court of Justice in accordance with the required procedure.[2]

iii. The discriminated company can apply to the member state where it is incorporated. This member state could bring the matter before the Court of Justice in accordance with Article 170. It is to be noted that proceedings before the Court of Justice are independent of the nationality of shareholders or of other persons entitled to Community treatment. It is also immaterial whether a matter is referred to the Court by a member state whose nationals are alleged to be victims or by another member state.

If the Court of Justice finds that the member state concerned has failed to fulfil an obligation under the Treaty, it may require

---

[1] Article 169/1 and 2 of the Treaty of Rome. See Valentine, *Court of Justice of Eur. Comm.*, vol. 1, pp. 374 ff.

[2] Article 170/1, Treaty of Rome; for the procedure to be followed in applying this Article, see the remaining sections 2–4 of the same Article.

in a binding way that the member state concerned take measures for the implementation of the judgment of the Court (Art. 171). For instance, if a British or American-owned German company applies for the establishment of a subsidiary under Community law in France, Italy or any other member state, and the administrative authorities of the second member state discriminate by refusing to complete the necessary formalities, this company may try to have a judgment of the Court of Justice on the matter in the manner discussed in the preceding paragraphs.

It can be concluded that the control of Community law applied by administrative organs of member states undoubtedly falls under the jurisdiction of the Court of Justice of the European Communities (Art. 164). While direct action is not possible by individuals or undertakings, the Treaty enables the Commission or any member state to refer the matter to the Court of Justice (Articles 160–170). In other words, individuals do not have a *locus standi* before the Court of Justice for bringing claims under Community law against member states. This recalls the similar arrangement under the European Convention for the Protection of Human Rights. Under Article 25 of this Convention, individuals may submit petitions to the Commission of Human Rights; beyond that stage, only the Commission or signatory states may bring a case before the European Court of Human Rights.[1]

The Court of Justice of the European Communities is another international judicial institution, besides the European Court of Human Rights, to which foreign investors may obtain access. It is responsible for the observance of Community law under which foreign investors are entitled to Community treatment. It is a specialized court—it deals with matters which do not fall within the competence of any other court, nor does its competence arise after the exhaustion of local remedies under municipal law, as is the case for the European Court of Human Rights. The Treaty of Rome enables the executive organs of the E.E.C. to address their acts directly to Community nationals or to foreigners entitled to Community treatment. Similarly, the Community Court of Justice is accessible, for matters specified by Community law, to individuals or legal persons.

[1] Article 48 of the European Convention for the Protection of Human Rights. See the relevant remarks, on the resistance of national sovereignty in relinquishing traditional positions, by R. Pinto: *Les Organisations Européennes*, Paris, 1963, p. 196.

Finally, it is to be noted that while municipal rules of expropriation do not fall within the ambit of Community law, by virtue of their effects on the proper functioning of the Common Market they may be caught by the jurisdiction of the Community Court of Justice. This also applies to direct or indirect measures of expropriation under which discriminatory treatment results in a breach of Community law.[1]

## Conclusions

1. The right of expropriation in the Common Market rests with the member states. The application of this sovereign right is governed by constitutional provisions which prescribe that expropriation must be effected in the public interest, based on due process of law and accompanied by compensation. This applies to the property of nationals as well as to that of foreigners in the respective member states. The doctrine of relative sovereignty thus governs the right of member states to expropriate private property;[2] there is agreement between limitations imposed by customary international law and those prescribed by the constitutional law of member states.

Under the current system, the question of 'equality of treatment' between nationals and foreigners cannot arise in the E.E.C. Incident to constitutional provisions, such treatment is prescribed: both nationals and foreigners are entitled to compensation. Independently from constitutional provisions, municipal courts and state practice with respect to international claims in cases of expropriation have recognized the principle that foreign property is protected under international law.[3] The recognition and application, by the member states concerned, of the principles of adequate, prompt and effective compensation is, however, a debatable one.

2. In addition to constitutional guarantees under municipal

---

[1] On indirect expropriation in general, see Wortley, *Expropriation*, p. 64; Nwogugu, *Legal Problems of Foreign Investment*, pp. 23, 73.

[2] A. Verdross: *Völkerrecht*, 3rd edn., Vienna, 1959, p. 8.

[3] Wortley, *Expropriation*, pp. 152 ff., especially pp. 155–6; same author, in: *Tulane Law Review*, vol. 35, 1961, pp. 740 ff., 762 ff.; Seidl-Hohenveldern, in: *Mélanges Séfériadès*, pp. 263–4; Nwogugu, *Legal Problems of Foreign Investment*, pp. 159 ff., especially p. 165; F. Ermacora: *Handbuch der Grundfreiheiten und der Menschenrechte. Ein Kommentar zu den österreichischen Grundrechtsbestimmungen*, Vienna, 1963, p. 170; Katzarov, *Théorie de la Nationalisation*, pp. 390–1; White: *Nationalization of Foreign Property*, 1961, pp. 183 ff.

law, foreign investments are protected in four member states (the exceptions being France and Italy) by the European Convention of Human Rights. This Convention and the Protocol to it of 20 March 1952 are of great practical importance, for they enunciate as positive law the protection of foreign property under international law (Article 1 of the Protocol). The observance of these substantive rules is, in addition, subject to the jurisdiction of the European Court of Human Rights which is in fact an international central court. As procedural law, the Convention of Human Rights enables this Court to ensure the uniform application of the given rules and excludes action by a contracting state as party and judge to a dispute at one and the same time.

The procedural rules of the Convention constitute a compromise between the main objective of its substantive rules, namely the protection of individuals against contracting states, and traditional rules of international law. First, action by the Commission and the Court of Human Rights is dependent on the exhaustion of local remedies. Secondly, a further traditional rule of international law is applied by the limitation that any natural or legal person may lodge a complaint with the Commission, but beyond that stage, individual complaints have to be represented before the Court by the Commission or by contracting states. The Commission or any contracting state may bring a case before the European Court of Human Rights irrespective of the individual victim's nationality. On the other hand, if an individual complaint is represented by a signatory state which claims that the given individual is its national, the preliminary question of nationality may arise under Article 48/1(b) of the European Convention of Human Rights.[1]

3. Rights that foreign investors have by virtue of Community law are subject to the jurisdiction of the Court of Justice of the European Communities. This Court is also an interstate judicial organ like the European Court of Human Rights. Responsible for the interpretation and uniform application of Community law in all member states, the Community Court can ensure the uniform observance of rights that investors enjoy under Community law. Many uncertainties and divergences that could easily arise under the competence of municipal courts can be consequently averted.

[1] On the question of nationality of claims, see Wortley, *Expropriation*; pp. 143 ff.; same author, in: *Tulane Law Review*, vol. 35, 1961, pp. 752 ff., Nwogugu, *Legal Problems of Foreign Investment*, pp. 100 ff., 108 ff.

Some of the remarks made with respect to the European Court of Human Rights apply similarly to the Community Court of Justice. Its jurisdiction is also characterized by a compromise. Natural or legal persons may bring a case before the Court in respect of Community organs; they may not do so, however, with respect to complaints they may have against member states in matters related to the application of Community law. The traditional approach to the relationship of individuals and states in international law applies therefore also to the jurisdiction of the Community Court. Member states have undertaken certain obligations under Community law towards natural or legal persons who are Community nationals or are assimilated to them. For instance, under Article 58, foreign-owned companies formed in accordance with the law of a member state will be entitled to national treatment in the other member states for setting up agencies, branches or subsidiaries. While a violation of this right by a member state falls under the jurisdiction of the Community Court, individual persons or companies affected by such a violation cannot, under Community law, appeal to the Community Court. Natural or legal persons cannot lodge a complaint with the Court against a member state. The interests of such persons have to be indirectly represented before the Court by the Commission (Article 169 of the Treaty of Rome), or by a member state (Article 170 of the Treaty). As in the case of the European Court, the member state which refers a case to the Community Court need not be the one whose national the natural or legal person concerned is (Article 170).

4. The legal system which ensures the protection of foreign investment in the E.E.C. recognizes the sanctity of private property both under municipal and international law. Consequently, the protection of foreign investment is possible (a) under constitutional provisions of municipal law, beyond the stage of local remedies; (b) under the Convention of Human Rights in the member states which are signatory parties and have accepted the compulsory jurisdiction of the European Court; (c) respect of investors' rights under Community law will be ensured by the Community Court of Justice. Furthermore, if a foreign investor's country and the Common Market country concerned have accepted the compulsory jurisdiction of the International Court of Justice, claims arising from expropriation may be entertained before the International Court by the investor's state against the

E.E.C. member state concerned.[1] In such a case, a preliminary question of crucial importance may be the effective nationality of the natural or legal person concerned.[2] As members of the United Nations Organization, the Common Market countries, with the exception of Germany, are *ipso facto* parties to the Statute of the International Court of Justice.[3] Only four member states of the E.E.C. have accepted, however, the compulsory jurisdiction of the Court, the exceptions being Germany and Italy.[4] The United States of America has accepted the compulsory jurisdiction of the Court but it is subject to reservations; American investment in four member states, France, Germany, Italy and the Netherlands, is protected by virtue of special clauses included in the respective treaties of Friendship, Commerce and Navigation.[5]

5. The system of protecting foreign investment and controlling investment disputes in the E.E.C. is an important aspect of the investment climate in the Common Market. As a result, the exposure of foreign capital to political risks is, at least in theory,

---

[1] Nwogugu, *Legal Problems of Foreign Investment*, pp. 237 f.; Wortley, *Expropriation*, p. 70; Seidl-Hohenveldern, in: *Mélanges Séfériadès*, p. 257.

[2] A precedent has been established by the decision of the I.C.J. in the *Nottebohm* case (I.C.J., Reports (1955), *Liechtenstein v. Guatemala*, p. 4). On this point, see Wortley, in: *Tulane Law Review*, vol. 35, 1961, pp. 752 ff.; Nwogugu, *Legal Problems of Foreign Investment*, pp. 103 ff. Seidl-Hohenveldern, in: *Mélanges Séfériadès*, p. 254; C. Parry: 'Some considerations upon the protection of individuals in international law', *Rec. ADI*, 1956/II), pp. 705 ff.; H. F. van Panhuys, *The Role of Nationality in International Law*, Leyden, 1959, pp. 156 f.

[3] Article 93/1 of the U.N. Charter. I.C.J., Yearbook 1963–64, p. 35.

[4] Article 36/2 of the Statute of the I.C.J.; on critical remarks concerning the present incapacity of individuals to use the I.C.J. directly and poor prospects therefor for the future, see Nwogugu, *Legal Problems of Foreign Investment*, pp. 237 f.; Seidl-Hohenveldern, in: *Mélanges Séfériadès*, p. 257. For declarations recognizing the compulsory jurisdiction of the I.C.J., see I.C.J. Yearbook 1963–64, pp. 218 ff.; Belgium, p. 220; France, p. 225; Luxembourg, p. 230; and the Netherlands, p. 231.

[5] For the U.S.–French Convention on Establishment see Treaties and International Agreements Series (T.I.A.S.), 4625; F.C.N. treaty with Germany, T.I.A.S., 3593; for the F.C.N. treaty with the Netherlands, T.I.A.S., 3942. On the protection of investments in bilateral treaties, R. Preiswerk: *La Protection des Investissements Privés dans les Traites Bilateraux*, Zurich, 1963; Nwogugu, *Legal Problems of Foreign Investment*, pp. 130 ff. The investment guarantee programme of the U.S. government does not include the member states of the E.E.C.; see U.S. Government Memorandum to Businessmen, State Dept., Agency for International Development, Wash., D.C., 1964, p. 53.

relatively small. This system offers a maximum of guarantee and predictability which must be the contribution that law can make to economic and social life; and while member states have the sovereign right to expropriate whenever they deem it appropriate in their public interest, the prospects that the current situation will continue, are favourable. In all member states some sectors of public utilities are already publicly owned and there is no large margin left for foreign enterprise to establish itself in these sectors. Sectors of basic industries are equally owned or controlled as public enterprise in countries like France or Italy, and both in these and in the remaining member states nationalization of further industrial sectors is not planned. Should such plans be envisaged in one or other member states, the interpenetration of municipal economies and of undertakings across municipal boundaries will make the expropriation of private economic sectors an increasingly complex matter. The progressive integration of municipal economies will tend to dissociate political considerations from economic ones with respect to expropriation. State monopolies and publicly owned enterprises will be subject to the economic law of the Treaty of Rome, as will private enterprise. As a result, member states will be subject to limitations in their control over the economic aspects of publicly owned industries in so far as the subservience of such industries to political objectives is concerned. In such circumstances, expropriation may be less attractive. The propensity to expropriate for political reasons may be less marked, owing to restrictions imposed by Community law on the economic control of undertakings in a manner contrary to the objectives of the Common Market. Moreover, in the case of an expected nationalization in one or another of the member states, the absence of certain obstacles within the economic union envisaged could easily unleash a flight of capital into the more secure member states. This could be averted, however, by joint action on the part of all member states, but such action would, on the other hand, affect the operation of the Common Market. The expropriation of manufacturing industries in a member state would be a more complex matter than it was before the establishment of the Common Market.

With the interpenetration of municipal economies the further application of the principle of effective link with respect to the nationality of companies may raise difficulties in case of an expropriation. If the nationalization of a given undertaking is effected, and thereby the rule of formal attachment (incorporation) of a company taken as criterion for its nationality, difficulties in ascertaining the nationality of that company may not arise. It will be immaterial, for instance, whether a company is incorporated in France but has a number of important centres of business throughout the Community. By virtue of its incorporation in France, that company will be a French company and if the French government decrees its nationalization, that company will be caught by the decree.

If, on the other hand, the doctrine of real seat is applied to the nationality of a Community company in case of a nationalization, more than one member state might possibly claim that company as its national. The concept of effective link for ascertaining the real seat of a company in order to determine, in turn, the nationality of a company is a confusing one, and if left to the interpretative power of municipal authorities, it can become even more confusing. Within the economic union envisaged and with current techniques of management and communications, a Community company can easily develop effective links and maintain real seats in two or more member states. In case of expropriation, it could make all the difference whether a company is decreed to be the national of the expropriating member state, or the national of another member state. As a national of the expropriating state, the company with the totality of its assets in the Community would be affected. As a national of another member state, that company might be affected only in so far as it has assets in the expropriating member state. This theoretical question may have concrete consequences. It is to be noted that a dispute between member states over this question, arising under an expropriation act, will not fall under the jurisdiction of the Community Court of Justice, for matters of nationalization are not governed by Community law (Article 222 of the Treaty of Rome). A solution may be sought by considering the question of corporate nationality in the Community as essential for the proper functioning of the Common Market. It could then fall under the general provisions of Article 100 which enables the Council to issue directives for the approximation of municipal laws in so far as such an approximation is necessitated by the proper functioning of the Common Market. A corresponding directive might then effect the application of uniform rules of formal nationality for companies in all member states or of uniform criteria as to the effective link of a company with a member state, and, as a result, of its nationality. In this manner, a legal question of preliminary importance to expropriation could be brought under Community law and consequently under the jurisdiction of the Community Court of Justice. According to a report on company law reform in the E.E.C.,[1] a Community company common as a type to all member states 'would end the necessity of choosing final nationality in international mergers'. If this quotation is to be understood as implying a company with a Community status, and consequently one not attached to a member state as the national of that member state, a few inferences can be made. First, the category of foreign companies in the member states would be increased by a Community-type of company which could become the first genuine type of international private commercial company incorporated under the law of an international organization, namely the E.E.C. Secondly, a Community-type of company could never be nationalized in its totality except in the case of simultaneous expropriation of its assets by all member states. It could never become extinct as a result of expropriation in a member state, because it is not a national of any member state. Finally, if a Community-type of company were to enjoy a better protection in case of nationalization as a non-national in any member state than would a national company, a drift towards the establishment of this type of company might well develop.

Community law does not govern the rules of expropriation in the E.E.C., but it has an impact on it. As a result, legal matters related to expropriation or nationalization will have to be examined, wherever necessary, in the light of Community law.

[1] *The Financial Times*, 11 June 1965, p. 5.

# PART TWO

# FOREIGN INVESTMENT AND THE LAW
## OF THE
## EUROPEAN ECONOMIC COMMUNITY

# CHAPTER X

# THE RIGHT OF ESTABLISHMENT

The law proper to the E.E.C. bears upon the status of foreign investment in more than one respect. It governs the freedom of movement or of establishment of foreign-owned enterprises within the economic union of the Common Market. Trade practices of foreign investors fall, in so far as they affect trade between member states, within the ambit of the rules of competition of the Treaty of Rome. The harmonization of municipal legislation in matters like company law, corporate taxation, the protection of industrial property, may affect the activities of foreign-owned undertakings. The converging economies of member states may induce the adoption of a common external policy including common rules applicable to investment from non-member countries. These topics will constitute the content of Part II of the study. Community law, as a currently developing body of legal rules, offers a relatively wide margin for speculative or theoretical approach, and in this part of the study, for obvious reasons, many of the speculative comments are based on the full implementation of the Treaty of Rome towards which the present transition is leading.

## ARTICLES 52–58 OF THE TREATY OF ROME AND THE ESTABLISHMENT OF COMPANIES

As we have seen in Part I, the initial entry of foreign investment into the member states of the E.E.C., the establishment and the form of business organization selected, and the re-transfer of capital and income are governed by municipal laws in each state; for these aspects of foreign investment in the Common Market, Community law is at present irrelevant and will be so until such time as the progressive economic integration of the six states will make a common monetary and economic policy towards non-member states necessary. Such a uniform policy towards other countries will, as we shall see later, necessitate the assimilation or harmonization of the existing rules of the member states.

In the meantime the problems facing foreign-owned enterprises already established in the E.E.C. which wish to make transfers and movements within the Common Market have to be considered, and in the questions raised in such cases, Community law does become relevant. Is the status of a foreign-owned enterprise in such a situation different from that of an enterprise seeking entry from a non-member state and establishment in the Common Market for the first time? May the already established enterprise avail itself of the provisions of the Treaty of Rome or must it continue to depend on the separate municipal rules of each member state?

Comments that follow on these questions must, perforce, be for the time being of more theoretical than practical importance, for as long as the right of establishment (Articles 52–58 and 220) is not fully implemented and the period of transition continues, the right to transfer companies from one member state to another, under Community law, cannot be of practical importance for foreign investors. Until then, foreign-owned companies, indeed all companies within the Common Market, must continue to use the existing separate municipal laws.

The right of establishment is, in the context of Community law, the right of nationals and of commercial or industrial legal entities assimilated to them, to move without legal restrictions set up for economic reasons, from the territory of one member state to that of another, for setting up or continuing a permanent commercial activity; it concerns independent, non-salaried activities.[1] It is related to one of the major objectives of the Treaty of Rome, namely the free movement of persons, services and capital.[2] Here we are concerned with the freedom of move-

---

[1] For a discussion of the right of establishment in general, see Campbell and Thompson, *Common Market Law*, pp. 46 ff., especially commentaries on Articles 52–58, pp. 233–7, also pp. 132–3; U. Everling: *Das Niederlassungsrecht im Gemeinsamen Markt*, Frankfurt/Main, 1963 (English edition: *Right of Estab. in the Common Market*, New York, 1964); H. K. Junckerstorff, ed.: *International Manual on the European Economic Community*, St. Louis, Miss., 1963, pp. 233 ff.; G. le Tallec: 'La Police des Etrangers dans les Etats Membres de la Communauté Economique Européenne et le Traité de Rome', *Rev. M.C.*, no. 72, September 1964, pp. 371 ff.

[2] Article 3(c) and Part II, Title III, Articles 48–73 of the Treaty of Rome. Aspects related to the free movement of wage-earning or salaried persons will not be discussed. Mention will be made of the free movement of services (Arts. 59–66) and of capital (Arts. 67–73) only where necessary within the discussion of the right of establishment. Bilateral treaties of friendship, commerce and navigation, or similar bilateral agreements between member states or between one of them and a non-member country, though mentioned

ment of nationals from non-member countries (or of companies
owned by such nationals) and the status of equality in this respect
which they may be accorded alongside nationals of the six member
states. The application of Articles 52–58 to the status of nationals
(physical persons) and companies from non-member countries
can be examined under four heads:

i. Nationals (physical persons) of non-member countries established in one of the member states and already exercising an
   economic activity there;
ii. Companies incorporated in non-member countries, with a
    branch in one of the member states;
iii. Companies constituted in accordance with the law of a member
     state but foreign-owned and not employing, as managers or
     directors, nationals of non-member countries;
iv. Companies constituted in accordance with the law of a member
    state but foreign-owned and employing nationals of non-
    member countries as managers or directors.

i. *Nationals of non-member countries established in one of the member
states and already exercising an economic activity there*

Article 52 sets out that 'restrictions on the freedom of establishment of *nationals* of a Member State in the territory of another
Member State shall be progressively abolished in the course
of the transitional period'.[1] The envisaged abolition is to be

---

where relevant, are not discussed here. The right of establishment does not
apply to persons exercising public authority (Art. 55/1). The Council is
authorized under Article 55/2 to exclude also other activities that normally
fall under the provisions of the Treaty.

[1] Article 52 does not distinguish between nationals of member states who
are *physical* or *legal* persons, and it could be assumed that the Article refers
to both. As there is, however, a separate Article 58 on companies and firms,
it can be concluded that the term 'nationals' in Article 52 refers to physical
persons to whom companies and firms will be assimilated in accordance with
Article 58. The Treaty of Rome defines Community 'nationals' with reference
to the municipal laws of member states (see also Article 7). For comments,
see Campbell and Thompson, *Common Market law*, pp. 209, 234; Groeben and
Boeckh, *Kommentar*. This distinction between natural persons and companies
is also found in the General Programme for the Removal of Restrictions on
the Freedom of Establishment (J.O.(C.E.), 1962, pp. 36/62 ff.). The General
Programme refers to *subjects* of member states (*ressortissants des Etats
Membres*). For a translation of the General Programme see Campbell and
Thompson, *Common Market Law*, Appendix 8, pp. 423 ff.

Existing restrictions shall be progressively abolished, and the introduction

P

extended to 'restrictions on the setting up of agencies, branches or subsidiaries by *nationals* of any Member State established in the territory of any Member State'.[1]

Since these provisions of Article 52/1 refer exclusively to 'nationals of a Member State'[2] and there are no provisions for the assimilation of natural persons, who are nationals of non-member countries and are established in a member state, to nationals of the six member states, it may be concluded that foreign nationals, as

---

of any new discriminatory measures will not be possible (Arts. 52–53). In accordance with the provisions of Article 54, setting up the procedure to be followed for the progressive abolition of existing restrictions, the Council of the E.E.C. has laid down a general programme (J.O.(C.E.), 1962, p. 32/62). A second general programme (ibid., p. 36/62) deals with the freedom of services (Arts. 49, 60 and 63). For the timetable and list of non-salaried professions, see ibid., pp. 38–39/62 and Annexes I (pp. 40–42/62), II (pp. 42–43/62), III (pp. 43–44/62) and IV (pp. 44–45/62). The system followed for listing the non-salaried activities is similar to the International Standard Industrial Classification of all Economic Activities (U.N., New York, 1958) but is adapted to industrial activities and conditions in the member states (*Stat. Indust.*, Stat. Office of the European Communities, 1961, vol. 2).

In accordance with Article 54/2 the Council issued three directives in 1964 for the implementation of the general programmes, related to procedures for the introduction of freedom of establishment and services in the industrial and handicraft professions (Dir. 64/427/CEE; J.O., 1964, p. 1863/64); and mining and quarrying (Dir. 64/428/CEE; J.O., 1964, p. 1871/64). The third directive (64/429/CEE; J.O., 1964, p. 1880/64) deals with details of transitional measures for the liberalization of industrial and artisan professions, in view of the diverging regulations in the municipal laws of the member states. For a survey of the directives see article by T. Oppermann in *Betriebsberater*, 20 May 1964, pp. 563 ff. (a French translation is in *Rev. M.C.*, no. 75, December 1964, pp. 544 ff.); also W. van Gerven: in *Journ. des Tribunaux*, 31 May 1964, pp. 357–62, which indicates the difficulties that are to be faced when co-ordinating municipal rules on diplomas and certificates and their mutual recognition in the member states (Art. 57/1). A similar opinion is expressed by M. Gaudet, in *Sociaal Economische Wetgeving*, 1961, pp. 52–68. For articles of earlier date see E. Schlachter: 'Nouveaux aspects de la liberté d'établissement dans le Traité de Rome', *Rev. M.C.*, no. 30, November 1960, and no. 33, February 1961; and H. G.: 'Droit d'établissement dans la C.E.E.', *Rev. M.C.*, no. 41, November 1961, pp. 410 ff.

[1] Author's italics.

[2] See Directive of the Council (J.O.(C.E.), 1964, pp. 845/64 ff.), Article 1 at p. 846 (persons to whom the right of establishment applies) mentions only nationals of a member state. In its consultative opinion, the Economic and Social Committee had expressed the view that the right of establishment should be extended to stateless persons (*apatrides*) and to refugees resident in the territory of the member states (J.O.(C.E.), 1964, p. 849/64).

physical persons, will not qualify under Article 52. Individual foreign investors engaged in business activities in one of the E.E.C. countries will continue to be subject to the separate municipal rules governing the establishment and business activities of aliens in the respective member states. For instance, whereas a German national established in Germany will qualify under Article 52 to set up a business in one of the other member states, a national of a non-member country established in Germany and intending to set up a business in another member state will be subject to the municipal rules on alien establishment in that member state. It is immaterial for Community law whether physical persons who are nationals of non-member countries are settled in a member state or come directly from a non-member state. Community law goes even further than that and distinguishes between nationals of the Common Market countries *established in one* of the member states, and nationals of the E.E.C. *not established* in the territory of any member state.[1] Article 52 will apply to Community nationals established in a member state.[2] Community nationals who are not resident in or are not established within the Common Market will be unable, under Article 52, to claim the freedom of establishment within the Common Market to set up an agency, a branch or subsidiary in the territory of one of the member states other than the member state of which they are nationals. Some authors have suggested that the term 'established in the territory of any Member State' implies a real (effective) link with the economic life of the given member state,[3] and it may be assumed that any person claiming the right of establishment as set out in Article 52 of the Treaty of Rome, must supply evidence in this respect. In the absence of such a link, persons resident outside the Common Market, regardless of their status as nationals or non-nationals of a member state, will be subject to equal treatment—they will not be entitled under Article 52 to the right of establishment within the Community. It may be assumed that in such a situation a national of a member state, coming from a

---

[1] Article 52, par. 1, last sentence.
[2] Groeben and Boeckh, *Kommentar*, vol. 1, p. 167 (commentary by H. Ehring); Junckerstorff, ed., *Manual*, p. 245; J. Audinet: 'Le droit d'établissement dans la C.E.E.', *J.D.I.*, vol. 86, 1959, p. 1011.
[3] Campbell and Thompson, *Common Market Law*, p. 234, comment that the terms 'established in the territory of any Member State' means having some effective link with the economy of the given member country.

non-member country and desirous of setting up an enterprise in the Common Market, will have to establish first in the member state of which he is a national and thus qualify under Article 52/1. It may be asked, however, at what stage of his residence in the member state of his nationality will he be considered as 'established in the territory' of that member state: what criteria would constitute, and at what time, an effective link with the economic life of that member state and which authority would be called upon to judge? As the requisite of an effective link is only implied by the terms 'established in the territory of any Member State' in Article 52, it would be difficult to maintain that it is a matter of implementation and falls therefore under the competence of the Community executive organs to establish the necessary criteria. Even if the term 'effective link' were included in Article 52, and all the more so in the absence of it, it will be necessary to consider the matter as a question of interpretation by the Court of Justice of the European Communities in accordance with Article 164 of the Treaty of Rome.

Article 52 of the Treaty, therefore, prescribes the concurrent application of two principles in ascertaining qualification to the right of establishment under Community law: (i) the principle of nationality, and (ii) the principle of an effective link with the economic life of any member state. Nationals of non-member countries, even if they qualify under the application of the second principle, will still be unqualified under the additional and concurrent requisite of nationality of a member state to have freedom of establishment within the Community.

ii. *Companies incorporated in non-member countries with a branch office in one of the member states*

Do such companies qualify under the Treaty of Rome for the right of establishment within the Community?

Article 58 contains the provisions for an answer in this respect. In its first paragraph, Article 58 sets out that for the purpose of applying the right of establishment, companies will have to be 'constituted in accordance with the law of a Member State . . .' This requisite is not the only one prescribed by Article 58, but it is by itself sufficient to clarify the status of companies incorporated in non-member countries, and the conclusion to be drawn is as follows.

Companies that have been incorporated as legal entities in

non-member countries will not qualify under the provisions of the Treaty of Rome. The fact that they have one or more branch offices in one or more of the member states will be, in this respect, irrelevant. A member state where such a company intends to set up agencies, branches or a subsidiary, will be free to apply its municipal rules governing establishment of companies from non-member countries. Hence, it would be advisable for a company from a non-member country to provide for qualification under Article 58/1 by setting up a subsidiary company in one of the member states.

iii. *Companies constituted in accordance with the law of a member state but foreign-owned and not employing, as managers or directors, nationals of non-member countries*

The situation of companies constituted in accordance with the law of a member state, even when foreign-owned, is different from that of nationals or companies from non-member states, already established, or, respectively, entertaining a branch office in the Common Market.

The Treaty of Rome does not apply the criterion of nationality[1] or the rule of control and ownership in determining the status of companies under the provisions of Article 58. It defines the term 'companies' as those constituted 'under civil or commercial law' of one of the member states, 'including co-operative companies and other legal persons under public or private law, with the exception of non-profitmaking companies'. Such companies, independently from their control or ownership, will be treated as legal entities within the Community, if they have been 'constituted in accordance with the law of a Member State' and have 'their registered office, central management or main establishment within the Community'. They 'shall, for the purpose of applying the provisions of [Chapter 2, The Right of Establishment], be assimilated to natural persons being nationals of Member States'.

Thus, in accordance with the provisions of Article 58 paragraph 1, companies constituted in one of the member states but owned or controlled by foreigners, partly or completely, will qualify for the right of establishment within the Community.

[1] Campbell and Thompson, *Common Market Law*, p. 47; Audinet, *J.D.I.*, vol. 86, 1959, p. 1015; Junckerstorff, *Manual*, p. 244; Everling, *Niederlassungsrecht im G.M.*, p. 40; N. Catalano: *Manuel de Droit des Comm. Européennes*, Paris, n.d., pp. 297 ff.

As a corollary to this rule, companies incorporated in non-member countries even when totally owned by nationals of the member states will not qualify under Article 58, because the rule of control or ownership is irrelevant[1] and the Treaty of Rome does not attach legal consequences to the nationality of persons owning or controlling a company.

As for the number of requirements, concurrent or alternate, that are necessary for a company to fall within the definition found in Article 58, authorities differ in their opinions. It is clear that as an essential requirement under Article 58/1, first sentence, 'companies' must be 'constituted in accordance with the law of a Member State . . .' Concerning the remaining alternative requirements, namely to have 'their registered office, central management or main establishment within the Community', the conclusion that the Treaty prescribes only two, or three requisites depends on the interpretation attached to the comma between the terms 'their registered office' and 'central management' in the text of Article 58/1. If the comma in question is interpreted as a substitution for *and*, then the prescribed requirements for a company to qualify under the Treaty are three: (i) incorporation in a member state, (ii) location of the registered office within the Community and (iii) location of the central management or main establishment within the Community. With the interpretation of the comma in question as standing for *or*, only two requirements would be necessary: (i) incorporation in a member state and (ii) location of the registered office *or* central management *or* main establishment within the Community.

The opinions submitted by the majority of authors consider the requirements enumerated in Article 58/1 as being non-cumulative and hence the latter case of two requirements will suffice to qualify a company under this Article.[2] One of the requirements,

[1] Groeben and Boeckh, *Kommentar*, vol. I, p. 168, n. 6, pp. 182–3, n. 5c, pp. 183–4.

[2] For various opinions, see Audinet, *J.D.I.*, vol. 86, 1959, pp. 1017, 1023; Campbell and Thompson, *Common Market Law*, p. 237; Groeben and Boeckh, *Kommentar*, vol. 1, p. 181, n. 3, p. 183, n. 5c; Junckerstorff, *Manual*, pp. 243, 244, 246; Stein and Nicholson, eds., *American Enterprise in the European Common Market*, vol. 2, p. 167; A. Piot: 'Du réalisme dans les conventions d'établissement', *J.D.I.*, vol. 88, 1961, p. 75; Y. E. Loussouarn: in *Rev. Trimestrielle du Droit Commercial*, 1959, p. 247.

For the non-cumulative theory, see Everling, *Das Niederlassungsrecht im G.M.*, p. 39; P. Leleux: in *Doing Business in the Common Market*, Chicago, 1963, p. 30.

the formation 'in accordance with the law of a Member State', is mandatory. The second requirement will be fulfilled by having the registered seat or central administration or principal place of business within the Community.

The author's opinion in the present study is that, in the light of the General Programme for the Removal of Restrictions on the Freedom of Establishment (1962),[1] two possibilities must be envisaged, one of them corresponding to three and the other to two requirements. Prior to the General Programme, it would have been possible to assume that after its creation 'in accordance with the law of a Member State . . .', it would have been sufficient for a company, in order to qualify—under the provisions of Article 58, to have its 'registered office' or 'central administration or principal place of business within the Community'. The General Programme includes, however, a requirement to be complied with where companies 'have only their registered office within the Community or an overseas country or territory . . .' According to the General Programme, the business activity of such companies 'shall show a continuous and effective link with the economy of a Member State or of an overseas country or territory . . . to set up agencies, branches or subsidiaries on the territory of a Member State'.[2] It is possible thus to envisage three requisites: (i) formation in accordance with the law of a member state; (ii) location of the registered office within the Community; and (iii) the existence of a continuous and effective link with the economy of a member state.[3] For the second possibility, i.e. if the 'central

[1] J.O.(C.E.), 1962, pp. 36/62 ff.

[2] Head I of the General Programme for the Removal of Restrictions on the Freedom of Establishment. For an English translation, Campbell and Thompson, *Common Market Law*, Appendix 8, pp. 423–4. The right of establishment with respect to associated countries and overseas territories is examined later in this chapter.

[3] The requisite of an effective link has been pointed out by a number of commentators on Community law: E. Wohlfarth and others: *Die Europäische Wirtschaftsgemeinschaft, Kommentar*, Berlin, 1960, p. 189. In the view of these authors, a company, to qualify under Article 58/1, must be necessarily constituted and established in the Community, but the form of establishment may be other than the location of its central administration or principal place of business within the Community; it may be in the form of a substantial part of its business being transacted within the Common Market.

For the General Programme, see J.O.(C.E.), 1962, p. 36/62, Title I, Beneficiaries. A similar requirement is found also in the General Programme for the freedom of services (ibid., p. 32/62 ff., Title I).

administration or principal place of business' of a company is 'within the Community', the requirement of 'a continuous and effective link with the economy of a Member State . . .' will not apply. The inference is that the location of the central administration or principal place of business within the Community will be considered tantamount to the existence of a continuous and effective link with the economy of a member state. Therefore, the requisites for the second possibility are only two in number: (i) formation in accordance with the law of a member state and (ii) the location of the central administration or principal place of business within the Community. It is noteworthy that both possibilities for a company to qualify under Article 58, with three and two requirements respectively, envisage the existence of an effective link. This corresponds to the same requirement implied under Article 52/1 for natural persons who are nationals of member states.

The reference of Article 58/1 to municipal law in the stipulation that companies must be formed 'in accordance with the law of a Member State' assumes the existence of a co-ordination between Article 58 and municipal company laws. This is currently not the case as far as the purpose of Article 58 is concerned. Article 58 refers to the E.E.C. as a whole by setting out that it will be sufficient for a company to have its registered seat, central administration or principal place of business *within* the Community. Under the present system of municipal company laws, to which Article 58/1 refers, the registered seat of a company must be in the member state where the company has been incorporated. The company laws of five member states (Dutch law is excepted) prescribe that the real seat of a company must correspond to its registered office. As it may be assumed that 'central administration' or 'principal place of business', as used in Article 58/1, refer to the real seat of a company, and as Article 58/1 refers to the laws of member states and requires that companies must be formed in accordance with one of them, it may be concluded that all requirements prescribed under Article 58 will have to be fulfilled under the present system, with reference to a single state for a given company; this member state will have to be the same for the application of all requisites, and these requisites cannot be less than three under the current municipal law of five member states, i.e. formation in accordance with the law of the member state concerned, and location of both registered and real seats in that member state. If this is true, Article 58 cannot be implemented in a manner which is envisaged by the inclusion of the phrase 'within the Community', unless the current system of municipal company laws is modified and co-ordinated with Article 58. While referring to the mandatory provisions of municipal laws under which the registered and real seats of a company must be identical and situated in the state of incorporation, Article 58/1 sets out that the registered office, central administration or principal place of business of a company must be 'within the Community'. In other words, under Article 58, if it were not for the requirements of municipal company laws to which the Article refers it should be possible for a company to be formed and incorporated in a member state, have its registered office in another member state, and its central administration or principal place of business in a third member state, as all three states would be within the Community. If emphasis is laid on an interpretation that the phrase 'within the Community' implies the E.E.C. as a whole and overrides the municipal legal boundaries set up by municipal company laws, the conclusion is that a conflict between the provisions of Article 58 and those of municipal laws exists and municipal laws will have to be co-ordinated with Article 58, which refers, however, to the mandatory requirements of municipal law. This question will be discussed in the section on the harmonization of municipal laws in their relevance to the topic of the present study. At this stage, it is sufficient to point out that the future interpretation of the phrase 'within the Community' by the Court of Justice, under Article 164 of the Treaty of Rome, can have a considerable effect on the scope of approximating municipal company laws and of co-ordinating them with the provisions of the Treaty 'to the extent required for the Common Market to function in an orderly manner . . .' (Article 3/1 (h)).

A further question of interpretation is raised by the term 'continuous and effective link'. It is implied by the Treaty of Rome in Articles 52 and 58, and mentioned in the General Programme for the Removal of Restrictions on the Freedom of Establishment, but neither the Treaty nor the General Programme contains a definition of it. A partial definition of a 'continuous and effective link' is given by the General Programme in negative terms: the nationality of partners, members of the managerial or supervising bodies, or of shareholders cannot constitute such a link.[1] In this

[1] J.O., 15 January 1962, p. 36 (also p. 32).

way, the requirement of a continuous and effective link is clearly restricted, in the opinion of Community organs, to the sphere of activities. Such a restriction still raises the question of criteria needed for the concrete application of the term. On a theoretical level a multitude of criteria may be considered in their application to companies, and in the absence of a definition in Community law the E.E.C. authorities may establish the criteria they deem suitable for the proper functioning of the Common Market; for the purpose of the present study, the term will be used with reference to the central administration or principal place of business or real seat of a company.

A further question raised by the term 'effective link' is that of its uniform application in the member states of the E.E.C. The expression 'effective (real or genuine) link' is frequently used by authors and legislators, but not infrequently in a confusing if not a conflicting manner as to its different meanings.[1] If the interpretation and application of this term were left to the administrative authorities and courts of member states, divergent views contradictory to the objectives of the Common Market could develop. As the term is related to Community law, it will have to be interpreted by Community organs whenever the question of its application under Community law arises.[2]

Observations in the preceding pages have been based on the assumption that the General Programme of 1962 for the removal of restrictions on the freedom of establishment has a law-creating effect. It is drawn up in accordance with Articles 54/1 and 132/1 (5) of the Treaty of Rome. While the validity of such an assumption may be questioned, there is no doubt that the General Programme reflects the official attitude of Community organs. As these organs have not only administrative and supervisory functions, but also a capacity to elaborate the specific application of many of the broad provisions of the Treaty and to adapt them to progressive integration, opinions expressed by the Council and

[1] See the critical remarks of Piot: *J.D.I.*, vol. 88, 1961, pp. 77–8; also Everling, *Das Niederlassungsrecht im G.M.*, p. 40.

[2] In accordance with Article 54/1. A clear definition of 'effective link' could also fall under Article 177/1 concerning the competence of the Court of Justice for the interpretation of the term. See Junckerstorff, ed., *Manual*, p. 246; Everling, *Das Niederlassungsrecht*, p. 40; le Tallec, *Rivista di Diritto Europeo*, 1961, p. 172; Schlachter, *Rev. M.C.*, no. 30, November 1960, p. 395; H. J. Meyer-Marsilius: *Das Niederlassungsrecht in der Europ. Wirtschaftsgemeinschaft*, Baden Baden, 1960.

Commission can be indicative of the manner in which provisions of the Treaty will be applied.

In conclusion, the main points concerning the right of establishment, on Community level, of companies owned or controlled by nationals of non-member countries may be summarized as follows:

1. Under the current situation, in order to qualify under Article 58 and with due regard to the mandatory requirements of municipal company laws, it is necessary to form a company in accordance with the law of a member state and have the registered seat of the company in that member state, and the real seat within the Community. While the constitution of a company in a member state and the location of its registered office and real seat in one or two member states should be of no consequence for the purpose of Article 58, and as we shall explain below also for current municipal company laws, the location of the real seat outside the Community of a company constituted in a member state may well bar qualification under the right of establishment in the whole of the Common Market. Municipal law in Belgium, France, Germany, Italy and Luxembourg apply the real seat theory with respect to the nationality of companies and if a company has been incorporated in one of these member states, both the registered office and real seat of the company are assumed to be in the member state concerned.[1] The company laws of these member states insist, as

---

[1] In Belgium any company with a real seat in that country is treated as a Belgian company (Article 197, Book I, Code de Commerce); L. Raape: *Internationales Privatrecht*, 4th rev. edn., Berlin, 1955, p. 190. For France, see G. R. Delaume: *American-French Private Int. Law*, no. 2 of Bilateral Studies in Private Int. Law, New York, 1953, p. 35; H. Battifol: *Traité élémentaire de Droit International Privé*, 3rd edn., Paris, 1959, p. 231. For an application of the doctrine of *siège réel*, see the decision of the *Tribunal Commercial* (Seine), 2 July 1912, D1913, 2, 165, quoted in *J.D.I.*, vol. 40, 1913, p. 1273. For Germany, see Section 5, Aktiengesetz. *Trading under the Laws of Germany*, publ. by the German-American Trade Promotion Office, New York, 1956, pp. 92–3; Schilling: 'Allgemeine Einleitung', note 47, in M. Hachenburg: *Kommentar zum Gesetz betreffend die GmbH.*, Berlin, 1956, p. 92. For an opposite opinion, see Schmidt: in *Groszkommentar zum Aktiengesetz*, Berlin, 1957, p. 40, no. 7 for Section 5; Raape, *Int. Privatrecht*, p. 190.

For Italy, in addition to the real seat being located in the country, the company must be incorporated under Italian law and maintain an effective link with Italy: Article 2509, Codice Civile. F. Capotorti: *La Nazionalità della società*, Naples, 1963, p. 208; B. Pallieri: *Diritto Internazionale Privato*, Milan, 1950, p. 139. See also Battifol, op. cit., p. 231, no. 8.

do Article 58 and the General Programme, that an effective link must exist between the given company and the economy of a member state. This opinion is obviously based on the assumption that the presence of the real seat of a company in a member state constitutes the required continuous and effective link, and it would indeed be difficult to imagine what other criteria could be more suitable for the meaning of this term.[1] Dutch law does not apply the 'real seat' doctrine.[2] A company created under Dutch law must have its registered office in the Netherlands but not necessarily its real seat. If, therefore, a company formed in the Netherlands is to qualify under Article 58, it must have its real seat not necessarily in the country but at least in a member state of the E.E.C. Under Community law and on the basis of current municipal laws, all companies, wherever incorporated, with their real seat in non-member countries, will not qualify under Article 58, irrespective of their ownership or control by nationals of member or non-member states.

As a corollary to the above remark, it can be said that companies formed in accordance with the law of a member state but having their registered office and real seat in different member states should qualify under Article 58. For the purpose of freedom of establishment *under Community law*, they will be under all circumstances Community nationals entitled to Community treatment. Member states would be unable to refuse the application of Article 58 to a company that has its registered office in one member state and its real seat in another, as under both theories of registered office or of real seat, the given company would be a Community national. The situation will be different if the real seat is outside the Community. In application of the real seat theory for ascertaining the nationality of a company in five of the member states, and by virtue of the principle of an effective link under Community law, a company with its real seat in a non-member country could be refused recognition as a Community

---

[1] On the seat of a company, see G. Kegel: *Internationales Privatrecht*, 2nd edn., Munich–Berlin, 1964, p. 206. A legal person will be duly recognized as such if it is legally incorporated in accordance with the law of its principal place of administration. This is presently the law in five of the Common Market countries; Netherlands is the exception. See E. Rabel: *Conflict of Laws*, 2nd edn., Ann Arbor, 1960, vol. 2, pp. 33, 39, 42–3, 50 ff., 68 ff.

[2] For Dutch law see R. D. Kollewijn: *American–Dutch Private International Law*, no. 3 of Bilateral Studies in Private Int. Law, New York, 1955, p. 15; also Groeben and Boeckh, *Kommentar*, vol. 1, p. 181, n. 3.

national. This line of argument can become invalid if the Community authorities set up other criteria than the real seat with respect to a 'continuous and effective link with the economy of a Member State . . .' This would, in turn, necessitate a co-ordination of municipal company laws with the freedom of establishment under Community law.

The right of establishment of Community law (Articles 52 ff.) marks a major development on the level of interstate law. It applies the same principles as bilateral treaties of establishment, but on a multilateral and regionally larger basis. Compared with the Draft Convention of the Hague Conference on Private International Law (7th Session 1951), it does not contain escape clauses. Article 1 of the Hague Draft Convention enunciates the application of the incorporation theory, while Article 2 offers a derogation thereto by its application of the real seat theory. Furthermore, in Article 7, the Draft Convention refers to certain rights but not necessarily to the right of permanent establishment. Community law provides in Article 58 of the Treaty of Rome for the application of the incorporation theory coupled with the principle of an effective link between a company and the economy of a member state, and companies qualified under Community law will be entitled to national treatment in the respective member states. Finally, the freedom of establishment will be ensured under Community law by the supervisory and judicial organs of the E.E.C. independently of possibly diverging opinions of municipal authorities. Such a centralized administrative and judicial system is a guarantee for the uniform application of Community law in all member states.

2. Foreign-owned undertakings formed in accordance with the law of a member state will qualify under Article 58 for Community treatment at an intermember level, whereas foreign-owned undertakings trying to enter the Common Market from a non-member state will continue to be subject to the respective municipal rules of member states.[1] In Belgium, foreign legal persons are recognized under Article 196 of the Co-ordinated Laws of 30 November 1935; in France, recognition of foreign companies is based on bilateral agreements or on special decrees similar to the basic model instituted by the Law of 30 May 1857, applicable to Belgian

[1] B. A. Wortley: *Legal Problems of the Common Market and European Free Trade Area* I.C.L.Q., Suppl. pub. no. 1, 1961, p. 29; Conard, in: *Michigan Law Review*, vol. 59, November 1960, no. 1, pp. 45 ff.

companies. In Germany and the Netherlands, customary rules apply.[1] In Italy, the corresponding provisions are in Article 16, paragraph 2 of the introductory provisions to the Codice Civile and Article 2505 of the same Code. In Luxembourg, the recognition of foreign legal entities is provided for in Articles 158–159 of the Law of 10 August, 1915.[2]

3. Under the current situation, each member state has still full discriminatory power to allow the establishment of foreign undertakings from third countries on its territory, but it is obviously impossible for individual member states to avert the circumvention of their rules by foreign enterprises. For instance, companies from non-member countries seeking establishment in France but hindered by strict French regulations, may have access under Community law to establishment in France by availing themselves first of the more liberal rules for alien establishment in one of the other member states. Hence the ultimate need for the co-ordination of municipal rules on alien establishment in all six member states seems to be indicated.[3]

Some authors have raised the question, whether the Treaty of Rome does not extend, in virtue of the 'most favoured nation' clause found in many bilateral treaties of establishment signed by member states with non-member countries,[4] the freedom of establishment to nationals and companies of the non-member states concerned.

The answer to the question is to be sought partly in Article

---

[1] B. Goldman: *Cours de Droit du Commerce et de la Concurrence dans les Communautés Européennes*, Paris, 1964, p. 135.

[2] Ibid., pp. 132, 133, 135; Groeben and Boeckh, *Kommentar*, vol. 2, p. 376.

[3] The growing need for co-ordination is being increasingly felt. See *The Financial Times*, 28 January 1965, p. 5: 'Foreign Capital in Europe'. The report refers only to the duty-free access of foreign investors to French markets by investing in other member states. It is to be added that the problem applies to the right of establishment and freedom of services as well, and with the progressive development of the economic union, no unilateral control or measure by one member state will be satisfactory. The liberality of Article 58 of the Treaty of Rome which confers a Community status to foreign-owned companies formed in the E.E.C. has been criticized by the French Minister of Industry, M. M. Maurice-Bokanowski: *The Financial Times*, 27 May 1965, p. 5.

[4] On bilateral agreements of establishment, see Goldman, *Cours de Droit du Commerce*, pp. 110 ff.; H. J. Walker: in *A.J.I.L.*, vol. 50, 1956, p. 373; Stein and Nicholson, eds., *American Enterprise in the Eur. Common Market*, vol. 2, p. 165.

234 under which: 'The rights and obligations arising from agreements concluded between one or more Member States on the one hand, and one or more third countries on the other hand before [the] Treaty came into force shall not be affected by the provisions of [the] Treaty.' One author has been of the opinion that the question 'is a very delicate [one] which cannot be decided until the Courts of Justice have had an opportunity of making a pronouncement'.[1]

The opinion submitted by the present author is that there is no common basis of comparison between the Treaty of Rome, on the one hand, and other international legal instruments of establishment. The Treaty of Rome is not an agreement of establishment but one of economic union. This is clearly enunciated in Article 234/3 according to which 'Member States shall, when carrying out the agreements referred to in the first paragraph of this Article, take into account the fact that the benefits granted under [the] Treaty by each Member State form an integral part of the establishment of the Community and are thereby inseparably linked with the creation of common institutions, the conferring of powers on such institutions and the granting of the same advantages by all other Member States.' The legal situation in which the right of establishment of Community law is to apply is, in its legal context and institutionally, quite different from the one in which bilateral treaties of establishment operate. The Community law of establishment will be operative between states which have accepted restrictions in their sovereign powers in applying or passing judgment on the right of establishment. They are not only bound under the maxim of *pacta sunt servanda*, but they will also be bound by the law of the Treaty as applied by institutions beyond the control of their sovereign authority. The implementation of the Community right of establishment is entrusted in the first place to the executive organs of the Community whose opinions and policy will be binding on member states in a form which is far beyond anything envisaged in bilateral agreements on establishment.

Under Article 234/3, the policy which will be followed by member states in case of conflicts is clear: under the Treaty, the member states are bound to consider the right of establishment and

---

[1] Audinet, *J.D.I.*, vol. 86, 1959, p. 1011. For the legal and economic context of the Treaty in relation to the 'most favoured nation' clause, see Junckerstorff, ed., *Manual*, p. 237.

all other advantages ensuing from the Treaty of Rome as an 'integral part of the establishment of the Community'. This implies also that member states are no longer in a position to extend similar advantages to nationals and companies of non-member countries, since the effect of such a policy would affect the other member states or the Community as a whole. Finally, in case of a possible litigation evolving around the 'most favoured nation' clause in its relation to bilateral agreements on establishment and the Treaty of Rome, a strong case could be made by arguing that non-member countries partners to bilateral agreements on establishment, for example between France and the United States or Germany and the United States, had tacitly consented to the contents of Article 234 of the Treaty, since wide publicity had been given to it and non-member states concerned had been silent since the beginning of the Common Market in 1958. The French-American convention of establishment was concluded in 1959;[1] it might well be maintained that this convention was concluded with the tacit recognition of relevant provisions of the already existing Treaty of Rome.

iv. *The right of establishment and the status of company managers or directors from non-member countries*

Since foreign investment is often accompanied by the appointment of foreign personnel as company managers or directors, it is necessary to consider the extent to which management, supervisory or top-level executive personnel from non-member countries must be included in the right of establishment within the Community.[2] Obviously nationals of member states, when employed in another member state are not regarded as 'foreign personnel' in the sense we have in mind; they will not be subject to any discriminatory treatment since they will be entitled, under the Treaty of Rome, to 'national treatment'.[3] Does the Treaty, however, apply also to managers and directors from non-member countries? It was shown above (pp. 201 ff.) that Article 52 cannot

---

[1] For the text of the convention, see *J.D.I.*, vol. 88, 1961, pp. 283 ff.

[2] Clearly, the question of foreign personnel is not a matter specific or exclusive for foreign-owned companies. It could equally concern companies without foreign capital. It is, however, more common to international investment accompanied by technical knowledge.

[3] Article 52, and Article 54/3(f); Stein and Nicholson, eds., *American Enterprise in the European Common Market*, vol. 2, p. 172.

apply to foreign nationals as physical persons. Can Article 54/3(f) apply to managerial personnel from non-member countries? Would a member state be entitled to refuse 'the entry of personnel [from third countries] belonging to the main establishment into managerial or supervisory posts' in agencies, branches and subsidiaries set up in its territory? If the answer is a negative one, then such foreign personnel will be subject to the municipal rules on alien residence and employment of the member states and thus not be governed by the Treaty.

A literal interpretation of the Treaty[1] provisions might well lead to an equivocal support of an affirmative or negative answer. In support of a negative viewpoint (foreign management personnel not included in the right of establishment), it could be argued that such personnel cannot qualify under Article 54/3(f) because they cannot be assimilated to nationals of member states under Article 52/1, which regulates the freedom of establishment of physical persons. The right of establishment of companies is governed by Article 58/1, under which companies are to be treated 'in the same way as individual nationals of Member States'. In both Articles there is, however, no reference, at least specifically, to management personnel from non-member countries. A forceful attempt could be made to extend the freedom of establishment to foreign management personnel by trying to assimilate managers and directors to labour, treated in Articles 48–51, but quite apart from objections to their assimilation to the category of salary earners, the text of the said articles and subsequent documents would not support such an attempt. While the text of Article 48/2 refers to 'Workers of the Member States' (without reference to nationality), Regulation 15 of the Council[2] relating to the first measures for effecting the free movement of workers within the Community, makes it clear that Article 48 applies to nationals of member states: 'Every national of a member state is entitled to accept salaried employment within the territory of another [member state] . . .'[3] Thus, the quoted text of the Treaty and

---

[1] On the interpretation of treaties, cf. Oppenheim, *International Law*, vol. 1, pp. 952 ff.; MacNair: *The Law of Treaties*, Oxford, 1961, pp. 364 ff.

[2] J.O.(C.E.), 1961, pp. 1073/61 ff.

[3] Regulation 15, Art. I/1 (translation by the author). For more general details on the free movement of workers, see Campbell and Thompson, *Common Market Law*, pp. 41 ff. Groeben and Boeckh, *Kommentar*, vol. 1, pp. 145 ff.

Q

subsequent documents would support the conclusion that managers and directors from non-member countries are not included in the right of establishment.[1]

It could be argued, on the other hand, that both the Treaty and subsequent documents regulate by inference the right of establishment also in respect to foreign management personnel. One such inference is to be found in the text of Article 58/1.[2] It may be assumed that the phrase 'formed in accordance with the law of a Member State . . .' applies also to provisions in the company law of a member state dealing with the appointment of directors and managers of a company. Such provisions on the inner organization of a company are to be regarded as an integral part of a country's company law. If, then, under the law of a member state the appointment of foreign personnel for management posts would be in conformity with the existing municipal regulations, the text of Article 58/1, 'in accordance with the law of a Member State', should apply equally to such foreign personnel. Foreign managers or directors would be just as much a part of the 'main establishment' to which Article 54/3(f) refers, as nationals from the member states, and hence be entitled to transfer for managerial or supervisory duties in agencies, branches and subsidiaries established in another member state.

In addition to the inference contained in the text of Article 58/1, additional support for an affirmative answer to our question can be sought in Article 54/3(f) within the context of the right of establishment, for, apart from its importance for the approximation or harmonization of municipal rules, the text of the said Article is also significant in respect to persons implied by 'the conditions governing the entry of personnel belonging to the main establishment into managerial or supervisory posts in . . . agencies, branches and subsidiaries' set up in the territory of a member state. It could be maintained that Article 54 contains not only procedural provisions as to how the right of establishment is to be progressively effected, but also important elements of sub-

---

[1] This is the conclusion reached by Leleux, *Doing Business in the Common Market*, p. 32.

[2] It should be remembered that the discussion in the present section of the study is based on the full implementation of the Treaty, as far as the right of establishment is concerned. Prior to that stage, and in the absence of regulations or directives by the Council, the municipal rules will, of course, continue to apply.

stantive Community law dealing with foreign personnel from non-member countries. The reasons are as follows.

Without Article 54/3(f), the freedom of nationals of member states to engage in non-wage-earning or unsalaried activities would still be adequately regulated by the Treaty. There are appropriate provisions in Article 52/2; it is laid down that such persons will enjoy national treatment by being subject to the same conditions as those applicable to 'nationals of the country where such establishment is effected . . .' It includes the qualification of nationals of member states to occupy top management positions in firms and companies. In the light of both Article 52 and Article 58, Article 54/3(f) would seem to be superfluous if it were not for the special problems related to management personnel from non-member countries. The status of such personnel is not specifically mentioned elsewhere in the Treaty; there is an inference relating to it implicit in Article 58. As for the substantive element pointing towards an affirmative rule that personnel from non-member countries will be included in the right of establishment, corroboration for it may be found in the reference in Article 54/3(f) to 'the progressive abolition of restrictions on freedom of establishment . . . both as regards the conditions for setting up agencies, branches or subsidiaries . . . and[1] as regards the conditions governing the entry of personnel belonging to the main establishment into managerial or supervisory posts in such agencies, branches and subsidiaries'. Under Article 53, 'Member States shall not introduce any new restrictions (for economic reasons) on the right of establishment . . . of nationals of other Member States.' Now under Article 58/1 companies are assimilated to nationals of member states, while Article 54/3(f) declares the progressive abolition of restrictions as regards the conditions governing the entry of personnel belonging to the main establishment into managerial or supervisory posts to be an integral part of the right of establishment. Hence, if foreign nationals are part of the management personnel of a main establishment, the conclusion is that the progressive abolition of restrictions should also apply to them. The text of the General Programme on the right of establishment seems to corroborate this conclusion. Under Head III, A, last paragraph, no restrictive provisions and practices of a limiting or hampering nature are to apply to 'the freedom of persons belonging to the principal establishment in a member

[1] Author's italics.

state to join the management or supervisory organs of its agencies, branches or subsidiary companies set up in another Member State'.[1] There is no reference therein to a distinction between nationals of member states and those of non-member countries. Section B of the same Head III of the General Programme excludes moreover the application of 'conditions which a legislative or administrative provision or an administrative practice place on admission to or the exercise of a non-wage earning activity and, even though applicable irrespective of nationality', result exclusively or mainly in a discrimination against foreigners who intend to exercise a non-wage-earning activity. It is, nevertheless, open to question whether a member state would still be entitled to discrimination against foreign personnel on grounds of non-recognition of diplomas, certificates and other evidence of qualification issued in or originating from non-member countries. Article 57/1 refers solely to 'the mutual recognition' of such evidence of qualification, and it could be argued that the term 'mutual' applies only to certificates, diplomas and other evidence of qualification issued only in the member states. It could, on the other hand, be argued that if foreign personnel were found duly qualified 'in accordance with the law' of the member state, under Article 58/1, at a company's main establishment, no further evidence of qualification should be necessary.

In conclusion, the right of establishment in regard to foreign personnel in the management and supervisory organs of a company formed in a member state under Article 58/1 should apply as follows:

1. The initial appointment of foreign nationals to managerial or supervisory posts in the main establishment of a company will be governed by the municipal rules of the given member state. Currently, foreign-owned enterprise is not subject to legal restrictions in appointing such personnel; uniform liberal rules apply. It is to be noted, however, that if a member state introduces restrictions in this respect, so that the appointment of foreign management personnel becomes difficult in that member state while the liberal policy of the remaining member states continues, the co-ordination of the relevant municipal rules in all member states may become necessary; foreign companies with subsidiaries and branches in various member states could otherwise circumvent, under the

[1] J.O., no. 2, 15 January 1962, p. 38; for English translation, Campbell and Thompson, *Common Market Law*, Appendix 8, p. 426.

Community law of establishment, the stricter rules of a given member state by proceeding first to the appointment of the desired personnel in the more liberal member states and transferring such personnel from there to the member state of destination.

2. Once admitted into the Common Market under the municipal law of a member state, as member of the managerial or supervisory personnel of a company formed in accordance with the provisions of Article 58/1, a national of a non-member country would not be subject to discrimination when transferring to managerial or supervisory posts in agencies, branches or subsidiaries of his company in other member states. Such a policy would be in line with the technical necessities of corporate activities and interstate investments. A contrary attitude would constitute an act of discrimination in terms of a distinction between companies formed in accordance with Article 58 but having, in the one case, community nationals as managerial personnel, and, in the other, foreign personnel. Such a distinction or discrimination does not seem justified under any provisions of the Treaty and would run counter to the technical necessities which prompt companies to transfer qualified personnel from one office to another.

3. A member state will be entitled, however, to object to the appointment of foreign personnel not attached to the main establishment of a company in the Community. The link between the right of establishment of Community law and a national from a non-member country is the requisite that such a person belong to the main establishment of a company. Direct appointment of such a person to a subsidiary, branch or agency of a company would be subject to the municipal rules of the given member state.

4. It seems, however, that the text of the Treaty will not allow the extension of this freedom to any developments envisaged in Article 220. By virtue of this Article, if the transfer of companies from one member state to another, under complete maintenance of their legal personality, were to become a possibility, unless otherwise provided in negotiations under Article 220, foreign management personnel would not be able to benefit—if Article 54/3(f) is interpreted, together with the last paragraph of Head III, A, of the General Programme, in isolation. In such a case it would be possible to argue that the texts refer only to transfers of personnel from the main establishment *to* agencies, branches or

subsidiary companies, but do not govern the total transfer of a company with its main establishment from one member state to another under complete maintenance of its legal personality. Since, on the other hand, Head III, Paragraph B of the General Programme (1962) for the Removal of Restrictions on the Freedom of Establishment[1] refers to the exclusion of all conditions resulting in restrictions to the right of establishment, the above distinction should not apply to a transfer of management personnel *from a main establishment to* agencies, branches or subsidiary company set up in another member state on the one hand, and, on the other, to a transfer *of the main establishment* together with its personnel from one member state to another. In the light of what is set out in Articles 58 and 54, with their frequent reference to branches, agencies and subsidiaries, it seems that the authors of the Treaty of Rome did not envisage, except in Article 220, the situation in which under a uniform company law or harmonization of company laws, the transfer of companies from one member state to another could take place without any change or adaptation in their legal personality.

### THE RIGHT OF ESTABLISHMENT IN ASSOCIATED COUNTRIES AND OVERSEAS TERRITORIES

Once established under municipal law in one of the member states of the E.E.C., a foreign-owned enterprise will be entitled to the Community right of establishment under Article 58 of the Treaty of Rome, which right refers to the *geographical* area in Europe of the six member states. In addition, however, foreign-owned enterprises operating in the Common Market will be further entitled to the right of establishment in associated countries and overseas territories, as set out in Article 132/5:

'In relations between Member States and the [associated] countries and [overseas] territories the right of establishment of nationals and companies shall be regulated in accordance with the provisions, and in accordance with the procedure laid down in the Chapter dealing with the right of establishment; this shall be effected on a non-discriminatory basis, subject to any special provisions made pursuant to Article 136.'[2]

[1] J.O.(C.E.), 1962, pp. 32/62 ff.
[2] Article 136 concerns procedural matters related to a transitional period. See also Article 8 of the Implementing Convention concerning the Associa-

We have already seen that the Community right of establish-ment includes foreign-owned enterprise. The application of Article 132/5 will be based on Articles 52–58 of the Treaty of Rome, which do not discriminate against foreign-owned enter-prise and rule out any discrimination, including any restrictions concerning foreign-owned companies in the Community. Accord-ingly, such companies will be capable of setting up agencies, branches or subsidiaries in the associated countries or overseas territories, without being subject to the domestic laws and regula-tions *applicable in those places* in respect of foreign investment originating from non-member countries, i.e. from countries out-side the E.E.C.[1]

Article 136 of the Treaty of Rome provided for the conclusion of an implementing convention annexed to the Treaty, for an initial period of five years after the establishment of the Common Market on 1 January 1958, on matters related to the association of countries and overseas territories with the Community. The im-plementing convention was signed on the same date as the Treaty of Rome, 25 March 1957. In Article 8, it stated that the right of establishment shall, in each of the countries or territories, 'be progressively extended to nationals, firms or companies of Mem-ber States other than that State having special relations with the country or territory concerned'.

By 31 March 1965, the E.E.C. had concluded treaties of associa-tion with Greece, Turkey, a number of African states and Mada-gascar. The treaty with Greece, signed on 29 July 1961, came into

---

tion with the Community of the Overseas Countries and Territories. Text in: *Treaty establ. the E.E.C.*, H.M.S.O., London, 1962, p. 141.

For a list of overseas countries and territories, see *Treaty establ. the E.E.C.*, p. 115. For an application of Article 58 with respect to French overseas territories, see Article 2 of the Decree no. 62-1514 of 27 November 1962 (J.O., 18 December 1962); Articles 1–2 of Decree no. 62-1954 of 29 December 1962 (J.O., 30 December 1962), fixing that for insurance business the condi-tions of establishment in French overseas territories are to apply to nationals of E.E.C. states other than France.

[1] For general material on aspects of association, see E.E.C. *Bulletin*, March 1964, no. 3-64, pp. 21–5, views on legal, economic and political aspects and the scope of association of the E.E.C. with the African States and Mada-gascar. For a study on Africa in relation to the Common Market, Th. Balogh, in: *Journ. of Common Market Studies*, vol. 1, no. 1, 1962, pp. 79 ff. For an earlier study on the same topic, E. Gambelli: *La C.E.E.*, Milan, 1960; also Catalano: *Manuel de Droit des Communautés Européennes*, p. 377.

force at the end of 1962,[1] that with Turkey came into force in
1964; the treaty with the associated African states and Madagascar
was signed on 20 July 1963 and is being currently implemented.[2]
Negotiations with a number of other countries, including Nigeria
and Austria, are proceeding.

In their respective agreements, Greece and Turkey agree to
base themselves on Articles 52 to 56 inclusive and Article 58
of the Treaty of Rome, in order to eliminate restrictions on the
freedom of establishment between them, respectively, and the
E.E.C.[3]

In a Decision concerning the association of countries and overseas territories with the E.E.C., the Council of the E.E.C. set out
in Article 25 that nationals and companies of all member states
shall be treated on a footing of equality in associated countries
and territories, in matters related to the right of establishment and
supply of services, provided the member state of nationals and
companies in question grants, on a basis of reciprocity, the same
rights to nationals and companies of the member state having particular relations with the country or territory in question, as well
as to companies of the country or territory in question.[4] Article 27
of the same Decision of the Council adds that the right of establishment in associated countries and territories concerns the access
to non-salaried activities and their exercise, the formation and
management of undertakings, notably of companies, as well as the
setting up of agencies, offices or branches.[5] Article 29/1 of the
Council's Decision of 11 June, 1964 corresponds to the content of
Article 58/2 of the Treaty of Rome; Article 29/2 is similar to
Article 58/1. According to Article 29/2, companies constituted in

[1] On the Greek economy in relation to the Common Market, P. L.
Reynaud, in: *Scienze Economiche e Commerciale*, 10th year, October 1963,
no. 10, pp. 975 ff.

[2] For surveys of the Convention of Association with African states and
Madagascar, cf. D. Olivier: *Rev. M.C.*, 6th year, 1963, pp. 480 ff., also ibid.,
an article by 'XXX', pp. 22 ff, especially p. 23. G. van Benthem van den
Bergh, in: *C.M.L. Rev.*, vol. 1, no. 2, September 1963, basic facts pp. 156 f.,
on the right of establishment pp. 162, 173.

[3] For the text of Association Agreement between Turkey and the E.E.C.,
see *Investment Guide to Turkey*, Investment Promotion Publ. Series, no.
E-13/64, Investment Promotion and Information Center, Dept. of Industry,
Istanbul 1964, pp. 165 ff., Art. 13, p. 167.

[4] J.O.(C.E.), 1964, p. 1476/64, Council Decision of 25 February 1964; also
J.O.(C.E.), 1960, p. 147/60 ff.

[5] J.O.(C.E.), 1964, p. 1477/64.

accordance with the law of a member state and having only their registered seat (*siège statutaire*) in a member state, must exercise activities that constitute an effective and continuous link with the economy of the given member state.[1] With reference to the non-cumulative requirements of Article 58/1 of the Treaty, it appears that, according to the Council, three requirements will after all be necessary: if a given company is (i) constituted in accordance with the law of a member state, and (ii) has only its registered office in that member state, these two requirements will have to be supplemented by a third one, namely an effective link with the economy of that member state. This clearly indicates that the enumeration of Article 58/1 is not meant to be exhaustive.

In a parallel Decision concerning the application of certain provisions on the right of establishment and payments to French overseas territories, the Council stipulates in Article 1 that Articles 52–58 of the Treaty of Rome shall be applicable to the said overseas territories under conditions provided for by the Council's Decision. Accordingly, the right of establishment is to be progressively extended to nationals and companies of the other five member states. All restrictions are to be eliminated within three years after the Decision of the Council comes into force, i.e. restrictions will be completely abolished by the middle of 1967.[2]

Thus, the right of establishment of the E.E.C. is favourable to foreign-owned enterprise not only in respect of the six member states, but also in relation to their associated countries and overseas territories. Establishment in one of the member states, in accordance with the municipal law of the given member state, will qualify a foreign-owned enterprise to the right of establishment in the remaining parts of the E.E.C. and in the associated regions outside it. The two basic principles which apply thereby are those of equality of treatment and of an effective link between the given enterprise and the member state where such enterprise is established. As a corollary to this rule, foreign undertakings established in one of the associated countries or overseas territories will have access for establishment in one or more of the E.E.C. countries.

[1] Ibid.
[2] Council, Decision of 25 February, 1964, in J.O.(C.E.), 1964, p. 1484/64.

## THE SUPPLY OF SERVICES: PUBLIC CONTRACTS

In the context of the Treaty of Rome, services are activities of a temporary character exercised across municipal boundaries, so that the supplier is established in a member state 'other than that of the person for whom the services are intended'.[1] There is no express definition for the term services as used in the Treaty. Article 60/1 sets out that the term shall include those 'normally provided against remuneration, in so far as they are not governed by the provisions relating to the free movement of goods, capital and persons'. Article 60/2 refers to an indicative enumeration: 'Services shall include in particular: (a) activities of an industrial character, (b) . . . of a commercial character, (c) artisan activities; (d) activities of the liberal professions.'

The right to supply services, as defined under Community law, is not accessible to nationals (natural or legal persons) of non-member countries, but foreign-owned undertakings incorporated in member states will be entitled to it. This distinction is in accordance with the right of establishment of Community law (Articles 52 ff.) which makes a similar distinction. The Treaty in Article 59/2 leaves, however, a margin for the possible extension of the right to supply services across municipal boundaries to nationals of non-member countries: 'The Council, acting unanimously, on the proposal of the Commission, may extend the provisions of [the] Chapter [on services[2]] to include services provided by nationals of a third country who are established within the Community.' This provision implies, similarly to Article 52/1, the requisite of a continuous and effective link between the given nationals of non-member states and also nationals of member states and the economy of the Common Market. Article 52/1 stipulates that nationals of member states can qualify under the Community right of establishment if they are already 'established in the territory' of a member state. Nationals of member states who are not established within the Community cannot be bene-

---

[1] Article 59/1 of the Treaty of Rome; also Articles 59–66. The supply of services includes the possibility that the person providing a given service may have to practice his activity temporarily in the state where the service is provided, 'under the same conditions as are imposed by that State on its own nationals' (Article 60(3)). For comments on the right to supply services under Community law, see Campbell and Thompson, *Common Market Law*, pp. 48 ff.

[2] Arts. 59–66, more specifically 60–61: types of services.

ficiaries of the right to supply services.[1] The requirements for companies when supplying services are the same as those set out in Article 58/1 for the right of establishment. In addition, the necessity of an effective link is indicated as another requirement by the General Programme concerning the supply of services.

The rule of Community treatment should apply in respect of public contracts also to foreign-owned undertakings irrespective of ownership, provided the undertaking concerned has an effective link with the economic life of the Common Market. There is no indication to the contrary in the text of the Treaty. There is, on the other hand, no express mention either of the elimination of restrictions in respect of foreign-owned firms, with respect to their capacity to enter into contracts with public authorities.[2] Community organs shall apply the principle of equal treatment '[as] regards investments financed by the Community in associated countries and territories', for 'participation in tenders and supplies shall be open on equal terms to all natural and legal persons who are nationals of Member states or of the [associated] countries and territories'.[3] This implies that foreign-owned

---

[1] Title I of the General Programme issued by the Council for the abolition of restrictions to the free movement of services within the Community: J.O.(C.E.), 1962, p. 32/62. The term 'establishment' means, in the context of the Treaty, a certain continuity of economic activities in one of the member states, in contrast to the term 'services' which may be in a member state other than the one where the centre of activities of a business undertaking is situated. See Campbell and Thompson, *Common Market Law*, p. 47; Stein and Nicholson, eds., *American Enterprise in the European Common Market*, vol. 2, pp. 184–6 for a general commentary on the contents of Article 60 of the Treaty.

[2] E.E.C. *Bulletin*, Supplement 5, 1964, pp. 19 ff. First draft directive concerning the participation of firms in the execution of building work for governments, local or regional authorities and other public corporations, submitted by the Commission to the Council on 16 March 1964. See also E.E.C. *Bulletin*, Suppl. 9/10-64, 1964, pp. 12 ff. of the Bulletin, and pp. 33–4 of the Supplement. For a comparative survey on contracts with and services to public administrative authorities, J. P. Hainaut and R. Joliet: *Les Contrats de Travaux et de Fournitures de l'Administration dans le Marché Commun*, vols. I–II, Brussels, 1963. Municipal rules on discriminating non-nationals will have to be eliminated in application of Community law: A. de Grand Ry, in: *Rev. M.C.*, nos. 37–38, June–August 1961. See Junckerstorff, *Manual*, p. 253; also the remark of J. L. Blondeel, in Friedmann and Pugh, *Legal Aspects of Foreign Investment*, pp. 61–2, footnote 50.

[3] Art. 132/4 of the Treaty, Part Four: Association of Overseas Countries and Territories.

undertakings established in the E.E.C. in accordance with Article 58/1 will be able to participate in such tenders and supplies of services. This would be in accordance with the content of Article 7 of the Treaty which prohibits 'any discrimination on the grounds of nationality . . .'

## THE FREE MOVEMENT OF CAPITAL WITHIN THE COMMUNITY

Closely linked with the freedom of establishment and of supplying services within the Community, is the movement of capital between the member states.[1] In this respect, the Treaty is more liberal towards nationals of non-member countries than in respect of their right of establishment and freedom to supply services. As we have seen already in the foregoing sections, nationals of non-member countries, i.e. natural persons, will not be qualified under the Treaty to avail themselves of the Community law of establishment, though the right to supply services across the national borders of member states may be extended to include nationals (natural or legal persons) of non-member countries established within the Community (Article 59/2). For the movement of capital, however, foreign nationals will qualify under Article 67/1 in their capacity as residents of member states, without 'any discrimination based on the nationality or on the place of residence of the parties or on the place where such capital is invested'. The usefulness of this provision for nationals of non-member countries, as far as their business activities are concerned, will be restricted by the fact that they will not enjoy the Community right of establishment. Abuse of the right set out in Article 67 can be averted by the application of Article 70/2 against capital movements which try to 'evade the rules of one of the Member States in regard to third countries'.[2]

---

[1] Since May 1960, the movement of capital within the Community is liberalized: the First Directive of the Council, with Annexes on the implementation of the provisions contained in Article 67. J.O.(C.E.), 1960, pp. 921/60 ff.; also E.E.C. *Bulletin*, no. 12, 1964, pp. 19–20.

[2] Wohlfarth, *EWG. Kommentar*, p. 175. Stein and Nicholson, eds., *American Enterprise in the Eur. Common Market*, vol. 2, pp. 175, 176, also p. 120; O.E.C.D., Code on the Liberalization of Capital Movements (as in January 1965).

## THE RIGHT OF ESTABLISHMENT AND DISINVESTMENT OF FOREIGN CAPITAL

The content of this section will be rather theoretical, as it will deal with a situation which may possibly arise in the E.E.C. after the transitional period.

The two ways in which foreign investment capital may enter a member state have already been examined: (i) directly from a non-member country; in such a case municipal rules on exchange control will govern both the investment and disinvestment of the given foreign capital; and (ii) through another member state, under the Community law of establishment (Article 58); for instance, a British-owned company established in Germany will be able to invest in France and set up a subsidiary there. Community law regulates, through the right of establishment, the intermember investment of foreign capital; it is, however, silent as to how the possible disinvestment of foreign capital that has availed itself of the Community right of establishment should be effected.

An easy solution would be the assertion that foreign capital should be transferred abroad, in case of disinvestment, through the country of its initial entry. To use the example suggested above, this would be Germany. Germany could, in turn, claim that the given investment capital, having been permanently transferred at intermember level to France, had ceased to be foreign capital *in* Germany and has consequently become foreign capital *in* France. In this case France would be considered responsible for the foreign exchange needed for the transfer of disinvested capital. France could argue, in turn, that it could not be responsible for this disinvestment since the given foreign capital had not entered its territory from 'abroad' under its municipal rules on foreign exchange applicable to foreign investment. The answers to the implied questions will depend on the extent of the interpretation given to the term 'establishment' in the context of the Treaty.

Referring to 'nationals of any Member State established in the territory of any Member State', Article 52 sets out that the right of establishment shall apply to 'the setting up of agencies, branches or subsidiaries' (Art. 52/1, last sentence), and shall include 'the right to engage in and carry on non-wage-earning activities,[1] to set up and manage undertakings and, in particular,

[1] Non-wage-earning activities comprise services (Articles 59–66 of the Treaty), trading in goods, manufacturing, banking: Groeben and Boeckh, *Kommentar*, vol. 1, n. 8 under Article 52; see also ibid., n. 9 under Article 221.

firms and companies (*sociétés*) within the meaning of Article 58/2'
on an equal footing with nationals of the country of establishment. Since companies and firms qualifying under Article 58/1
are to be 'treated in the same way as individual nationals of
Member States', it is clear that the provisions of Article 52 will
also apply to companies.

Such an assimilation presupposes, however, the recognition,
throughout the Community, of the legal personality of companies
and firms formed in accordance with the law of a member state.
Recognition is implied in Article 58 and explicitly mentioned in
Article 220 of the Treaty of Rome. There is, however, a difference
in the meaning attached, in Articles 58 and 220, to the term 'establishment' with reference to companies, a distinction which is
relevant to the question of disinvestment of foreign capital that
enters a member state through another member state.

Article 58 implies the capacity of companies as legal persons to
set up agencies, branches or subsidiaries in a member state and
thus corresponds to the current *interstate* practice of recognizing
foreign companies as legal entities. When the Treaty of Rome is
fully implemented, the current *interstate* practice will become *intermember* (Community) law under which the mutual recognition of
Community companies and firms will be independent of any
bilateral agreements or unilateral municipal rules. While Article 58
implies the capacity of Community companies as legal persons, it
does not regulate their transfer from one member state to another,
for purposes of establishment, without the necessity of modifying
or completely transforming their legal personality. In other words,
under Article 58, companies in the Common Market are to be
recognized as legal persons with a capacity to set up business or
subsidiaries in a member state other than the member state where
they have been incorporated. This appears to be the scope of the
term 'establishment' as used in Article 58—it refers to the right
to set up business or subsidiaries in another state, but not the
right of complete transfer from one member state to another.

Article 220 seems, on the other hand, to have a wider meaning
attached to 'establishment', because it refers to 'the maintenance of
[the] legal personality' of firms or companies as defined in
Article 58, 'if their registered office is *transferred*[1] from one country to another . . .' These terms imply clearly the capacity of companies to transfer from one member state to another *without*

[1] Author's italics.

having to modify their legal personality and adapt it to the domestic law of the given member state. In this respect, the Treaty acknowledges the fact that the current situation and inter-member rules of establishment in the E.E.C. cannot satisfy the requirements of the Treaty and provides that, for that purpose, 'Member States shall, in so far as necessary, enter into negotiations with each other with a view to ensuring for the benefit of their nationals [and legal persons assimilated to them] . . . the mutual recognition of firms or companies . . .'[1]

Let us assume that with the full implementation of the Treaty the mutual recognition of firms or companies has been effected. A company formed in Belgium with foreign capital from a third non-member country, may move its registered office and the centre of its activities to, say, Germany without having to introduce any changes in its statutes in order to adapt itself to the provisions of domestic law in Germany.[2] If this foreign-owned company intended, after a number of years, to disinvest and re-transfer abroad the capital originally brought first from a non-member country to Belgium and subsequently to Germany, the question would arise as to which member state, Belgium or Germany, would be bound by law to provide the necessary foreign exchange needed for the repatriation of the invested capital. Belgium, in our example, could decline an obligation in this respect on grounds that the foreign-owned company, originally formed under its domestic law, had become, by transferring its registered office to Germany, a German company. Germany could, in our example, argue in turn, that it could not incur any obligation towards nationals of non-member countries as a result of the initial foreign investment effected under Belgian law. This hypothetical situation suggests how, with the progressive implementation of the Treaty of Rome, it will be necessary to effect also a corresponding approximation or harmonization of municipal regulations on foreign investment in the member states. Provision could be made to provide for such an approximation or harmonization in connection with negotiations envisaged under Article 220.

[1] For comments on Article 220 see: Stein and Nicholson, eds., *American Enterprise in the Eur. Common Market*, vol. 2, p. 170; Audinet, *J.D.I.*, vol. 86, 1959, pp. 1019–21; Groeben and Boeckh, *Kommentar*, vol. 1, p. 182, no. 5b, last par., pp. 183, n. 5c.

[2] The hypothetical situation of the example considered here involves also the question of diverging company laws. The difficulties involved therein are surveyed in chapter XII on harmonization.

*Possible solutions*

1. An agreement at Community level that any member state authorizing the initial establishment of foreign investment from a non-member country in its own territory will be responsible for the disinvestment of it by providing the necessary foreign exchange. Of course, while the favourable foreign exchange position of the E.E.C. countries continues, the question is not a serious one.

2. An arrangement that the member state in which a question of disinvestment arises should be responsible for effecting the transfer abroad of the capital funds involved.

3. As a possibility of a far distant future, a monetary union of the E.E.C. would make the question superfluous by having a uniform foreign exchange, investment and disinvestment system for all of the member states.

So far, during the transitional period, the questions outlined here have not yet arisen, owing to the fact that foreign investors do not need to invest in a given member state via another member state, but can avail themselves of the liberal policy of the six countries and thus have direct access from a non-member country to the member state in question. Similarly, disinvestment and re-transfer of funds abroad can at present be effected directly, without the necessity of disinvesting via another member state.

CONCLUSIONS

The Community law of establishment regulates the intermember movement of persons, services and capital. It distinguishes between Community and foreign nationals and bars the latter from the right of establishment. It entitles, however, foreign capital to Community treatment in accordance with the provisions of Article 58. The criteria applicable to this are those of investment for the formation of companies and firms in accordance with the law of a member state, and the existence of a link with the economic life of the E.E.C. The elusive and complicated criteria related to the nationality of investors are excluded from application, eliminating thus the need for a complicated machinery of administrative control which would otherwise be necessary. Under the Community right of establishment, entry into one of the member states is, for a foreign investor, tantamount to access to all member states of the E.E.C., and, in addition, to the associated countries and overseas territories. The advantage implied thereby cannot be underestimated as far as the attractiveness or investment climate of the E.E.C. to foreign capital is concerned.

The right of establishment provides also for all of the accessory provisions that are necessary for economic activities throughout the E.E.C.—capital movements and the transfer of managerial personnel from one member state to another. While some of the clauses in the Treaty, for example, Article 54/3(f), and the term 'maintenance of [corporate] personality' in Article 220 will need elaboration on the part of the E.E.C. executive organs, the principles of liberalism and Community treatment in their extension to foreign investment are clearly defined and constitute important foundations of legal security and predictability. These elements are important for the assessment of investment climate in a region like the E.E.C., and it may be suggested that the Treaty of Rome, in its articles on the right of establishment, both corroborates and consolidates the liberal policy that its member states currently apply towards foreign investment.

The right of establishment involves, however, the question of alignment or harmonization of municipal laws in their relevance to companies and hence also to foreign investors. In this respect, a margin of necessities exists, which is examined in greater detail in chapter XII. In the light of the situation in March 1965, in the opinion of the present author, the extent to which harmonization will be necessary concerns not so much the needs of foreign-owned enterprises as those of Community enterprise. Under pressure exerted by the financially and technologically more powerful American firms operating in certain industrial sectors of the Common Market, industrial quarters in France and Germany have been suggesting the necessity of some harmonization as one of the means for promoting the competitiveness of Community enterprise in comparison with foreign undertakings. Some of the remarks made in this connection are closely linked with the inter-member freedom of establishment and mergers.

R

# CHAPTER XI

## THE RULES OF COMPETITION

It is relevant to ask how and to what extent the rules of competition of the Treaty of Rome (Articles 85 ff.) can affect the operations of foreign investors in the E.E.C. These questions concern primarily the co-ordinated activities of foreign firms and their subsidiaries in the Community. The situation of foreign principals and of their subsidiaries involves special relationships, and it may be asked whether the nature of these relationships could affect the way in which the Community law of restrictive practices would apply to them. In discussing this question, only related aspects of Community law will be covered, and no comprehensive survey of the still developing, and in many respects intractable, law of the E.E.C. will be made.[1] The intricate question of relationship between municipal and Community law will not be discussed, nor the details of the system of registration reviewed. This has been adequately done in specialist studies cited.

We propose, however, to discuss another question which may seem at first unconventional—one which has never been raised in connection with Articles 85 ff. nor indeed envisaged by the authors of the Treaty of Rome. It concerns the function of Articles 85 ff. as possibly regulating competition between foreign undertakings, on the one side, and domestic enterprises, on the other. It seems appropriate to raise this question in view of the fact that, in the three years 1963-5, some industrial quarters in the

[1] For surveys and studies of the law of restrictive practices in the E.E.C. see: A. Campbell: *Restrictive Trading Agreements in the Common Market*, London, 1964; F. Honig and others: *Cartel Law of the E.E.C.*, London, 1963; T. C. Clark, in *Journ. Amer. Bar Assoc.*, vol. 49, 1963, pp. 837-9; P. Pujade: in *Aspects of European Integration* (an Anglo-French symposium), London, 1962, pp. 88 ff.; *I.C.L.Q.*, Suppl. Publ. no. 6, 1963; P. Verloren van Themaat, pp. 18 ff., H. Schumacher, pp. 65 ff.; P. Verloren van Themaat: in *New York Univ. Law Review*, vol. 38, 1963, pp. 435 ff.; W. L. Fugate, ibid., pp. 458 ff.; G. Nebolsine, ibid., pp. 479 ff., G. J. Weiser, ibid., pp. 496 ff.; M. M. van Notten, ibid., pp. 525 ff.; Int. Bar Association, 9th Conference (Edinburgh 1962), pp. 151 ff.; A. K. Lewis and J. A. Kemp: *Registration of Commercial and Licence Agreements in the Common Market*, London, 1962; H. van den Heuvel, *A.J.C.L.*, vol. 12, 1963, pp. 172-93.

E.E.C. have expressed concern about the threat of domination by foreign-owned enterprise in certain industrial sectors of the Common Market, referring chiefly to highly competitive American firms. The object of the following discussion will be to discover whether the concern expressed can be related to the Community rules of competition, and whether, in case of need, Community law could cope with the problem of regulating competition between financially and technologically strong foreign-owned firms and Community enterprises.

The main objective of Community law on restrictive practices is to provide for 'a harmonious development of economic activities' through 'a system ensuring that competition in the Common Market is not distorted'.[1] The proposed system is set out in broad terms in Articles 85 ff. of the Treaty. Based primarily on a functional approach or on the principle of effect, the broad formulation of the rules enunciated is well adapted to the necessities of a progressive economic integration, and it involves the evolution of a new framework of reference in which it is inadvisable to fix details in advance. As the integration progresses and, in its different stages, varying economic forces assert their positive or negative influence, it becomes indispensable that basic principles be applied with flexibility. A too formal and legalistic approach would clash with the requirement of flexibility in promoting and co-ordinating the objectives of the Common Market, while an exaggeratedly pragmatic approach would have defeated the purpose of security and predictability as a necessary object of these legal rules.

Thus, 'all agreements between undertakings, all decisions by associations of undertakings and all concerted practices . . . shall be prohibited as incompatible with the Common Market' if they are 'liable to affect trade between Member States' and are 'designed to prevent, restrict or distort competition within the Common Market or which have this effect' (Article 85/1). The application of this provision to restrictive practices hinges upon the *adverse* effect that such practices may have upon trade *between member states*. Applying the same functional approach and referring to the same types of practices, namely 'any agreement or type of agreement between undertakings, any decision or type of decision by associations of undertakings, and any concerted practice or type of concerted practice', paragraph 3 of the same

---

[1] Articles 2 and 3 par. 1(f) of the Treaty of Rome.

Article 85 states that the provisions of the above-quoted paragraph 1 may be declared inapplicable if these practices help 'to improve the production or distribution of goods or to promote technical or economic progress, whilst allowing consumers a fair share of the resulting profit' without involving unnecessary restrictions and without eliminating competition 'in respect of a substantial part of the goods concerned'.[1]

A similar functional approach is found in the provisions of Article 86 on the 'dominant position.' This article does not rule out a dominant position by 'one or more undertakings' but 'any improper exploitation' thereof 'within the Common Market or within a substantial part of it'. Any such improper exploitation 'shall be deemed to be incompatible with the Common Market and shall be prohibited, in so far as trade between Member States could be affected by it'. Article 86 refers then to a (non-exhaustive) list of practices which 'in particular' would be tantamount to improper exploitation (imposition of unfair prices; restrictions in production, marketing and research; agreements with unequal terms; and the inclusion, in agreements, of additional obligations unconnected with the content of a given contract).

The broad terms of Articles 85–86 obviously leave a wide margin for their concrete interpretation and implementation. Accordingly, the Council of the E.E.C has been empowered under Article 87/1 to issue 'the necessary regulations or directives to put into effect the principles set out in Articles 85 and 86. The Council shall decide on these . . . on a proposal of the Commission and after consulting the Assembly'. The law-making function of the regulations or directives is indicated in paragraphs 2(b) and 2(c) of the same Article 87, according to which, the regulations or directives shall be designed 'to decide exactly how Article 85/3 is to be applied . . . [and] to define, where necessary, the extent to which the provisions of Articles 85 and 86 are to be applied in the various economic sectors'. The implementation and supervision of the principles laid down in Articles 85 and 86 are entrusted to the Commission under Article 89/1 of the Treaty. It is thus obvious that the currently developing law[2] of restrictive practices in intermember trade

[1] For commentaries, Groeben and Boeckh, *Kommentar*, vol. 1; Campbell, *Restrictive Trading Agreements*, pp. 8 ff.; Honig, *Cartel Law*, pp. 8 ff.
[2] A broad meaning is being attached to the term 'law' in this sentence. The Community law on restrictive practices would be, strictly speaking,

within the E.E.C. will be based not only on the broadly formulated rules of Articles 85 ff. but also on the subsequent regulations, directives, statements and opinions issued or respectively expressed by the executive organs of the E.E.C., and on the decisions of the Court of Justice of the European Communities.[1]

Concerning the relationship of foreign principals and their subsidiaries in respect of restrictive trading agreements between them, a number of comments may be submitted on the basis of the situation as in March 1965.

## The terms 'undertaking' and 'association of undertakings'[2]

These terms, as used in Articles 85–86, are not defined by the Treaty of Rome or by regulations issued subsequently by the Council in implementation thereof.[3] It could be questioned whether a legal or economic interpretation of them would influence the compatibility or incompatibility of restrictive trading agreements with Community law, concluded between foreign principals and their respective subsidiaries in the E.E.C. In concrete terms, it could make all the difference if a principal and its one or more subsidiaries were considered to be, because of their economic interdependence, a single entity or undertaking for the purpose of Article 85. At the present stage of developments, as far as Community rules on restrictive practices are concerned, the legal or economic interpretations of the terms 'undertaking' and 'association of undertakings' are immaterial.

---

Articles 85–94, especially Articles 85–86, of the Treaty of Rome. Since, however, these Articles are vague and their precise legal significance cannot be ascertained without the implementation rules issued by the Council and views set out by the Commission in Communications, it becomes necessary to include under 'law' the relevant documents and views of the E.E.C. executive organs. See Campbell and Thompson, *Common Market Law*, comments on p. 247 (under Article 85); Honig, *Cartel Law*, p. 2.

[1] A note on regulations issued up to March 1965 is appended to this chapter.

[2] 'Undertaking' is the term used in the English translation published by H.M. Stationery Office, Art. 85, p. 32. The term 'enterprise' is used in Campbell and Thompson, *Common Market Law*, pp. 246–7 (text of Art. 85 and comments), and by Honig and others, *Cartel Law of the E.E.C.*, p. 7, text of Art. 85 and commentary pp. 8 ff.

[3] D. G. Valentine, *Court of Justice of the Eur. Communities*, vol. 1, p. 290. *C.M.L. Rep.*, vol. III, Part II, pp. 352–3, for a discussion of the term 'enterprise' (*Sorema v. High Authority*).

Agreements between principals and their respective subsidiaries could, as a result of their adverse effect on trade between member states, fall within the ambit of Articles 85 and/or 86. The term 'undertaking' may be assumed to include any person or persons, natural or legal, capable of exercising a business or economic activity, and capable of concluding agreements.[1] If principals and their subsidiaries are considered as different (separate) undertakings, the provisions of Article 85/1, applicable to practices *between* undertakings, would become operative. If, on the other hand, principals and their subsidiaries are treated as a single entity, the question of 'improper exploitation . . . of a dominant position' could arise under Article 86. Thus, it may be said that an exemption from the provisions of Articles 85–86 cannot be dependent on a definition of the term 'undertaking' in its application to the relationship of principals to their respective subsidiaries.[2] As indicated above the decisive criterion, on which the application of Articles 85–86 will depend, will be the fact that the intended restrictive practices are 'liable to affect trade between Member States and . . . are designed to prevent, restrict or distort competition within the Common Market or . . . have this effect'. The legal or economic relationship of undertakings which participate as principal and subsidiary in such practices will be

---

[1] See comments in Campbell and Thompson, *Common Market Law*, p. 247; Honig, *Cartel Law*, pp. 8–9. For a discussion of the term in relation to municipal and Community law, see O. Gandenberger: 'Was ist ein Unternehmen' in which the author examines the term within the context of German cartel law.

J. de Rochemont: 'La notion d'entreprise dans le droit des Communautés Européennes', *Droit Européen*, no. 33, 1964, pp. 306–22. The author surveys the meaning of the term in French legal usage, in the texts of the three Community treaties and in the deliberations of the Court of Justice of the European Communities.

[2] In a few cases, the Court of Justice of the European Communities had to deal with the definition of the term 'enterprise': *Kloeckner Werke A.G. v. The High Authority* (Case 17–61), *Mannesmann A.G. v. The High Authority* (Case 19–61), and *Hoesch A.G. v. The High Authority* (Case 20–61). The Court adopted the view that for tax purposes each subsidiary had to be deemed to be a distinct legal entity. Owing to the particular nature of the legal issue involved (liability for equalization payments due on the use of scrap metal), the Court's decision could hardly be applied to Article 85 of the Treaty of Rome. The treatment of an enterprise can vary greatly and even be contradictory between the application of different sets of legal rules, e.g. for taxation, contracts, etc.

immaterial. All subsequent regulations and statements issued respectively by the Council and Commission, in implementation of Articles 85–86, refer to the nature of and relationship established by restrictive trading agreements between undertakings and not to the legal or economic interdependence of the latter. In Regulation 17 of the Council, the first implementing one, Article 1 refers to agreements, decisions and concerted practices that constitute the object of Article 85/1, and to any abuse of a dominant position within the meaning of Article 86. It declares them as prohibited without prior decision to this effect being required. Article 2 of the same regulation deals with negative clearances that the Commission may issue at the request of the undertakings, or associations of undertakings, concerned. The negative clearance will be based on the merits of the trading agreements and not on the nature of relationship that exists between the undertakings.[1] The first Statement of the Commission (November 1962) on the application of Article 85 of the Treaty to certain exclusive distribution agreements refers to the market position, and states that the provisions of Article 85/1 will not apply for a period of three years, i.e. until November 1965, to agreements in which the participating undertakings do not occupy a dominant position in the Common Market or within a substantial part of it.[2] In its statement on exclusive agency contracts made with commercial agents (1962), the Commission sets out the rules which will be applied to distinguish between commercial agents and 'independent traders'. Again, the rules will be applied independently of the nature of any other relationship between the undertakings concerned.[3] Finally, Regulation no. 19/65/CEE of 2 March 1965 enunciates the rules that will be applied when issuing collective or block exemptions to certain categories of agreements and concerted practices, in application of Article 85/3 of the Treaty.[4] Reference therein is once more to categories of agreements and not to categories of legal or economic relationships between undertakings.

[1] See Campbell, *Restrictive Trading Agreements*, pp. 32 ff. for an English translation of the relevant Articles and commentaries; also Honig, *Cartel Law*, pp. 42 ff.

[2] Campbell, ibid., pp. 119 and 104.

[3] Campbell, ibid., pp. 128–9, 133.

[4] J.O.(C.E.), 1965, pp. 533/65 ff.

*'Trade between member states'*

Restrictive practices will be caught by Article 85 if they (i) constitute in effect an agreement,[1] (ii) are liable to affect[2] trade between member states and (iii) have as their object the prevention, restriction or distortion of competition within the Common Market.[3] All three mentioned requirements of Article 85/1 are based on the principle of effect: the qualification of restrictive practices will not depend on their formal or other characteristics as an agreement but on their effective impact on trade within the Community. Hence, the term 'agreement' will have to be interpreted comprehensively.[4] The remaining requirements (ii) and (iii) above in-

---

[1] The agreements referred to in Article 85, par. 1(a)–(e) are indicative and not exhaustive, all the more since the text lists them with the indication 'in particular': Campbell, *Restrictive Trading Agreements*, pp. 8–9.

[2] 'Liable to affect' should be interpreted in the sense liable to affect harmfully or adversely, as implied by the German, Italian and Dutch texts (German: *beeinträchtigen*, Italian: *pregiudicare*, Dutch: *ongunstig beinvloeden*); the French corresponding term does not convey the suggested meaning as well as do the other three languages. Furthermore, the logical relationship between par. 1 and par. 3 of the same Article points towards the suggested interpretation: par. 3 refers to agreements that may have a positive or beneficial effect on the trade of the Community and as such exempts them from the prohibition set out in par. 1 which can thus refer to agreements that are liable to have an *adverse* effect on trade between member states. See par. 1 of Article 92 where the terms 'adversely affects trade between Member States' are used. P. Verloren van Themaat, in: *New York Univ. Law Rev.*, vol. 38, 1963, pp. 45 f.

[3] This third requirement can be interpreted as complementary to the terms 'trade between Member States' in the sense that Article 85 deals solely with trade *between* member states *within* but not *outside* the Common Market. This invites a comment which is legally a relevant one though academic in nature: restrictive practices that aimed at the export trade of one or more member states, adversely affecting the exports of one in favour of exports from the other(s) in a given foreign market, even though involving nationals of one or more member states, would not be caught by the provisions of Article 85/1. This is at least the conclusion that can be drawn from the interpretation of the third requirement in par. 1 of Article 85, in conjunction with the phrase 'trade between Member States'. See M. R. Kruithof: 'The application of the Common Market Anti-Trust Provisions to international restraints of trade', *C.M.L. Rev.*, vol. 2, 1964, p. 72; A. Deringer: 'Les règles de concurrence au sein de la C.E.E.', *Rev. M.C.*, 1963, p. 87; Wohlfarth and others, *EWG. Kommentar*, p. 244.

[4] For comments in favour of an extensive interpretation, see Campbell and Thompson, *Common Market Law*, p. 247; Honig and others, *Cartel Law*, pp. 9–10; furthermore, agreements, decisions for restrictive practices need not have concrete adverse effects on trade. The intention for the same effects would be sufficient by themselves.

dicate that restrictive trading agreements concluded within or outside the Community, by firms established in a member state or in a non-member country, will be subject to Article 85 if they affect trade within the Community at an intermember level.[1] As a corollary to this rule, restrictive trading agreements will not be subject to the provisions of the Treaty of Rome if they concern the trade either *in* one of the member states or between one or more member states and non-member countries. Thus, in a negative (i.e. authorizing) clearance issued by the Commission in 1964 in respect of an exclusive dealing agreement between a French company and a British firm, the Commission's decision was based on the consideration that the agreement did not split the E.E.C. into different markets, that is, at the level of trade between member states, nor was there any other reason to intervene under Article 85/1.[2] In another negative clearance issued in 1964 in accordance with Article 2 of Regulation no. 17 to a Dutch Engineering and Contractors Association (DECA), the Commission based their decision on a similar consideration. The argument backing the negative clearance was to the effect that the DECA, comprising four building and construction firms with associates and subsidiaries situated in Belgium, Italy and Germany, co-ordinated building and construction orders from outside the Common Market. While Article 85 applies to practices affecting goods as well as services, neither the purpose of the given agreement nor its effects involved, the Commission argued, the prevention, restriction or distortion of competition *within* the Common Market —the effects of the agreement concerning the DECA affected markets lying outside the Common Market, and therefore territories outside the ambit of the Treaty of Rome; there was no indication that the said co-operation agreement had had any effect on competition *in* the E.E.C.[3] In a further and similar negative clearance (1964) involving a Belgian and an American company, the Commission maintained that the agreement in question did not deal with territorial restrictions or protection, by imposing

---

[1] See E.E.C. Commission: *Guide Pratique* concernant les Articles 85 et 86 du Traité instituant la C.E.E. et les Règlements d'Application, Brussels, 1962, p. 10, part II, section III/2, categories of agreements subject to notification. Kruithof, *C.M.L. Rev.*, vol. 2, 1964, pp. 75, 92. See also Question 1, par, 6 of Form B of Regulation no. 27, J.O.(C.E.), 1962, pp. 1118/62 ff.

[2] J.O.(C.E.), 1964 (no. 136, 26 August).

[3] J.O.(C.E.), 1964 (no. 173, 31 October).

activities limited to a specified area, or with the right to buy or sell other competing products. The Commission found that it was a non-exclusive concession and did not involve territorial protection, adding that no objections had been submitted by interested parties after notice had duly been given in the Official Gazette of the Community.[1] On the basis of these decisions it may be said that, in application of the principle of effect, restrictive trading agreements between foreign firms and their subsidiaries in the E.E.C. will fall under Article 85 if they affect *intermember* trade. If they do so adversely, then they will belong to the category of prohibited practices referred to in paragraphs 1 and 2 of the same Article. If they affect intermember trade without, however, preventing, restricting or distorting competition, they will be governed by the provisions of paragraph 3 of the same Article 85 and of the regulations issued in implementation thereof.

## 'Dominant position'

The position of foreign firms and their co-ordinated activities with subsidiaries or other undertakings in the Common Market could also fall, in addition to the provisions of Article 85, under the meaning of Article 86. Here again, it will be irrelevant whether the registered office or main establishment of a given undertaking or undertakings is situated inside or outside the Common Market, if the undertakings concerned occupy a dominant position and improperly exploit it in respect of trade between member states.[2]

The term 'dominant position' is not defined by the Treaty, nor has it been defined so far by the executive organs of the E.E.C.[3] The same absence of definition applies to the nature of legal or economic relationship between several undertakings which together command a dominant position. This lack of definitions may not be, however, of crucial importance, since the Treaty does not prohibit them *per se* nor their exploitation in a manner which may be conducive to better production or distribution of goods, or to better technical or economic progress. That in this situation

[1] J.O.(C.E.), 1964, p. 1426/64. Cf. also Decision 64/233/EEC, J.O.(C.E.), 1964, p. 915/64.

[2] Campbell, *Restrictive Trading Agreements*, pp. 15 ff.; Honig and others, *Cartel Law*, pp. 35 ff.

[3] Honig, ibid., p. 36. Also E.E.C. Commission, *Guide Pratique*, part I, section II; Summary of discussions of the Round Table of the Assoc. Française d'Etude de la Concurrence, December 1963: report by R. Foures, *Droit Européen*, no. 53, 1963, pp. 523–6.

a wide margin of assessment and evaluation for a given case may exist is obvious, whereby the merits of a dominant position in terms of their adverse effect on intermember trade will be the decisive element, not the bare fact that a dominant position *per se* exists. The simple existence of a dominant position would not entail, under the Treaty, any legal consequences. More than that, it would be superfluous to speak, in the context of the Treaty, of a dominant position without having in mind its abuse. Without its 'improper exploitation', the existence of a dominant position in the E.E.C. would become irrelevant for Community law.

With reference to the flexible interpretation that can be given to the term 'dominant position' by the executive organs of the E.E.C., it can be said that the Council and the Commission will not only be exercising a law-making function but will also have the capacity to shape to a considerable extent the policy of mergers and concentrations within the Common Market. By issuing the necessary regulations under Article 87, it will be possible to promote and control economic and industrial concentration in accordance with the harmonious development of the Community. The notions of 'cartel' and 'concentrations' are, in fact, relative ones in the E.E.C.[1] and with the expanding dimensions of trade and mass production markets, they will have to be both adapted and standardized in accordance with the requirements of the economic union. In this respect, the manner in which Article 86 will be interpreted and implemented by the Council and Commission will have an important regulatory effect, corresponding to the purpose of the Treaty. In yet another respect, however, the application of Article 86 by the Community organs may have a possible function to fulfil, namely, in respect of the relationship between Community undertakings (firms owned by Community nationals) and foreign-owned enterprise. Both regulatory functions of Article 86 will be examined, first on the level of economic activities between member states.

One of the main objectives of the Common Market is 'to promote throughout the Community a harmonious development of economic activities, a continuous and balanced expansion, an increased stability, an accelerated raising of the standard of living and closer relations between the Member States' (Article 2). The implication of this Article is that, among others, the growth and

[1] H. von der Groeben, reported in E.E.C. *Bulletin*, no. 12, 1964, p. 51. *Cartel*, vol. 14, no. 3, July 1964, p. 123.

expansion of the economies of the member states will be co-ordinated, in such a way that none of them secures a dominant position incompatible with the objectives of the E.E.C. If such an unbalanced situation were to develop, its effects would be tangible, among other forms, as the dominant position of undertakings from a given member state in a given economic sector and the improper exploitation of that position with adverse effects on trade between member states. To avert it, the provisions of Article 86 would become applicable. The function of Article 86 could thus be the elimination both of the undesirable dominant position held by certain undertakings in relation to others, and of the improper exploitation on the part of certain economic sectors of a given member state in relation to other member states; as well as the promotion of mergers and concentrations both in and between member states in accordance with the objectives of the Treaty.

The concept of dominant position may be adapted, indeed, not only in respect of the need in the growing Common Market for the advantages of mass production and better technical and economic progress, but also in respect of meeting and co-ordinating competition from firms from non-member states with subsidiaries established in the E.E.C.[1] In other terms, one of the regulatory functions of Article 86 could be that of co-ordinating the size and financial and technological strength of foreign-owned firms that are operating in the Common Market with the interests of the Community.

Turning again to the expansion of certain American firms in the E.E.C., it has been pointed out that the financial and technological resources of these firms are factors threatening the competitiveness of relevant Community undertakings. A number of suggestions for improving the position and competitiveness of Community firms have been made, concerning various legal matters such as company law, investment allowances and also control of inflowing foreign investment capital. These aspects are reviewed later in this study, but here we might examine whether foreign-owned firms, mainly American, with their financial and technological strength, could be controlled under Community law to prevent them from gaining an undesirably dominant position.

In certain respects the Treaty of Rome may be interpreted as a body of rules aiming at the co-ordination of growth and inter-

[1] H. von der Groeben, reported in E.E.C. *Bulletin*, no. 12, 1964, p. 51.

penetration of the economies of the six member states. For this
purpose, the Treaty is adequately equipped with all the necessary
clauses to ensure the proper functioning of the Common Market.
It lacks, however, the necessary legal instruments to cope with the
confrontation of the Community economy by that of a non-
member state, in the form of competition by foreign investment
within the E.E.C. The problem would not arise if it were not for
the fact that the foreign companies concerned are better equipped
with financial resources (e.g. 'cheaper' money in the United States)
and higher technological standards. In addition, they have the
benefit of accumulated experience of lengthy activity as large
companies in mass markets. In fact, there are in the Treaty itself
no suitable clauses that would enable the Council and the Commission to deal with the question of massive competition on the
part of firms from non-member states, operating through subsidiaries, except under the provisions of Articles 85 and 86 and
possibly under Articles 100 ff. While the first two Articles permit
action by the Community authorities under the Common Market
rules of competition, it would be much more difficult to do
so under Article 100: it would be necessary to prove under
Article 100 that the activities of foreign-owned subsidiaries are
interfering with the 'operation of the Common Market' and that,
therefore, municipal legislation affecting them must be regulated
in accordance with the objectives of the Community. The Council
could then, on a proposal of the Commission, 'issue directives for
the approximation of such legislative and administrative provisions of Member States' concerning the establishment of operations of foreign investors in so far as they adversely affect the
proper functioning of the Common Market. The present situation would not, however, permit such an interpretation—there
has not been any evidence so far that foreign investments as such
have had an adverse effect on the proper functioning of the E.E.C.
On the contrary, there is evidence in support of the argument
that they have made valuable contributions to its economy.

Returning to the possible application of Articles 85 and 86 in
regulating competition between foreign-owned enterprises, on
the one hand, and domestic enterprises, on the other, it must be
said that in application of the Community treatment set out in
Article 58, foreign-owned firms or subsidiaries can never be the
object of any action as 'foreign' firms under Articles 85–86. If they
exercise restrictive practices, they will be subject to the provisions

of Article 85 like all other firms in the E.E.C. without distinction as to ownership. If one or more foreign-owned firms undertake 'any improper exploitation' of a dominant position within the Common Market or within a substantial part of it, Article 86 will become operative. Could then foreign-owned enterprises develop a dominant position in the E.E.C. to the point where they could eliminate domestic competition while not being caught by the provisions of Articles 85 and/or 86? The potential threat of such a dominant position has already been claimed by some industrial quarters in the E.E.C., especially in France and Germany. Arguments have been thereby based on considerations of national or Community economic interests.

While it seems very doubtful that this question could be answered in the affirmative, it may nevertheless still be asked, under what circumstances could the broadly enunciated rules of Articles 85 and 86 be interpreted and implemented by the Council and Commission, so as to check any undesirable take-over by foreign-owned firms of certain industrial sectors in the E.E.C.? First of all, it is to be noted that in the period 1960–5 the situation of foreign investment has not taken a form which would warrant the intervention of the Community authorities on grounds that it has an adverse effect on trade between member states. Secondly, it is unlikely that one or a few foreign-owned undertakings would, in the economy of the E.E.C., be in a position to develop a monopolistic position, because they would not be able to do so without affecting trade between member states. In such a case they would be caught by the provisions of Articles 85 and/or 86. In other terms, the rules of competition of the E.E.C. would be adequate to meet any deliberate threat to fair competition on the part of foreign enterprise in the Common Market, since among other rules, paragraph 3 of Article 85 would be operative—it provides for controls against the elimination of 'competition in respect of a substantial part of the goods concerned' in a given industrial or commercial sector. This would apply to the Common Market as a whole or to a 'substantial part of it' (Article 86) which may lie within the confines of a single member state.[1] It may be concluded, therefore, that the concern expressed by domestic industrial quarters about the dominant position of foreign-owned (American) firms in certain economic sectors of the E.E.C. has not yet corresponded to a situation in which 'improper exploita-

[1] E.E.C., *Guide Pratique*, part I, section II, par. 3.

tion' or practices detrimental to the proper functioning of the Common Market were involved. Community law, not condemning a dominant position *per se* nor discriminating between a dominant position by foreign-owned or domestic undertakings, cannot intervene in support of the complaints that have been thus far voiced in certain industrial quarters. Community law does not prohibit one or more firms from acquiring a dominant position in a given industrial sector nor does it distinguish in this respect between domestic and foreign-owned undertakings.

### FUTURE PROBLEMS

The above conclusion should not, however, lead to the belief that the presence of highly competitive foreign-owned firms in the E.E.C. does not pose any problems. Problems do exist but they do not belong, at least thus far, to the domain of the law on restrictive practices. They concern aspects of adjustment on the part of domestic enterprises and municipal legislation related to them more than they concern measures of coercion to be applied against foreign investment. They even necessitate a new approach that would fully grasp all the implications that an economic union brings with it. In this respect, foreign investing firms have so far developed a more integrated approach to the developing Community than have domestic enterprise or municipal legislators. Municipal legislative and psychological barriers established along traditional border-lines are constituting, more and more, for the industries concerned, a hindrance in meeting the invigorating challenge of foreign-owned enterprises.[1] As long as foreign-owned undertakings dominate industrial sectors in which they excel, in accordance with Community rules on competition, they will not be subject to action under the Treaty of Rome. Domestic enterprise desirous to take the challenge implied thereby will have to see to it that barriers to their competitiveness in relation to foreign-owned undertakings are overcome on the levels of municipal legislation and of faster progress in economic integration. Domestic firms interested in mergers that are being dictated by technical and economic forces in the wake of the progressive integration are hampered by the current system of company law in the Common Market; the law of industrial investment needs to be improved in some of the member states, e.g. France; a new

[1] *Cartel*, vol. 14, no. 3, July 1964, p. 123.

approach towards intensive and large-scale research as a basis of economic progress in the Community is needed.

## AID GRANTED BY MEMBER STATES

Foreign investments in the E.E.C. have benefited from aid granted by member states (e.g. Belgium and Italy) for projects deemed to be favourable to the economic development of the country. Such aid may, however, under Articles 92 ff. of the Treaty of Rome, distort competition in the E.E.C. 'in so far as it adversely affects trade between Member States' (Article 92/1). The implication of the relevant provisions is that while Articles 85 and 86 of the Treaty directly govern the restrictive trading agreements also of foreign-owned undertakings, projects of foreign investors may, in addition, be indirectly caught by Articles 92 ff. of the Community rules on competition, whenever foreign investment projects are dependent on state aid. This means that the executive organs of the E.E.C. will have a power to influence indirectly the flow of foreign investment capital whenever state aid is thereby involved.

In a concrete case involving Belgian state aid to the Ford Tractor Company (Belgium) in Antwerp, the Commission decided on 28 October 1964,[1] that the Belgian government should withdraw the aid which was in the form of interest rebates. These had been granted in accordance with the Law of 17 July 1959, for the promotion of economic expansion and the establishment of new industries. Having examined the plans of the Ford Tractor Company (Belgium) in Antwerp (a plant for assembling tractors and producing equipment for them), and the difficulties that Community firms had encountered in recent times in that branch of industry, the Commission suggested that the aid furnished by the Belgian government for the establishment of a new production plant was incompatible with the Common Market. The Commission took its decision in accordance with the procedure laid down in Article 93/2 of the Treaty.[2]

This decision of the Commission is quoted here in so far as it concerns a project involving the participation of foreign-owned

---

[1] J.O.(C.E.), 1964 (no. 195, 28 November).
[2] For comments in connection with Article 93, see Valentine, *Court of Justice of the Eur. Communities*, vol. 1, pp. 268 f., 279 f.

capital. Otherwise, neither the relevant provisions of the Treaty of Rome nor the decision of the Commission have so far dealt with foreign-owned undertakings as such. It is, however, obvious that the executive organs of the E.E.C. possess a competence under Articles 92 ff. to influence foreign investment projects indirectly when these happen to be dependent on aid by the governments of member states. Under Article 93/3 the Commission is empowered to do so, since it 'shall be informed, in sufficient time to enable it to submit its comments, of any plans to grant or modify grants of aid'. If the given project is judged to be 'incompatible with the Common Market within the meaning of Article 92', the Commission can take action under Article 93/2, and 'The Member State concerned shall not put its proposed measures into effect until [the initiated] procedure has resulted in a final decision.' The procedure may, however, be suspended until the Council makes its attitude known, at the request of a member state. Once taken, the decision of the Commission must be complied with, otherwise the decision may be referred to the Court of Justice by the Commission or by any interested member state, notwithstanding the procedural provisions of Articles 169 and 170. In 1964, the Commission discussed the effects of an application of Article 93/3 which provides for compulsory notification of state aids. A draft regulation will be prepared in accordance with the provisions of Article 94.[1]

CONCLUSIONS

The present section ends with some observations on (i) the Community rules of competition in their relation to foreign principals and their subsidiaries in the E.E.C., and (ii) the position of the same rules in respect of international anti-trust law.

Legal rules on restrictive practices are rules of economic law—they regulate competition in economic life—and the manner in which they are drafted can depend largely on whether the objectives they serve are currently existent or belong mainly to the future. If a proposed law of restrictive practices is to be created for maintaining and regulating an already existing system of competition, it will be possible to make detailed and specific rules, because the current situation will represent a picture of the conditions under which the implementation of the rules will have to

[1] E.E.C. *Bulletin*, no. 12, 1964, p. 17.

s

function. If, however, the economic situation in which rules of competition are to function is not yet in existence, but is envisaged only as a future objective in an instrument like the Treaty of Rome, then the drafting of detailed rules will become a debatable matter. The multitude of economic factors and their impact on the market are difficult to assess. In the case of the Treaty, the economic situation of the six member states involves a transitional period.

The economic union which is being created in implementation of the Treaty will continue to have a fundamental impact on the national economies involved in it. It is unpredictable in its many details. The development of mass markets and mass production is having an inevitable effect on the size of undertakings. Markets are developing from national to continental size and the foundations of a new system of competition are being laid. According to the objectives of the Treaty, the transformation envisaged is not to be left to the whim of economic forces; it will have to proceed in accordance with the multiple aims of the Treaty, protecting the economic interests of the member states and promoting their harmonious development in a continuous and balanced manner. These multiple and, in many respects, historically unique functions make it practically impossible, and at most of academic interest, to have elaborate and detailed rules of competition. The market in which they have to operate is still largely inexistent and difficult to assess in its many details. Thus, while including rules of competition in the Treaty, it was necessary to strike a compromise between the two extremes of a strongly legalistic approach and a dominantly pragmatic one, and to choose a method that enables the lawyer and economist to see eye to eye. The amount of unpredictability involved in it, pointed out by lawyers, is by far the lesser evil compared with the confusion or harm that might have been caused by a rigidly legalistic approach. The functional approach adopted by the authors of the Treaty is, in respect of restrictive practices, the one most adapted to the situation of the E.E.C. It was necessary to give to the executive organs of the E.E.C., in matters related to competition, a law-creating competence in addition to the administrative one. As the Community law of restrictive practices develops, the system of notification and exemption of trading agreements will be important for the control and supervision of competition in the E.E.C., in accordance with criteria established by regulations of the Council. The opinion of the Commission will be in this respect of major importance.

In respect of restrictive trading agreements between foreign firms and their subsidiaries established in the E.E.C., the situation may be summarized (March 1965) as follows:

1. The extent of legal or economic relationship between a principal and its subsidiary is immaterial for the rules of competition;

2. Restrictive trading or licensing agreements that do not affect trade between member states will not be caught by the provisions of Articles 85–86 of the Treaty. They may fall, however, under the respective municipal laws of member states;

3. If they affect trade between member states, the exemption or prohibition of restrictive practices will depend upon their adverse effect on trade between member states. This is a matter of qualification for which the Commission has sole competence, subject to review by the Court of Justice of the European Communities.[1] It is, therefore, advisable to comply with the requirements of notification. If an agreement is found to be caught by the provisions of Article 85/1, it could be declared 'automatically . . . null and void', and could entail, on grounds of negligent or wilful infringement, a liability to substantial fines and penalties.[2] Application for a negative (i.e. exempting) clearance in respect of an agreement, and the non-application of Article 85/1, is to be made on Form A; for any notification of trading agreements under Article 85/3, Form B will have to be used. For certain exclusive concession agreements which do not contain clauses especially liable to distort competition within the Common Market, a simplified notification may be effected on Form B.1.[3] According to the Manual on restrictive trading agreements, an application for negative clearance on Form A and notification on

---

[1] Article 9/1 of Regulation 17. Also E.E.C., *Guide Pratique*, 1962, part I (IV). For an English translation of the relevant Article 9 of Regulation 17 and of part I (IV) of the Manual, Campbell, *Restrictive Trading Agreements*, pp. 44–5, p. 172. Also Honig and others, *Cartel Law*, pp. 61 ff.

[2] Article 85/2 of the Treaty of Rome; Articles 15–16 of Regulation 17. Campbell, ibid., pp. 53 ff., 37 f., 35; Honig, ibid., pp. 28 ff., 70 ff.

[3] For details and the forms, see Regulation No. 27 of the Commission (Forms A and B), and Regulation No. 153 of the Commission (Form B.1). For commentaries with English translations of the regulations, Campbell, ibid., pp. 75 ff., pp. 80 ff. (Form A), pp. 87 ff. (Form B), pp. 106 ff. (Form B.1); also on the same, Honig, ibid., pp. 79 ff., 133 ff.

Form B can be filed with the Commission at one and the same
time.[1]

The more transparent or the simpler a restrictive trading agreement is, the easier will it be to predict its exemption under
Article 85/3. For example, agreements that are bipartite and
satisfy, in addition, the remaining criteria set out by the Council
in its Regulation no. 19/65 of 2 March 1965 fall under the category of practices qualified for block exemptions.[2] For multipartite or multipurpose agreements, the situation is much more
complicated. For this reason it is wise to seek the opinion of the
Commission on multipartite agreements dealing simultaneously
with price maintenance, rights to use patents, technical knowledge or manufacturing processes, and containing clauses on the
joint application of standards and research. In this respect, a vague
but nevertheless important guideline may be the opinion of the
Commission, that if exclusive agreements have an adverse effect
on the application of the Treaty to intermember trade and restrict
its effectiveness in regard to competition, such an adverse effect
will have to be based on economic reasons which must in turn be
justified as necessary to the main content of a trading agreement.[3]
Expanding this principle, it may be submitted that the benefits of a
restrictive trading agreement to the economic life of the E.E.C.
must outweigh the adverse effects it may include, subject to the
approval of the Commission. The same remark applies in respect

[1] E.E.C., *Guide Pratique*, part II (IV, par. 1).
[2] J.O.(C.E.), 1965 (no. 36, 6 March), especially Article 1; also Campbell,
*Restrictive Trading Agreements*, pp. 36, 105; *Guide Pratique*, part II (II, 3);
Article 4/2 of Regulation No. 17 of the Council (1962); Regulation No. 153
of the Commission (1962), Article 1.
[3] See the decision of the Commission concerning the exclusive distribution
agreement between the Grundig Verkaufs-GmbH, and Société Consten
(France), no. 64/566 EEC of 23 September 1964, J.O.(C.E.), 1964, p. 2545/64.
For critical and other comments, *C.M.L. Rev.*, vol. 1, 1963–64, pp. 218 ff.;
T. Schapira: in *J.D.I.*, vol. 92, 1965, p. 67; H. D. Hennings: *Die Welt*, no. 17,
21 January 1965, p. 9. For a detailed report on the case, *C.M.L. Rep.*, vol. 3,
part 12, December 1964, pp. 489 ff. An appeal against the decision has been
lodged with the Court of Justice of the European Communities (J.O.(C.E.),
1965, p. 9/65). Thus, an opinion of the Court of Justice on the interpretation
of Articles 85–86 of the Treaty will be forthcoming. See also request for an
interlocutory ruling lodged with the Court, on 16 October 1964, for the case
47/64, *Vermeulen's Handelsmaatschapij v. Alfred Faber GmbH.*, E.E.C. *Bulletin*,
no. 12, 1964, p. 61.

of Article 86, under which a negative clearance may be sought on grounds that a dominant position, while existent, does not involve in the given case an abuse of it.[1]

The following observations may be made on the Community rules of competition in respect of international anti-trust law.

Since the Treaty of Rome is an instrument of public international law, its rules of competition, regulating interstate trade, correspond to international anti-trust rules. Attempts to produce an international regulation of restrictive practices go back to the period of the League of Nations.[2] In the post-war period, the same topic was discussed at the United Nations Conference on Trade and Employment held at Havana, November 1947–March 1948, and in the final act of the Conference, in the so-called Havana Charter, clauses on restrictive practices were included under chapter V.[3] The relevant Articles 46–54 dealt with the enumeration of restrictive practices and related definitions (Articles 46/3 and 54), provided for a consultation and investigation procedure (Articles 47–49 and 53) and set out the rights and obligations of states in matters related to restrictive practices (Articles 50–52). Compared with the attempts of the Havana Charter to compromise between traditional concepts of state sovereignty and exigencies of international trade, the Treaty of Rome marks with its rules of competition a decisive breakthrough in the development and implementation of international anti-trust law.[4] It incorporates principles that are well suited to the objectives of an economic union. The practices it is called to regulate and control are more comprehensive in Articles 85–86 ff. than those listed in Article 46 of the Havana Charter. The practices listed in the former are by way of example while those mentioned in the Havana Charter seem to be exhaustive (Article 46/3). Referring to practices, the Havana Charter states that these 'are . . .' while the Treaty of Rome sets out that restrictive practices caught by Article 85/1 'shall, in particular, include . . .' Furthermore, from the view-point

---

[1] Regulation No. 27 of the Commission (1962), Article 4, and E.E.C., *Guide Pratique*, part II (II, 1, last par.).

[2] Cf. E. Lebée: 'Trusts et Cartels Internationaux', *Rec. A.D.I.*, vol. IV, 1927, pp. 147 ff.; E. Gunther, *Kartelle und Monopole im modernen Recht*, vol. 2, Karlsruhe, 1961, pp. 553 ff., 561 ff.

[3] U.N. Conference on Trade and Employment (21 November 1947–24 March 1948), Havana, Cuba. Final Act and Related Documents (April 1948); also Domke: in *I.C.L.Q.*, 1955, pp. 129 ff.

[4] W. Friedmann, *The Changing Structure of Int. Law*, pp. 184 f.

of legal technique, the Treaty of Rome presents the advantage of listing the restrictive practices by private firms or state authorities under a single heading; the Havana Charter deals with them in a number of Articles dispersed in the text. For example, in addition to Articles 46–54 under chapter V, earlier Articles refer to subsidies (Articles 25 ff.) and dumping (Article 34). The most significant contribution of the Treaty of Rome is, however, the fact that it provides for a centralized machinery of control and supervision, entrusted to the executive organs of the E.E.C. under the judicial control of the Court of Justice of the European Communities. The member states have to follow and implement the Community policy. With the competence that the Council and Commission of the E.E.C. have in developing and implementing the law, we have a system of international anti-trust law which transcends the sovereign powers of the member states and is in this respect much more than an interstate law of restrictive practices, particularly so as the highest instance responsible for the judicial control of the system is an international and not a municipal court.[1] Finally, it can be said that the experience accumulated by the implementation of the Treaty will be a valuable contribution to the drafting of international legal instruments regulating restrictive practices in interstate or regional trade. The designation of Community law as 'international' in respect of restrictive practices must be subjected, however, to one reservation—as long as the member states of the E.E.C. remain, for the purpose of international law, legally and politically separate entities, the E.E.C. rules of competition will indeed be an international anti-trust law for the member states. Should, however, the economic integration of the Common Market lead to political union so that the E.E.C. becomes an international legal entity representing its member states in all spheres of international life, the rules of competition of the E.E.C. will become, as a result, its internal or 'municipal' law.

NOTE

REGULATIONS CONCERNING THE RULES OF COMPETITION
ISSUED UP TO MARCH 1965

Regulation No. 17, 6 February, 1962, The First Implementing Regulation pursuant to Articles 85–86 of the Treaty of Rome. For a survey of its contents,

---

[1] See the remarks of H. von der Groeben, in: *Opera Mundi—Europe*, no. 279, 19 November 1964, p. 7.

see Campbell, *Restrictive Trading Agreements*, pp. 29 ff.; Honig and others, *Cartel Law of the E.E.C.*, pp. 42 ff. J.O.(C.E.), 1962, pp. 204/62 ff.

Regulation No. 26, J.O.(C.E.), 1962, pp. 993/62 ff., deals with the application of certain rules of competition to the Production of and Trade in Agricultural Products.

Regulation No. 27, J.O.(C.E.), 1962, pp. 1118/62 ff., the first implementing regulation pursuant to Regulation No. 17.

Regulation No. 49, 29 June, 1962, J.O.(C.E.), 1962, p. 1571/62, amending Regulation No. 26.

Regulation No. 59, 3 July, 1962, J.O.(C.E.), 1962, pp. 1655/62 ff., amending Regulation No. 17.

Regulation No. 141, 26 November, 1962, J.O.(C.E.), 1962, pp. 2751/62 ff., relating to the non-applicability of Regulation No. 17 to Traffic.

Regulation No. 153, 21 December, 1962, completing and modifying Regulation No. 27.

Regulation No. 99, 25 July, 1963, J.O.(C.E.), 1963, p. 2268/63, relating to the hearing provided for in Article 19 par. 1 and 2, of Regulation No. 17.

Regulation No. 118, 5 November, 1963, J.O.(C.E.), 1963, p. 2698/63.

Regulation No. 19, 2 March, 1965, J.O.(C.E.), 1965, pp. 533/65 ff., concerning the application of Article 85/3 of the Treaty of Rome to certain categories of agreements and concerted practices. Article 1 of the regulation sets out that the Commission is authorized to issue block exemptions to specified trading agreements.

In addition a manual for firms on the Community law of restrictive practices has been published. The following statements have been issued by the E.E.C. Commission:

First Statement on Exclusive Distribution Agreements (1962), J.O.(C.E.), 1962, p. 2627/62.

Second Statement on Exclusive Distribution Agreements (1962), J.O.(C.E.), 1962, p. 2628/62.

Third Statement on Patent Licensing Agreements (1962), J.O.(C.E.), 1962, p. 2628/62.

Second Statement on Patent Licensing Agreements (1962), J.O.(C.E.), 1962, p. 2628/62.

Statement on Exclusive Agency Contracts made with Commercial Agents (1962), J.O.(C.E.), 1962, p. 2687/62.

Statement on Patent Licensing Agreements (1962), J.O.(C.E.), 1962, p. 2922/62.

For translations of the documents listed above, see Campbell, *Restrictive Trading Agreements*.

# CHAPTER XII
## HARMONIZATION OF MUNICIPAL LEGISLATION

The need for the approximation of municipal rules is considered in the Treaty of Rome. A number of Articles refer to harmonization when dealing with specific matters, while a general clause on approximation is found in Article 100, which refers to 'such legislative and administrative provisions of Member States as directly affect the establishment or operation of the Common Market'.[1] All Articles concern the alignment of municipal laws to the extent necessary for the proper functioning of the Common Market, as stated in the programmatic clause of Article 3/1(h), and confer the necessary powers on the executive organs of the E.E.C. to issue directives.

There is no reference to foreign investment in the specific or general clauses on approximation of laws in the Treaty of Rome and in the absence of such specific reference, the establishment of a link between the harmonization of municipal laws and foreign investments may seem at first far-fetched. The current situation (March 1965) in respect of foreign investments in the E.E.C. and the problems they raise, together with the opinions expressed on them, show however that such a relationship does exist, and it is the purpose of the present chapter to illustrate it and submit a few suggestions on it.

No survey or exposition of Community law in its comprehensive application to harmonization of municipal laws is undertaken here; aspects of harmonizing municipal rules will be treated only in so far as they show a relevance to the status and activities of foreign-owned firms in the Common Market. The points to be treated will follow the systematic order already used in this study:

[1] Articles 27 (customs matters), 54/3(g) (guarantees demanded from companies), 56/2 (right of establishment), 57/2 (non-wage-earning activities), 66 (services), 99 (indirect taxation), and 117 (social systems). For comments see Groeben and Boeckh, *Kommentar*; Campbell and Thompson, *Common Market Law*; Pujade, *Aspects of Eur. Integration*, p. 105. For further comments on Article 100 see B. A. Wortley: in *Nederlandse Tijdschrift voor Internationaal Recht*, 1962, pp. 530 ff.

economic sectors inaccessible or conditionally accessible to foreigners, exchange control regulations, company law, taxation and the law of patents; though because of the nature of the main topic of harmonization, an overlapping between these different points will sometimes be inevitable.

Firstly, a statement on the basic terms used in this section is necessary. 'Co-ordination' and 'harmonization' will be used as synonymous with the general concept of 'approximation'. They will refer to aligned but separately existent bodies of municipal rules, whereas the term 'unification' will denote the creation of a single body of rules uniformly applicable in all member states of the E.E.C. All these terms are generally synonymous in the text of the Treaty of Rome but they represent, nevertheless, a rising scale from 'co-ordination' to 'harmonization' to 'unification'.[1] The last term is not expressly used in the Treaty but is implicit, for instance, in Article 220, though without any indication as to whether the implied unification ought to be *factual*, i.e. laws separately existent but uniform in effect, or *formal*, i.e. separate laws replaced by one single law.

## THE APPROXIMATION OF MUNICIPAL RULES ON ECONOMIC SECTORS INACCESSIBLE OR CONDITIONALLY ACCESSIBLE TO FOREIGN INVESTORS

We have already seen in Part I, how member states of the E.E.C. individually apply rules that govern the exclusion or conditional participation of foreign investors in certain economic activities deemed to be of public or national importance. Member states like France and Italy make the participation of foreigners in the economic activities in question dependent on domestic partnership, reciprocity, long residence in the country and considerations of national interest. The relevant municipal provisions refer to foreign nationals without distinguishing between Community nationals and others from non-member countries.

The Treaty of Rome has introduced, on the other hand, a distinction between nationals of member states and nationals of non-member countries. It stipulates, for example, that the right of

[1] For a definition and discussion of the terms, see Pujade, in: *Aspects of Eur. Integration*, pp. 104–5; G. Phillips: 'Erscheinungsformen und Methoden der Privatrechts-Vereinheitlichung' (Thesis, Univ. of Mainz), 1963, pp. 52 ff., 59 ff., 76 ff., 82 ff.

doing or setting up business within the Community shall apply to physical and legal persons who are nationals of member states (Articles 52, 58). It has in this way established the principle of Community treatment, under which Community nationals will be entitled to national treatment in the respective member states; but municipal rules governing the access of foreigners to certain economic activities do not make the distinction introduced by Community law. These municipal rules will obviously not in future be applicable to Community nationals; and the necessary amendments to the municipal laws in question will have to be effected by providing for the application of the term 'foreigners' in them only to nationals of non-member countries. Whatever the policy of individual member states towards nationals of non-member countries may be, the application of certain principles in municipal rules will no longer be possible with respect to Community nationals. They will be incompatible with the standard of Community treatment under the Treaty of Rome. For instance, the principle of domestic partnership, or the insistence that nationals of other member states accept domestic participation in the business they plan to set up in the given member state, is incompatible with the principle of national treatment applicable under Community law. The principle of reciprocity is self-evident in the principle of Community treatment, though in its formal aspects only, as a member state will be under no obligation to treat other Community nationals better than its own nationals.[1] The requirement of long residence in the country for access to a given economic activity is untenable under the provisions of Community law, as is the principle of national interest, considered in the right of establishment (Articles 52 ff.); and it is somewhat of a strained interpretation to claim that the principle of national interest could be maintained by a member state, in respect of other Community nationals, by referring to the concept of public security mentioned in Article 56. Under paragraph 1 of this Article, the right of establishment 'shall not invalidate any legislation, regulations and administrative rules providing for special treatment for foreign nationals on the grounds of public policy, public security and public health'.[2] An exception could be construed under Article 223/1(b), according to which any member

[1] Article 52/2 of the Treaty of Rome.
[2] It is to be assumed that here the term 'foreign' refers to Community nationals.

state may take 'whatever measures it considers necessary for the protection of the essential interests of its security, and which are connected with the production of or trade in arms, munitions and war material . . .' A member state could bar access to armaments industries as necessary for the protection of the essential interests of its security, even to Community nationals, while its own nationals could have access to it. However, such an exception under Articles 56 or 223/1(b) to the Community law of establishment will be subject to the control of the Council who will have competence to issue directives by a qualified majority (Article 56/2) for the co-ordination of matters falling under Article 56, and to decide by a unanimous decision (Article 223/2 and 3), the list of products to which the provisions of Article 223/1(b) shall apply. With a few exceptions, Community law replaces for Community nationals those rules which govern the access of foreigners to certain economic activities.

While providing for a few possible exceptions that member states may maintain or introduce, with the approval of the E.E.C. Council, to the Community right of establishment, the Treaty of Rome does not interfere with the right of member states to apply the rules that they deem suitable for their policy towards investors from non-member countries. Nationals (natural or legal persons) of non-member countries applying for establishment will continue to be subject to the municipal rules of the member state where they intend to set up business. For instance, a company incorporated in the United Kingdom and owned by British nationals will be subject to French municipal regulations when applying for the establishment of a subsidiary in France. However, if the same British company or the same British nationals already participate or own a company incorporated in Germany with its real seat in Germany in accordance with German company law, and apply for the establishment in France of a branch office or subsidiary of their German company their application will be governed by Community law (Article 58 in conjunction with Article 52), under which French authorities will be unable to apply at their discretion their municipal rules on foreign ownership.

The legal implications of this situation are obvious. Through the right of establishment under the Treaty of Rome, each of the six member states of the E.E.C. controls the access of nationals of non-member countries to all other member states of the

Common Market. If member states want to avert the circumvention of their municipal laws by foreign investors in so far as prohibitions or conditions of access to certain economic activities are concerned, standards of treatment, uniform for all member states, for nationals of non-member countries will have to be applied at the initial stage of investment in any one of the member states. Beyond this initial stage, foreign investors become assimilated, under Article 58 of the Treaty, to Community nationals with a right to Community treatment.[1] Of course, the practical possibilities for the exploitation of the situation described above are limited and hardly of a nature that could disturb the proper functioning of the Common Market, but the legal possibilities are there. The establishment of foreign investors in a member state can no longer be effectively controlled by the municipal rules of that member country alone. A solution will have to be sought, when the need arises, in the harmonization of the respective policies and legislative standards of all member states. Since such a co-ordination cannot be initiated, in case of need, by the executive organs of the E.E.C. under any of the articles on the right of establishment or on the harmonization of specific matters governed by special articles, it will fall under the general provisions of Article 100. Under that Article, the Council shall, 'by a unanimous decision, on a proposal of the Commission, issue directives for the approximation of such legislative and administrative provisions of Member States as directly affect the establishment and operation of the Common Market'. Under paragraph 2 of the same Article, if the intended directives involve in their implementation the amendment of legislation in one or more member states, the Assembly of the Community and the Economic and Social Committee shall be consulted.[2]

Article 100 has a wide margin of application as it includes within its ambit the approximation of any legislative and administrative rules in the member states that affect the functioning of the Common Market and are not specifically governed by other articles in the Treaty. This wide margin of application is balanced, however,

[1] For a criticism of this system by the French Industry Minister, see *Financial Times*, 27 May, 1965, p. 5.

[2] For commentaries see Groeben and Boeckh, *Kommentar*; Wohlfarth and others, *EWG. Kommentar*; Campbell and Thompson, *Common Market Law*; Catalano, *Manuel de Droit des Comm. Eur.*, pp. 347 ff.; Pujade, *Eur. Integration*, p. 105.

by a rigorous machinery of political and technical control. To counteract the possibility of a too far-reaching interference in the municipal legal systems on the part of the Community executive, Article 100 stipulates that the Council shall issue directives 'by a unanimous decision' and 'on a proposal of the Commission'. Furthermore, if the intended directives concern the laws of one or more member states, the Assembly and the Economic and Social Committee of the E.E.C. will have to be consulted. This type of political and technical control will also apply to approximation affecting municipal laws on the establishment and activities of foreign investors in so far as such an approximation is necessitated by the operation of the Common Market.

The above remarks apply similarly to the co-ordination of exchange control regulations governing the entry and disinvestment of foreign capital and the transfer of income therefrom. Under the impact of the progressive economic union, no individual member state will be in a position to use exchange control regulations as an effective instrument for controlling foreign investments, without the co-ordination of similar measures in the other member states. The more liberal policy of a single member state will be sufficient to render ineffective restrictive measures by other member states, as a result of the Community right of establishment. Under that rule, natural or legal persons who are nationals of non-member states are, it is true, excluded, but not companies owned by them and incorporated in one of the member states in accordance with Article 58. As for action for the approximation of exchange control regulations in so far as it concerns the proper functioning of the Common Market, its possible need is hinted by Article 72: 'Member States shall keep the Commission informed of any movement of capital to and from third countries which they know about.' While this implies an obligation for member states to keep the Commission informed, the article does not empower the Commission to initiate action except to 'address to Member States any comments which it deems appropriate' on the subject of capital movements to and from non-member countries. There is no reference to co-ordination of exchange control regulations in Article 73: 'If movements of capital lead to disturbances in the operation of the capital market in any Member State, the Commission shall, after consulting the Monetary Committee, authorize such State to take protective measures in the field of capital movements, the conditions and details of which the

Commission shall determine.' Reference in this section 1 and the remaining section 2 of Article 73 is to measures in respect of individual member states for coping with a situation of a transitory nature. As far as the current situation is concerned, the approximation of exchange control rules in the member states does not raise any problems. Exchange control in its current form is in fact harmonized since it is characterized by the same liberal policy in all member states and there is no probability that it might undergo any change as long as the current favourable position in the balance of payments of member states continues. Should the need arise, however, action in this respect should become possible under the general provisions of Article 100 discussed above.

### THE APPROXIMATION OF MUNICIPAL COMPANY LAW IN ITS RELEVANCE TO FOREIGN INVESTMENT

Paradoxically, this topic is a most ardently debated one in connection with foreign investments in the E.E.C. though at first glance it is not a directly relevant one. It does not concern, for instance, the improvement of the current situation for the purpose of attracting foreign investment or improving the current investment climate, currently among the best in the world; nor is the approximation of company law related to difficulties that are peculiar only to foreign investors and do not apply to domestic undertakings. The need for approximation of municipal company laws has been demonstrated by the problems of competition between Community firms and American firms.

It is first necessary to examine what the problems of competition between firms in the Community and American firms are in the current situation, and to what extent the existing system of municipal laws is or is not contributing towards solving these problems. A word of warning is, however, necessary in this respect: the question of competition between American and Community firms is a very complex one; it has many aspects, legal, economic, technological, etc. Because of this, solutions to it cannot lie predominantly in the sphere of legal matters, and the observations that follow should not mislead the reader into believing that a reform of company law in the E.E.C. can by itself improve the situation completely. This law reform is, however, an essential step in the contribution of lawyers to the development of the E.E.C. and its legal system and it raises many questions of a technical nature. Our observations are arranged thus, in terms of: the position of Community firms under the current situation of company law; approximation under the provisions of the Treaty of Rome; and the extent of contribution that a reform of company law can make towards solving some of the problems.

When referring to the position of Community firms in relation to foreign-owned undertakings, a number of points should be noted. First, the reference applies only to a number of industrial sectors such as the fields of electronics, chemicals, motor-car manufacturing and farming machinery, in which competition by foreign-owned firms is keen. Secondly, the concern of such Community firms is not about foreign-owned undertakings as a whole but about American-owned companies which have been investing and expanding in the E.E.C. Finally, discussions on competition by American-owned firms in the industrial sectors in question do not concern all American firms but mainly those that are considered to be 'giants' on an international scale.

Since the inception of the Common Market and increasingly since 1963, industrial quarters in the E.E.C. have been noting the accelerating pace with which American private investment capital has been entering the E.E.C. and the manner in which American-owned subsidiaries have been developing and expanding their activities throughout the Community. Much of the American private investment has been mobilized in the fields of technology-intensive and capital-intensive industries. The financial and technological strength and the efficiency of American-owned subsidiaries have created a serious challenge for their counterpart Community firms. With no corresponding financial and technical resources at their disposal, the industrial quarters concerned and authorities of the member states in the E.E.C. have been discussing some possible remedies for improving the competitive position of Community firms. Suggestions have, in this respect, concerned improvements in the financing and research facilities of Community industries, and, through the reform of company law, by adapting the companies to the changing economic and technical conditions of the progressive Common Market. It has been pointed out that large American companies are better equipped to satisfy the developing mass market of the E.E.C. than are Community firms, which have been developing and operating within the narrower confines of municipal law and municipal markets. Without disregarding other factors, the existence of

municipal legal frontiers is hampering the expansion and adjustment of Community firms to the changing conditions of economic life in the E.E.C.

A summary comparison of the size and strength of internationally active American firms with corresponding European companies reveals the existence of a number of disparities. A survey
published by the *Union des Industries de la Communauté Européenne*
(UNICE: Brussels), on the size of companies in the major industries in Western Europe and the United States,[1] shows that
annual sales of the 20 largest American companies correspond in
value to the entire gross national product of Germany, while
those of the five largest American companies alone represent the
gross national product of Italy. General Motors, the largest company in the world, has sales which exceed the German Federal
budget and are equal to the combined sales of the 13 largest
companies in Germany, while the same company's motor car
production rivals that of the motor car industry of the entire
E.E.C. General Motors is itself an important investing company
in the E.E.C. While the business figures of American companies
may be taken as an indication of their financial strength and size,
their position in industrial research may be considered as an
indication of their technological strength. As we have seen already the largest American companies investing in Europe are
those which do 88 per cent of the industrial research undertaken
in the United States.[2]

In the light of these facts and with reference to the position of
Community firms, it has been suggested that a well-developed and
dynamic market like the E.E.C. requires large entities which are
financially stronger and can resort more easily to self-financing,
and which have, moreover, easier access to capital markets than do
smaller bodies.[3] Not least, they are more able to support a system
of industrial research that can cater for the continuous need for
improvement and rationalization in developing new products and
new processes. Thus, a concentration of financial resources and of
effort seems to be required to meet the changing conditions of the
Common Market, a concentration that cannot be undertaken,
however, within the financial and legal limitations of municipal
frontiers. It is against this background that the contribution that

[1] Quoted in *European Community*, no. 5, May 1965, p. 10.
[2] See also other relevant statistics on pages 17 ff.
[3] UNICE Report, quoted in *European Community*, no. 5, May 1965, p. 10.

a reform of company law could make to promote the necessary adaptation has been discussed in the UNICE Report, where it was also pointed out, that whatever the merits of such a reform may be, its contribution could be but one among many that would deal with factors of a legal, economic, technological and psychological nature.

How does the existing system of municipal company law function in the E.E.C. and what are its limitations with respect to greater mobility, co-operation and concentration needed by Community firms? As we have seen the system is characterized by the existence of six different sets of municipal laws, which have certain basic principles in common but sufficient dissimilarities, on the other hand, to make them into separate substantive laws. Apart from administrative formalities which must be complied with in the territory of each member state, requirements for the minimum number of incorporators and shareholders, minimum corporate capital, publicity and disclosure of financial information, guarantees for the protection of shareholders and third parties vary from one member state to another. The nationality and capacity of companies to do business in the territory of a member state other than that of their incorporation is governed by rules of private international law. With the exception of the Netherlands, each member state insists that foreign-owned companies must have their registered and real seat within that member state. Under Dutch company law the registered seat of a company may not be identical with its real seat.

While the present system is satisfactory in so far as the interstate activities of companies are concerned, it falls short of satisfying the legal and technical requirements of the progressive economic union. In the current practice, no difficulties have been encountered by companies of member states when setting up agencies, branch offices or subsidiaries in a member state other than that of their incorporation. The right of establishment or freedom to carry on business without obstacles throughout the E.E.C. goes, however, beyond the limits of the possibilities offered by the present system. As at March 1965, the transfer of a company and of its registered seat from one member state to another is not possible without liquidating it in the member state of incorporation, and then incorporating it in the member state of its destination. In this process, administrative formalities are to be complied with and fees must be paid and the elements of time,

T

266 LEGAL ASPECTS OF INVESTMENT IN THE E.E.C.

effort and money are not negligible. The transfer of a corporate seat cannot be decided on technical and economic grounds alone, and has to be considered also in the light of the existing legal barriers between the six municipal systems. Secondly, however technically or economically urgent or necessary co-operation or joint research between firms of different member states may be, the existence of municipal legal barriers has again to be considered and the Community rules of competition that govern trade between member states have to be respected. Finally, mergers of undertakings can be effected only within the boundaries of each of the municipal systems; they are technically not feasible between firms incorporated under the law of different member states. For instance, in Germany, mergers are only possible where all the companies concerned have their registered seats (i.e. are incorporated) in Germany.[1]

Thus, industrialists in different member states are finding that they have to cope with the limitations of current legal realities while having to adapt themselves to the expanding economy of the Common Market. For instance, a German and a Belgian company had to arrange their co-operation in the form of two separate companies in Germany and Belgium, respectively, whereas under a uniform legal system they would have effected a merger in the form of a single company.[2] Apart from administrative inconveniences and technical and economic disadvantages involved in the present system in matters related to mergers between companies registered in different member states, competition is hampered or distorted both between Community firms and any financially and technologically stronger American firms, and between Community firms themselves. The present system favours the concentration of firms within the economically and geographically larger member states, without offering similar possibilities to firms in the smaller member states, where firms have fewer opportunities for concentration and co-operation in the economy of their country.[3]

[1] Sec. 247/2 of the German Law for Joint-Stock Companies (Aktiengesetz); 1937, as amended.

[2] *Cartel*, vol. 14, no. 3, July 1964, p. 119; *Opera Mundi— Europe*, no. 294, 4 March, 1965, p. 1; *Die Welt*, no. 49, 27 February, 1965, p. 9. See in this connection, the remarks of Professor Hansen, managing director of Farbenfabriken Bayer, in: *The Times*, 4 May, 1965, p. 19.

[3] For an example, see the Volkswagen–Daimler link: *Financial Times*, 24 October 1964, p. 1.

In contrast, the Treaty of Rome provides for the right of Community firms to carry on business within the E.E.C. in a manner that is more comprehensive than the scope of the systems operative under municipal law. It provides for a system which is not only adaptable to the technical and economic requirements of the progressive Common Market, but one which is also free from such legally rather elusive criteria as that of control or ownership in its application to companies under Article 58. Its objectives with respect to the mobility of companies is similar to the aims of the draft Convention concerning the recognition of the legal personality of foreign companies, associations and foundations (The Hague, 1951).[1] This draft Convention also provides for the recognition of companies in the contracting states (Article 1) and for the maintenance of their legal personality in cases of mergers and transfers of the registered office across municipal boundaries (Articles 4/2 and 3/1 respectively). It leaves, however, a wide discretionary power of recognition to the contracting states under application of the 'real seat' doctrine (Article 2) and in respect of legal capacity, e.g. to hold property (Article 5; see also Articles 6 and 7). It neglects the technical necessity of approximating municipal laws. The Treaty of Rome does not leave the interpretation of its provisions on the recognition of companies to the discretionary sovereign power of member states, but places them under the administrative and judicial control of Community organs.[2]

With due consideration for disparities between the objectives of the Common Market and the limitations of a system with six different municipal laws, the alignment of municipal company laws is envisaged in broad terms by the Treaty of Rome. In accordance with the programmatic statement of Article 3/1(c) on the intermember abolition of obstacles to the free movement of persons, services and capital, Article 54/3(g) provides for the co-ordination 'to the necessary extent' and alignment of 'the

---

[1] Conference de La Haye de Droit International Privé, Actes de la 7e Session (1951), Articles 1 and 2, p. 385. For an English text, *A.J.C.L.*, 1952, pp. 277 ff.; also H. Dölle: in *Zeitschrift für auslandisches und internationales Privatrecht*, vol. 17, 1952, pp. 161 ff. For comments on Articles 1–2 of the Draft Convention, see also Stein and Nicholson, eds., *Amer. Enterprise in the Eur. Common Market*, vol. 1, pp. 166–7.

[2] Articles 145, 155, 164, 171, 177. For comments on these, Groeben and Boeckh, *Kommentar*; Campbell and Thompson, *Common Market Law*; Wohlfarth and others: *EWG. Kommentar*.

guarantees which Member States require within the meaning of Article 58/2, so as to protect the interests both of Member States and outsiders'. Article 220 refers to 'the mutual recognition of firms or companies as defined in Article 58, second paragraph, the maintenance of their legal personality, if their registered office is transferred from one country to another, and the possibility of mergers between firms or companies which are subject to different domestic laws'.

The intended scope of alignment of municipal company laws, possibly ranging from minimum co-ordination to formal unification, is not clearly indicated by the texts of Articles 54 and 220, nor can uniform deductions be made from the contents of Articles 52 and 58. Much can depend on the definitions that are attached to terms like 'establishment' or 'approximation', 'harmonization' or 'unification' as starting points for the interpretation of the articles in question. In addition, conclusions reached may depend on the way in which the articles are arranged or grouped as a framework of reference. In the first place, if a comprehensive meaning is attached to the term 'establishment' within the framework of Articles 52, 54 and 58 in its application to companies, as meaning not only the capacity of companies to set up agencies, branch offices or subsidiaries in member states other than the one of incorporation, but also the capacity of maintaining their legal personality while transferring the registered office from one member state to another, Article 220 may seem, with respect to companies, to be substantively redundant or to be meant as a *procedural* clause that puts member states under the obligation to conclude the convention(s) necessary for the full implementation of substantive rules included in Articles 52 ff. It may be a question of opinion whether the term 'establishment' has a restricted meaning in the context of Articles 58 and 52 and a comprehensive one only for the purpose of Article 220; but the inclusion of its comprehensive meaning in the Treaty is a necessity both for the objectives of the E.E.C.[1] and for improving the situation of Community companies in their competition with large and strong foreign firms. If the authors of the Treaty had but a restrictive interpretation of the term in mind, they were then only codifying as Community law what is already the general practice in Western Europe. There are no major difficulties in the current system of establishing agencies, branch offices or subsidiaries both in the

[1] Articles 2 and 3 of the Treaty of Rome.

Common Market and in other countries.[1] This system is operating more or less satisfactorily in a framework in which the process of an economic integration is not involved.

The main objective of the E.E.C. is the creation of an economic union. In its application to a municipal system, the term economic union implies the capacity of companies to transfer within it their seat or centre of activities. Under the economic union that the existing municipal system represents (in the individual member states of the E.E.C.) there is no restriction on the right of companies to transfer, within the territory of the same country, their seat in accordance with the necessities of their activities. If the term 'economic union' as a major objective of the E.E.C. is to be defined in the same way as economic union under an individual municipal system, the legal status of commercial legal entities within the territory of the Community cannot be expected to be more restricted than it is traditionally within the territory of an individual national economy.

Secondly, it is in conjunction with the activities of the Community, enumerated in Article 3, that the exclusion of a comprehensive meaning for 'establishment' within the framework of the Treaty becomes untenable. For this purpose, the programmatic clauses (c) and (f) of Article 3 are sufficient to suggest together a wider meaning for the term. According to these clauses, the activities of the E.E.C. shall include, among others, 'the abolition, as between Member States, of obstacles to the free movement of persons, services and capital' and 'the establishment of a system ensuring that competition in the Common Market is not disturbed . . .' If Community companies did not have the full freedom of establishment, including the right to transfer their registered seat from one member state to another, or to effect mergers across municipal boundaries, an obstacle distorting competition in the Common Market would exist, because companies of larger member states would be enabled to enjoy a larger freedom of establishment and mergers within their own wider geographical frontiers than would companies in member states with smaller territories.

Finally, in the light of the fact that the transfer of the registered seat of companies from one member state to another under main-

---

[1] W. Fikentscher and B. Grossfeld, in: *C.M.L. Rev.*, vol. 2, no. 3, December 1964, p. 259; also H. Arnold, in: *Aussenwirtschaftsdienst des Betriebs-Beraters*, 9th year (1963), pp. 221 f.

tenance of their legal personality is mentioned in Article 220, it can be concluded that the term 'establishment' cannot have a restricted meaning within the framework of the Treaty in the sense that it solely applies to the right of companies to set up agencies, branches or subsidiaries in a member state other than the one where they are incorporated. However varying the content of the term 'establishment' may be in the different provisions of the Treaty, it can, nevertheless, be concluded that the Treaty refers also to the transfer of registered seats and maintenance of the legal personality of companies at a Community level.

Furthermore, with the gradual integration of the Community the economic and technical need for the development of larger companies at a Community level is growing and it may in this respect be asked, what developments does the Treaty of Rome envisage as improvements upon the current situation in accordance with the needs of a progressive economic integration? For this purpose, Articles 58 and 54 will have to be examined first.

'Companies and firms (sociétés) formed in accordance with the law of a Member State' and satisfying one further requisite, viz., 'having their registered office, [or] central administration or principal place of business within the Community', will be treated 'in the same way as individual nationals of Member States'. According to the General Programme of 1962 on the abolition of obstacles to the right of establishment,[1] companies with only their registered office (*siège statutaire*) within the Community or in one of the overseas associated countries or territories must also have, for qualification under Community law, an effective and continuous link between their activities and the economy of a member state or an overseas associated country or territory.

As the above provisions now stand, they contain self-limiting elements that conflict with the requirements of the current municipal laws of five member states; co-ordination is obviously necessary. If Article 58/1 had read (author's amendments in italics): 'Companies and firms (sociétés) formed in accordance with the law of a Member State and having their registered office, central administration or principal place of business within *the member state of incorporation* shall . . . be treated in the same way as individual nationals of Member States,' and if the phrase 'formed in accordance with the law of a Member State' (Article 58/1) means 'formed *and operating* in accordance with the law' of that member

[1] J.O.(C.E.), 1962, pp. 36/62 ff.

state, then Community law would coincide with municipal law on company qualification under Article 58, and there would be no need for a co-ordination between the two systems on this point. But according to Community law, it should be sufficient for a company to be formed in accordance with the law of a member state and to have its registered office in a member state and an effective link with the economy of *any* member state, or to have its registered office, central administration or principal place of business *within* the Community, in order to qualify under Article 58. In other words, there is under Community law a dissociation of the registered seat from the real seat of a company, an approach which corresponds far better to the economic realities of the developing Common Market. Under it, companies in the E.E.C. would have the possibility of registering their seat in a member state but have their centre of business or administration anywhere *within* the Community in accordance with their economic needs. They could even have a number of administrative centres in different member states availing themselves of modern technical facilities of communication and management. In this connection, it may be asked whether the application of an identity of registered and real seats or their confinement to a single member state really corresponds any longer to the developing realities of the economic union that the Common Market progressively represents. While being dependent on a municipal authority for acquiring their legal personality, companies in the E.E.C. and many other companies that are internationally active are finding it more and more difficult to observe the laws of the country where they are incorporated as their business activities are no longer confined to the territory of that one state.

In municipal company law, insistence on the identity of the registered and real seats is based on the assumption that companies incorporated in a state confine their main activities to the area circumscribed by the municipal law of that state. While this approach has been adopted and applied in many municipal systems, systems like those of the United Kingdom and the Netherlands have recognized that it could not appropriately be applied to British and Dutch companies with wide trade ramifications overseas. The theory of identity of registered and real seats cannot always be satisfactorily applied to companies engaged in large-scale interstate trade operations.

Now that in a region like the E.E.C. internal trade barriers are disappearing, the activities of companies are expanding and ramifying, reference to them will possibly have to be made in terms of the Common Market as a whole, and not of a single member state. In other words, for economic purposes many companies will be operating as Community companies in the economic sense of the term, and economic and legal necessities incident to their operation will differ from those traditionally encountered in trade between states separated by political, economic and legal barriers. As envisaged by the Treaty of Rome, there will be an interpenetration and integration between the six municipal economies and in view of the current and future needs of Community industries, it will be impractical to maintain certain of the legal barriers that are embodied in municipal company laws. In this connection it is justified to ask what functional usefulness insistence on the identity of the registered and real seats of a company will have with reference to the territory of a member state. The doctrine of 'real seat' is based on elusive criteria and leaves a wide margin of assessment. The Community rules do not apply it as identical with the registered seat of a company and in so doing take into due consideration the technical needs of companies operating in the Common Market as a whole. With the opportunities that the Common Market and its law offer to companies, it will become more and more difficult using traditional criteria to ascertain the real centre of gravity in activities deployed by large companies. For them, the framework of reference will have to be the Community as a whole, as stipulated in Article 58/1 with the terms 'within the Community'. Beyond the stage of incorporation, further insistence on the identity of real and registered seats of such companies with reference to the territory of a single member state would be formal rather than real and difficult to maintain in the light of economic changes that are taking place in the Common Market.

In the light of these arguments as to the greater appropriateness of the wording of Article 58/1 and returning to the question of co-ordinating municipal company laws and the provisions of Article 58, it may be suggested that the laws of five member states where the doctrine of 'real seat' is applied should be altered to align with the requirements of Community law. Without such a co-ordination, the phrase 'within the Community' will either be meaningless or mean 'having its registered office and real seat in the same member state'. Moreover, because Dutch company law does not apply the 'real seat' theory, the conflict between Article 58 and the municipal company law of the five other states will involve an element of discrimination. A company formed in accordance with Dutch company law could be refused recognition under the municipal laws of the other member states, if it happened to have its 'real seat' outside the Netherlands.

Concerning the procedure for initiating the co-ordination of the municipal company laws under discussion, as there are no specific provisions applicable to it, it would have to be effected in accordance with the general clause of Article 100.

A number of comments will be now submitted in connection with the scope of Article 54/3(g) which empowers the executive organs of the E.E.C. to draft and issue (in accordance with the provisions of Article 54/2) directives for co-ordinating and rendering of equal value the guarantees required of companies under the respective municipal systems. It can be asked whether this Article implies a scope of approximation that includes the legislation dealing with the capacity of companies to transfer their registered seat from one member state to another while maintaining their legal personality.

The answer is to be sought in Article 52/1 in which the terms 'freedom of establishment of nationals of a Member State in the territory of another Member State' are used. Article 58/1 implies a reference to these terms when it stipulates that companies as defined under it shall 'be treated in the same way as individual nationals of Member States'. According to Article 52/2, 'freedom of establishment shall include the right to engage in and carry on non-wage-earning activities, to set up and manage undertakings and, in particular, firms and companies (sociétés) . . . under the conditions laid down for its own nationals by the law of the country where such establishment is effected . . .'

It is first to be assumed that reference to 'individual nationals' in Article 52 implies physical persons, as there is a special corresponding article on commercial legal persons in the same chapter on the right of establishment, viz., Article 58. Under this article, companies are to be assimilated to individual nationals (natural persons). With reference to this assimilation, it could be argued that the right of establishment equally applies to natural and legal persons, including the right of companies to transfer their registered seat from one member state to another while maintaining their legal personality. Such an argument is hardly tenable, however, as it disregards both the differences between the status of physical and legal persons in current interstate legal relations, and the contents of Article 220 of the Treaty, in which specific reference is made to the intermember transfer of registered seats and the maintenance of the legal personality of companies. With due consideration of the legal vacuum that presently exists in these matters, Article 220 provides for negotiations between member states for the conclusion of an agreement on them.

The recognition of the legal capacity of physical persons to set up commercial activities in countries other than that of their nationality is an old and well-established institution in international trade. The same remark applies to the capacity of companies to set up agencies, branches or subsidiaries in countries other than that of their incorporation. A novel legal situation is implied, however, when the interstate transfer of the registered seat of a company under maintenance of its legal personality is considered; it is certainly a novel situation as far as practice in the member states of the E.E.C. is concerned, where interstate transfer has to be effected in the form of a dissolution of the original legal personality of the given company and its creation anew under the law of the country of destination. A law for the complete transfer of companies from one member state to another does not exist in the Common Market; it has yet to be developed and possibly codified in a convention in accordance with Article 220. It may be concluded, therefore, that the scope of Articles 52–58 does not include the right of companies to transfer their registered seats from one member state to another while maintaining their legal personality; and furthermore, that the scope of co-ordination or approximation envisaged in Article 54/3(g) corresponds only to the necessity of aligning municipal rules on the establishment of agencies, branches or subsidiaries and guarantees required for them.[1] The alignment of municipal company laws dealing with the right of companies to transfer their registered seats to another state while maintaining their legal personality

---

[1] As integration progresses and the regulatory competence of Community organs increases, so does the scope of application of Article 54/3(g); Fikentscher and B. Grossfeld: *C.M.L. Rev.*, vol. 2, no. 3, December 1964, p. 259; the scope of Article 54/3(g) cannot include the co-ordination of rules which have to be yet created, viz., for the intermember transfer of the registered seat while maintaining its legal personality.

will have to be effected in accordance with the respective clauses of Article 220.

The manner in which the relevant provisions of Article 220 could be implemented by means of a convention raises a great number of questions, on some of which observations will be now submitted.

First, their implementation will necessitate the creation of a new body of rules under which Community companies will be able to maintain their legal personality while transferring their registered seat from one member state to another, or while effecting mergers across national boundaries. Apart from giving full effect to the term 'right of establishment' in its comprehensive meaning and in accordance with the objectives of the E.E.C., the new rules will be, in addition, tantamount to a major development in interstate or international company law. Experience accumulated under it may be very valuable for the development of a special body of rules applicable to the status of international companies. Further remarks on this point will follow when we deal with the status of large companies that are active in international investment and involved in important activities in a number of states. These remarks will be made in the light of similarities that exist between some of the problems of approximation or unification of company law in the Common Market, on the one hand, and the development of a special body of legal rules applicable to international companies, on the other.

Secondly, the manner in which the provisions of Article 220 may be implemented evolves around the term 'unification'. This term is implicit in Article 220 if one agrees that its implementation can be nothing short of a unification, if not in form, then at least in effect. With reference to company law, its unification is not directly envisaged by the Treaty of Rome,[1] nor is the unification of any other specific matter prescribed by the Treaty. The alignment of municipal laws is to be effected whenever the need for it arises and only to the extent that is necessary for the proper functioning of the Common Market.[2] The initiative in this respect is within the competence of the Community executive organs,

---

[1] In this connection, see the remarks of M. Wang: 'Die Europäische Aktiengesellschaft in der EWG', no. 27 in *Arbeiten aus dem juristischen Seminar der Universität Freiburg (Switzerland)*, Freiburg, 1964, pp. 146, 148–9.

[2] Articles 3(h) and 100 of the Treaty of Rome. For comments, Catalano, *Manuel de Droit des Comm. Eur.*, pp. 254, 347 ff.

subject to a technical and political control as specified for various matters as indicated at the beginning of this chapter. As, however, the scope of approximation will be based on the objectives and the necessities of the Common Market, it may be concluded that the alignment of municipal norms may include at least some *factual* unification under which separately existing bodies of municipal rules governing similar matters would have a uniform effect in the respective member states. As far as the contents of Article 220 are concerned, including important aspects of company law, even a formal unification would be possible as member states could codify the respective rules in conventions and subsequently assimilate them to their municipal laws.

Finally, the implementation of Article 220 is, in its relevance to company law, connected with the question of *desirability* and *feasibility* of factual or formal unification.[1] The first term, 'desirability', is related to the economic, political, psychological and other non-legal objectives which an intended unification must correspond to and serve. Thus, the desirability of a reform extending up to unification of company law in the E.E.C. has been expressed in industrial quarters; such a desirability is further indicated by the needs of Community enterprises that have to face the financial and technological strength of large American companies. Of course, a uniform company law in the E.E.C. would not contribute to the solution of all their problems, but it could make a valuable contribution by facilitating co-operation and concentration across municipal boundaries. The second term, 'feasibility', is in the first place a legal term, as it refers to the existence or non-existence of a certain legal technique which could be used with respect to given 'desirable' objectives. For instance, within the current context of the international legal situation, however 'desirable' the creation of a special status for internationally active companies may be for the quarters concerned, the 'feasibility' of such a special status is not a possible one with respect to private commercial companies—there is no suitable framework as yet to handle it in the current techniques of international economic law. It should be finally noted that the clear delineation of the two terms 'desirability' and 'feasibility' as defined above is not always possible; they may easily overlap in their meaning. For instance, the unification of company law in the

[1] Philips, 'Erscheinungsformen and Methoden der Privatrechts-Vereinheitlichung', pp. 99 ff.

Common Market may be a *desirable* one from the point of view of industrialists,[1] and could be a feasible though complicated one from a lawyer's angle, but it could be both *undesirable* and *unfeasible*, except through successive stages, because of psychological and other barriers in different member states.

The reform of company law, maintained as desirable by industrial and other quarters in the Common Market because of the position of Community undertakings in competition with large American firms active in the E.E.C., will have to be effected either through (i) *formal unification*, or (ii) *approximation* of currently existing laws to the extent needed within the framework of the Community, or (iii) creation of a two-tiered system, basically similar to the one envisaged by the creation of a Community patent law, which will exist side by side with municipal laws. Formal unification is a gigantic task and of extreme academic interest, but of limited usefulness in comparison with the immense effort it would require and the unpredictable effect it would have on some of the economic patterns peculiar to the member states, and of little current interest for the functioning of the Common Market. It would not be advisable to attempt the creation of a uniform law or code of all types of companies without having a clear picture of the economic and other realities in which they would have to function. As in the case of Community rules on competition and their progressive development, lawyers will have to see eye to eye with economists.

Of far more direct interest for the proper functioning of the Common Market in respect of the position of Community companies is the approximation of current company laws in the respective member states. Current work in this respect is progressing on Community level. A directive for co-ordinating and rendering equivalent the guarantees required in the member states of companies as defined in Article 58 and in accordance with Article 54/3(g) of the Treaty is being prepared.[2] It will deal with matters related to publicity requirements, authority of company agents and the nullity of three types of companies: joint-stock companies (German: *Aktiengesellschaften*, French: *sociétés anonymes*); limited liability companies (German: *Gesellschaften mit beschränkter*

---

[1] Fikentscher and Grossfeld, *C.M.L. Rev.*, vol. 2, no. 3, December 1964, p. 262.

[2] For a discussion of them, see Fikentscher and Grossfeld, *C.M.L. Rev.*, vol. 2, no. 3, December 1964, pp. 259 ff., 264 ff.

*Haftung*, French: *sociétés à responsabilité limitée*); and partnerships with limited liability shares (German: *Kommanditgesellschaften mit Aktien*, French: *sociétés en commandite par actions*). This is the first step towards the approximation of company laws since the General Programme of 1962 concerning the abolition of obstacles for the right of establishment.[1] In addition, a team of government experts is elaborating a convention in accordance with Article 220 (1, sub-par. 4) of the Treaty for the mutual recognition of companies and legal persons,[2] and work on the question of mergers was due to begin in March 1965.[3] With reference to the draft directive and other work in progress for the approximation of municipal company laws, it may be said that an alignment of municipal rules may amount in the long run to a *factual* unification if the effect of the separate municipal laws becomes uniform in all member states and a major change will have been effected with the conclusion of a convention that will enable Community firms to maintain their legal personality while transferring their registered seat from one country to another or to effect mergers between firms of different member states.[4] Many technical problems will have to be solved first. For instance, what will the status of a French company be after transferring its registered seat to Italy? Will it continue to be French or will it have to be considered as an Italian company? The easiest solution will probably be to consider a company a national of the member state where it has its registered seat. For this purpose, in case of a transfer across national frontiers the maintenance of corporate legal personality could be effected by a simple procedure of registration and compliance with guarantees specially required in the given member state, instead of initiating an involved procedure of incorporation as it is prescribed under the current system. In this respect it will be, however, particularly important to avoid a situation in which disparities due to different factors could start a drift of registered offices from one member country to another as a result of comparative advantages in the member state of destination.

[1] For the General Programme, J.O.(C.E.), 1962, pp. 36/62 ff.
[2] E.E.C. *Bulletin*, no. 8, 1964, p. 32.
[3] E.E.C. *Bulletin*, no. 1, 1965, p. 29.
[4] Y. E. Loussouarn: 'La Condition des Personnes Morales en Droit International Privé', *Rec. ADI*, vol. I, 1959, pp. 548 ff.

*Suggestions for the future*

All the above possibilities of reforming or improving company law in the E.E.C. would still fall short of satisfying a major need of Community industries both in respect of the expanding mass market of the E.E.C. and of competition with large and strong American firms, namely the development of larger Community undertakings with legal capacity and uniform validity throughout the Common Market. It has been suggested that this could best be done by the creation of a public company of a Community type to meet the need for larger undertakings, in a double-tiered system in which municipal company laws would continue to operate.[1] This type of corporate entity would have a legal personality uniformly recognized under all six municipal systems and would be able to raise capital by offering shares to the public in all six member states.[2] Finally, it would be an adequate instrument for mergers and concentrations.

Such a Community company would indeed be the most immediate and economical remedy in promoting the development of larger firms. It could be the first step for the gradual development of a Community code of company law which could evolve parallel to the needs of the progressive integration. As a type of legal entity which is apart from those long established under municipal law, it could have a structure acceptable both with respect to the needs of Community business and to municipal legal standards in the different member states. Finally, it could without great difficulty be subjected to the judicial control of a

---

[1] See M. Vasseur, in: *Journ. of Business Law*, 1964, pp. 358 ff., 1965, pp. 73–4. On the need for concentration and mergers for better competition with firms from abroad, see the statements of E.E.C. Commission-member, Herr von der Groeben in an address to the European Parliament in Strasbourg (*Financial Times*, 17 June 1965, p. 5); the statements of Professor Hallstein, President of the E.E.C. Commission (*The Times*, 18 June 1965, p. 18); opinions of E.E.C. Commission-member Signor Colonna di Paliano, (*Opera Mundi—Europe*, no. 309, 17 June 1965, p. 12); also the opinion of M. Bestrand and M. P. Uri, reported ibid., p. 5.

[2] Vasseur, *Journ. Bus. Law*, 1965, p. 75. For a note of the French Government to the E.E.C. Commission on a reform of company law in the Common Market, *Financial Times*, 30 March 1965, p. 5. For detailed discussion on a commercial company of a European type, Congrès International pour la Création d'une Société Commerciale de Type Européen: Report in the *Rev. M.C.* (Supplement), no. 27, July–August 1960; also *Le Droit Européen*, nos. 21–2 (1960); and D. Thompson, in: *I.C.L.Q.*, vol. 10, 1961, pp. 851–76.

court at Community level, thus guaranteeing uniformity in the interpretation and application of its law. It has been suggested for this purpose that one should consider the establishment of a commercial division at the Court of Justice of the European Communities.[1]

Two conflicting views have been expressed at official levels. On the one hand, the attitude of the French government favours a system under which, on the basis of a convention, each member state would provide for an identical type of 'European' company and incorporate it under its own law. According to the French viewpoint, this company would be subject to the jurisdiction of national courts. On the other hand, another opinion favours action under the Community Council. The Council would elaborate a European company statute which would give a company incorporated under it equal rights under Community law in all member states and would subject it to the final jurisdiction of the Community Court of Justice.[2]

Both proposals are motivated by the need (i) to eliminate obstacles to the freedom of establishment and (ii) to stimulate joint enterprises and mergers between firms that have to face competition from non-member countries. It is submitted here that the French plan for standardization within the framework of existing municipal company laws should be considered for encouraging co-operation across municipal boundaries between medium-sized undertakings, while the mobility of large enterprises should be promoted by a uniform type of European company independent of the legal and administrative barriers currently attached to municipal company law. On formal grounds, the administration of the law could be subjected to municipal authorities; its judicial control should be, however, vested in the competence of the Community Court. In the absence of a central and uniform interpretation and application of the law, the law of the proposed European company could suffer the same difficulties as do many international agreements in the hands of municipal courts. Furthermore, the establishment of a central authority, responsible at Community level for granting European status to applying companies or to new formations, could be very instrumental in regulating competition between large and small undertakings in the Community. The creation and supervision of a Community type

---

[1] Vasseur, *Journ. Bus. Law*, 1965, p. 79.
[2] *The Financial Times*, 11 June 1965, p. 5.

of company is a legal matter which falls within the ambit of Community affairs and hence of Community law. As a question of principle, it cannot be left to the administrative authorities of member states nor subjected to the exclusive competence of national courts. Thus far, the effectiveness of the Treaty of Rome has been due not least to the existence of interstate administrative and judicial organs. A company of Community type could best serve the interests both of the Common Market as a whole and of its individual member states by virtue of its ultimate supervision and control by Community organs.

It is relevant to comment at this point on prospects of an international company for private commercial activities, similar to the one proposed for the Community as a whole. A comparison of the two types can explain why prospects in the E.E.C. are better and how in the E.E.C. the legal problems concerned are different from those outside it. Commercial legal entities are the main forms in which international investments are effected, and any progress in their international uniformity and legal capacity across state boundaries could make a valuable contribution to the development of a law of international investments.

The term 'international company' is a general and ambiguous one.[1] It is sometimes used for companies that carry on activities under the same name in different countries. In this sense General Motors is an international company; but it is not so in the legal sense, as activities of the principal company are carried on by separate legal entities in various countries, each different and legally distinct from the principal. A principal–subsidiary relationship through participation of capital or management control does not yet correspond to the legal definition of an international company as a single, private, commercial legal entity uniformly recognized and able to transfer its registered seat or effect mergers across municipal boundaries. Nor can ownership or participation by nationals of different countries correspond to the legal meaning of a private international company. The same remark applies to legal entities that function as public utilities; profit-making is not their primary purpose and they are owned or controlled by state-owned undertakings or public authorities. They serve, in the first place, public interests, and have been created by special interstate agreements.

[1] I. Seidl-Hohenveldern: 'European Companies', *Journ. Bus. Law*, 1959, p. 120.

U

Discussions on the status of international companies or associations must distinguish between state-owned or state-controlled international companies, and private international companies; there are problems peculiar to each category. In the case of publicly owned or controlled international companies, public interest in two or more countries in a particular field of economic activity or public utility is involved. This is reflected by the fact that undertakings of this category are often established, by inter-state agreements, for a specific purpose. This includes the delimitation of the geographical boundaries, scope of activities and powers of the undertaking in question. Their legal status and structure can be, so to say, 'static' as the element of freedom for geographical and economic expansion, so characteristic of international commercial companies, is absent. Naturally, changes in their status or structure, however 'static', are possible; but these are governed by decisions beyond the private initiative of personnel responsible for their management, and have to be coordinated with reference to many public interests. That this type of publicly controlled international undertakings raises less problems than privately owned profit-making international companies is proven by developments in the post-war period in which, by way of examples and in their chronological order, companies like Eurofima,[1] the International Moselle Company,[2] Eurochemic,[3] have been created. They are publicly owned international companies.

Private ownership is not sufficient, in turn, to satisfy the defini-

[1] European Company for the Financing of Railway Equipment, created by the Convention of 20 October 1955 (Eurofima Convention): U.N.T.S., vol. 378, p. 255. See Seidl-Hohenveldern, *Journ. Bus. Law*, 1959, pp. 126 f.

[2] Created by a convention between France, Germany and Luxembourg, 27 October 1956, for dredging the Moselle river between Coblenz and Thionville. For text see *J.D.I.*, vol. 85, 1958, p. 265.

[3] European Company for the Chemical Reprocessing of Irradiated Fuels. For the Statutes and other documents related to the establishment of Eurochemic, see O.E.E.C. Special Publication. For a survey of the activities of the company, O.E.C.D. *Observer*, no. 13, 1964, pp. 27 ff. For a detailed study on state-owned international undertakings, see H. Drück: *Gemeinsame Unternehmungen in Staaten-Verbindungen*, no. 9 in the series of the Inst. für Völkerrecht, Univ. of Göttingen, Studien zum internationalen Wirtschafts-recht und Atomenergierecht, 1962. Also P. Lepaulle: 'Betrachtungen über die internationalen Gesellschaften', *Archiv für die civilistische Praxis*, 159. Jg., 1960, p. 126.

tion of an international commercial company, comparable with private commercial companies under municipal law. Under municipal law, commercial companies are free to expand or reduce their activities and may raise capital the way they deem it suitable. For instance, in two companies created by international agreements between some member states of the Common Market, the utilization of private capital is possible, but it is subject to the application of equity between nationals of the respective countries as shareholders of the companies.

Article 7/1 of the Franco–Italian Convention on the construction and operation of a tunnel under the Mont Blanc (14 March 1953) sets out that the operation of the tunnel shall be assigned to a company in which a French and an Italian company shall each subscribe 50 per cent of the capital, and the board of directors of which shall be composed of an equal number of representatives of the two national companies.[1] In the Franco–German company which co-ordinates the selling of coal from the Saar and Lorraine basins, and which was formed in accordance with Article 84 of the Franco–German Treaty of the Saar (27 October 1956), both physical and legal persons of French or German nationality may participate as shareholders on an equity basis.[2]

Obviously, the status of companies like these cannot correspond to the needs of private free enterprise across state boundaries. Any legal limitations as to where a commercial company should, for economic and technical reasons, have its seat or raise capital cannot adequately satisfy the need for mobility of commercial companies. One of the main functions of municipal law is to promote that mobility to the extent compatible with public interest, and if a corresponding mobility does not seem feasible on an interstate level, with respect to the interests of the states concerned, then the chances for the development of private international companies, in the strictly legal sense of the term, are minimal.

The question of the interstate status of companies has never been raised as concretely as by the Treaty of Rome in its rules on

---

[1] U.N.T.S., vol. 284, pp. 223 ff.

[2] Traité sur le Règlement de la Question Sarroise, Art. 84/1. For an English translation, see *J.D.I.*, vol. 84, 1957, p. 775. See also J. Bärmann: 'Supranationale Aktiengesellgeschaften?', *Archiv für die civilistische Praxis*, 156. Jg., 1957, pp. 156 ff.; Seidl-Hohenveldern, *Journ. Bus. Law*, 1959, pp. 127-8.

establishment. Not only is the recognition of companies for set-ting up agencies, branches or subsidiaries envisaged (Article 58), but there is also concrete reference to the capacity of Community firms to transfer their registered seats across national boundaries while maintaining their legal personality (Article 220/1, sub-par. 3), and to the possibility of mergers between companies subject to different domestic laws (ibid.). References to companies in both Articles 58 and 220 apply specifically to *commercial* companies, as 'firms or companies whose objects do not include the making of profit' are excluded.[1]

Prospects within the E.E.C. are far more favourable for the de-velopment of a Community company for private commercial activities than for a homologous form outside the Community. An interstate agreement, the Treaty of Rome, exists as a basic instrument for progress, which contains the essential requisites by providing for a common interstate economic policy with many political and social effects ancillary to it. The alignment of national economies cannot but induce the gradual alignment of municipal laws governing economic matters. The Treaty provides for a Community or interstate common court, under which the uniform application and interpretation of interstate norms can be effected. Natural or legal persons who would be shareholders of a Community type of company would have a common status as Community nationals and would not be distinguished or dis-criminated against as nationals of different states. Moreover, a common capital market would be developed under Community law. Not least, the executive organs of the E.E.C. would be able to act as co-ordinating and supervisory agencies by controlling the pace of a uniform progress throughout the Community. They have the competence to issue the necessary directives. Many technical problems, such as corporate taxation, supervision, ac-counting systems, could be tackled from the angle of the Com-munity as a whole.

Compared with the favourable legal and administrative arrange-ments of the Community for the development of a type of inter-national commercial company, the prospects for a similar development outside the E.E.C. are weak. It would not be suf-ficient to define the status of international companies in a con-vention and provide for their uniform incorporation under the authority of the respective countries or of a central agency like

[1] Article 58/2 of the Treaty of Rome.

the United Nations Organization.[1] This would be but a beginning;[2] beyond the stage of an initial interstate agreement, it would be essential to provide for the development of a uniform judicial practice. This would have to be done in the form of a central judicial organ in charge of a uniform interpretation of the given convention. If this were left to municipal courts divergent opinions would develop. In the interest of the states concerned and of the public at large, it would be just as essential to have a body of workable rules governing the restrictive practices of international companies. Any control machinery should be in position to check the abuse of any dominant position. Even at the present stage, in which municipal boundaries act as legal and economic barriers to the expansion of companies, some corporations are sufficiently strong, for instance, to improve or upset the balance of payments of some states.[3] Other problems related to taxation, accounting systems and other matters, would have to be similarly tackled on a basis of uniformity. With reference to all of these questions, it becomes clear what advantages and potential possibilities the legal and administrative arrangements envisaged in the Treaty of Rome present. Its system is based on the conclusion that the assessment of facts and rules affecting trade between member states cannot be left to the individual judgment of the states concerned,[4] and it marks a distinct departure from the principle of decision and action at individual municipal levels.

Finally, the development of international commercial companies is just as much a matter of political decision as of legal technique. It involves the willingness of states, as in the case of the Common Market, to co-ordinate their municipal economies and policies ancillary to them. In the absence of such a willingness, economic and legal problems involved in the creation of an international company would become insuperable and the usefulness of such a company a doubtful one in the light of the current international situation. In contrast, the situation in the E.E.C.

[1] H. Martyn: *International Business. Principles and Problems*, London–New York, 1964, p. 288.

[2] On legal techniques of unification of municipal laws, see Philips, 'Erscheinungsformen und Methoden der Privatrechts-Vereinheitlichung', pp. 141 ff., 148–9.

[3] *The Economist*, 17 October 1964, 'Companies outgrow Countries', p. 271.

[4] See the remarks of H. von der Groeben with respect to trading agreements affecting trade between the member states of the E.E.C., in: *Opera Mundi—Europe*, no. 279, 19 November 1964, p. 7.

has the essential economic and legal requisites for the creation of a Community company. The Community law on the right of companies to carry on business across municipal boundaries goes further than any system so far proposed or envisaged by international agreements.[1]

The proposed creation of a company of a Community type could make a contribution by eliminating one legal barrier to the expansion and concentration of Community firms. It would enable them to adapt themselves to the expanding market of the E.E.C. and to competition with large American firms, in so far as company law can make a contribution in this respect. On the other hand, the new type of company would equally offer advantages to foreign undertakings. For operations on a Community-wide scale, it would no longer be necessary to establish separate companies for operating manufacturing plants in the member states concerned, requiring at present a separate incorporation in each of the member states concerned.

### HARMONIZATION OF FISCAL LEGISLATION

The distorting effect of municipal fiscal frontiers has been considered in the Treaty of Rome (Articles 95 ff.). After detailed preparatory work, a uniform system of tax on added-value is being currently elaborated and will be introduced in a single operation.[2]

[1] Conférence de La Haye de Droit International Privé, Actes (7th Session, 1951), Draft Convention concerning the recognition of the legal personality of foreign companies, associations and foundations. Council of Europe: Doc. AS/EC (49) 20, 16 December 1949 (on interstate recognition of European public and private companies): Doc. AS/EC (4) I (Memorandum on European Companies by the Secretary-General (30 May 1952); Report to the Consultative Assembly on behalf of the Committee on Economic Questions (24 September 1952), CE Doc. 71, pp. 833 ff.; in this connection, see Wang, 'Die Europäische Aktiengesellschaft in der EWG', pp. 43-4; Seidl-Hohenveldern, *Journ. Bus. Law*, 1959, pp. 122 ff. International Chamber of Commerce: Model Bilateral Agreement on the Status of Foreign Establishments, Brochure no. 20 (revised text), 1947; for an earlier text, C.I.C. Copenhagen Congress (1939), Doc. no. 10.

For discussions on the legal situation of international associations, Institut de Droit International, *Annuaire*, Bath Session (1950), vol. 43-1, pp. 547 ff. Discussions go back to 1910 and 1923 when a draft convention was adopted (ibid., pp. 618 ff.; also vol. II, pp. 335 ff.). International Law Association, 46th Conference, Edinburgh (1954), pp. 364 ff.

[2] Article 99/1 of the Treaty of Rome. For a discussion of turnover-tax harmonization and preparatory work undertaken therefor, J. Reugebrink: *Omzetbelasting en E.E.C.* Deventer 1963.

The appropriate legislative instruments will be promulgated by member states before 1 January 1968 and will enter into force before the end of the transitional period in 1969. The system to be introduced is similar to the one already in force in France (*taxe sur la valeur ajoutée*). It will therefore mean a change, in the other five member states, from the 'cascade' to the new system. Under the 'cascade' system, a small charge is levied on the *total* value of an article every time it changes hands during production, a transaction ending with the final consumer.[1] In contrast, the new system of tax on added-value corresponds to a levy exactly proportionate, at each stage of transaction, to the value added to the prices of goods and services.[2]

For manufacturers, the transition from the 'cascade' to the new system will mean that, as far as turnover tax is concerned, there will be no advantages in the vertical concentration of firms in order to reduce the number of separate operations subject to turnover tax. Under the new system of added-value, the levy on manufactured goods will not be affected by the size and organization of the firms concerned.[3]

The proposed system of harmonizing turnover taxes in the E.E.C. may be considered the first stage of further progress in this respect, parallel to the progressive integration. The overall impact of the envisaged economic union will align economic conditions in the member states and, with the interpenetration of economies, municipal systems of taxation will also have to align and thus develop greater similarities.[4] As a result, new patterns of comparative advantages may gradually develop in respect of double taxation agreements with non-member countries and investment income from the E.E.C.

## UNIFORM PATENT LAW

Work on a Draft European Patent Convention has reached an advanced stage (March 1965). It envisages the creation, for the E.E.C., of a uniform patent system of a supra-national nature, in

[1] E.E.C. *Bulletin*, no. 8, 1964, p. 33; *Financial Times*, 29 April 1965, p. 5.

[2] J.O.(C.E.), 1964 (no. 111, 13 July) for opinions addressed to the member states.

[3] *Financial Times*, 29 April 1965, p. 5.

[4] G. S. A. Wheatcroft: in *Bulletin for Int. Fiscal. Doc.*, vol. 18, no. 2, 1964, pp. 45 ff.; also ibid., no. 5, 1964, J. J. Hansen, on the harmonization of indirect taxes in the E.E.C., pp. 177 ff.

accordance with the Paris Union for the Protection of Industrial Property.[1] Alongside this uniform system, the municipal systems will continue to exist.

Access to the benefits of the uniform patent system for nationals of non-member countries will depend on its accessibility for such countries.[2] The major advantages of the uniform system would be a single registration of patents in a form valid for all six members and the elimination of some of the disadvantages experienced under the present substantive rules of some member states.[3] Under the current system, patenting in the E.E.C. involves compliance with six different administrative procedures in the respective member states, in addition to drawbacks due to differences in substantive rules.

While adherence by non-member countries to the Draft European Patent Convention would present obvious advantages for their nationals, it would at the same time raise a number of technical problems, as it would entail the Convention prevailing over existing municipal patent laws[4] in the non-member countries concerned.

Indications are that opinion in the E.E.C. favours an initial limitation of the proposed Convention to member states of the Community only. Non-member countries will be able to join it subsequently.[5] In the light of the current situation (March 1965), it may be assumed that the system of patenting in the E.E.C. will not be modified in 1965 as far as nationals of non-member countries are concerned.

### GENERAL CONCLUSIONS

The approximation of municipal laws in the E.E.C. is relevant to the status of foreign investors in the member states in so far as,

---

[1] Cf. G. Oudemans: *The Draft European Patent Convention—A Commentary with English and French Texts*, London, 1963, pp. 2 ff. For an English text of the Paris Convention (International Convention for the Protection of Industrial Property, 20 March 1883) as amended at Brussels (14 December 1900), at Washington (2 June 1911), at the Hague (6 November 1925), at London (2 June 1934), and at Lisbon (31 October 1958), see Campbell and Thompson, *Common Market Law*, Appendix 6, pp. 402 ff.

[2] Oudemans, *Draft European Patent Convention*, p. 5.

[3] C. J. De Haan, in: *Doing Business in the Common Market*, Chicago, 1963, pp. 100 ff.; ibid., S. Delvalle, pp. 107 ff.

[4] Oudemans, *Draft European Patent Convention*, p. 5.

[5] *Opera Mundi—Europe*, no. 281, 3 December 1964, p. 7.

under the impact of the Treaty of Rome, a relationship is established between divergent municipal standards governing the establishment of foreigners. This relationship (and the consequent need for co-ordination) result from the application of two divergent principles by municipal laws and Community law respectively.

Municipal rules governing the access of foreigners to certain economic activities or to business activities in general in the given state are based on the principle of control or ownership, in accordance with which foreign investments are judged in the light of desirability or non-desirability of foreign ownership. Rules vary, however, from one member state to another. Community law applies, on the other hand, the principle of Community treatment to physical or legal persons who are nationals of member states and desire to carry on business in a member state other than the one where they have their centre of activities. We have seen that this concerns not only legal persons (undertakings or firms) owned by nationals of member states but also those owned by nationals of non-member countries. As a result, it is impossible for an individual member state to maintain an effective policy towards the establishment and investments of nationals from non-member countries, without agreeing about a common policy with the remaining member states. In the absence of an aligned policy towards foreign investments, nationals of non-member countries can avail themselves of the more liberal policy of one member state and once established there, claim the right of Community treatment, under Article 58, for companies owned by them. It is noteworthy in this respect that the co-ordination necessitated by the divergences of municipal rules concerns the interests of member states and not those of foreign investors.

The greatest relevance to our topic lies in the approximation, reform or development of company law in the Common Market, a relevance due to the financial and technological strength of American firms with which Community undertakings have to compete. Opinions expressed in this respect have pointed out that while many different factors would have to be considered when referring to the competitive position of Community firms, a reform of company law could promote the formation of larger Community undertakings. Such undertakings would correspond both to the changing conditions in the E.E.C. and to better competitive positions in respect of foreign firms.

Observations submitted earlier in this section suggested that, in the current situation, the recognition of foreign companies did not present major difficulties for setting up agencies, branch offices or subsidiaries in the different member states. Currently planned directives for the alignment of guarantees required from companies in the member states would not, therefore, introduce a substantial change; they will, nevertheless, have a formal effect of integrating under Community law what is still an application of rules by municipal authorities who, in the absence of a specific directive, could use their discretionary power.

The main contribution of company law towards responding to the needs of Community undertakings would be made by the creation of a Community company common to all member states. This would enable Community firms to move their registered seats from one region of the E.E.C. to another, in accordance with economic or technical necessities while maintaining their legal personality. Above all, it would pave the way for mergers and the creation of larger entities. On the level of conflict rules, it would eliminate conflicts due to the gravitation of companies between different systems of company law.[1]

The creation of a Community company would mark a major advance towards a type of international company in the strictly legal sense of the term. In contrast to the situation outside the E.E.C., the economic conditions in the Common Market, the objectives of the Rome Treaty and the institutional arrangements it offers are, it is suggested, all propitious for the creation and workability of a Community company. The disproportion between the potential future and the imperfections of the current transitional period are considerable, it is true, and much creative effort will be required by lawyers; but their efforts 'and perhaps also their boldness, should be on the same scale as those of engineers and economists'.[2] The contribution that could be achieved

[1] E. Simonetto: in *Rivista Internazionale di Scienze Economiche e Commerciali*, vol. 12, 1965, p. 93. For studies on the conflicts of municipal company laws, see: T. Ravá: 'Le problème de la comparaison et l'unification du droit des sociétés par actions', Rapport Prelim. July 1951, Inst. Int. pour l'Unification du Droit Prive, U.D.P., 1951, Etudes XXVI, Sociétés Commerciales, Doc. 2; M. Wang: 'Die Europäische Aktiengesellschaft in der EWG'; B. Goldman: 'The law of international companies', *J.D.I.*, vol. 90, 1963, pp. 321 ff.; J.-P. Calon: 'The international company—elements of a general theory', *J.D.I.*, vol. 88, 1961, pp. 694 ff. For a proposal of transnational enterprises, D. P. Kircher: *Harvard Business Review*, March–April 1964, pp. 6 ff.

[2] J.-P. Calon, op. cit., p. 733.

thereby could be a major one to the international law of foreign investment.

In conclusion, it might be said that the points discussed in this chapter have a more direct relevance to the E.E.C. as a host region for foreign-owned undertakings, than to the interests of foreign investors themselves. This is, however, a legal aspect of foreign investment where the interests of investors and of host countries overlap.

PART THREE

SUMMARY AND
SPECULATIONS ON THE FUTURE

# CHAPTER XIII

# THE INVESTMENT CLIMATE OF THE EUROPEAN ECONOMIC COMMUNITY

## INVESTMENTS IN THE E.E.C. AND THE FOREIGN BUSINESSMAN

Apart from non-legal aspects of foreign investment in the E.E.C. such as comparative costs of labour, differential rates of fiscal charges and availability of production resources, it can be said that a question of major legal interest for a foreign investor is the way in which he can best organize his operations in the E.E.C. while attending to his other activities outside the Common Market. This involves proper arrangements from the outset, including compliance with the requirements of company law in the member states concerned. This point is of particular importance in the E.E.C. as Community law refers also to municipal company law with respect to the freedom of setting up agencies, branches or subsidiaries in accordance with Article 58 of the E.E.C. Treaty. The observations which follow refer in particular to action that foreign businessmen must take if they wish to qualify for Community treatment under the Treaty of Rome. Exchange control regulations, taxation, particulars of municipal company law and employment of aliens have already been discussed in Part I.

If a foreign businessman or company is not interested in future expansion within the Common Market in the form of agencies, branches or subsidiaries in different member states, there will be no need to comply with the requirements of Article 58 of the E.E.C. Treaty in order to qualify for the freedom of carrying on business under Community law in the different member states. If, however, he wishes to have such a possibility in hand, then it is advisable to qualify under Article 58 by establishing a subsidiary in accordance with the law of a member state and by having, in addition, both the registered and real seats within the Community. This suggestion is submitted with reference to the current systems (1965) of municipal company laws to which

Article 58 refers. Under those laws, the overriding requirement is that a company incorporated say, in France, must have both its registered office and real seat in that country, in order to qualify as a French and therefore a Community company. The company laws of all six member states prescribe that the registered office must be in the member state concerned, otherwise incorporation may be refused. Subsequent transfer of the registered office abroad is tantamount to a loss of legal personality as a national of the member state.

As all the member states except the Netherlands apply the doctrine of 'real seat' to the nationality of a company, the location of the real centre of management of say, a French company in the United Kingdom could result in the treatment of that company as a British national. Such a conclusion can easily be avoided by setting up management premises in the member state where the company has been incorporated and consequently has its registered office, and by maintaining the minimum of local staff and management personnel. Obviously, the criterion of control (nationality of shareholders) of a Common Market company is irrelevant for the purpose of both municipal company laws and Community law. What matters is compliance with the formal requirement that a company, incorporated in a given member state, must also have its real seat in that state in addition to its registered office. Dutch law does not prescribe the location of the real seat of a Dutch company in the Netherlands. This fact is, however, immaterial under the current system for the remaining member states. The result is that a Dutch company with its real seat say, in London, may be denied recognition as a Community company under the laws of the remaining member states and thus not qualify under Community law. Although there is a conflict between Article 58 of the E.E.C. Treaty and the current company law of five member states in the absence of harmonization of the company laws of these states, it is the requirements of municipal law that will have to be observed. On the other hand, the need for such a harmonization is not an urgent one, as the current liberal policy of member states does not discriminate between Community and other companies. Should the provisions of Article 58 continue to apply however, while the liberal policy of member states to allow non-Community companies to establish activities in their territory were to be restricted, foreign investors and companies without a subsidiary in the E.E.C. in accordance with

Article 58 of the E.E.C. Treaty, may find access to the Common
Market a difficult problem. This remark applies equally to all the
benefits that accrue to foreign investors under the Community
right of establishment.


## THE STATUS OF FOREIGN INVESTMENT IN THE E.E.C.

Some sectors of economic activities are subject to state monopolies in certain member states; for example France and Italy;
public enterprise controls to a large extent public utilities in all
member states; and public participation in manufacturing industries in member states like France, Germany and Italy is extensive
and ramified. Nevertheless, a wide field is open and accessible
to foreign capital, and foreign enterprises with high technological standards have availed themselves extensively of this large
margin.

The scope of public participation or control in economic life
includes the industries and public utilities considered to be of
national or public interest (power generation and supply, communication, banking). This scope has a settled pattern in the
E.E.C. It is not the object of current political controversies as to
whether, in a given member state, public enterprise should be extended through further nationalization or not; and as, on the other
hand, the margin for foreign participation in these hardly exists,
the question of control of public utilities or of basic industries
does not arise with respect to foreign investment. Foreign capital
has a delineated sphere of activities not subject to changes in the
foreseeable future. In this way, the question of sovereignty over
natural resources is an immaterial one for aspects of foreign investment in the member states of the E.E.C.[1] In a diversified
market like the Community, foreigners can invest extensively in
the manufacturing industries; and while the participation of
foreign capital for the exploitation of natural resources is a possibility in a member state like the Netherlands (for example, natural
gas) the question of need for foreign capital in developing urgently
needed basic resources is not a primary one in a well-developed
region like the E.E.C. Concern expressed in member states like
France or Germany is not related to the issue of sovereignty over
natural resources, but to the extent of foreign participation and

[1] Resolution no. 1803 (XVII) of the U.N. General Assembly, 14 December
1962, on permanent sovereignty over natural resources.

x

control in technologically important industries such as chemicals and electronics.

Foreign exchange rules and the favourable economic situation of member states enable investors in the E.E.C. to secure guarantees for the regular transfer of investment income and of disinvested capital. In three member states, Belgium, Italy[1] and Luxembourg, investors can choose between an official exchange market (and a transfer guarantee attached thereto) and a free exchange market without a transfer guarantee. In all member states, the incidence of transfer of investment income on the balance of payments is not an obstacle to foreign investment as a whole. In a member state like France, the long-term effect of an individual investment project on the country's balance of payments is taken into consideration when issuing the required authorization; this is, however, a rule applicable to the merits of individual projects and not to foreign investments as a whole. The foreign exchange position of the E.E.C. is favourable as an incentive to investment and municipal rules on foreign exchange function in accordance with this favourable position.

The legal distinction between foreign investors, on the one hand, and nationals of a given member state, on the other hand, is made at the level at which application is made in accordance with foreign exchange regulations and administrative formalities ancillary to it. At this stage of admission into the member state concerned, a foreign investor is treated in his status as such, as opposed to nationals of that member state. Beyond that stage, foreign investors become assimilated to nationals in so far as the specific project of their investment is concerned.

Under the company laws of member states, foreign investors can organize their activities without intervention as to domestic participation. Excluding other practical considerations, they may organize companies with 100 per cent foreign ownership. Managerial posts may be occupied by foreigners; the recruitment of foreign technical personnel is not restricted by a distinction between foreigners and nationals, but by considerations of necessity or availability of the personnel needed in the member state concerned.

In taxation, foreign investors are not subject to penal rates. Differential rates are based on administrative or technical reasons.

[1] A free exchange market practically exists in Italy, as authorized banks can carry on the spot exchange transactions.

Numerous double taxation agreements govern the fiscal status of foreigners.[1] Equality of treatment in this manner is applied under company law as well as in matters dealing with taxation. Company and taxation laws are not instruments for discrimination or for deterring foreign investment in the E.E.C. With equality of treatment prescribed under them, it can be said that they act as important investment incentives. Moreover, other incentives to industrial and economic investment apply without discrimination between foreign-owned enterprises and others owned by nationals.

The advantages of a non-discriminatory treatment of foreign investments once foreign capital begins to operate in the E.E.C. are manifold. There is no cumbersome administrative machinery of control with the threat of constant interference. Foreign enterprises can operate with a minimum of bureaucratic formalities. It is submitted that the application of non-discrimination to the activities of foreign investors beyond the stage of their establishment in the given member states is one of the most valuable merits of the current system in the E.E.C. It implies the viewpoint that beyond the stages of initial control, authorization and establishment, the application of special provisions to the operations of foreign-owned undertakings is not a practical one in a region like the E.E.C.

In the legal system of the E.E.C., a further attractive aspect of foreign investment is the status that foreign-owned undertakings will enjoy under Community law. Wholly or partially foreign-owned companies formed in accordance with the law of a member state and having their registered office, centre of management and activities in the E.E.C., will be able to establish agencies, branches or subsidiaries in the different member states. Their status will be governed by Community law and not by municipal rules which will continue to apply to new investment coming from a non-member country and seeking establishment in the E.E.C. for the first time. In other words, investment in one member state will entail under Community law not only access to all markets of the economic union envisaged by the Treaty of Rome, but also the right to invest under Community law independently of municipal

---

[1] Cf. A. R. Albrecht: 'The taxation of aliens under International Law', *B.Y.I.L.*, vol. 29, 1952, p. 170, for discrimination due to administrative reasons or particular circumstances. On double taxation see Nwogugu, *Legal Problems of Foreign Investment*, pp. 47 ff.

rules applicable to investment from non-member states. In addition, similar rights will apply with respect to associated countries and overseas territories. Investment in the Common Market entitles foreign capital, therefore, not only to national treatment in the member state and in so far as the given investment project is concerned, but also to Community treatment under the law of the E.E.C. There is no discrimination under Community law; beyond the stage of regulations on foreign exchange and the authorization needed to set up any activity in a member state, the nationality of foreign investors becomes immaterial once they start their activities. For the purpose of Community law, the nationality of shareholders is immaterial for the qualification of a company formed in accordance with Article 58/1 of the Treaty of Rome. The application of considerations of nationality and foreign control with regard to the freedom of establishment of Community companies would have acted as a strong deterrent to foreign investment. Apart from complexities due to questions of settling the formal and effective nationality of shareholders, some machinery of administrative control would have been necessary, and not least, both foreign investors and nationals of member states would have been greatly restricted in their attempts to co-operate. With the non-discrimination of foreign-owned undertakings, Community law is similar to the municipal laws which provide for equality of treatment beyond the stage of initial establishment. This concordance of municipal and Community laws as far as the status of foreign investors after establishment in the E.E.C. is concerned, is a basic element of co-ordination between municipal and Community rules; and it may be considered one of the major contributions of law to the favourable investment climate of the Common Market. Legal aspects of foreign investment in the Common Market do not raise any special problems as far as the rights and interests of foreigners are concerned, but a few problems exist on the side of Community enterprises which have to compete with American companies in the current legal system.

The survey of law for the protection of foreign investment in the E.E.C. showed how rules in municipal and international law had many similarities in common. The sanctity of foreign and domestic private property is recognized in all six member states and anchored in constitutional provisions. The protection of foreign property is part of the basic norms of municipal laws. This protection is not governed by standards of ordinary laws such as a normal legislative act or ministerial decree and therefore capable of exposure to political influences. As part of the respective constitutions, the protection of foreign property in the E.E.C. is subject to the same requirements as those which govern the amendment of constitutional norms.

The sanctity of private property under municipal law is governed by the rule that expropriation must be in the public interest, based on law and subject to legally ascertained compensation. This rule is common to all six member states and it has definitely the character of a rule of international law in the E.E.C. Examples that were quoted showed how municipal courts and governments of member states had applied this principle in cases of both domestic and foreign expropriations. Discussions on the application of 'equal treatment' to nationals and foreigners in the E.E.C. are superfluous as the principle of compensation applies to nationals and foreigners without distinction. With regard to prompt, adequate and effective compensation, neither municipal laws in their constitutional provisions nor the Protocol (20 March 1952) to the European Convention of Human Rights mention it explicitly by using the terms 'prompt, adequate and effective' though these terms may be assumed to be implied by the idea of just compensation set out in municipal law and the European Convention of Human Rights. Compensation paid for post-war nationalization in France and Italy may be considered as a minimum standard as it falls short of the cumulative requirements of promptness, adequacy and effectiveness.[1]

While municipal rules on the protection of private property are subject to the jurisdiction of municipal courts, two international courts, namely the Community Court of Justice and the European Court of Human Rights, also have jurisdiction with respect to rights and interests of foreign investors. The status of foreign-owned enterprise under Community law is subject to the jurisdiction of the Community Court of Justice. In this way, an important legal aspect related to trade and economic activities across state boundaries is subjected to the competence of an international, independent central court. This fact provides a good example for the independence of interstate law from municipal authorities. The impartial and uniform application of Community law is thus guaranteed. It is true that natural or legal persons do not have a

---

[1] In France, foreigners affected by nationalization after 1945 were better treated than French nationals.

*locus standi* before the Community Court of Justice in claims or complaints against member states. Procedural rules under the Treaty of Rome provide, however, sufficient means for seeking a remedy in this respect before the Court.

The second international judicial organ affecting the status of foreign investors in the E.E.C., the European Court of Human Rights, has a jurisdiction which includes the protection of foreign property in cases of expropriation. As an international court it will apply general principles of international law with respect to expropriation, as provided in the Protocol to the Convention of Human Rights. This Protocol establishes in a declaratory manner the prior existence of general principles of international law with respect to expropriation for all contracting states. For contracting states that have accepted the compulsory jurisdiction of the European Court of Human Rights, these general principles are positive law applicable within the territories of the states concerned. With the exception of France and Italy, the member states of the E.E.C. have accepted the jurisdiction of the European Court and the law which this Court will apply. The implication of this acceptance is that for these four member states of the E.E.C., the protection of foreign property is based on international law and remedial procedure thereunder. Independently of the treatment which these four member states, Belgium, Germany, Luxembourg and the Netherlands, may apply in respect of their own nationals, they are bound to apply to foreigners the rules of the European Convention for the Protection of Human Rights.

On the procedural level, the right of natural and legal persons is restricted to that of lodging a petition with the Commission of Human Rights. They may not directly appear before the European Court.[1] The fact that they may independently take procedural action leading to the submission of their case before an international court is, however, a development of great importance. In this respect, the European Convention of Human Rights effects a certain recognition of natural and legal persons as subjects of international law for the purpose of the Convention. As far as the contracting states which are parties to the Convention of Human Rights are concerned, discussions on this topic are thus carried to a higher level of development where the legal status of individuals in international law is viewed in the light of a functional approach. According to this approach, with the

---

[1] See however the *Lawless Case*, referred to at page 183 above.

development of closer social and economic ties across municipal boundaries, certain individual rights cannot be properly contained and ensured by municipal law and judicial organs thereof, but must be subjected to international judicial institutions that correspond to new relationships between individuals and states as traditional subjects of international law. Finally, it must be said that all of the provisions ensuring the protection of foreign investment in the E.E.C. would not be sufficient to guarantee the sanctity of foreign property, if it were not for that intangible conclusion that all law must be able to inspire, the conviction that legal rules include a willingness to honour accepted obligations. Without this highly intangible but equally essential element behind law, none of the provisions that govern the status and protection of foreign investment in the E.E.C. as elsewhere would be of much value. It is highly characteristic of the E.E.C. that this willingness to respect foreign property is not expressed in a single legal instrument, e.g. in an investment code, but permeates the municipal as well as international legal practice of the member states. This, more than political statements or promises in the form of single legislative acts, is tacitly or explicitly expressed in a multitude of rules that affect the status of foreign investors.

While the legal aspects of investment climate in the E.E.C. are satisfactory as far as the rights and interests of foreign investors are concerned, some problems exist with respect to the competitive capacity of Community firms against large American companies. It may be asked in this connection, whether these problems are related to the current legal system and whether law can make a contribution towards solving them. Opinions on this question suggest that such a contribution can be made, as discussed in chapter XII under the heading on the harmonization of laws in the E.E.C. Before submitting concluding suggestions in this respect, it is appropriate first to evaluate the situation for foreign investments in the Common Market, as seen by investors and by official and economic circles in the member states.

## ATTITUDES IN THE COMMON MARKET

The attitudes both of foreign businessmen and of officials and businessmen in the E.E.C. countries towards foreign investment in the Common Market can be valuable indicators as to the adequacy of existing laws on foreign enterprise, and in reviewing some opinions we may see how much legal rules contribute to-wards or detract from the investment climate in the E.E.C. Laws can easily destroy a favourable investment climate; they have their limitations in creating or maintaining it.

Views expressed by foreign investors reveal the factors that motivate a foreign enterprise to enter the Common Market. The attitudes of authorities and domestic enterprises in the host coun-tries show the extent to which the current legal system on foreign investment corresponds with official or public consensus, and per-mit a more thorough discussion on the desirability or undesir-ability of corrective modifications to the current legal rules. Three main questions are dealt with here: Why do foreign investors in-vest in the Common Market? To what extent are official quarters in the E.E.C. concerned about foreign enterprise? To what extent does domestic enterprise welcome or complain about foreign enterprise?

It must be pointed out that current discussions or complaints about foreign enterprise in the Common Market concern, in fact, American investments, and not foreign investments as a whole. In other words, private capital inflow from the United States is the subject of discussions while capital inflow from other coun-tries like the United Kingdom, Sweden or Switzerland, much smaller in magnitude than American investments, is not an object of concern. Reasons behind this peculiar situation will be men-tioned in some of the opinions quoted herein and discussed in the conclusions.

*Why do foreign investors invest in the Common Market? What type of foreign enterprise invests in the Common Market?*

Since the bulk of foreign investment in the E.E.C. consists of capital from the United States, the overwhelming majority of opinions cited herein concerns American enterprise. The same opinions are equally representative of investors from the United Kingdom, Sweden, Switzerland and other countries exporting private investment capital to the E.E.C.

Considerations that motivate the American businessmen and companies to invest in the Common Market may be summarized as follows:

There are great similarities between the lines that economic development has taken in the United States and those anticipated in Western Europe (including the Common Market). The parallels concern not only the production and consumption of goods, but also industrial technology and consumers' tastes.[1] Investors can do business under conditions familiar to them. The high and still growing purchasing power of the consumers is attractive.[2] High standards of efficiency in skilled labour and experts needed for business activities (lawyers, tax experts, accountants, managerial personnel and so on) are available. There are extensive facilities for doing business. The networks of transportation and communications are good.[3]

There are no currency restrictions and exchange needed for international transactions, for the transfer of profits and royalties, is obtainable.

There are no fiscal discriminations and various investment incentives apply equally to domestic and to foreign-owned enterprise.[4] Once authorized to be established (in one of the member states), foreign-owned enterprise is not subject to any restrictions or discriminations.

Preferential trading areas like the Common Market necessitate the establishment of undertakings inside the customs-union in order to maintain and expand the market share hitherto claimed.[5] The customs-union makes the existing and currently integrating markets all the more attractive. A single investment in one of the member states is tantamount to investment in and access to formerly separate tariff areas and markets.[6] Profit margins are good.

The E.E.C. is a politically stable area.

The E.E.C. is suitable as a cost-saving base for export operations to other markets abroad.[7]

---

[1] J. C. de Wilde: 'International financing of industrial development', *Commercial Banks in Relation to Medium- and Long-Term Credit*, Vienna, 1964, p. 143. For the European car market as an example, *The Financial Times*, 11 February 1965, p. 3; also *Newsweek*, 8 March 1965, p. 46.

[2] Belgium or the Netherlands alone have a market equal to the total size of markets in many of the new countries of Africa taken together and representing an area several hundred times larger than the Netherlands; see J. P. Cole, *Geography of World Affairs*, p. 141.

[3] N. Willatt: *Times Review of Industry*, March 1963, p. 13.

[4] Ibid. Also *Brit. Trade Journal*, Suppl., 6 December 1963, p. 48.

[5] *United States, an economic survey*, O.E.C.D., Paris, November 1963, p. 11.

[6] Krause and Dam, *Federal Tax Treatment of Foreign Income*, p. 66.

[7] Krause and Dam, loc. cit.

American private investments abroad (in this case the E.E.C.) promote American exports, as investments effected will promote exports incidental to their operations abroad. Investments abroad contribute to the strength of the dollar.[1]

Certain commodities can be produced at more competitive prices in other industrial countries (including the member states of the E.E.C.) than in the United States.[2]

Experience gained in activities abroad may be valuable for competition at home, by the introduction, for example, of new patents and packaging. Profits earned abroad may act as insurance against difficulties and competition at home. Activities abroad are protective against competitive threats both in the United States and abroad.[3]

(According to a French opinion on factors behind American investment abroad) American enterprises, under pressure by anti-trust laws, cannot invest further in the United States and have to use available capital in enterprise abroad in favourable markets like the E.E.C.[4]

It would be difficult to distinguish clearly between the economic and the legal reasons why American businessmen and companies invest in the E.E.C. Economic and legal components of investment climate may be involved in these at one and the same time. Evidently, a favourable investment climate implies the importance of both categories. These in turn are mutually interdependent, since any economic order, in the strict sense of the term 'order', cannot exist in modern industrial society without its counterpart of a legal order. This last would not, however, by itself be conducive to a favourable investment climate if basic economic and other standards were non-existent and hence could not assist in the concrete implementation of the legal rules.

Some of the above remarks seem, nevertheless, to reflect more on the legal than the economic aspects of investment climate in the E.E.C. Thus, reference to the absence of any discrimination in-

[1] U.S. Secr. of Commerce J. T. Connor, quoted in *Le Monde*, 17 March 1965, p. 21.

[2] H. Kronstein: *The Corporation Take Over*, A. Hacker, ed., New York–London, 1963, p. 158.

[3] G. D. Bryson: *Profits from Abroad*, New York, 1964, pp. 50–1, 53, 55 ff., 62; for a businessman's approach to factors analysed when selecting a country, see pp. 191 ff.

[4] *Entreprise*, no. 490, 30 January 1965, p. 45.

dicates an awareness that in the Common Market member states, foreign-owned enterprise, once established, is subject to national treatment on a footing of equality with domestic enterprise. Likewise, the attraction that the progressive economic integration of the E.E.C. offers to the foreign investor can be explained in the light of Community law which extends the application of Community treatment, without discrimination, also to foreign-owned enterprises established in one of the member states. Finally, the remark that investments are effected because the E.E.C. is a politically stable area should be related to the effectiveness of the respective municipal orders and to the absence of pending major political or social issues like the imminent threat of nationalization. In fact, the view that investors can undertake activities under conditions familiar to them betrays an awareness of the fact that the sectors of public and private enterprise are currently clearly delineated and no major issues apt to provoke upheavals are pending. All in all, a salient characteristic of the investment climate in the E.E.C. contains a minimum of heterogeneous factors which would interfere with proper investment and managerial planning essential to modern industrial life.

The size of the American and other foreign undertakings that invest in the E.E.C. corresponds to that of medium and large enterprise.[1] There is, however, a close connection between firms that spend extensively on research and development in the United States, and firms that invest for operations abroad. For instance, a company like I.B.M. spends alone £60m yearly on research and one of the results of such extensive research budgets is the fact that the American computer industry, which has interests in the E.E.C., controls some 70 per cent of the world market for computers.

Since 1960 there has been a shift from reliance on wholly owned subsidiaries to co-operation with local knowledge and local capital. These collaborations are being increasingly regarded as essential to success, and as a possible way of dealing with resentment towards foreign enterprise.[2] Most American companies which have invested in Western Europe (including the E.E.C.) are confident in the long-term future for investments in the area.

[1] *Times Review of Industry*, March 1963, article by N. Willatt, p. 13.
[2] In *Europe* (a Financial Times Survey) 7 December 1964, G. Owen on increased investment by the U.S., p. 16. Bryson, *Profits from Abroad*, pp. 145–146, 152 ff. and 202.

According to some reports, American manufacturing companies will spend more than a thousand million dollars for investments in the Common Market during the period 1964–6. They do not want to be excluded from the advantages of being inside its 'rich' market for imports into the E.E.C. are being subjected to the impact of external tariffs and other factors. The climate for investment in Europe, in general, is considered to be very good, as political stability continues and incomes are more broadly distributed, thus strengthening the spending power of its large population.[1]

### Opinions expressed at Community level

Under the Treaty of Rome, the executive organs and other institutions of the E.E.C. do not have any powers to take action that affects the status of foreign investments in the member states. A number of statements have, however, been made on their part, which correspond to the general pattern of attitudes in the Common Market.

The very first question addressed in 1958 to the E.E.C. Commission by a member of the European Parliamentary Assembly, concerned foreign investments in the Common Market. M. M. Debré asked whether the Commission's attention had been turned to current foreign investments and investment projects of foreign enterprise, especially of American firms.[2] Desirous of availing themselves of the related provisions of the E.E.C. Treaty on the right of establishment foreign investors could invest freely in one or the other of the regions of the Common Market, and in the absence of any supervision on the part of the Commission, M. Debré remarked, such investments could disturb the economic as well as political and social equilibrium. He asked whether it was not urgent to envisage, in agreement with the member states, strict supervision to provide for equality in the benefits and burdens resulting from foreign investments.[3]

In their reply, the Commission stated that maximum develop-

---

[1] Kenneth Rush, *Opera Mundi—Europe*, no. 296, 18 March 1965, p. 7. According to *Neue Zürcher Zeitung*, 9 February 1965, Blatt 10, American investment in Europe had considerably increased following the discussion of possible curbs on foreign investments.

[2] As pointed out earlier, discussions evolve, under the term foreign investment, actually around *American* investments.

[3] J.O.(C.E.), 1958, p. 25/58.

ment, within the Community, of private investment from non-member countries was to be favoured. The Commission added that any discouragement in this respect was to be avoided and explained that they were, nevertheless, aware of the problems that may arise as a result of a too great concentration of such investments in a given member state or industry. The Commission then referred to the provisions of Article 72 of the Treaty which defines the modalities of co-operation between the six member states of the E.E.C. in the field of foreign investments. According to this Article, 'Member States shall keep the Commission informed of any movements of capital to and from third countries which they know about. The Commission may address to Member States any comments which it deems appropriate on this subject.' The Commission concluded their parliamentary reply to M. Debré's question by stating that the Commission would take action, whenever necessary, to issue opinions to the governments of the Member States and collaborate with them for a common policy.

In June 1959, Professor W. Hallstein, President of the Commission, made the following statement at a National Press Club luncheon in Washington, D.C.: 'It seems to me that our Community has received no more gratifying vote of confidence than American industry's rapidly mounting investment in the Common Market . . . We welcome this import of capital and "know-how" from America, and we hope in the future to see a reciprocal movement of European investment to your country . . .'[1]

In reply to a further question related to foreign investments in the Common Market, the Commission commented that there were no provisions in the Treaty of Rome enabling the Commission to oppose foreign investment projects in the E.E.C.[2]

The more frequent attention drawn to investments from the United States and growing concern about them in 1963-4 are reflected in more frequent statements, at Community level. At a joint meeting between the institutions of the European Communities, in a speech by Mr de Block on behalf of the Council, it was stated that policy towards foreign investment had been in keeping with the E.E.C.'s open character and that this policy would continue to be so at least until the end of the transitional period.[3]

[1] Quoted in Stein and Nicholson, eds., *American Enterprise in the European Common Market*, vol. 1, p. 28.
[2] J.O.(C.E.), 1962, p. 894/62.          [3] E.E.C. *Bulletin*, no. 1, 1964, p. 7.

Whereas in the last-mentioned statement a possible time-limit to the current liberal policy towards foreign investment in the E.E.C. was vaguely suggested, the Seventh Report of the Monetary Committee (1 March 1965) indicated in more clear terms that, if the present influx of capital into the Community were to continue, there would be a danger of fresh balance of payments surpluses. Such surpluses would be conducive to new inflationary pressure; and other measures failing, fundamental importance would have to be attached to the restriction of excessive imports of capital from countries outside the E.E.C., concluded the report of the Monetary Committee in March 1965.[1] In this connection, it is important to add that the Committee is referring to a particular problem raised by foreign investments on the level of the monetary situation; as such it does not concern the merits of foreign investment as a whole.

In reply to another question by a European Parliamentarian, the Commission stated in December 1964 that its members followed with utmost attention the evolution of foreign investments in the Common Market.[2] The Commission also added that it had not been possible to collect from member states sufficiently complete and detailed information which would allow a thorough study of the problem. In the opinion of the Commission, foreign investments as an aggregate were not a negligible factor in the general economic progress of the Common Market and had constituted an appreciable source of capital supplies for member states. The Commission concluded that they did not in any way doubt the efficiency with which Community enterprise would be able to react to competition from non-member countries within the framework of the Treaty of Rome. The Commission would continue to follow developments with greatest attention.

The opinions expressed by the Commission justify the conclusion that foreign investments, in the first place from the United States, did not present any global problems for the E.E.C., though the situation may not be uniform for all sectors of economic activities, such as in the automobile industry.[3] A technical difficulty in evaluating the current situation seems to be, for the Commission, the lack of adequate data. For this reason, the Commission ordered that a new study be undertaken, to be ready in

[1] J.O.(C.E.), 1965, pp. 640/65, par. 30.
[2] J.O.(C.E.), 1964, pp. 3725-6/64.
[3] *The Financial Times*, 28 January 1965, p. 5, and 4 February 1965, p. 5.

May–June 1965. The experts responsible for the study were to try to discover the exact extent of foreign participation in all sectors of economic activities within the E.E.C. This is not an easy task since investments in general and foreign investments, in particular, are not easy to identify for various reasons. The current lack of adequate information is partly due to the reluctance of some member states in providing all the information needed for composing an accurate picture of foreign participation in the respective national economies and industrial sectors.

In February 1965, Professor W. Hallstein, President of the E.E.C. Commission, referred again to the advantages that Europe had derived and still derives from the influx of American capital (some 1,700m US dollars in 1964), but he said he opposed a concentration of such capital in any one economic sector.[1] Concerning action to remedy the situation to the necessary extent, Professor Hallstein underlined his hope that the problem concerned should be discussed by the American authorities in conjunction with the deficit of American balance of payments. In an interview given to *Entreprise* (Paris), Professor Hallstein said the question of American investments in the E.E.C. had been raised and hence a reply would have to be found.[2]

In conclusion it may be said that the Commission has, since 1958, increased the attention paid to the evolution of foreign enterprise, in the first place American capital, in the E.E.C., and with a special study undertaken, in 1965, the outlines of a common policy by all member states may slowly emerge. Professor Hallstein's remarks reveal an awareness of the complications that would have to be faced if action were to be taken by member states of the Common Market, both in the absence of corresponding clauses in the Treaty or protocols annexed to it, and in the framework of bilateral treaties on establishment concluded by individual member states with third countries. Mention should also not be omitted of the possible impact that unilateral action against foreign enterprise in the Community would have on investments by E.E.C. member states in non-member countries.

*Official attitudes in the member states of the Common Market*

What has been written so far might be considered as an extensive comment on the *positive* attitude of the E.E.C. member states

[1] *Le Monde*, 6 February 1965, p. 5.
[2] *Entreprise*, no. 496, 13 March 1965, p. 31.

towards foreign investment. The conclusion suggested by large and increasing figures of foreign capital is corroborated by the well-defined and non-discriminatory treatment of foreign enterprise in sectors of activities accessible to them. We shall now refer to some official attitudes not previously mentioned.

In Belgium, foreign enterprise has been considered by the government as a valuable asset for the diversification of the country's economy, the introduction of new techniques and creation of new activities.[1] The alignment of investments, both foreign and domestic, with governmental objectives in economic development has not caused difficulties.

The situation is somewhat different in France and not wholly devoid of discrepancies. It is not easy to distinguish in terms of causes and effects. Thus, while fiscal burdens carried by undertakings in France are claimed to be the heaviest in the Common Market countries, participation of American capital in French economic life seems to be greater than in any single country in the world.[2] The Minister of Finance, M. G. d'Estaing, has been of the opinion that American investment had tended to select certain sectors of the French economy thus threatening to interfere with governmental control over employment, and also economic planning.[3] The government desires to encourage the establishment of foreign enterprise and technology in development regions of the country, but nevertheless, it considers that national economic planning and control must safeguard strategic sectors of the country's economy against foreign ownership.[4] It is also believed that the long-term effect of foreign investments on the balance of payments position of France cannot be favourable. President de Gaulle deplored, in his 1965 New Year's address, the invasion of American capital.[5] According to press reports, foreign investments were mentioned at the Rambouillet meeting between Chancellor Dr Erhard and President de Gaulle.[6] It is fully recognized that unilateral controls introduced by one of the member states

[1] O.B.R., 1964, no. 64-15, p. 14.

[2] A. H. Diamond: *Digest of French Taxes and Business Organization*, 1958, p. 2.

[3] M. C. MacLennan: 'The Common Market and French Planning', *Journ. C.M. Studies*, vol. III, no. 1, October 1964, p. 39.

[4] Ibid. Also E. Bock: in *The Banker*, May 1963; *Neue Zürcher Zeitung*, no. 301, 1 November 1964, Blatt 11 verso, and *Cartel*, vol. 14, no. 3, July 1964, p. 108 (on the Machines Bull affair).

[5] *New York Herald Tribune*, European edn., 1 January 1965, p. 1.

[6] *The Financial Times*, 28 January 1965, p. 5.

cannot be satisfactory in regulating the inflow of foreign investment, since foreign companies, once unilaterally authorized to
establish in one of the member states, can gain access to the
remaining member states under the provisions of Community law.

Comments expressing concern about foreign investments, again
mainly in respect of American enterprise, have come from private
quarters in Germany; official statements like the one by the Minister of Economic Affairs of the Land Nordrhein-Westfalen, have
been generally favourable.[1] The same remark applies to official
attitudes in Italy, where a special law encouraging foreign investments has been operative since 1956 and where it is realized that
domestic capital is not sufficient to finance all of the economic
development envisaged.

In Luxembourg, the government has welcomed the participation of foreign enterprise in efforts to diversify the country's economic production and create new and efficient undertakings. Such
a diversification has been envisaged in view of the country's past
dependence largely on iron and steel production.[2] In the Netherlands, authorities have favoured foreign enterprises that are not
labour intensive, introduce new technological standards and contribute to the internationally competitive position of the country's
industry.[3] An economic official of the Dutch government is
reported to have said: 'The threat of American colonization is
poppycock. [American] companies have to obey our laws, pay
our taxes . . .'[4]

These official attitudes are marked by a lack of uniformity—
opinions diverge from one member state to another. Furthermore,
a politically and economically larger member state like France
seems to be much more concerned about the influence of foreign
enterprise on her economic life and about the domination of
foreign capital in some sectors of industrial production than
smaller member states like Belgium and the Netherlands. In fact,
opinions expressed to the author in Belgium, Luxembourg and
the Netherlands were concerned about the economic benefits that
foreign investment brought. They were not based on any political considerations but seemed to be motivated by overwhelm-
ingly economic criteria.

---

[1] *Die Welt*, no. 55, 6 March 1965, p. 9.
[2] *W.T.I.S.*, 1962, no. 62-75, p. 6.
[3] *O.B.R.*, 1964, no. 65-1, p. 1.
[4] *Newsweek*, 8 March 1965, p. 47; *Cartel*, vol. 14, no. 3, July 1964, pp. 120-1.

*Opinions reflecting attitudes of E.E.C. businessmen and industrialists*

Information available on attitudes on the part of businessmen and other private quarters in the E.E.C. mainly concern controversial issues related to foreign enterprises, and thus do not convey a complete picture of the whole situation which is one marked by smooth functioning in most respects. There are, however, some aspects which have become objects of concern, related not to foreign investment *per se*, but to some of the problems to which it gives rise. These concern the competitive pressure to which domestic enterprise is exposed by the presence of efficient foreign undertakings, and whether such competition is salutary and fair.

In France, U.S. firms control 90 per cent of the production of synthetic rubber, 65 per cent of farm machinery production and almost all the electronics industry. In view of these facts, Baron Hottinger, Head of the French delegation at the 19th Congress of the International Chamber of Commerce in Mexico (1963), was of the opinion that 'foreign investments should not take control of key-sectors of the French economy, but [they are] welcome, even indispensable'. A similar attitude led in 1963 to controversies when the American food-canning company, Libby's, began the implementation of a large investment project in the south of France. Fear of foreign domination in the food-canning sector was the main argument that was advanced against the project.[1] In 1965, it turned out that the contribution made by Libby's had been particularly valuable since it had averted the submersion of numerous sectors of the French food market by products originating from the other members of the Common Market.[2]

Referring to the competition that French firms have to sustain in relation to foreign firms, aspects frequently pointed out concern the actual size of French firms which are in most cases too small in comparison with the dimensions indicated by technical requirements.[3] A leading French firm, which may be the first in its branch, is ten times smaller than its comparable American enterprise. Facilities for financing investments are inadequate and fiscal charges too large to lead to competition with foreign enterprise. Wherever necessary, the door should not be opened too

[1] Cf. G.-Y. Bertin, in: *Cartel*, vol. 14, no. 2, April 1964, p. 61.
[2] *Entreprise*, no. 493, 20 February 1965, p. 27.
[3] *Entreprise*, no. 492, 13 February 1965, p. 47.

widely to foreign competitors and thus lead to the elimination of small French undertakings before they have had time to adjust themselves to the changing conditions.[1]

The introduction by American investment of better technological standards has, naturally, been to Europe's advantage. They have led to higher productivity and modernization of industrial processes, but the challenge they bring must be met.[2] With larger waves of American investments to be expected in the future, according to an industrial expert, French companies should be induced to concentrate and thus avoid the risk of being taken over by American capital.[3] American firms should be induced to divide the investment capital between themselves and French partners, thus sharing managerial power. Moreover, American firms should undertake to make better use of the potential research skill in France, by conducting research work within their subsidiaries in France. This is already being done by some American firms. Other measures directed at restricting American enterprise in France could otherwise be as damaging to Europeans themselves as they could to Americans.

Asked about their preferences in associating themselves with German or American firms, French entrepreneurs had been 43 per cent in favour of association with German undertakings; 34 per cent were in favour of association with Americans, 18 per cent with other nationalities and 5 per cent did not reply.[4] Asked about their preference for American firms, respondents said it was based on political considerations, on the fact that the technological capacity of Americans was immense and of international standards. Some believed that the farther away a principal company was based, the better would it be for the autonomy of its subsidiary in France. Others emphasized the contribution that Americans made in capital and in technical knowledge. An association with Americans offered the best prospects for new markets, since Americans had experience in operating in mass markets and their financial resources were considerable.

Referring to the intention of the government to apply stricter

[1] For an example concerning the food industries. See Bertin, *Cartel*, vol. 14, no. 2, April 1964, p. 78.

[2] *Cartel*, vol. 14, no. 3, July 1964, p. 122.

[3] *Entreprise*, no. 477, special issue, 31 October 1964, the interview with A. Chalandon, p. 7.

[4] *Entreprise*, no. 477, Special number, 31 October 1964, p. 236.

criteria in authorizing the entry of American capital into France, above all by favouring investment in new enterprises as against investment in the form of take-overs of existing firms, opinions expressed doubt about the efficiency of such measures. Not by protectionist measures, but by intensive research programmes should the challenge of American enterprise be met, in addition to the concentration of those undertakings which must of necessity be affected.[1] Some of the American firms operating in Europe are not necessarily large, but they are highly specialized.

A further interesting remark, made by the same author, concerns the acquisition in the E.E.C. of assets by American firms which, under the anti-trust rules of the United States, would be excluded from their acquisition in the U.S.A. This remark raises a series of highly complicated technical questions, but it refers to one of the basic facts that are behind the complaints of European businessmen about American enterprise in the E.E.C.: the issue of competition on unequal terms between E.E.C. firms and American firms. American firms can compete in the E.E.C. without being subject to financial and other limitations that affect the competitive position of Community firms, a point to be taken up in some detail below. In anticipation, it might be said that municipal and Community rules on competition regulate restrictive trading practices of undertakings; but the Treaty of Rome fulfils another major function: it governs not only competition between firms as they operate from the respective member states, but also competition between the six different national economies which constitute the Common Market and on whose proper co-ordination the functioning of the Common Market depends. There are, however, no provisions in the Treaty of Rome for regulating the competitive position of firms that originate in countries outside the E.E.C. and enjoy there non-aligned conditions of financing, concentration and research.[2]

In Germany, private views have been voiced in critical terms about American enterprise. After the Volkswagen–Daimler agreement for closer co-operation was announced, it was stated that united efforts against American competition in the automobile industry were not only in Germany's but also in Europe's interest.[3] In the German press, the need for better statistical cover-

---

[1] P. Uri, *Le Monde*, 24 February 1965, p. 16.
[2] Two articles by P. Uri, *Le Monde*, 23–24 February 1965.
[3] *Die Welt*, no. 251, 27 October 1964, p. 10.

age of foreign enterprise in the E.E.C. has also been noted.[1] An article in *Frankfurter Allgemeine* of 25 February 1965 (p. 1), signed by J. Eick, has scrutinized, in critical terms, the behaviour of some American investors: in the opinion of the writer, American investors export with their capital the American way of life. This consists, he continues, in living isolated, and in disregarding the living habits of the local population; they behave as if everything should be done the way it is done at home in the United States. Washington should consider how to bridle some of the American giant undertakings, otherwise resentments like this will be generated. On the other hand, a report in the monthly published by the American Chamber of Commerce in Germany,[2] states that 'German executives in industry and finance are almost unanimous that U.S. investment has been, ever since 1945, and continues to be a beneficent factor in increased economic and technical strength . . . in France, the attitude in all the large enterprises is exactly the same.'

## CONCLUSIONS

The opinions and attitudes reviewed here reveal a number of important points in relation to the investment climate of the E.E.C. and its possible future trends.

Official and private opinions welcome the valuable contribution made by foreign enterprise in the member states but are, on the other hand, aware of a number of adjustments that seem to be necessary. These adjustments concern the optimum co-ordination necessary between the interests of investors and nationals of the host countries. The former do not hesitate to qualify the investment climate as very good. Their comments have nothing to do with standards of differential treatment as these do not exist in the E.E.C. but refer to minor points of co-operation between foreign and domestic enterprises. Faced with the choice between sole ownership or co-operation with local skill and capital, foreign investors have been more and more making use of co-operation with nationals and capital of the host country.

Foreign investors, chiefly American firms, entering the Common Market for economic activities are very often highly specialized and technologically well-equipped undertakings which know

---

[1] Ibid., 6 February 1965, p. 10. Also, the statements of Dr. H. J. Abs, in *The Financial Times*, 8 February 1965, p. 1.

[2] *Commerce in Germany*, March 1965, no. 135, p. 8.

what the Common Market offers them, and what they in return can offer to the markets of the E.E.C. The enterprises in question have well-financed research programmes, features which are lacking in the activities of many European firms.

The state authorities, while welcoming foreign investors, are also aware of the interests that should not fall under the control of foreign undertakings. Here, the politically and economically stronger members, France for example, are more sensitive than the smaller members of the E.E.C. Moreover, it seems that current legislation restricting the access of foreigners to certain sectors of activities does not wholly correspond to the aspirations of both authorities and the public at large. Thus, while legally not formulated, an unwritten rule, that certain vital industries should not be dominated or substantially controlled by foreign capital, does seem to exist. No legislative action is however being recommended and it is difficult to see in the light of Community law, what the meaning of unilateral legislative action directed at a control of foreign enterprise should or could be. In this connection, it is noteworthy that interest in foreign investment has been increasingly growing, culminating in the current study (March 1965) recommended by the Commission of the E.E.C. This study will outline the possibilities of co-ordinated action on foreign investment to be taken in case of need. Difficulties of a legal nature are, however, full of technical complexities as a result of unilateral legislation, bilateral establishment agreements, as well as the Treaty of Rome, all of which exist side by side, and cannot be wholly co-ordinated without the consent of non-member states that are parties to bilateral establishment agreements. The shift of interest in matters of foreign investments has been, however, towards the Community level.

Opinions entertained by private businessmen in the E.E.C. welcome the participation of foreign enterprise in their respective national economies. They appreciate the technological and other innovations that foreigners bring with their capital. They have, on the other hand, a feeling that they have to face hard competition from foreign enterprise, especially from the United States, and on unequal terms. While accepting the welcome challenge of competition, which can be in the economic interest of the Common Market, certain domestic firms and some municipal authorities note the absence of a system which would enable domestic enterprises to adjust themselves to the new situation. Private businessmen do not favour protectionism, but they feel the need for measures which would, where needed, put domestic enterprise on a footing of equality with American firms as far as financial and research resources are concerned.

Some opinions have been expressed on the need to persuade the American firms concerned 'to work on a basis of equality . . . instead of taking over whole companies, or even entire advanced branches of industry . . .'[1] For their part, domestic enterprises in the E.E.C. should intensify their research programmes for technological progress, the inadequacy of which would possibly entail the 'technological satellization' of Europe in accordance with the law of the mightier dominating the rest.[2]

On the institutional or procedural level, the problem comes down to one of co-ordination and co-operation (i.) between the E.E.C. as a whole and the United States as the non-member country involved in the current situation, and (ii.) between the six member states themselves, at Community level. The need for co-ordination and co-operation at Community level, by all member states, is felt by their respective governments. It marks progress towards a new, and necessary, approach which deals with the Common Market as an organic whole and not just the sum of six municipal systems. This point concerns the basic difference in the approach of many foreign and domestic firms to activities in the E.E.C. Foreign firms entering the Common Market have been quick to grasp the opportunities that the progressive integration towards a single large market has offered them, and with experience in operating within large consumers' markets, they have been able to plan accordingly. Many domestic undertakings on the other hand have taken a long time to look at the Common Market in terms of exactly what it implies as a single large market, instead of an area of intermember trade as another form of import–export trade under more favourable tariff conditions.

---

[1] *The Guardian*, 4 February 1965, p. 11.

[2] *Rev. M.C.*, no. 75, December 1964, p. 568 (on the statement of M. Pleven at the European Parliament in November 1964). See the opinions of Marcel Demonque, in: *Entreprise*, no. 486, 2 January 1965, p. 19.

# CHAPTER XIV

## THE CURRENT SITUATION AND SPECULATIONS ON THE FUTURE

On the foreign investor's side, the current situation is marked by an absence of the problems that are commonly related to investments in the developing regions of the world. Political risks are practically non-existent. The transfer of investment income is not subject to restrictions. Once established in a member state, foreign investors can depend on the effectiveness of national and Community treatment as set out under municipal and Community laws respectively. Policy towards foreign investors seeking establishment in the respective member states is liberal and foreign capital has availed itself amply of that liberalism since the establishment of the Common Market in 1958.

The absence of legal problems on the investor's side does not correspond, however, with a similar situation on the side of the host member states. A number of problems, resulting from competitive pressures, exist which, though not yet critical, nevertheless affect the interests of certain domestic undertakings in the E.E.C.

Significantly, the concern expressed so far about competition is not directed towards foreign enterprise as a whole and it does not deal with the questions of basic principles usually met in discussions about investments in developing regions, such as permanent sovereignty over natural resources, or the exclusion of foreign enterprises from influence over production resources or important industries, though the view has been expressed in the E.E.C. that a national economy must not necessarily suffer damage as a result of such influence.[1] Discussions on the current situation in the E.E.C. deal with the aggregate effect of many complex factors which are restricting the mobility of Community firms to

---

[1] See the prefatory note of the Bundesbank to a list of foreign investors in Germany. Reported in *The Financial Times*, 11 June 1965, p. 5; also the opinion of von Falkenhausen, president of the association of German banks, favourable to American investments in the Common Market, reported in the *Kurier* (Vienna), 10 April 1965, p. 6.

meet the challenge of their strong American counterparts. As the factors concerned are both legal and non-legal in nature, it is appropriate to review the adequacy of the present legal system in the E.E.C. to ensure fair competition between Community firms and their foreign counterparts operating in the Common Market. The proposition taken here as a departing point for the observations which follow is that the present system is not wholly adequate within the framework of the progressive Common Market in which domestic firms have to expand from national to Community dimensions.

One of the implied but very essential functions of the E.E.C. Treaty is the co-ordination of competition between the respective economies of member states (Article 2 of the Treaty of Rome). Extensive interpenetration is expected to develop between national economies and firms from different member states, and the Treaty would be expected to function so that extraneous factors distorting competition in a developing Common Market would be checked and eliminated. Firms participating in the uniform market must have uniform conditions of competition, such as aligned legal capacity, fiscal treatment, access to financial resources for development and research.

In the system of economic integration envisaged by the Treaty of Rome, external relations with respect to foreign investments in the Common Market are not specifically governed by Community law; the assumption behind this attitude was probably that foreign investments within the Community would never assume the magnitude they have done since 1960. The penetration of the Common Market by foreign capital, it was thought, would be marginal and would not involve the impact of extensive investment from a single country like the United States. As a result, investments from countries like the United Kingdom, Sweden or Switzerland and their limited extent compared with American investment continue to be noted without concern; even if firms from these countries benefit from disparities between different municipal systems, their impact on the Common Market remains relatively insignificant.

The situation of American firms is, however, different. Their massive participation might be likened to that from a *seventh* member state of the E.E.C., in which the benefits of the Common Market are used without those firms being subject to the restrictions, legal and economic, imposed by Community law and by the aggregate situation in the E.E.C. While American firms are competing in the Common Market, they can simultaneously organize themselves financially and technologically outside the E.E.C. They have access to cheaper financial resources;[1] they have benefited from the favourable provisions of double taxation agreements and from fiscal legislation at home, under which profits earned abroad have been taxable only when returned to the parent company in the form of dividends;[2] favourable tax-havens have been used as operational bases; arrangements have been used between principal and subsidiary companies regarding intercompany pricing, licensing agreements, shifting of expenses and other devices for maximizing profits in ways possible only in international trade; they have accumulated an immense reservoir of technological progress due to better research and development facilities at home. Obviously, these advantages are not open to Community firms operating within the Community or else are open to them only to a limited extent. The inequalities of a situation like this contain the elements for a distortion of competition within the Common Market, a distortion which is significant since it involves the impact on E.E.C. economies of conditions in a non-member state, through extensive investment from that state.

Measures to improve the current situation may be pragmatic or systematic. The situation is related to the balance of payments deficit of the United States, and the American government has resorted to pragmatic measures by appealing to businessmen to 'exercise voluntary restrictions in lending money or making investments abroad in the developed countries'.[3] This does not,

---

[1] Seventh Report of the E.E.C. Monetary Committee, J.O.(C.E.), 1965, p. 637/65 (par. 15). See also the lecture by Kristensen (Secretary-General of the O.E.C.D.) given in Hanover, favouring lower interest rates in Europe and higher rates in the U.S.A., reported in the *Kurier*, 17 April 1965, p. 9. On the higher costs of bankers in Europe as compared with the U.S.A., see Constantin von Velsen's lecture in Hamburg on 28 January 1965, reported in *Commerce in Germany*, no. 135, March 1965, p. 9. For local financing facilities in Belgium, France, Germany and the Netherlands respectively, see J. F. McDaniels, ed.: *International Financing and Investment*, New York, 1964, pp. 280 ff., 287 ff., 328 ff., 306 ff.

[2] The late President J. F. Kennedy, 'Our Federal Tax system', House of Representatives, Doc. no. 140, 87th Congress, 1st Session, 3 May 1961, quoted in American Government—Readings and Documents, P. H. Odegard, ed., New York, 1964, pp. 590–1.

[3] *The Financial Times*, 11 February 1965, p. 11; also, ibid.,(p. 1; *The Financial Times*, 19 February 1965, p. 12; *The Economist*, 27 February 1965, p. 853,

however, solve the particular problems of Community undertakings, even if it slows down the acquisition by American investors of industrial assets in the E.E.C. For a solution to these problems, legal, economic and financial measures in the E.E.C. will have to be envisaged, measures which can be related to international law, on the one hand, and to internal or Community law, on the other.

Measures with respect to the external legal relations of the Common Market are neither desirable nor feasible. Any attempt to bar the access of American capital into the Common Market would be a case of flagrant discrimination between foreign investment from the United States and from other countries. It would at the same time affect the position of Common Market countries as capital exporters. Moreover, it would constitute a breach of the establishment agreements that member states like France, Germany and Italy have concluded with the United States. Finally, it would not provide for the changes needed within the Community.

One theoretical possibility would be to attempt a co-ordination of direct or indirect aids and subsidies that foreign governments grant to companies expanding abroad. Apart from the technical complexities that would have to be overcome in this respect, owing to the absence of adequate theoretical preparatory work, such an attempt would also have to overcome the barriers of international, economic and legal policies; it is not a feasible solution, nor proportional to the magnitude of the limited problems that domestic enterprise in the E.E.C. has to face.[1]

The contribution that law can make in improving the competitiveness of Community undertakings will have to be sought within the Community. The financial needs of the undertakings concerned for developing into Community firms is related to their ability to get the required resources on capital markets within the Community. For this purpose, it will be necessary to amend municipal laws in such a way that European capital can be mobilized quickly and easily on integrated money markets within the Community.[2] Such a uniform capital market would, by providing

---

letter by H. W. Singer; *The Financial Times*, 3 March 1965, p. 13; ibid., 16 June 1965, p. 13.

[1] See the statement of E.E.C. Commission-member Sig. Colonna di Paliano, reported in *Opera Mundi—Europe*, no. 309, 17 June 1965, p. 13.

[2] See the conclusions of M. Bertrand and M. P. Uri from the debate at the 'Round Table Conference on the Problems of Europe', 15th meeting,

the institutional arrangements necessary for mobilizing savings within the Community and putting them to work, assist Community undertakings in their needs and fill the gap that has stimulated the demand for American money within the Community.[1] Legal aspects of capital markets in the E.E.C. are thus involved in the current situation of foreign investment within the Common Market.

A further legal aspect which, if improved, could help to promote the competitive position of Community undertakings, concerns the field of industrial research and development. Investment in the E.E.C. is accompanied by a considerable inflow of technical knowledge in the form of patents and licensing agreements. This reflects the nature of industrial activities in economically advanced regions of the world, where firms must maintain their market position or conquer new markets by improving their products and by developing new ones. The inflow of foreign technical knowledge has been interpreted as the result of a 'technological gap' between standards abroad and within the Community. The need for encouraging research effort has been pointed out with reference to declining figures of domestic patents in some member states. For example, in France, whereas 41·45 per cent of filed patents were of French origin in 1956, the corresponding figure for 1962 was 34·54 per cent, a declining trend that has been correlated to the increasing flow of American investments in the E.E.C. after 1960.[2] There is a growing realization that the expanding Community market cannot be catered for by industrial research undertaken on a national scale. In March 1965, France favoured the establishment of a Community policy for scientific and technical research.[3] The French government, in its note to the E.E.C., referred to the harmonious development of economic activities as one of the objectives of the E.E.C. and interpreted it as implying the need for common efforts in scientific and technical research. While the Treaty does not contain any precise procedural clauses in this respect, this matter could be included in the general ambit of Article 100, on the approximation of laws to the extent neces-

---

Brussels, 8–9 June 1965, reported in *Opera Mundi—Europe*, no. 309, 17 June 1965, p. 5.

[1] *The Financial Times*, 11 February 1965, p. 11.

[2] *Le Monde*, 7–8 February 1965, p. 9. See also chapter VII, page 158 above, for French expenditure on foreign patents.

[3] *Le Monde*, 20 March 1965, p. 20.

sary for the proper functioning of the Common Market. The
French government's note showed an awareness that the vulner-
ability of certain technologically intensive industries in the E.E.C.
is inversely related to the pace of scientific and technological development. A reform of the institutional and legal system of
scientific and industrial research in the E.E.C., could make, in
this respect, a valuable contribution. The re-orientation of scientific and industrial research is an involved process and slow to
yield quick results. It is, however, one of the cornerstones on
which the technical progress of an economically and industrially
well-developed region like the E.E.C. may well depend in general
and one of the by-products of the necessary reform could be the
higher efficiency of Community firms in competing with technologically well-equipped foreign firms.

A third legal aspect related to the problems of Community
firms in their competition with their foreign counterparts is that
of reforming the current system of municipal company laws. The
municipal legal barriers which at present hamper the mobility and
development of companies on a Community-wide scale should be
overcome by the provision of a common type of stock company
such as was discussed in chapter XII. The administrative application of its law could be left to municipal authorities, but the
judicial control of it should be subjected to the competence of
the Community Court of Justice. A law which transcends the
boundaries of member states and which is created for the purpose
of bringing the economies of those states closer to each other
should not be left to the interpretation and control of separate
municipal courts. The unifying function of law depends not least
on the unifying judicial function of a central court. The interests
of the Community as a whole require a fresh approach to legal
problems related to the current situation of foreign investment in
the E.E.C. The promotion of such an approach could be one of
the important contributions that lawyers can make to the E.E.C.
Legal developments in the E.E.C. with respect to capital markets,
industrial research and corporate mobility should facilitate a Community approach by industrialists to their Community problems.
In the absence of such an approach it is feared that psychological
attitudes in the E.E.C. will continue to cling to municipal limitations while competitive foreign enterprise will continue to reap
the benefits of a wider outlook.

The extension of Community treatment to foreign-owned

undertakings has been criticized on the grounds that it gives a Community status to foreign companies which establish themselves in the Common Market.[1] This criticism implies a reference to or possible preference for the principle of control or ownership, as the criterion for the qualification of undertakings as Community firms. It is submitted that while the Treaty of Rome extends Community treatment to foreign-owned undertakings in the manner specified by Article 58, this treatment could be restricted, by an amendment of Article 58, to Community-owned firms only, i.e. to companies controlled and owned by Community nationals. Such an amendment is technically feasible under Article 236; its benefits to Community undertakings and to the Common Market as a whole would be of a very debatable value, however, as the control of undertakings availing themselves of Article 58 would necessitate an administrative machinery which would be charged with distinguishing between Community-owned and foreign-owned undertakings by applying such criteria as those of effective nationality. Secondly, such a system would run counter to the interests of Community nationals, in an extreme case, by making any co-operation between them and foreign investors almost impossible. Standards of differential treatment would have to be established, including the extent to which foreign investors may participate in undertakings that qualify under Article 58. Such an amendment of Article 58 would not violate obligations incurred under bilateral establishment treaties. The general purpose of such an amendment to Article 58 remains, however, an impractical one. The current situation in the E.E.C. with respect to competition between foreign and Community firms does not require nor can it be radically improved by action *against* foreign investment. It requires action *for* Community undertakings aiming at an improvement of their financing and research facilities and at increasing their mobility and capacity to co-operate, transfer or merge across national boundaries.

[1] Statements of M. M. Maurice-Bokanowski, French Minister of Industry, reported in *The Financial Times*, 27 May 1965, p. 5.

# APPENDIX A
# ECONOMIC AND DEMOGRAPHIC DATA

### TABLE 1
*Area and population, mid-1963*

|  | Area in sq. km. | Population in thousands |
|---|---|---|
| E.E.C. | 1,167,500 | 178,518 |
| U.S.A. | 9,363,400 | 189,375 |
| U.S.S.R. | 22,402,200 | 224,764 |
| World | 135,773,000 | 3,270,000 |

### TABLE 2
*Area and population of E.E.C. member states, 1963*

|  | Area in sq. km. | Population in thousands |
|---|---|---|
| Belgium | 30,500 | 9,290 |
| France | 551,200 | 47,840 |
| Germany | 248,500 | 57,606 |
| Italy | 301,200 | 51,491 |
| Luxembourg | 2,600 | 324 |
| Netherlands | 33,500 | 11,967 |

Source: E.E.C., *Basic Statistics of the Community*, 5th edn., 1964.

### TABLE 3
*External trade figures of the E.E.C., 1963*

|  | Imports | Exports |
|---|---|---|
|  | (in million dollars) | |
| E.E.C. | 40,350 | 37,545 |
| World | 142,300[1] | 152,090 |

[1] Excluding Eastern bloc.

327

## TABLE 4

### Average annual growth rates of gross national product at constant prices

In percentage of aggregate g.n.p.

|  | 1952–62 | 1963–4[1] |
|---|---|---|
| Belgium | 3·1 (1953–62) | 5·0 |
| France | 4·7 | 5·1 |
| Germany | 6·7 | 6·2 |
| Italy | 6·3 | 2·7 |
| Luxembourg | — (not available) | — |
| Netherlands | 4·9 | 5·5 |

Source: E.E.C., *Basic Statistics of the Community*, 5th edn., 1964, Tables 64, 65.
[1] Cf. the O.E.C.D. *Observer*, no. 14, February 1965, p. 13.

## TABLE 5

### Industrial growth

|  | 1962 current prices | 1970 constant 1961 prices | Gross national product growth percentage |
|---|---|---|---|
|  | g.n.p. in 1,000m dollars | | |
| Belgium | 12·7 | 17·4 | 3·2 |
| France | 71·5 | 93·2 | 4·6 |
| Germany | 84·2 | 113·0 | 6·7 |
| Italy | 39·5 | 52·2 | 6·3 |
| Luxembourg | 0·5 | 0·7 | 4·3 |
| Netherlands | 13·1 | 16·7 | 4·9 |
| E.E.C. | 221·5 | 293·1 | 5·6 (weighted average) |

Source: The Chase Manhattan Bank: *The New European Market: A Guide for American Businessmen*, January 1964, p. 21.

## TABLE 6

### General indices of industrial production (excluding construction)

*1958 = 100*

|  | 1963 |
|---|---|
| Belgium | 130 |
| France | 130 |
| Germany | 136 |
| Italy | 169 |
| Luxembourg | 113 |
| Netherlands | 130 |
| E.E.C. | 139 |

Source: E.E.C., *Basic Statistics of the Community*, 5th edn., 1964, Table 42.

TABLE 7

| | Gross national product at market prices per capita, 1963 (in dollars) | Structure of g.n.p. at current prices (percentage) | | |
|---|---|---|---|---|
| | | Agriculture, forestry, fishing | Mining, quarrying, manufacturing industries, construction | Other activities |
| Belgium | 1,500 | 7·0 | 39·2 | 53·8 |
| France | 1,671 | 8·7 | 45·8 | 45·5 |
| Germany | 1,641 | 5·2 | 52·6 | 42·2 |
| Italy | 899 | 15·5 | 41·9 | 42·6 |
| Luxembourg | 1,606 (1961) | 7·5 | 55·7 | 36·8 |
| Netherlands | 1,212 | 8·8 | 41·4 | 49·8 |

Source: The O.E.C.D. *Observer*, no. 13, December 1964, pp. 22–3.

TABLE 8

*Domestic capital investment in 1960, in percentage of gross national product*

| | |
|---|---|
| Belgium | 17·5 |
| France | 17·4 |
| Germany | 23·7 |
| Italy | 22·3 |
| Luxembourg | 20·9 |
| Netherlands | 23·5 |
| E.E.C. | 21·1 |

Source: *The New Europe and its Economic Future*, based on *Europe's Needs and Resources*, by J. F. Dewhurst, J. O. Coppock, P. Lamartine Yates, *et al.*, statistics by B. Mueller, 1964, p. 125.

TABLE 9

*Average per capita income of some E.E.C. countries, the U.K. and U.S., before and after the First World War (in pre-war dollars)*

| | 1914 | 1925 |
|---|---|---|
| Belgium | 182 | 141 |
| France | 182 | 124 |
| Italy | 105 | 63 |
| U.K. | 237 | 265 |
| U.S. | 337 | 388 |

Source: *A Comparison of the Wealth and National Income of Several Important Nations* (Italy, France, Belgium, U.K. and U.S., before and after the War, Rome, 1925, Table between pp. 39 and 40.

z

APPENDIX A

TABLE 10

*Economically active population*

|  | Year | Total (in 1,000) | Percentage of population |
|---|---|---|---|
| Belgium | 1963 | 3,590 | 39 |
| France | 1963 | 19,237 | 40 |
| Germany | 1963 | 25,614 | 44 |
| Italy | 1963 | 19,800 | 40 |
| Luxembourg | 1960 | 128 | 41 |
| Netherlands | 1961 | 4,324 | 37 |

Source: E.E.C., *Basic Statistics.*

TABLE 11

*Employment in agriculture, industry and other sectors, 1963*

|  | Agriculture (per cent) | Industry (per cent) | Other Sectors (per cent) |
|---|---|---|---|
| Belgium | 6·5 | 46·7 | 46·8 |
| France | 20·7 | 40·1 | 39·2 |
| Germany | 13·5 | 49·0 | 37·5 |
| Italy | 27·0 | 41·2 | 31·8 |
| Luxembourg | 21·0 | 45·2 | 33·8 |
| Netherlands | 9·9 | 42·1 | 48·0 |

Source: The O.E.C.D. *Observer*, no. 13, December 1964, pp. 20–1.

# APPENDIX B

# FOREIGN INVESTMENT DATA

TABLE 1

*American investment in the E.E.C., in the period 1959–61, in percentages of gross capital formation in industrial sectors*

|  | 1959 | 1960 | 1961 |
|---|---|---|---|
| Belgium-Luxembourg | 1·5 | 2·6 | 1·9 |
| France | 1·5 | 1·5 | 1·4 |
| Germany | 2·3 | 2·5 | 3·1 |
| Italy | 0·9 | 0·9 | 2·0 |
| Netherlands | 3·8 | 2·5 | 2·2 |

Source: J.O.(C.E)., 1963, p. 977/63, Table 4.

TABLE 2

*Value of American investments[1] in Europe at the end of 1962*

|  | Petroleum per cent | Manufacturing per cent | Others per cent | Total in million dollars |
|---|---|---|---|---|
| Belgium-Luxembourg | 20 | 61 | 19 | 283 |
| France | 25 | 58 | 17 | 1,006 |
| Germany | 26 | 65 | 9 | 1,472 |
| Italy | 42 | 43 | 15 | 540 |
| Netherlands | 44 | 32 | 24 | 370 |
| E.E.C. | 30 | 56 | 14 | 3,671 |
| Western Europe | 26 | 56 | 18 | 8,607 |

Source: The Chase Manhattan Bank: *The New European Market—A Guide for American Businessmen*, January 1964, p. 39.

[1] Data represent cumulative totals of net capital investments and undistributed subsidiary earnings.

## TABLE 3

### Where American firms are investing in Europe

| | Belgium[1] | France | Germany | Italy | Nether-lands | E.E.C. | Western Europe |
|---|---|---|---|---|---|---|---|
| | *in million dollars* | | | | | | |
| Machinery (non-electric) | 54 | 63 | 57 | 54 | 29 | 257 | 382 |
| Electrical machinery | 28 | 43 | 22 | 43 | 14 | 150 | 215 |
| Household appliances | 1 | 16 | 9 | 8 | 4 | 38 | 58 |
| Transport equipment | 14 | 32 | 6 | 18 | 8 | 78 | 107 |
| Heavy equipment | 7 | 14 | 8 | 4 | 3 | 36 | 53 |
| Office machinery | 6 | 10 | 11 | 4 | 5 | 36 | 63 |
| Instruments and watches | 5 | 19 | 27 | 14 | 20 | 85 | 123 |
| Basic metals and products | 27 | 21 | 24 | 21 | 11 | 104 | 136 |
| Research and engineering | 6 | 17 | 9 | 6 | 7 | 45 | 58 |
| Petroleum and other fuels | 8 | 12 | 10 | 13 | 5 | 48 | 63 |
| Chemicals | 67 | 52 | 50 | 54 | 47 | 270 | 348 |
| Rubber | 6 | 9 | 3 | 5 | 4 | 27 | 32 |
| Paper | 7 | 15 | 8 | 6 | 4 | 40 | 67 |
| Textiles and clothing | 15 | 9 | 9 | 12 | 14 | 59 | 87 |
| Food, beverages and tobacco | 14 | 19 | 16 | 14 | 15 | 78 | 114 |
| Glass | 6 | 1 | 1 | 5 | — | 13 | 18 |
| Finance | 4 | 15 | 10 | 6 | 3 | 38 | 52 |
| Distribution | 2 | 3 | 2 | — | — | 7 | 13 |
| Hotels | 4 | 4 | 3 | 1 | 1 | 13 | 19 |
| Marketing and publicity | 3 | 8 | 6 | 4 | 1 | 22 | 36 |
| Other services | 11 | 11 | 4 | 5 | 8 | 39 | 56 |
| Others | 14 | 11 | 16 | 12 | 5 | 58 | 81 |
| Total | 309 | 404 | 311 | 309 | 208 | 1,541 | 2,181 |

Source: The Chase Manhattan Bank: *The European Markets*, January 1964, p. 40.
[1] Belgium includes Luxembourg.

## TABLE 4

*Regional analysis of U.K. direct investment and earnings, 1961–2, excluding oil and insurance companies*

|  | 1961 | 1962 |
|---|---|---|
| In E.E.C. |  |  |
| In £ million | 24·8 | 30·7 |
| Per cent | 11·7 | 19·6 |
| Total in world |  |  |
| In £ million | 211·6 | 156·9 |
|  |  | (figures for 1962 are incomplete) |

Source: *Board of Trade Journal*, 15 November, 1963.

## TABLE 5

*Swedish subsidiaries in the E.E.C.*

|  | No. of subsidiaries | |
|---|---|---|
|  | In the E.E.C. | In the world |
| Engineering | 176 | 635 |
| Mining | 4 | 9 |
| Timber, pulp, paper | 24 | 49 |
| Paper-processing, printing | 7 | 22 |
| Chemicals and pharmaceuticals | 37 | 121 |
| Textiles | 8 | 23 |
| Quarrying and building | 12 | 33 |
| Leather, plastics and rubber | 7 | 22 |
| Trading firms | 27 | 104 |
| Food | 4 | 15 |
| Agencies, service trades, communications | 15 | 3 |
| Banks, insurance | 2 | 8 |
| Holding companies | — | 6 |
| Power stations | — | 1 |
| Total | 323 | 1,084 |
| Per cent | 30 | 100 |

Source: B. Ekman: 'Swedish industry goes abroad', *Featuring Sweden*, no. 4, 1964, p. 30.

### TABLE 6

*American direct investments in the E.E.C.*
*in million dollars*

|  | *1950* | *1960* | *1961* |
|---|---|---|---|
| E.E.C. | 637 | 2,644 | 3,041 |
| World total | 11,788 | 32,778 | 34,684 |

*In percentage of U.S. investment in the world*

| E.E.C. | 5·4 | 8·1 | 8·8 |
|---|---|---|---|

Source: J.O.(C.E.), 1963, p. 976/63.

### TABLE 7

*American direct investments in E.E.C. countries at the end of 1957*
*and 1961, in million dollars*

|  | *1957* | *1961* | Percentage increase |
|---|---|---|---|
| Belgium-Luxembourg | 192 | 256 | 33 |
| France | 464 | 840 | 81 |
| Germany | 581 | 1,170 | 102 |
| Italy | 252 | 467 | 85 |
| Netherlands | 191 | 308 | 61 |
| E.E.C. | 1,680 | 3,041 | 81 |

Source: J.O.(C.E.), 1963, p. 977/63.

# BIBLIOGRAPHY

## BOOKS

*Annuaire Suisse de Droit International*, vol. 7, Zurich, 1950.

ANON. *A Comparison of the Wealth and National Income of several important Nations (Italy, France, Belgium, the United Kingdom and the United States) before and after the [first world] War*, Rome, 1925.

BANCA NAZIONALE DEL LAVORO. *Guide for Foreign Investors in Italy*, Rome, 1962.

BANCO DI ROMA. *Foreign Private Enterprise in Italy*, 2 vols., Rome, 1959.

BANK FOR INTERNATIONAL SETTLEMENTS, BASLE. *Eight European Central Banks, A Descriptive Study*, London, 1963.

BANQUE INTERNATIONALE A LUXEMBOURG. *Luxembourg and the Common Market. Establishment of New Industrial Enterprises*, Luxembourg, 1959.

BATTIFOL, H. *Traité élémentaire de Droit international privé*, 3rd edn., Paris, 1959.

BEBR, G., *Judicial Control of the European Communities*, London, 1962.

BELGIAN MINISTRY OF ECONOMIC AFFAIRS AND ENERGY. *Digest of Special Laws designed to promote industrial investments in Belgium*, Brussels.

BERTIN, G.-Y. *L'Investissement des Firmes étrangères en France*, 1945–62, Paris, 1963.

BLÜMLICH, W. and FALK, L. *Einkommensteuergesetz*, 9th edn., 2 vols., Berlin, 1964.

BÖCKSTIEGEL, E.-H. 'Die allgemeinen Grundsätze des Völkerrechts über Eigentumsentziehung. Eine Untersuchung zu Artikel 1 des Zusatzprotokolls zur Europäischen Menschenrechtskonvention', *Neue Kölner Rechtswissenschaftliche Abhandlungen*, vol. 27, Berlin, 1963.

BOCZEK, B. A. *Flags of Convenience*, Cambridge, Mass., 1962.

BOOY, D. *Belastingsrecht in wording, de ontwikkeling van de belastingsontwerpen en de vergelijking met het bestaande recht*, Arnhem, 1964 (loose-leaf).

*Britannica Book of the Year for 1963*, London.

BROWN, W. M. *The External Liquidity of an Advanced Country*. Princeton Studies in International Finance, no. 14, Princeton, 1964.

BRYSON, G. D. *Profits from Abroad*, New York, 1964.

CAMPBELL, A. *Restrictive Trading Agreements in the Common Market*, London, 1964.

CAMPBELL, A. and THOMPSON, D. *Common Market Law. Texts and Commentaries*, London, 1962; First Supplement, 1963.

CAPOTORTI, F. *La Nazionalità della Società*, Naples, 1963.
CASSA PER IL MEZZOGIORNO. *Dodici Anni, 1950–1962*, vol. 1, Bari, 1962.
CATALANO, N. *Manuel de Droit des Communautés Européennes*, Paris, n.d.
CHASE MANHATTAN BANK. *The European Markets. A Guide for American Businessmen*, New York, 1964.
CHATELAIN, J. *La Nouvelle Constitution et le Régime Politique de la France*, 2nd rev. edn., Paris, 1959.
CHENOT, B. *Les Entreprises Nationalisées*, Paris, 1956.
CHEYNET, P. *Tableaux Comparatifs des Impôts et Taxes, applicables aux Sociétés Commerciales dans les Pays du Marché Commun*, Paris, 1963.
CHURCH, E. M. *Business Associations under French Law*, London, 1960.
COLE, J. P. *Geography of World Affairs*, 3rd edn., London, 1964.
CONTIMART. *The Italian Market*, A Contimart Report, no. 7, Zurich, 1962.
COUNCIL OF EUROPE. *The Rights of the European Citizen*, Strasbourg, 1961.
COURTNEY, P. 'Investment across the Atlantic,' in *European American Survey*, publ. The European Movement, Brussels, 1957.
CREDIT DU NORD. *Foreign Investment in France*, Paris, 1963.
CREDITO ITALIANO. *Useful Information for Investing Capital in Italy*, Rome, 1961.
DECHERT, C. R. *Ente Nazionale Idrocarburi. Profile of a State Corporation*, Leyden, 1963.
DELAUME, G. R. *American-French Private International Law*. Bilateral Studies in Private International Law, no. 2, New York, 1953.
DELVALLE GOLDSMITH, S. 'Difficulties facing American business in patent applications in Europe', in *Doing Business in the Common Market*, Commerce Clearing House, Chicago, 1963, pp. 107–13.
DEWHURST, J. F., COPPOCK, J. C., YATES, P. L. and others. *Europe's Needs and Resources. Trends and Prospects in 18 Countries*, New York, 1961.
—— *The New Europe and its Economic Future*, New York, 1964.
DIAMOND, A. S. *Digest of French Taxes and Business Organization*, 1958.
*Dictionnaire des Sciences Economiques*, Paris, 1956.
DRÜCK, H. *Gemeinsame Unternehmungen in Staaten-Verbindungen*, Studien zum Internationalen Wirtschaftsrecht und Atomenergierecht, no. 9, Univ. Göttingen Inst. für Völkerrecht, 1962.
EINAUDI, M., BYE, M. and ROSSI, E. *Nationalization in France and Italy*, Ithaca, 1955.
ELY, N. *Summary of Mining and Petroleum Laws of the World*, U.S. Dept. of the Interior, Bureau of Mines, Washington, 1961.
ERMACORA, F. *Handbuch der Grundfreiheiten und der Menschenrechte. Ein Kommentar zu den österreichischen Grundrechtsbestimmungen*, Vienna, 1963.

ERRERA, J., SYMON, E., MEULEN, J. VAN DER and VERNAEVE, L. *Euratom: Analyse et Commentaires du Traité*, Bibliothèque de l'Institut Belge de Science Politique, Brussels, 1958.

*Europa Yearbook* 1962 and 1964, London.

EUROPEAN ECONOMIC COMMUNITY. *Europe's 60 Largest Companies* (1961), Luxembourg, 1963.

E.E.C. COMMISSION. *Régime juridique des Transports ferroviaires, routiers, et fluviaux dans les Etats membres de la C.E.E. Situation au 1er juillet 1962*, Luxembourg, 1962.

E.E.C. STATISTICAL OFFICE. *Basic Statistics of the Community*, 5th edn., Luxembourg, 1964.

EVERLING, E. *Das Niederlassungsrecht im Gemeinsamen Markt*, Frankfurt/Main, 1963. English edn.: *The Right of Establishment in the Common Market*, New York, 1964.

FATOUROS, A. A. *Government Guarantees to Foreign Investors*, New York, 1962.

FECHNER, R. *Grundriß des Steuerrechts*, 3rd edn., Berlin, 1960.

FEDERATION OF BRITISH INDUSTRIES. *Taxation in Western Europe. A Guide for Industrialists*, 6th rev. edn., London, 1964.

FIRST NATIONAL CITY BANK OF NEW YORK. *The European Common Market*, New York, 1958.

FLORIO, F. *Nazionalità della Nave e Legge della Bandiera*, Milan, 1957.

FOIGHEL, I. *Nationalization. A Study in the Protection of Alien Property in International Law*, Copenhagen, 1957.

FREDERICQ, L. *Traité de Droit Commercial Belge*, vols. 4–6, Ghent, 1950.

FRIEDMANN, W. G. *The Changing Structure of International Law*, London, 1964.

FRIEDMANN, W. G. and PUGH, R. C. (eds.). *Legal Aspects of Foreign Investment*, London, 1959.

GAMBELLI, E. 'I paesi e i territori d'oltremare e la Communità', in *La Communità Economica Europea*, Milan, 1960, pp. 111–33.

GARCIA, F. L. (ed.). *G. C. Munn's Encyclopedia of Banking and Finance*, 6th edn., Boston, Mass., 1962.

G.A.T.T. *International Trade 1964*, 1964.

GERMAN-AMERICAN TRADE PROMOTION OFFICE. *Trading under the Laws of Germany*, New York, 1956.

GOLD, J. *The International Monetary Fund and Private Business Transactions. Some Legal Effects of the Articles of Agreement*, I.M.F., Washington, 1965.

GOLDMAN, B. *Cours de Droit de Commerce et de la Concurrence dans les Communautés Européennes*, Paris, 1964.

GROEBEN, H. v. D. and BOECKH, H. v. *Kommentar zum EWG-Vertrag*, 2 vols., Baden-Baden, 1958.

GROOT, W. E. DE, ENGELBERTS, A. J. and VERDENIUS, A. A. *Nederlandse Belastingwetten*, 2 vols., 6th edn., Alphen aan den Rijn, 1965.

GUBBELS, B. *Die steuerliche Abschreibung im In- und Ausland,* Institut Finanzen und Steuern, Heft 76, Bonn, 1964.

GUNTHER, E. *Kartelle und Monopole im modernen Recht,* Karslruhe, 1961.

HAAN, C. J. DE. 'The proposed E.E.C. Patent Convention: problems and prospects', in *Doing Business in the Common Market,* Commerce Clearing House, Chicago, 1963, pp. 100–6.

HACHENBURG, M. *Kommentar zum Gesetz betreffend die Gesellschaft mit beschränkter Haftung,* Berlin, 1956.

HACKER, A. (ed.). *The Corporation Take-over,* New York, 1963.

HAINAUT, J. P. and JOLIET, R. *Les Contrats de Travaux et de Fournitures de l'Administration dans le Marché Commun,* 2 vols., Brussels, 1963.

H.M.S.O. *Treaty establishing the E.C.S.C., Paris, 18 April 1951,* London, 1962.

HERMANN, C., HEUER, G., HEINING, A. and SCHILLING, O. VON. *Kommentar zur Einkommensteuer und Körperschaftssteuer,* 10th edn., Köln, 1964.

HOBSON, C. K. *The Export of Capital,* London, 1914 (republ. 1963).

HONIG, F., BROWN, W. J., GLEISS, A. and HIRSCH, M. *Cartel Law of the European Economic Community,* London, 1963.

INSAM, N. 'Der Wirtschaftsausbau Siziliens. Probleme, Ziele und Maßnahmen eines wirtschaftlich rückstandigen Landes', doctoral thesis, Univ. of Vienna, 1961.

INSTITUT DE DROIT INTERNATIONAL. *Annuaire,* Bath Session, 1950, vols. 43-I, 44-II.

INTERNATIONAL BAR ASSOCIATION. *Report,* 9th Conference, Edinburgh, 1962.

—— Records of the Conference on International Aspects of Nationalization, 1954.

INTERNATIONAL BUREAU OF FISCAL DOCUMENTATION. *Guides to European Taxation, vol. 1. The Taxation of Patent Royalties, Dividends, Interest in Europe,* Amsterdam, 1963.

INTERNATIONAL CHAMBER OF COMMERCE. *Model bilateral agreement on the status of foreign establishments.* Brochure no. 20, revised text, Paris, 1947.

INTERNATIONAL COURT OF JUSTICE. *Yearbooks 1953 to 1964,* Leyden.

INTERNATIONAL LAW ASSOCIATION. *Report,* 46th Conference, Edinburgh, 1954.

INTERNATIONAL LEGAL MATERIALS. Current Documents, American Society of International Law, Washington, D.C.

INTERNATIONAL MONETARY FUND. *14th Annual Report on Exchange Restrictions,* Washington, 1963.

INVESTMENT PROMOTION AND INFORMATION CENTRE. Dept. of Industry, Istanbul. *Investment Guide to Turkey.* Investment Promotion Publ. Ser. no. E-13/64, Istanbul. 1964.

JUNCKERSTORFF, H. K. (ed.). *International Manual on the European Economic Community*, St. Louis, Miss., 1963.

KATZAROV, K. *Théorie de la Nationalisation*. Travaux et Recherches de l'Institut de Droit Comparé de l'Univ. de Paris, no. 17, Neuchâtel, 1960.

KAUFMANN, H. (ed.) *Kommentar zum Gesetz gegen Wettbewerbsbeschränkungen*, Köln, 1958.

KEGEL, G. *Internationales Privatrecht* 2nd edn., Munich–Berlin, 1964.

KIRKPATRICK, J. *Le Régime Fiscal des Sociétés belges par Actions*, Brussels, 1963.

KISS, A.-C. *Répertoire de la Pratique française en Matière de Droit International Public*, vol. 1, Paris, 1962.

KOHLER, E. L. *A Dictionary for Accountants*, 3rd edn., New Jersey, 1963.

KOLLEWIJN, R. D. *American-Dutch Private International Law*. Bilateral Studies in Private International Law, no. 3, New York, 1955.

KRAUSE, L. B. and DAM, K. W. *Federal Tax Treatment of Foreign Income*, Washington, 1964.

LANGEN, E. *Kommentar zum Kartellgesetz*, 3rd edn., Neuwied/Rhein, 1958.

LELEUX, P.. 'The right of establishment within the E.E.C. Harmonization of company laws', in *Doing Business in the Common Market*, Commerce Clearing House, Chicago, 1963, pp. 22–35.

LEWIS, A. K. and KEMP, J. A. *Registration of Commercial and Licence Agreements in the Common Market*, London, 1962.

LEWIS, T. H. (ed.). *The Business Encyclopedia and Legal Advisor*, 5 vols., 6th edn., London, 1956.

McCORMICK CROSSWELL, C. *International Business Techniques. Legal and Financial Aspects*, New York, 1963.

McDANIELS, J. F. (ed.). *International Financing and Investment*, New York, 1964.

McNAIR, LORD. *The Law of Treaties*, Oxford, 1961.

—— Preface to *The Rights of the European Citizen*, publ. Council of Europe, Strasbourg, 1961.

MARMOL, C. DEL. *La Protection contre les Abus de Puissance Economique en Droit belge*, Liège, 1960.

MARTYN, H. *International Business. Principles and Problems*, London–New York, 1964.

MEYER-MARSILIUS, H. J. *Das Niederlassungsrecht in der europäischen Wirtschaftsgemeinschaft*, Schriftenreihe zum Handbuch für europäische Wirtschaft, Heft 12, Baden-Baden, 1960.

MIGNOT, M. A. 'Le Traité de Rome et les monopoles fiscaux de tabac', *Recherches Economiques de Louvain*, no. 7, September 1964.

*Moody's Municipal and Government Manual: American and Foreign*, New York, 1964.

340 BIBLIOGRAPHY

MORSELLI, E. *Le Imposte in Italia*, 7th edn., Padova, 1962.

MOYES, A. and HAYTER, T. *World III: A Handbook on Developing Countries*, New York, 1964.

MÜLLER, H. and GRIES, G. *Kommentar zum Gesetz gegen Wettbewerbsbeschränkungen*, Frankfurt/Main, 1958.

MÜLLER-HENNEBERG, H., SCHWARTZ, G. and others. *Gesetz gegen Wettbewerbsbeschränkungen. Kommentar*, Köln, 1958.

NETHERLANDS MINISTRY OF ECONOMIC AFFAIRS. *Guide to the establishing of industrial Operations in the Netherlands*, The Hague, 1961.

NWOGUGU, E. I. *The Legal Problems of Foreign Investment in Developing Countries*, Manchester, 1965.

OPPENHEIM, L. *International Law. A Treatise*, H. Lauterpacht, ed., vol. 1, 8th edn., London, 1963.

O.E.C.D. *Code of Liberalization of Invisible Operations*, Paris, December 1964.

—— *Statistics of Balance of Payments 1960–61*, Paris, 1962.

—— *Economic Surveys: The United States*, Paris, November 1963.

—— *Guide to Legislation on Restrictive Business Practices: Europe and North America*, 4 vols., Paris, 1964.

OUDEMANS, G. *The Draft European Patent Convention. A Commentary with English and French Texts*, London, 1963.

*Oxford Economic Atlas of the World*, Oxford, 1954.

PALLIERI, B. *Diritto Internazionale Privato*, Milan, 1950.

PANHUYS, H. F. VAN. *The Role of Nationality in International Law*, Leyden, 1959.

PAUWELS, V., VANDIJK, L. and ROELANDT, R. *Traité des Impôts sur les Revenus*, Brussels, 1963 (loose-leaf).

PEASLEE, A. J. *Constitutions of Nations*, 3 vols., 2nd edn., The Hague, 1956.

PENNINGTON, R. R. *The Principles of Company Law*, London, 1959.

PHILLIPS, G. 'Erscheinungsformen und Methoden der Privatrechts-Vereinheitlichung', thesis, Univ. of Mainz, 1963.

PINTO, R. *Les Organisations européennes*, Paris, 1963.

PREISWERK, R. *La Protection des Investissements privés dans les Traités bilatéraux*, Zurich, 1963.

PUJADE, P. 'The harmonization of conditions of competition', in *Aspects of European Integration. An Anglo-French Symposium*, P.E.P., London, and Institut de Science Economique Appliquée, Paris, pp. 88–119.

RAAPE, L. *Internationales Privatrecht*, 4th rev. edn., Berlin, 1955.

RABEL, E. *Conflict of Laws*, vol. 2, 2nd edn., Ann Arbor, 1960.

RASCH, H. *Wettbewerbsbeschränkungen gegen Kartell- und Monopolrecht. Kommentar zum Gesetz gegen Wettbewerbsbeschränkungen*, Berlin, 1958.

RAVA, T. *Le Problème de la Comparaison et l'Unification du Droit des Sociétés par Actions*. Rapport préliminaire, juillet 1951. Institut International pour l'Unification du Droit Privé, Etudes XXVI, Sociétés Commerciales, doc. 2.

REUGEBRINK, J. *Omzetbelasting en E.E.C.*, Deventer, 1964.

RICHMAN, P. B. *Taxation of Foreign Investment Income*, Baltimore, 1963.

RIDLEY, F. and BLONDEL, J. *Public Administration in France*, London, 1964.

ROBERTSON, A. H. *European Institutions. Co-operation, Integration, Unification*, London, 1959.

—— *The Council of Europe. Its Structure, Functions and Achievements*, 2nd edn., London, 1961.

—— *Human Rights in Europe*, Manchester, 1963.

ROBINSON, R. D. *International Business Policy*, New York, 1964.

RYN, J. VAN. *Principes de Droit Commercial*, vol. 1, Brussels, 1954.

SCHMIDT, W. and ANDREAS, K. 'Bank deutscher Länder und die angeschlossenen Landeszentralbankern', *Enzyklopädisches Lexikon für das Geld-, Bank- und Börsenwesen*, vol. I, Frankfurt/Main, 1957.

SEIDL-HOHENVELDERN, I. *Internationales Konfiskations- und Enteignungsrecht*, Beitrage zum auslandischen und internationalen Privatrecht no. 23, publ. Max-Planck Institut für ausländisches und internationales Privatrecht, Tübingen, 1952.

—— 'Judicial Protection of Foreign Investments', in *Mélanges Séfériadès* (publ. Ecole des Sciences Politiques '*Panteios*' d'Athènes), 2 vols., Athens, 1961, vol. 1, pp. 251–66.

SINNER, J. *Code de la Lègislation fiscale Luxembourgeoise*, 4 vols., Luxembourg, 1964.

—— *Etudes Fiscales*, Luxembourg, 1963.

STEIN, E. and NICHOLSON, T. L. (eds.). *American Enterprise in the European Common Market. A Legal Profile*, 2 vols., Ann Arbor, 1960.

*Topham's Company Law*, 12th edn., London, 1960.

TROTABAS, L. *Finances Publiques*, Paris, 1964.

U.S. DEPT. OF COMMERCE. *Survey of Current Business*, vol. 43, Washington, 1963.

—— *Statistical Abstract of the United States*, Washington, 1964.

U.S. STATE DEPARTMENT. Agency for International Development. *Memorandum to Businessmen*, Washington, 1964.

VALENTINE, D. G. *The Court of Justice of the European Communities*, 2 vols., London, 1965.

VERDROSS, A. *Völkerrecht*, 3rd edn., Vienna, 1959.

VOTAW, D. *The Six-legged Dog: Mattei and E.N.I. A Study in Power*, Berkeley–Los Angeles, 1964.

WALINE, M. *Traité élémentaire de Droit administratif français*, 5th edn., Paris, 1950.

WANG, M. *Die europäische Aktiengesellschaft in der europäischen Wirtschaftsgemeinschaft*, Arbeiten aus dem juristischen Seminar der Univ. Freiburg (Switzerland), no. 27, Freiburg, 1964.

WAUTERS-DE NEEFF, C. *Code des Lois sur les Sociétés par Actions en vigueur dans les Pays du Marché Commun*, Brussels, 1964.

WHITE, G. *Nationalization of Foreign Property*, London 1961.

WHITE, W. W. and RAVENSCROFT, B. G. *Patents throughout the World*, New York, 1963.

WILDE, J. C. DE. 'International financing of industrial development', in *Commercial Banks in relation to Medium- and Long-term Credit*, Vienna, 1964, pp. 140–59.

WOHLFARTH, E., EVERLING, U., GLAISNER, H. J. and SPRUNG, R. *Die europäische Wirtschaftsgemeinschaft. Kommentar*, Berlin, 1960.

WOLFF, M. *Das internationale Privatrecht Deutschlands*, 3rd edn., Berlin, 1954.

WORTLEY, B. A. *Expropriation in Public International Law*, Cambridge, 1959.

—— (ed.). *The United Nations. The First Ten Years*. Manchester, 1957.

ZOLOTAS, X. *Monetary Equilibrium and Economic Development*, Princeton, 1965.

## ARTICLES AND OTHER REFERENCES IN PERIODICALS

ALBRECHT, A. R. 'The taxation of aliens under international law', *B.Y.I.L.*, vol. 29, 1952, pp. 145 ff.

ARNOLD, H. 'Die Angleichung des Gesellschaftsrechtes in der europäischen Wirtschaftsgemeinschaft', *Außenwirtschaftsdienst des Betriebs-Beraters*, 19. Jg., 1963, pp. 221 ff.

AUDINET, J. 'Le droit d'établissement dans la C.E.E.', *J.D.I.*, vol. 86, 1959, pp. 982–1049.

BAILEY, R. 'Nationalization and Professor Hallstein', *The Spectator*, 6 April 1962, pp. 434–5.

BALOGH, T. 'Africa and the Common Market', *Journ. Common Market Studies*, vol. 1, 1962–63, pp. 79–112.

BÄRMANN, J. 'Supranationale Aktiengesellschaften?', *Archiv für die civilistische Praxis*, Jg. 156, 1957, pp. 156–211.[1]

BENTHEM VAN DER BERGH, G. VAN. 'The new Convention of Association with African States', *C.M.L. Rev.*, vol. 1, 1963–64, pp. 156–82.

BERTIN, G.-Y. *Direction*, no. 94, April 1963, pp. 401–11.

—— 'Towards an international market. Foreign investment in the food trades', *Cartel*, vol. xiv, April 1964, pp. 61 ff.

BOCK, E. 'New flows in the world capital market', *The Banker*, May 1963, pp. 319–27.

BOMPARD, E. 'The Italian banking system', *Journ. Inst. of Bankers*, vol. 86, no. 4, August 1964, pp. 276–89.

BRONDEL, G. 'La politique énergétique de la Communauté Européenne' *Rev. M.C.*, 7me année, no. 69, May 1964, pp. 225–33.

CALON, J. P. 'The international company. Elements of a general theory', *J.D.I.*, vol. 88, 1961, pp. 695 ff.

CARTOU, L. 'Le Marché Commun et les capitaux', *Rev. de Science financière*, vol. 55, 1963.

CASTBERG, F., in *Annuaire de l'Inst. de Droit International*, vol. 44-II, 1952, pp. 264–5.

CLARK, T. C. 'Antitrust principles and the Common Market', *Journ. Amer. Bar Assoc.*, vol. 49, 1963, pp. 837 ff.

DENIAU, J. 'Objectives and the constitutional structure of the E.E.C.', *I.C.L.Q.* Suppl. Publ. no. 1, 1961, pp. 1–7.

DERINGER, A. and others. 'Les règles de concurrence au sein de la C.E.E.', *Rev. M.C.*, 6me année, 1963, pp. 37 ff., 84 ff., 126 ff., 172 ff., 256 ff., 301 ff., 347 ff., 440 ff., 488 ff.

DÖLLE, H. 'Die 7. Haager Konferenz', *Zeitschrift für ausländisches und internationales Privatrecht*, vol. 17, 1952, pp. 185 ff.

DOMKE, M. 'Foreign nationalizations', *A.J.I.L.*, vol. 55, 1961, pp. 585 ff.

—— 'Notes on the United Nations Convention on Restrictive Practices', *I.C.L.Q.*, vol. 4, 1955, pp. 129 ff.

EGGERS, E. R. 'How U.S. firms invest in the E.E.C. economy', *Commerce in Germany*, no. 131, November 1964, p. 26.

—— 'Investment in Europe . . . with an American Accent', *Opera Mundi—Europe*, no. 269, 10 September 1964, pp. 5–12.

EKMAN, B. 'Swedish industry goes abroad', *Featuring Sweden*, no. 4, 1964, pp. 28 ff.

FAY, S. B. 'State ownership in Germany', *Current History*, vol. xviii, March 1950, pp. 129–33.

FIKENTSCHER, W. and GROSSFELD, B. 'The proposed directive on company law', *C.M.L. Rev.*, vol. 2, 1964–65, pp. 259–70.

FITZMAURICE, SIR GERALD, in *Annuaire de l'Inst. de Droit International*, vol. 44-II, 1952, pp. 274–5.

FOGARTY, M. P. 'Co-determination and company structure in Germany', *British Journ. of Industrial Relations*, vol. 2, no. 1, March 1964, pp. 79–113.

—— 'Companies beyond Jenkins', *Planning* (P.E.P.), vol. xxxi, no. 486, February 1965.

FORSYTH, M. 'The Parliament of the European Communities', *Planning* (P.E.P.), vol. xxx, no. 478, March 1964.

FOURES, R. ' "La position dominante" en droit français et en droit européen', *Le Droit Européen*, 6me année, no. 53, 1963, pp. 323–6.

FREDERICQ, L. 'De veranworderlijkheid van de beheerders in de naamloze vennootschap', *Rechtskundig Weekblad*, 24 November 1957, pp. 537 ff.

FUGATE, W. L. 'The Common Market and the United States Anti-trust Laws', *New York Univ. Law. Rev.*, vol. 38, 1963, pp. 458 ff.

GAUDET, M. 'Aspects juridiques de la liberté d'établissement dans le Marché Commun', *Sociaal-Econ. Wetgeving*, 2nd yr., 1961–62, pp. 52–68.

GERVAIS, J. 'Les capitaux étrangers en France', *La Vie Française*, 20ᵉ année (1964), no. 979–80, 28 février et 3 mars 1964, pp. 8 and 7 respectively.

GERVEN, W. VAN. 'Les droits d'établissement et de prestation de services dans le Marché Commun', *Journ. des Tribunaux* (Brussels), 31 May 1964, pp. 357 ff.

GOLDMAN, B. 'The law of international companies', *J.D.I.*, vol. 90, 1963, pp. 321 ff.

GRAND RY, A. DE. 'L'harmonisation des législations au sein du Marché Commun en matière de marchés publics', *Rev. M.C.*, 4me année, nos. 37–8, June–August 1961, pp. 247 ff., 282 ff.

HALLSTEIN, W. *Entreprise*, no. 496, 13 March 1965, p. 31.

HENNINGS, H. D., in *Die Welt*, no. 17, 21 January 1965.

HEUVEL, H. VAN DEN. 'Civil-law consequences of violation of the antitrust provisions of the Rome Treaty', *A.J.C.L.*, vol. 12, 1963, pp. 172 ff.

HISSENHOVEN, A. VAN, in *Rev. de la Banque* (Brussels), 27th year, no. 4, 1963.

HUFFSCHMID, B., in *Documents, Revue des Questions Allemandes*, 19th year, no. 1, January–February 1964.

JANSEN, J. J. 'Harmonization of indirect taxes in the E.E.C.', *Bull. International Fiscal Documentation* (Amsterdam), vol. 18, no. 5, 1964, pp. 177 ff.

JONES, C. 'The vital public sector—Nationalisation in Western Europe', *European Community*, May 1965, pp. 6–7.

KIRCHER, D. P. 'Now the transnational enterprise', *Harvard Business Rev.*, March–April 1964, pp. 6 ff.

KOROWICZ, M. ST. 'The problem of the international personality of individuals', *A.J.I.L.*, vol. 50, 1956, pp. 533 ff.

KREMP, H. 'Kein Ausverkauf der EWG-Wirtschaft', *Mitteilungen der Handelskammer Hamburg*, no. 5, May 1963, pp. 170–2.

KRUITHOF, M. R. 'The application of the Common Market Antitrust provisions to international restraints of trade', *C.M.L. Rev.*, vol. 2, 1964–65, pp. 69–94.

LE TALLEC, G. 'Le droit d'établissement et les prestations de services des sociétés', *Rivista di Diritto Europeo*, July–September 1961, pp. 270 ff.

—— 'La police des étrangers dans les états membres de la C.E.E. et le Traité de Rome', *Rev. M.C.*, 7me année, no. 72, September 1964, pp. 371–80.

LEBEE, E. 'Trusts et cartels internationaux', *Rec. A.D.I.*, 1927–IV, pp. 147–246.

LEPAULLE, P. 'Betrachtungen über die internationalen Gesellschaften', *Archiv für die civilistische Praxis*, Jg. 159, 1960, pp. 126 ff.

LIPPMAN, R. D. 'American business interests and a uniform Common Market Trademark Law', *A.J.C.L.*, vol. 12, 1963, pp. 255 ff.

LOUSSOUARN, Y. E. 'La condition des personnes morales en droit international privé', *Rec. A.D.I.*, 1959–I, pp. 443–551.

—— 'Dispositions du Traité de Rome relatives aux sociétés', *Revue trimestrielle de Droit Commercial*, 12ᵉ année (1959), pp. 246–56.

MACLENNAN, M. C. 'The Common Market and French planning', *Journ. Common Market Studies*, vol. 3, 1964–65, pp. 23–46.

MEISSNER, G. 'Using a loan as GmbH capital', *Commerce in Germany*, no. 135, March 1965, pp. 20–1, and no. 136, April, 1965, pp. 16–17.

MORDACQ, P. 'Les investissements américains en France',—*La documentation française*, in *Problèmes Economiques* no. 818, 3 September 1963, pp. 14–18.

MORERA, R. 'Considérations sur la clause d'exclusivité', *Le Droit Européen*, 6me année, no. 53, 1963, pp. 297–305.

MÜNCH, F. 'Les effets d'une nationalisation à l'étranger', *Rec. A.D.I.*, 1959–II, pp. 411–503.

NEBOLSINE, G. 'Foreign enterprises under the Common Market Antitrust Rules', *New York Univ. Law Rev.*, vol. 38, 1963, pp. 479 ff.

NIEHUS, R. J. 'Setting up business in Western Germany: tax considerations', *The Accountant*, vol. 147, 1962, pp. 412 ff.

NOTTEN, M. M. VAN. 'Know-how licensing in the Common Market', *New York Univ. Law Rev.*, vol. 38, 1963, pp. 525 ff.

OLIVIER, D. 'La Convention d'Association entre la C.E.E. et les états Africains et Malgache Associés, signée à Yaounde, le 20 juillet 1963', *Rev. M.C.*, 6me année, December 1963, pp. 480–7.

OPPERMANN, T. 'Die Durchführung der EWG-Niederlassungs- und Dienstleistungsprogramme seit 1961', *Der Betriebs-Berater*, 19 Jg., 1964, pp. 563–70.

—— 'L'application des programmes généraux de la C.E.E. concernant la liberté d'établissement et la libre prestation des services', *Rev. M.C.*, 7me année, no. 75, December 1964, pp. 544–59.

OSTERKAMP, K. 'Die Organisation der italienischen Energiewirtschaft', *Die öffentliche Wirtschaft*, Jg. 13, no. 1, 1964, pp. 43–5.

OWEN, G. 'Increased investment by the U.S.', *Europe: A Financial Times Survey*, 7 December 1964, p. 16.

PARRY, C. 'Some considerations upon the protection of individuals in international law', *Rec. A.D.I.*, 1956–II, pp. 653–725.

PIOT, A. 'Of realism in conventions of establishment', *J.D.I.*, vol. 88, 1961, pp. 39–85.

REYNAUD, P.-L. 'Inchiesta sull 'economica greca e il Mercato Commune, *Riv. Intern. Scienze Econ. e Commerciale*, vol. 10, 1963, pp. 975 ff.

ROCHEMONT, J. DE. 'La notion d'entreprise dans le droit des communautés européennes', *Le Droit Européen*, 6me année, no. 53, 1963, pp. 306–22.

SAVATIER, R. 'Le Marché Commun au regard du droit international privé', *Rev. critique du Droit International Privé*, vol. 48, 1959, pp. 237 ff.

SCHAPIRA, J. 'La décision Grundig-Consten', *J.D.I.*, vol. 92, 1965, pp. 67–80.

SCHLACHTER, E. 'Nouveaux aspects de la liberté d'établissement dans le Traité de Rome', *Rev. M.C.*, 3me année, no. 30, November 1960, pp. 392–6.

SCHUMACHER, H. 'The system of enforcement [of antitrust law]. 3, The European Economic Community', *I.C.L.Q.* Suppl. Publ. no. 6, 1963, pp. 65–77.

SEIDL-HOHENVELDERN, I. 'European companies', *Journ. Business Law*, 1950, pp. 120 ff.

SIMONETTO, E. 'Sulla necessità di una disciplina internazionale uniforme in materia di società commerciale', *Riv. Intern. Scienze Econ. e Commerciale*, vol. 12, 1965, pp. 86 ff.

SUETENS, L. P. 'Belgian anti-trust law in action', *C.M.L. Rev.*, vol. 2, 1964–65, pp. 325–39.

THOMPSON, D. 'Project for a commercial company of European type', *I.C.L.Q.*, vol. 10, 1961, pp. 851 ff.

UCKMAR, V. 'L'imposition des revenus dans le régime fiscal italien', *La Fiscalité du Marché Commun*, no. 9, July 1964, pp. 203 ff.

URI, P. *Le Monde*, 23 February 1965, p. 14, and 24 February 1965, p. 16.

VALLÉE, P. H. DE. 'Les investissements américains en Europe', *L'Information* (Paris), 14, December 1962, pp. 9–10.

VASSEUR, M. 'A company of European type', *Journ. Business Law*, 1964, pp. 358 ff., and 1965, pp. 73 ff.

VERLOREN VAN THEMAAT, P., in the introduction to 'Antitrust and the Common Market: a Symposium', *New York Univ. Law Rev.*, vol. 38, 1963, pp. 435 ff.

—— 'The antitrust policy of the European Economic Community', *I.C.L.Q.* Suppl. Publ. no. 6, 1963, pp. 18–26.

WALKER, H., Jr. 'Provisions on companies in United States commercial treaties', *A.J.I.L.*, vol. 50, 1956, pp. 373–93.

WEISER, G. J. 'Antitrust policy and industrial property in the European Economic Community', *New York Univ. Law Rev.*, vol. 38, 1963, pp. 496 ff.

WHEATCROFT, G. S. A. 'Modern trends in taxation', *Bull. International Fiscal Documentation* (Amsterdam), vol. 18, no. 2, 1964, pp. 45 ff.

WILLATT, N. 'The Dilemma for American Investors', *Times Review of Industry and Technology*, March 1963, pp. 11 ff.

WORTLEY, B. A. 'The general principles of private international law', *Rec. A.D.I.*, 1958-II, pp. 91–257.

—— 'The protection of property situated abroad', *Tulane Law Review*, vol. 35, 1960–61, pp. 739 ff.

—— 'Harmonization of law in the European Economic Community', *Nederlandse Tijdschrift voor Internationaal Recht*, vol. 9, 1962 (Special Issue), pp. 529–36.

—— 'The need for more uniformity in the law relating to the international sale of goods in Europe', *I.C.L.Q.* Suppl. Publ. no. 1, 1961, pp. 45–57.

# INDEX

348

354 INDEX

loans, incentive, 3, 136 ff.
Luxembourg
Belge-Luxembourgeois Economic
Union, 53
company law, 70, 89–93, 96, 99 ff.
employment of aliens, 144
entry and repatriation of capital, 53
exchange control regulation, 52–3,
55, 100, 162, 298
expropriation, 169
foreign investment in, 22, 313
foreign legal entities, 214
Institut Belge-Luxembourgeois de
Change, 46, 53
investment incentives, 141–2
law on patents, 158–9; on restrictive practices, 155
*milliardaires*, 128, 130
public enterprises and utilities, 27,
44–5
state-owned industries, 27

main office, location, 36, 38, 41,
145–6, 206–7; *see also sections on*
company law *under individual
countries*
management, managers, 36–7, 100–1,
143, 162, 216–19, 298 f.; *see also
sections on* company law *under
individual countries*
right of transfer within E.E.C.,
145, 221, 233
manufacturing industries, 18, 20 ff.,
41, 97, 332 f.
markets, 102, 245, 250, 279, 305, 315
mergers, 102, 113, 115, 195, 233, 243,
247, 266, 268, 278 f., 284, 290
*milliardaires*, 128, 130
mining, mineral exploitation, 28,
30 f., 35, 38, 84, 171, 202n., 283
mobility of enterprise, 62, 267, 283,
321, 325
monetary union, 232
monopolies, 147, 152, 154
state, 26 f., 193, 297; *see also under
individual countries*
'most favoured nation' clause, 214 ff.
motor industry, 28, 30 f., 97, 170,
263 f., 310, 316

municipal courts and Community
law, 186
municipal law, 3
company law, 61 f., 97–103, 265,
277 f., 283; *see also under individual countries*
expropriation, 167, 172, 174, 189
functioning in E.E.C., 265 ff.
harmonization, 61, 102, 199, 231,
233, 256 ff., 277, 286 ff., 325
protection of foreign investor,
174 ff., 191
real seat theory, 211–12
restrictions on competitiveness,
102–3, 245, 247
right of establishment, 200, 205 f.,
208 f., 211, 213 f., 260 f.
unification, 102, 257, 275–7, 278

national interest, 39, 40n., 175–6, 258
nationality, principle of, in establishment of companies, 145, 194,
204–6, 209, 211 f., 278, 283, 296,
300, 326
of claims in disputes, 183–4, 187,
190 f., 193 ff.
of investors, 232
nationalization, 164, 170, 174 f.
and foreign enterprise, 175–6, 194
compensation, 170 f., 172 f.
*see also* expropriation
natural resources, 297, 320 f.
Netherlands
banking, 27, 43
company law, 93–7, 101
Convention of Human Rights, 302
Dutch Engineering and Contractors Association, 241
Economic Competition Com-
mittee, 156n.
employment of aliens, 144
entry and repatriation of capital, 54
exchange control regulations, 54
expropriation, 169, 171, 173 f.
foreign investment in, 22–3, 55, 313
indirect investment, 55
investment incentives, 142
law on patents, 158–9; on restrictive practices, 155–6